1-3-87

LOVE, LIGHT, AND A DREAM

Television's Past, Present, and Future

JAMES ROMAN

PRAEGER

Westport, Connecticut
London

Library of Congress Cataloging-in-Publication Data

Roman, James.
  Love, light, and a dream : television's past, present, and future
/ James Roman.
    p.   cm.
  Includes bibliographical references and index.
  ISBN 0–275–95180–4 (alk. paper)
  1. Television broadcasting—History. I. Title.
PN1992.2.R66 1996
  384.55′4′09—dc20   95–47213

British Library Cataloguing in Publication Data is available.

Library of Congress Catalog Card Number: 95–47213
ISBN: 0–275–95180–4

First published in 1996

Praeger Publishers, 88 Post Road West, Westport, CT 06881
An imprint of Greenwood Publishing Group, Inc.

Printed in the United States of America

The paper used in this book complies with the
Permanent Paper Standard issued by the National
Information Standards Organization (Z39.48–1984).

10 9 8 7 6 5 4 3 2 1

Contents

Acknowledgements

There are a number of people whose help I'd like to acknowledge: Janet Hulstrand for her editorial assistance and Tricia Grosso, Harmony Stookesbery, and Eloise Jackson for their help with research and organization. As always I'm indebted to my wife Mardee and my children, Matthew, Joshua, and Heather, who were always supportive and understanding during the time I spent researching and writing this book.

Introduction

Those earliest flickers of phosphorescent images excited an international public and created unsurpassed wealth for those fortunate enough to have had a "vision" for television. Television—a word that has taken on new meaning and a technology that is in transition.

Even today, television is still an experimental medium. While it has come a long way from the fuzzy images transmitted by Farnsworth and Zworykin, television continues to evolve into new technological and substantive dimensions.

America's first generation with television created a love affair with sight and sound. Viewers were enraptured by the electronic pictures and entertained by the talent that performed right in their living rooms. At times the "medium was the message," with audiences watching anything, as long as it was on television. During those nascent years television explored new dimensions in programming and technology, creating a hybrid environment for the consumption of both high culture and kitsch. Sid Caesar and Arturo Toscanini shared the same electronic proscenium, while Ed Sullivan entertained the public with opera and circus acts.

At the same time that producers and programmers pondered the limits of audience taste, engineers pursued the technological dimensions of the televised image. CBS and RCA developed competing color television systems, and NBC's *Bonanza* became the first regularly scheduled network series to be broadcast in color. Soon larger picture tubes were manufactured, stretching the electronic canvas and providing an illusion of greater viewing dimension.

While the technological aspect of television changed, so did the nature of programming. The cathode ray tube became a mirror reflecting the concerns, hopes, and dreams of American culture. During the 1950s, television was an electronic test tube, broadcasting popular sitcoms, variety programs, quiz shows, documentaries, and live Congressional hearings to an avid viewing public.

During the 1960s, television lost its innocence and became embroiled in the political climate of the decade. Politicians, activist groups, and community leaders all embraced the technology and used it to reach the public. Television touched a responsive chord and became a medium for dissent among a disenchanted audience.

The 1970s and early 1980s reflected a critical change in the direction of American television. During the 1970s, networks adopted new programming genres, specifically the miniseries, which became an integral component of national television. Advances in rocketry and satellite technology forged new frontiers in space and programming. Ad hoc networks could be formed by various stations linked via satellite, bypassing the traditional network hookup and standard programming sources.

Television in the 1970s was also defined by a new political vulnerability. American citizens were held hostage in Iran, and soon television too became a sort of electronic hostage. Stations and networks eager for material were manipulated by the Iranian captors who proved adept at organizing and distributing televised coverage of the crisis. Increasingly both in our society and abroad, television has become a participant, sometimes even an instigator, of events rather than an innocent bystander.

The 1970s and 1980s also saw the development of alternative video distribution technologies. Cable television, pay television, satellite, and video cassettes and disks have dramatically altered the traditional pattern of program distribution. As a result, television has become decentralized and more consumer oriented.

As we move toward the twenty-first century, television will change from a medium of passive entertainment to one of interactive information management. Very likely it will be the Rosetta Stone of the Information Age, providing important clues to the myths and images of our culture. The changes in the art, industry, and technology of television will have a profound effect on American society. In many ways, television will also become a critical tool in the democratic process, enfranchising those with the knowledge and ability to enter its virtual world of form and function.

This book provides the reader with an understanding of important developments in the history of television, while offering a timely look at the regulatory and policy issues now impacting on the evolving role of television in our society.

1

Synergy: A Consolidation of Hardware and Software

Of all the developments that have helped to shape the communications industry in the United States over the past two decades, none has had a greater impact than the dizzying pace of aggressive corporate mergers and acquisitions. In 1979 the Gannett Company acquired Combined Communications Corporation for $340 million, which was the largest media deal up to that time.[1] But during the 1980s, the laissez-faire politics of the Reagan administration made way for a host of media acquisitions and mergers that rippled through the broadcasting industry, each seeming to set new records for purchase amounts. Corporate trading has eclipsed the million-dollar mark, and with Japanese investments in American media, the trend toward acquisition and investment continues, now headed toward the billions.

Indeed, the 1980s served as a harbinger to the wild wooing of media giants in the 1990s. In 1994 the aggressive bidding for Paramount by Viacom and QVC resulted in victory for Sumner Redstone's Viacom in a deal worth $9.7 billion. Viacom, with holdings as diverse as MTV Networks and Showtime, forged an alliance with Paramount, a diversified company with entertainment interests in publishing, film, and sports. In 1994 a potentially crucial merger, which would have combined the protocols of cable television and the telephone, collapsed when Telecommunications Incorporated (TCI) and Bell Atlantic announced the termination of their agreement. The $33-billion deal was undone by a combination of factors including an FCC-mandated cut in cable rates and a personality clash between two very different executives, John C. Malone of TCI and Raymond W. Smith of Bell Atlantic.[2]

As a result of these mergers, the entertainment industry has entered the 1990s with only vague distinctions remaining between what were once competitive industries. Television and film have become inexorably linked in the production and distribution marketplace, and the term "synergy" has become the high-tech catchword for the 1990s—instead of hardware and software being defined as two distinct areas, a marriage between the two is viewed as having a greater total effect than the sum of each.

A "corporate personality" has also emerged due to the interest of the Japanese in American media and technology. This corporate posture reflects a global consolidation that has influenced American industry, creating a synergism between the Japanese and their orientation toward hardware, and Americans with their instinct for the successful creation of software.

THE NETWORKS EVOLVE: MERGERS AND ACQUISITIONS

The year 1986 proved to be a benchmark one for media acquisitions, mergers, and threatened takeovers. The drama began with a joint announcement by the American Broadcasting Company (ABC) and Capital Cities Communications of an intended merger that was eventually valued at $3.5 billion. And one of the most spectacular media acquisitions in 1986 was made when General Electric (GE) purchased RCA and its television network, the National Broadcasting Company (NBC), for $6.3 billion.

While many equate GE with the manufacturing of consumer appliances, its influence goes far beyond the American household. GE is the tenth largest corporation in the United States and is a primary defense contractor and manufacturer of jet engines, nuclear reactors, missiles, and locomotives. In addition, the corporate slogan "We bring good things to life" is suggestive of GE's involvement in almost every aspect of America's production and distribution of one of its most precious resources, electricity. And although GE attempts to maintain a pristine corporate image for its public, it nevertheless has been involved in some shady schemes. These range from the deliberate tampering with light bulbs to cut their life span by a third and increase sales during the Depression to bid rigging and forgery.[3] These instances of the abuse of power have raised questions about GE's suitability as a broadcast licensee, but they seemed to have little impact on the FCC, which provides oversight of such mergers.

The 1980s and early 1990s proved to be a turbulent time for network television. In addition to the instability brought about by both friendly and hostile takeovers, television executives feared losing their audiences to competing technologies such as video and cable TV. In this climate of uncertainty, advertising revenues decreased.

CBS

CBS, once the network leader in broadcast television, suffered the most during these times. Perhaps the greatest unnerving effort to take over the network came from Jesse Helms, the right-wing senator from North Carolina. Helms threatened to lead a group of conservative financiers, who were disgruntled with CBS liberalism, in a takeover of CBS stock. Although the attempt failed, the negative publicity and the realization that the network was vulnerable to unfriendly suitors left CBS in a precarious state.

One of the most audacious attempts at a corporate takeover of CBS was made by Ted Turner. In late 1986 the outspoken patriarch of cable broadcasting announced his intention to acquire the CBS network. Turner had criticized CBS for its liberal viewpoint and violent programming and felt that his leadership would change things. Although industry observers viewed Turner's offer of a no-cash settlement—with indebtedness secured via high-risk "junk bonds"—as an empty gesture, his previous corporate success forced CBS executives to take his threat seriously. In an effort to thwart Turner's hostile takeover attempt, the CBS Board of Directors approved a corporate purchase of 21 percent of CBS shares for close to $1 billion. In addition, the chairman of Loews' Corporation, Laurence A. Tisch, was persuaded to increase his company's interest in CBS from 12 percent to almost 25 percent equity. With the corporate acquisition of more CBS stock, it became difficult for an unfriendly outside suitor to acquire controlling interest in the company. After Tisch had successfully thwarted the attempted hostile takeover of CBS, he joined with CBS president William Paley in a comprehensive reorganization of the company.

With a reputation for being thrifty, Tisch decided that CBS was bloated with personnel and swiftly terminated over a thousand employees.[4] He also closed several news bureaus and sold the CBS book- and music-publishing subsidiaries. Perhaps his most startling move was the announcement that CBS would sell one of its crown jewels, its record division. CBS Records was the envy of the industry, with consistently high profits and top recording artists under contract. Indeed, while the network's radiance was fading, the record division was glowing, offsetting the red ink created by a third-place television network. The successful suitor was the Sony Corporation, which paid $2 billion for CBS Records in 1987.

Naturally, the changes Tisch made at CBS angered quite a few employees, especially those within the news division. Veteran newscasters were dismissed, and the news budget was dramatically reduced. The unhappiness at CBS News was exemplified by a 1988 announcement made by news anchor Dan Rather and Don Hewitt, executive producer of *60 Minutes*, stating their interest in buying CBS News. Although the purchase never materialized, this announcement by two prominent CBS employees clearly suggested a mood of uncertainty at the network.

As it entered the 1990s, CBS had embarked on an ambitious financial and management reorganization plan. It announced a $2 billion stock buy-back program and a thorough review of corporate policy conducted by the management concern of McKinsey and Company. CBS's problems, however, were not quite over: a $100 million baseball licensing contract blunder and mediocre coverage during the Persian Gulf War showed that the network still had a long way to go in recapturing its former dominance in the industry. CBS's reliance on past accomplishments was underscored in 1991, when the network successfully challenged its competitors with a "special" prime-time programming schedule derived from the reworking of two "Golden-Age" programs, *Ed Sullivan* and *I Love Lucy*, along with a reunited cast from *M*A*S*H* and reruns of the *Bob Newhart Show*. These programs generated badly needed high ratings and served as a fitting monument to William Paley and the glory days of CBS under his leadership.

Beginning in 1991, the sparkle in the CBS crown returned; the network finished first in the prime-time ratings for three consecutive seasons.[5] Its success was attributed to a number of factors, including more consistent programming leadership, a record-breaking 1994 Winter Olympics telecast, and overall increasing audience shares for network television.

The mid-nineties, however, presented new challenges to CBS's leadership. Ratings fell to an all-time low for the 1995 season, putting the network back into third place. Their loss of the network broadcast rights for National Football League (NFL) games to NBC and Fox was a startling blow. As a result of this loss and aggressive investment by Fox in New World Communications Group, CBS failed to keep control of eight affiliated stations, losing them to Fox, including stations in Dallas, Detroit, Atlanta, and Cleveland.

Hoping to recoup their dominance from Fox, CBS announced a merger with the Quality, Value and Convenience (QVC) Cable shopping network, led by Barry Diller, a brilliant television and film entrepreneur. That deal failed to be consummated because of both business and personal complications.[6] CBS, however, was not satisfied to be a mere bystander as Fox or any other television network pulled the rug out from under its stable of affiliated stations. In July, 1994, CBS announced an agreement with Group W for a long-term (ten-year) affiliation agreement with Group W television stations in five cities, and in 1995 CBS spent more than $1 billion for a seven-year basketball deal.[7]

The network's fortunes were dealt another blow when Howard Stringer, president of the CBS Broadcast Group, resigned in 1995. Stringer had a long and distinguished career at CBS and was credited with helping to turn the network around. He left to assume a leadership position of a tele-TV joint interactive-video venture funded by Pacific Telesis Group, the Bell Atlantic Corporation, and NYNEX Corporation. His departure gave even more credence to the investment community's sense that Lawrence Tisch was very serious about selling the network.

Fox Television Network

One man who is no stranger to the world of mergers and acquisitions is Australia's Keith Rupert Murdoch. In 1988 Murdoch's company, The News Corporation Ltd., purchased Triangle Publications from Walter Annenberg for $3.2 billion. With its 112 editions and the third-largest weekly circulation (behind *Modern Maturity* and *Reader's Digest*), *TV Guide*, the crown jewel of Triangle, is a leader in mass-market magazine publishing. Although Murdoch built his empire in Australia and London by securing a number of newspapers and magazines, it has been his American acquisitions that have attracted attention. Prior to his procurement of Triangle Publications, Murdoch had bought the *Boston Herald American*, the *Chicago Sun Times*, the *New York Post*, *New York* magazine, the *Village Voice*, *New West*, *New Woman*, and Harper and Row. His aggressiveness in publishing is surpassed by an even more consuming drive to acquire television stations and movie studios. In his quest to become a media mogul, Murdoch bought Twentieth Century Fox from Marvin Davis for $575 million and then for a mere $2 billion acquired the Metromedia Stations headquartered in New York City. His grand design is to establish a fourth commercial television broadcasting network, Fox Broadcasting, to compete with CBS, NBC, and ABC. The network, which started in 1986, has more than 150 affiliates, including the nine Fox–owned and operated stations.

In 1994, Murdoch's genius for timing and opportunity brought about two of the most radical broadcasting deals of the decade. For the first time, Fox became a player in the high-profile world of sports broadcasting when it outbid CBS and the other networks for the NFL's NFC games by offering $1.56 billion over four years, or $400 million more than CBS, which had been broadcasting the games for the last thirty-eight years. While a sports franchise is important to network television, the parties realized the risks involved and the heavy financial losses endured from broadcasting baseball and football games. Both NBC and CBS entered the NFL negotiations firmly committed to reducing broadcast licensing fees.

Fox, however, dramatically changed the negotiating process when it bargained with an open checkbook and a high-priority corporate agenda. And shortly after acquiring the National Football Conference rights, Fox Sports landed exclusive network television privileges for National Hockey League (NHL) games for $155 million over five years.

Murdoch knew that the football franchise would help to legitimize Fox as a competitive national broadcast network. He also expected to discount any losses from the deal by parlaying the NFL acquisition into a strategic marketing coup. In May 1994, Fox announced that it had reached an agreement with New World Communications Group Inc., which effectively would add the group's entire stable of twelve stations to the Fox affiliate family. The biggest loser in this deal was CBS, which lost eight of its affiliates to Fox, while ABC lost three, and NBC, one.

New World's major investor, billionaire Ronald Perelman of Revlon fame, accomplished two goals in the Fox deal. One was a long-standing desire to become a significant force in the entertainment industry; the other was to infuse his station group with a large sum of cash. Fox provided the cash when Murdoch pledged to invest $500 million in New World.

Although Fox seems to be poised on the threshold of competitive success, it is still a long way from achieving parity with the other networks. It does not have a network news presence, and its daytime, prime-time, and late-night programming do not measure up to the competition. However, Murdoch has shown a willingness to endure substantial losses in order to meet his goals and prove to the world that he can build a competitive fourth network.

While Rupert Murdoch has demonstrated keen business acumen, he has also proven to be a skilled tactician. Entering the U.S. market and creating a synergy between film, television, and publishing required an ambitious confrontation with a myriad of government antitrust rules and regulations. To the chagrin of the three broadcast networks, Fox was immune from the infamous FCC financial interest and syndication ("Fin/Syn") rules, which severely restrict a network's ownership of programming distributed on its facilities and place limitations on the network's ability to participate in the syndication of those programs. A 1991 FCC ruling defines a network as a broadcasting service that distributes more than fifteen hours of prime-time programming a week: thus, as long as Fox stayed below the fifteen-hour prime-time allotment, it remained exempt from the rules. However, when Fox exceeded the limit, it managed to negotiate a waiver to the rules, raising the ire of the broadcast networks. Then the Fin/Syn rules were abolished altogether in 1995.

Murdoch's negotiating ability was also tested concerning his ownership of both a newspaper and a television station in the same city. This situation, known as cross-ownership, is prohibited by FCC policy. In fact, Murdoch's cross-ownerships involved *four* properties in *two* cities: the *Boston Herald* and WFXT-TV in Boston and the *New York Post* and WNYW-TV in New York. For some time, however, Murdoch was given a waiver that allowed him to own and operate these properties while he actively campaigned for a relaxation of the cross-ownership rules so that he could retain them all. In late 1987, however, with a little sleight of hand by Senators Ernest F. Hollings and Edward Kennedy, legislation was added to a large appropriations bill signed by President Reagan. The legislation prohibited the FCC from repealing or altering its cross-ownership rules and prohibited any extensions or waivers to the rule. Consequently, Murdoch was forced to sell the *New York Post* to Peter Kalikow, in February 1988. Although Murdoch filed a suit against the legislation that was ultimately successful, his was a Pyrrhic victory, since he had already sold the properties in question.[8] But he reacquired the *New York Post* after it teetered on the verge of bankruptcy. In April 1989 the FCC determined that Murdoch could transfer ownership of WFXT-TV, the Boston station, to a trust administered by Edward W. Brooke, a former senator from Massachusetts, and Hugh L. Carey, former governor of New York. Under the terms of the agreement, Mr. Murdoch retained beneficial ownership, which included profits from the sale of the station and dividends awarded by the trustees. Murdoch was barred from the day-to-day operation of the station, and WFXT-TV is prohibited from affiliating itself in any way with the Fox Television network stations.

The early 1990s proved to be perilous financial times for media moguls like Rupert Murdoch. Saddled with excessive short-term debt and facing billion-dollar loan repayment, Murdoch was forced to restructure his debt by negotiating with the 150 banks and insurance companies that he is indebted to. To meet these payments, Murdoch sold off nine of his American magazine holdings for $600 million in 1991.

Consumed with his vision to create a global media empire, Murdoch has surmounted a number of challenges and has succeeded in fulfilling his agenda for controlling a significant portion of production and distribution on the information highway. In 1995 he won a landmark FCC decision against the rules that prohibit more than 25 percent foreign ownership of radio and television stations. Murdoch, a naturalized American citizen, argued that his was not foreign ownership, but the FCC claimed that the Fox–owned and operated stations were, since 99 percent of the Fox stations' equity is owned by the News Corporation, an Australian holding company. In an effort to resolve the issue, the FCC asked Fox to either show how its network served the public interest or reorganize. In May 1995, Fox Television announced that it would restructure itself to meet the government foreign ownership concerns.[9] Shortly after settling the FCC requirement, Murdoch announced a $2-billion agreement with long-distance telephone carrier, MCI, for a joint global venture in content and distribution.

Time Warner

Corporate instinct is a unique phenomenon that involves an ability to predict the direction of future business trends. Sensing a shift in the entertainment industry and feeling a need to advance a new business posture, in 1989, Time and Warner Communications announced their intention to merge.

Time's move of aligning itself with Warner presented it with several opportunities and advantages that made the merger attractive. The leaders of Time believed that the merger would thwart a hostile takeover of their compnay. In addition, an agreement with Warner was in consonance with Time's financial agenda: both companies owned cable systems, produced feature-length films, and had various publication subsidiaries. Time owned HBO, and Warner owned one of the most successful record companies in the nation. Apparently the merger between Time and Warner had been contemplated for some time, because the companies had already exchanged shares, with Warner owning 12.5 percent of Time, and Time 9.5 percent of Warner. According to the terms of the deal, Warner's owners were to hold 60 percent of the combined company.

Like other diversified media conglomerates, Time Warner has not been immune to the vagaries of an uncertain economy. Servicing a massive debt of $8.8 billion while remaining sensitive to the concerns of shareholders became a difficult juggling act to sustain. Steven Ross's Time Warner found a solution to this problem when in 1991 the Toshiba Corporation and the Itochu Corporation announced a $1.6 billion investment inTime Warner, effectively acquiring 12.5 percent ownership in the company's cable, HBO, and film business, and resulting in a new limited partnership, Time Warner Entertainment.

The two Japanese companies are well-established multinationals: Toshiba and its consumer electronics boast annual sales of $33 billion, and Itochu, the world's largest trading company, has a hand in everything from uranium to clothing, and annual sales in eighty-seven countries of $150 billion. As with other Japanese investments in American media, the rationale has been to build on their technological expertise by learning how Americans create enetertainment and unifying that knowledge with technological advances. There is little doubt that Time Warner, with its interests in motion pictures, television, publishing, cable television, television production, and music, will be a major global force in the media during the nineties and beyond.

Interestingly, the two personalities most closely associated with the founding of these two companies could not be more opposite in character. Although both men had humble beginnings, Steven J, Ross, a former funeral-parlor and parking-garage manager, led Warner with a flamboyant and extravagant style, while Henry Luce (who died long before the merger), founder of Time and the son of missionaries, was almost miserly in his corporate and personal life. Because of his compensation (between $34.5 and $78 million a year), lavish life-style, and a failed $3.5 billion rights offering, Ross was motivated to make this Asian connection. And while the Japanese are noted for their deep pockets, they also have a pecuniary instinct that could be reflected in Time Warner's free-spending mentality.

After Steven Ross's death in 1992, Gerald Levin took over the company. Levin's personality was in stark contrast to the glitzy, show-biz style of Ross. He is a low-profile executive whose style and demeanor is more evocative of the classroom than the boardroom. Although making an attempt at more visibility, he is clearly uncomfortable in the frenzied publicity of the businesses in which Time Warner is so firmly established.

Because of Levin's low-key leadership style, Time Warner has been perceived as being vulnerable to a corporate takeover. In 1994, Seagrams Inc. took an increased equity position in Time Warner. Edgar Bronfman Jr., the heir to the Seagrams fortune, was known to be interested in the company and had powerful West Coast friends who were willing to help him achieve his goal. In 1995, however, Seagrams purchased 80 percent of MCA, putting its 15 percent share of Time Warner on the auction block.

Levin has committed Time Warner to the development of a fifth broadcast television network—WB television network, which premiered in January, 1995—a highly speculative endeavor, given the present broadcasting environment. With Fox becoming a more viable player in network television and Paramount also vying for fifth-network status—United Paramount Network also made its debut in January 1995—the feasibility of Time Warner's success in this venture is greatly diminished.

There are other businesses, however, where Time Warner is making more realistic attempts to compete. Although 1994 federal cable rate cuts forced the company to reduce its cable capital spending by $100 million, the Time Warner cable subsidiary has embarked on an ambitious interactive television project in Orlando, Florida. Levin's commitment to making Time Warner cable the largest multiple system operator (MSO) in the nation was dramatically realized in early 1995 when the company announced the acquisitions of Houston Industries and Cablevision Industries.[10] These new holdings increased Time Warner's cable subscriber base to 11.5 million, almost as large as TCI's.

Developing sophisticated video distribution technology is a priority for Time Warner; however, providing an effective interface with existing technology is also high on their corporate agenda. In 1994 the company was the first to announce that it would use its cable technology to provide telephone service to residential and business customers. The competitive telephone service was implemented in Rochester, New York.

Another matter that Levin must be concerned about is the decline in earnings for the Warner Music Group. Although consistently a leader in U.S. market share, the Warner Brothers music label has relied heavily on some of its more established talent, like Madonna, to generate high profits for the division. In the past Madonna has produced $1.35 billion in revenue since her 1983 debut album, but her recent performance has been more lackluster. Her popularity was not enhanced by her tasteless 1994 network television appearance on *Late Show with David Letterman* or by the publication of *The I Hate Madonna Handbook*. In addition, the Warner Music Group experienced a change in senior executive management that may have been prompted by public and congressional displeasure of its "gangsta" rap music, featuring violent and degrading lyrics.[11]

Turner Network

He's popped up in some unusual places—at the helm of a racing yacht, in conversation with Cuba's Fidel Castro, and on the cover of *Time* magazine—but surprise and audacity are no strangers to Robert Edward "Ted" Turner III. Adept at making deals, Turner revived his father's bankrupt billboard business and acquired a number of media properties that challenged the traditional precepts of the media industry. He created the first cable superstation by taking a local station, WTBS-Atlanta, and distributing its signal via satellite to cable systems around the country. Turner also challenged the monopoly of network news in 1980 by creating the first twenty-four-hour news channel, Cable News Network (CNN), which was a step ahead of the broadcasters in covering the Persian Gulf War. He made headlines again when he attempted a takeover of CBS Inc., and when that effort failed he purchased MGM from Kirk Kerkorian mainly for its vast film library.

That deal cost Turner $1.5 billion and submerged his empire in an enormous debt. In order to make the debt manageable, Turner was forced to sell large blocks of equity in his company to several large cable corporations that formed a consortium of thirty-one cable companies. He also had to give up some of his power to a fifteen-member board of directors, which provides oversight for any expenditures over $2 million. In order to launch Turner Network Television (TNT), Turner had to convince his board of directors that the new programming service was a sound investment, and they agreed with him, stipulating only that Turner reinvest 80 percent of revenue earned back into programming.

As a result of his acquisition of the MGM film library, Turner was embroiled in yet another controversy, when he set out to colorize the black and white films in the collection. The colorization process uses computers to add color to black-and-white films with the purpose of increasing their marketability.

Creating a synergy among cable television, motion pictures, broadcast television, and video technology has become a dominant theme in Ted Turner's quest for diversification. In 1993, Turner purchased two movie studios, Castle Rock Entertainment and New Line Cinema Corporation. Castle Rock, which had produced the 1993 Clint Eastwood hit, *In the Line of Fire*, and has respected producer/director Rob Reiner as a principal, is being positioned by Turner as a major player in theatrical film production. Turner's purchase of Hanna-Barbera and his 1992 launch of the Cartoon Network were bold moves that helped to secure Turner's position as a leading entertainment provider.

It is apparent, however, that Ted Turner is not satisfied with being an "also-ran" in the vast stakes of media domination. He would like to be a primary bidder for sports franchises and Olympic Games; instead he has had to be satisfied with the leftovers from network television. Turner truly aspires to be owner of a broadcast network, and he's willing to make the personal and professional sacrifices that will enable him to achieve his goal. In 1995, Turner broke off talks with General Electric in his attempt to acquire a whole or a part of NBC. However, that same year Turner entered into an agreement with Time Warner to sell it the 82 percent of Turner Broadcasting that it didn't already own.

Like other media moguls who have taken note of McLuhan's prophecy of the "global village," Turner has set his sights on the international media marketplace. He has created an international presence for some of his domestic operations, such as CNN International, TNT Latin America, TNT and Cartoon Network Europe, and Cartoon Network, Latin America. Turner, always restless for greater growth, is now hoping to expand his influence into rapidly developing Asian markets.

Disney

The Walt Disney Company has a substantial investment in both broadcast and cable television. Disney stunned Wall Street and the telecommunications industry in July 1995, when it announced an agreement with Capital Cities/ABC to purchase that company for $19 billion. The combination of these two giant entertainment companies marks an industry watershed in creating entertainment synergism between broadcasting, cable, film, and telephone technology. After the acquisition, Disney became the eleventh-largest American corporation in the Fortune 500 and the largest media company. As a result of the merger, Disney has created the essence of the vertically integrated company controlling production, distribution, and exhibition of its product.[12] Disney owns the Buena Vista and Touchstone film production companies, Walt Disney television, and the Disney Channel cable television station, whose programming includes both vintage animated features and original productions. In January 1989, Disney extended its programming reach by purchasing an independent television station, KCAL-TV, the lowest-rated independent television station in Los Angeles, for $320 million.[13] Disney, which produces a number of successful syndicated television programs, is using the station as a home base for the development of original programming and the distribution of its syndicated television programs.

Disney has been aggressive in the syndicated television programming marketplace and has achieved notable success with its animated series *Ducktails*. If anyone doubts Disney's goal of becoming one of the most productive television program syndicators, an examination of its programming investment speaks to its commitment. Disney's syndicated afternoon programming block of sixty-five programs costs $110 million, or $400,000 per half-hour episode. In addition, the Walt Disney Company is spending $30 million to promote the programming series and will feature their animated stars in future Disney theatrical films.

Disney has also worked at assuring a profitable after-market for its feature films. In the summer of 1989, it purchased an equal share of Viewers Choice, a New York–based pay-per-view company. Its partners in the venture are American Television and Communications, Continental Cablevision, Cox Communications, Newhouse Broadcasting, Telecable, and Viacom Cable. As part of the deal, Touchstone and Hollywood Pictures agreed to provide feature films to the pay-per-view company.

Another technique devised to generate additional profits from Disney theatrical features is the video "sell-through market," in which feature films are sold directly to consumers on video cassettes. This mode of distribution was successful for Disney and made *Pretty Woman* the top-selling video for 1990, earning Disney a $40-million profit. In a bold marketing move, Disney in 1994 released the *Return of Jafar*, its sequel to *Aladdin*, directly to video, bypassing theatrical distribution.

Disney's commitment to television was also evidenced by its expenditure of more than $100 million to retain the exclusive services of the most accomplished writer/producer teams in the business. These teams were essential to the success of series like *Roseanne*, *The Golden Girls*, and *My Two Dads*. This effort shows that Disney is devoted to revitalizing its network television production subsidiaries, Buena Vista, Touchstone, and Walt Disney Television, into a prominent force in prime-time network television program production.[14] Indeed, Disney's commitment to broadcast television and the network hierarchy was clearly enunciated by its acquisition of Capital Cities/ABC.

Perhaps Disney's most visible failure was the aborted acquisition of Jim Henson Associates. In 1989 the two companies announced that Disney would purchase Henson's Muppets for $150 million. In addition to acquiring the exclusive rights to the vast Muppet television library, Disney would also own exclusive merchandising rights to Muppet characters. To many, the deal seemed to be an arrangement fit for fantasy land: until the untimely death of Jim Henson in 1990. After his death the parties could not come to terms, and eventually Henson's family filed a lawsuit charging Disney with copyright/trademark infringement, corporate greed, and exploitation. Finally the parties settled out of court.

Viacom

One of the most protracted and tense corporate bidding wars ever to consume the American entertainment industry occurred during the five months between September 1993 and February 1994, when Viacom and QVC were posturing against one another for the ultimate prize, Paramount Communications. Viacom's bid of nearly $10 billion made it the victor and created the second-largest media/entertainment giant after Time Warner. Viacom, which billionaire Sumner Redstone bought in 1987 for $3.4 billion, has interests in cable and broadcast television, while Paramount is most noted for its motion picture studio but also is diversified, with interests in publishing and sports franchises.[15] Perhaps the most difficult challenge facing Viacom is the melding of two diverse corporate units into a cohesive whole for more profitable economies of scale. To that end, in 1994 Viacom management announced a restructuring of its divisions, creating the Viacom Entertainment Group, which includes Paramount Pictures, Paramount and Viacom television program production and distribution, and the Paramount and Viacom broadcast groups.

Blockbuster Entertainment

One of the key players in the Viacom/Paramount deal was Wayne Huizenga, CEO of Blockbuster Entertainment. Eager to position his company as a major media broker, Huizenga agreed to sell Blockbuster to Viacom for $7.97 billion in Viacom stock.

Confronting a high-tech future where "video on demand," the ability for cable subscribers to view movies in their home anytime they wish, could eat into video rental profits, Huizenga created his own brand of synergism. Blockbuster has diversified into the music retailing business; it acquired several large chains, making it the third-largest music retailer in the country. In a unique attempt to create a new niche market in the music retailing business, Blockbuster joined with IBM to develop a "music on demand" retailing option for consumers. The joint venture, called New Leaf, allows consumers to make their own compact disks on site at a kiosk in the music store. Eventually Blockbuster hopes to expand the technology to create a video version.

Having secured a firm foothold in the video and music business, Huizenga pursued his quest for an integrated company by buying a third of Republic Pictures Corporation (RPC) and a majority of the Spelling Entertainment Group, a major producer of television programs.

Huizenga owns a number of high-profile sports franchises that also factor into his entertainment empire. He plans to build a huge sports and entertainment park on twenty-five hundred acres of land northwest of Fort Lauderdale, which he intends to make into one of the country's major entertainment attractions.

SYNERGY

While the consolidation of American media and entertainment properties was becoming a prominent theme in U.S. business, the Japanese were studying the marketplace for investment. Having already established a conspicuous American position in the distribution of electronic hardware, Japanese businessmen sensed the need to move into the software market. While Japanese manufacturers had handily captured the American market for hardware, their talent for producing and packaging entertainment software was seriously deficient. To make up for this, some Japanese investors simply acquired that which they could not create.

The first entertainment company to fall under Japanese control was CBS Records. An established leader in the recording industry with a stable of top artists, it was irresistible to Sony, which bought it for $2 billion in 1987. Encouraged after this creative plunge, Sony pressed ahead and purchased Columbia Pictures from the Coca-Cola Company for $5 billion.

The Sony foray into the American entertainment industry aroused the interest of another Japanese global giant, the Matsushita Electric Industrial Company. Founded in 1918 with a $50 stake by Konosuke Matsushita, the company grew from a modest manufacturer of electric light sockets to an international conglomerate, swallowing up companies like JVC and Quasar. At the time of his death, Konosuke Matsushita left an estate worth $1.88 billion.

Matsushita's successor, Akio Tanii, a powerful figure in international business, had watched Sony's move into the American creative community with both interest and suspicion. The idea of creating a symbiotic relationship between electronic hardware and software was an enticing prospect to Tanii, and in 1990 the Matsushita Electric Industrial Company acquired MCA Inc., in the process becoming the owner of Universal Pictures, Geffen Records, theme parks, a publishing house, and Los Angeles real estate.

With no prior experience in the creative aspect of entertainment production, the Japanese companies initially made few personnel changes in their respective studios. However, they soon learned that the Japanese style of management was not well suited to the high-risk, glitzy life-style of Hollywood show business. In 1994, Sony announced a $2.7 billion write-off from its 1989 acquisition of Columbia Pictures Entertainment, and Matsushita hired the high-powered financial consultant Michael Ovitz and the investment banking concern of Allen & Co. to help it out of its quagmire.[16]

In April 1995, Matsushita announced that it was selling 80 percent of MCA, Inc. to the Seagrams Company for $5.7 billion in cash. Edgar Bronfman Jr., the CEO of Seagrams, had a long-standing interest in the entertainment industry, having acquired 15 percent equity in Time Warner. Apparently there were significant cultural and professional differences between Yoichi Morishita, president of Matsushita, and Lew Wasserman, MCA's chairman, and Sidney J. Sheinberg, its president.

NOTES

1. Ben H. Bagdikian, *The Media Monopoly*, 2 ed. (Boston: Beacon Press, 1987), 24.

2. Kevin Maney, *Megamedia Shakeout* (New York: John Wiley & Sons, 1995), Chapter Three.

3. In 1985 the company pleaded guilty to forging one hundred thousand employee time cards to transfer expense from a private contract to a Department of Defense project.

4. Christopher Winans, *The King of Cash* (New York: John Wiley & Sons, Inc.), 1995.

5. 1990–91, 1992–93, and 1993–94.

6. In 1995 Barry Diller purchased controlling interest in Silver King Communications, the sixth largest television-group owner in the nation.

7. In July 1995 Westinghouse bought CBS for $81 a share, for a total price of $5.4 billion. The FCC approved the acquisition in November 1995.

8. Geraldine Fubrikant, "Murdoch Selling 9 U.S. Publications for $600 million," *New York Times*, 26 April 1991, A1, D15.

9. In July 1995 the FCC announced that Fox's ownership structure is acceptable because it is in the public interest.

10. Houston Industries was acquired for $2.3 billion, and Cablevision for $2.2 billion.

11. As this book went to press Time Warner made a $8.5 billion offer to acquire Turner Broadcasting System Inc. In 1995 Time Warner Inc. sold back 50 percent of its stake in Interscope Records, which featured gangsta rap performers.

12. The terms of the deal require that Disney pay $65 plus one share of Disney stock for each share of Capital Cities/ABC. For that, Disney gets a television network and, as a special trophy, ESPN, a distinguished international sports distribution franchise.

13. Disney acquired ownership of KABC-TV in Los Angeles as part of its merger with Capital Cities/ABC and agreed to divest itself of KCAL-TV to comply with then current FCC ownership rules.

14. Chairman Michael Eisner's commitment to making Disney the preeminent entertainment company was evidenced by his hiring Michael Ovitz, chairman of the Creative Artists Agency (CAA), as president of Disney.

15. After the Paramount acquisition, Sumner Redstone sold off Madison Square Garden, the Knicks, and the Rangers to Cablevision and ITT for $1.075 billion. In 1995, Viacom announced a complex transaction spinning off its cable systems and transferring $1.7 billion of debt to a new company. TCI acquired the shares of the new company for $350 million and assumed the debt. TCI then gained control of Viacom's 1.2 million cable subscribers.

16. Responding to its heavy losses, Sony's President Nabuyuki Ideo in 1995 forced the resignation of Michael P. Schulhof, President and Chief Executive of Sony Corporation of America.

2

Strategies for Success: Networks and Independent Stations

Over the course of its history, television has gradually become accepted as a legitimate purveyor of the arts of comedy and drama while it has sustained its image as an effective tool for the dissemination of news and information. But as thousands of hours of programming flicker endlessly across millions of cathode-ray tubes and liquid crystal displays, the most prominent symbol that defines the industry is the dollar sign.

Although network television revenues have suffered from competition with cable and videocassettes and from shrinking advertising budgets, they are still a potent force in the industry. They control most station affiliates and national news coverage, own and operate stations, and wield powerful lobbying efforts.

NETWORK AFFILIATES

A television station affiliated with a national network has the enormous financial resources of a diversified entertainment company behind it. Each network affiliate draws upon its parent network for programming—approximately five thousand hours annually—and for scheduling, promotion, and advertising services. A station affiliated with a network enters into an agreement with the network that defines the responsibilities of each party. This contract addresses a number of points including program distribution, scheduling of financial renumeration, program logs, program substitution, and indemnification (which protects the network-affiliated station from any suits emanating from network programming).

It is the network's responsibility to arrange for the distribution of its programming to its affiliates around the country. Distribution of programs is by one of two formats—wire or satellite. Since the days of radio, the networks have relied almost exclusively on the use of AT&T telephone lines for the dissemination of programming. Satellites, however, have provided an efficient alternative to traditional wire distribution, and all four commercial networks are now involved in distributing their programming schedules via satellite.

The terms of network/station contracts do provide the station affiliate with the option of rejecting any of the network programs. This option, however, must be exercised at least seventy-two hours before the program is scheduled for broadcast. If a program is rejected by the affiliate, then the network has the right to offer the rejected program to any other station in the same market. In practice, an affiliated station would be unlikely to exercise this option frequently because of the loss of revenue and the need to provide substitute programming. In addition, there is the ever present possibility that the network might be antagonized to a point where it would abandon the station after expiration of the contract.

In order for a group of television stations to function as a network, they must have a consistent programming schedule for each time zone across the country. This means that affiliated stations agree to broadcast the programs locally in their market on the day and in the time period that the network specifies. This scheduling consistency allows the network to build audience loyalty and sell national advertising. If affiliated stations reject network programming or delay such programming for broadcast during a different time period, then the network structure begins to crumble and advertisers can no longer rely upon comprehensive national or regional coverage. For example, in 1993 CBS was faced with the formidable task of clearing affiliate time for its new program, *The Late Show with David Letterman*. This was difficult because a considerable number of CBS affiliates had contractual obligations to broadcast other programs in the 11:30 p.m. (Eastern) time slot.

Remuneration

There are two ways that the affiliate station earns revenue from the network. The first is via direct payment from the network to the station. This payment is based on the amount of time that the station reserves for network programming and the market size and audience reach of the affiliated station. These payments vary; a station in a large city can earn as much as $1 million a year, while a small station's network earnings may be only several hundred thousand dollars. Fox has over 150 affiliated stations, while ABC, NBC, and CBS each have over 200 affiliates. Except for

Fox, each of the networks distribute over $100 million of annual compensation to their affiliates.

With increased concerns about trimming budgets, the networks have been searching for ways to decrease the costs of affiliate compensation. In May 1989, NBC took a bold step and announced a new performance-based affiliate compensation plan. Starting in January 1990, all NBC affiliates had their compensation computed according to two statistical variables; audience size for local programs broadcast between 4:00 and 8:00 p.m., and demographic breakdown. The 4:00–8:00 p.m. time period is critical to network programming because it provides a local audience flow to network prime-time programs. Demographics are also important because advertisers are particularly interested in reaching the eighteen-to-thirty-four-year age group. In a concession to its affiliated stations, NBC guaranteed that affiliate compensation for any station would not vary by more than 20 percent annually.

CBS and ABC have now also adopted performance-based affiliation agreements. In 1992, however, CBS nearly caused a revolt among its affiliated stations when it announced that the network would begin charging them for programming. Attempting to reverse an $85.8 million loss in 1991, the network proposed a maximum charge of 25 percent of annual compensation for stations in the one hundred biggest markets. After a tense confrontation with CBS affiliates, the network backed down from its program compensation plan, although it did initiate a plan to further decrease their affiliate payments. But CBS's CEO Tisch's frugality backfired in 1994, when Rupert Murdoch, CEO of Fox, engineered the defection of twelve CBS affiliates to the Fox station line-up. This raid caused a realignment in the network affiliate hierarchy as CBS moved to substitute the twelve stations it lost by replacing them with affiliated stations from other networks.

Network-affiliated stations naturally dislike any attempts to cut their network compensation, as these payments account for 5 to 25 percent of their annual revenue. Although the affiliated stations would rather have a more stable reimbursement program, they are well aware of the value of network compensation in an increasingly competitive marketplace. Two cases illustrate this point. KGMB, a CBS affiliate in Honolulu, was informed by the network that it would lose its $300,000 annual payment because of the excessive number of local preemptions by the station. In the meantime, two local independent stations had approached CBS offering to pay the network for the privilege of affiliation. A similar case occurred with WTVQ, a Lexington, Kentucky ABC affiliate.

The second source of affiliate revenue is generated by the availability of commercial spots reserved for the affiliate within and adjacent to network programs. These commercial spots can be sold to local advertisers for a premium because of their position either within or adjacent to the network program. Local advertisers can thus enjoy the benefit of being associated with a network and its programming and the wide exposure that it will generate for them.

While the complexities of the affiliate/network agreement are numerous, there is an additional variable that must be considered. The networks do not actually broadcast the programs they distribute; their affiliates do. Networks are program providers that supply the product and distribution technology to the affiliated stations, which actually show the programs in their local markets. Thus, the local affiliated station is responsible for program content, not the network. Since networks do not broadcast programming, they are not licensed by the FCC, but their affiliates are. It is the affiliate's license that would be placed in jeopardy if network programming violated an FCC regulation; therefore, according to the terms of the contract the network agrees to indemnify, or protect, the broadcaster from any damages, claims, or liabilities that the network program may cause.

Scheduling Strategy

The network views its obligation to affiliates as not merely a business contract but as a bond of mutual support and trust. To this end the network attempts to build a strong program schedule that will generate revenue for both parties. In formulating the schedule, the network must consider several key variables: demographics, audience flow, and program format.

The term "demographic" refers to the type of audience that is expected to view a particular program. The audience population is categorized according to various features—age, sex, income, and other characteristics—for purposes of program scheduling. For example, a network may schedule a children's program prior to adult programming hoping that the adult audience will leave the set tuned to the station that was selected by the child.

Another programming technique that relies upon the inertia of the viewer is the audience-flow strategy, which is based upon the assumption that the audience is passively watching television. To hold the audience, the network must offer programming that will sustain their interest. If programs within the evening schedule are too different from each other, this philosophy goes, the viewer may change the channel. Therefore the network plans "block programming," offering shows of similar format, like situation comedies, during a certain time period. This strategy has worked successfully, with popular sitcoms scheduled back to back.

New programs present unique scheduling difficulties for the network because their impact upon a particular scheduling period is unknown. One strategy is to place the new program between two successful ones, a practice known as "hammocking." This technique offers a strong lead-in that provides audience flow to the new entry and gives the new program an opportunity to build an audience and sustain a viable ratings posture during the first weeks of the season.

The fall 1989 season offered an interesting case study on a network's competitive programming strategy. CBS, for years the acknowledged leader of prime-time television, had been smarting from the ratings superiority of its rivals, NBC and ABC. In an attempt to avoid the disastrous programming strategy that had befallen the network in the fall 1988 season, CBS decided that the fall 1989 prime-time network programming schedule would shift its emphasis from viewers eighteen-to-thirty-four, to the thirty-five-and-over age group. The network selected programs whose prominent characters were well into their thirties or forties. Unfortunately, this gamble on older rating demographics did not prove successful and resulted in the forced resignation of Kim LeMasters, the CBS head of entertainment, and the cancellation of several series. CBS did regain its ratings in the 1990s, with some of their programs—*Murder ,She Wrote, Dr. Quinn,* and *In the Heat of the Night*—appealing to older audiences.

Program Development

While the network may use scheduling strategies to help insure audience stability, the most effective means for establishing successful programs is during the production development process. One cost-effective technique is the use of derivative programming or "spin-offs" from successful network series. For example, the series *Happy Days* inspired other successful programs such as *Laverne and Shirley* and *Mork and Mindy.* Another proven strategy is to create crossover appearances by favored series characters. By doing this, a character from a popular program can appear on a less successful program and generate higher ratings. Occasionally networks engage in a practice called "stunting," which may be used effectively during a week when national ratings surveys are made. Stunting refers to abrupt changes in the normal daily program schedule and usually includes movie-length versions of regularly scheduled series, miniseries, specials, and theatrical film presentations.

New program development is a rigorous business not well suited for the fainthearted. Typically the three networks receive five thousand to six thousand new program proposals annually. Many of these come from established production companies whose talent pool includes writers and

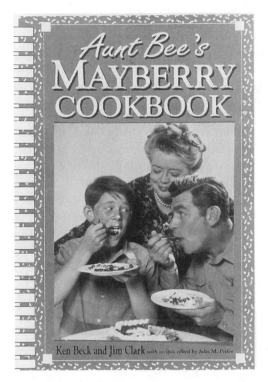

Syndicated sitcoms may provide additional sources of revenue, such as book. *Aunt Bee's Mayberry Cookbook* was named after a character from *The Andy Griffith Show.* Courtesy of Rutledge Hill Press.

producers that have network production experience and previous network programming success. Some critics blame the lack of program diversity on the network's bias toward prominent production companies and the television divisions of the major Hollywood studios. However, it is these companies that have the financial resources, talent, and business connections needed to demonstrate a credible programming posture with the networks.

After an initial review process, the networks select approximately five hundred scripts for further development. At this stage, the network is cautious about investing vast sums of money in unrealized programs, so they resort to the "step deal." Money is provided to the production company on a step-by-step basis, and funding may cease at any stage along the way. Normally the first step is authorization for an expanded treatment or a script. If the network continues to be interested, it may order additional scripts or authorize expanded rewrites. Although well-known writers command hefty fees, the money is better spent this way than on an expensive, failed pilot.

By far most of the submissions that networks receive are for half-hour situation comedies ("sitcoms"). Sitcoms are one of the most popular programming formats in television today because some of them have the ability to last for decades and generate hundreds of millions of dollars in syndication profits.

Those sitcoms that pass the test of time are known within the industry as "evergreens." Although many sitcoms are profitable in syndication, only a few have the qualities needed to become evergreens. Those qualities include ample program inventory to avoid rerun burnout, an avoidance of overly faddish speech or style, and a unique and creative performance standard. Sitcoms like *I Love Lucy*, *M*A*S*H*, *The Andy Griffith Show*, and *The Dick Van Dyke Show* all have these enduring qualities. The merchandising revenue associated with long-running sitcoms can be enormous: although *The Andy Griffith Show* concluded its run on network television in 1968, *Aunt Bee's Mayberry Cookbook*, named after the popular character in the program, recently sold over eight hundred thousand copies.

Another variable that impacts upon the afterlife of a sitcom is the number of venues available for distribution. Cable television has helped to extend the run of many sitcoms, and CD-ROM, along with interactive video, may also add to the endurance of the format.

The costs associated with the program development process are considerable, especially when there are no guarantees that a program will be selected for the network schedule. There is a significant difference in the cost of producing a pilot for a one-hour drama and a half-hour sitcom. On average the sitcom will cost approximately $750,000 to 1 million, while the drama may cost between $1 and 3 million. Usually, in an effort to achieve the best program pilot possible, the production company exceeds the network's budget allocation; this is referred to as deficit financing. In addition to the big budgets that producers lavish on their pilots, they also bring in specialists—writers, directors, and producers who have exceptional skills in developing successful pilots—to help them.

In many cases, prime-time network dramatic series producers prefer a two-hour pilot because of the enhanced production values generated by a budget of close to $4 million. Usually, two-hour pilots stand a better chance of being picked up by the network because of the cost and effort already invested. Often, even after the pilot becomes a series, the production company spends more to produce the program segments than the network provides for in its license fees. This loss is seen as a long-term investment by the producer, who expects to recoup the original investment plus considerable profits in program syndication.

Even after the producer has surmounted the hurdles of review by the network and has received the network's permission for pilot production, there are still no guarantees that the show will make it to the regular network schedule. The three networks may commission fifty pilots for approximately two dozen vacant time periods for the new season. After the pilots are produced, a number of variables are used to select the programs for the season schedule, and quality is not the only factor.

Sometimes pilot programs are test marketed, and measurements are compiled on viewer preferences. Although the research methodology used to obtain these audience reactions is inconclusive, it is one factor in the program selection process. Another important factor is the competition with the other networks. A pilot may be chosen because it offers an alternative to a program on another network and will hopefully attract that program's audience.

Ratings and demographics are also significant variables in the program selection process. Audience preferences for particular types of programs and the success of certain program themes will also be important determinants. Indeed, the advertiser's concern about reaching a specific audience may be an influencing factor in pilot selection.

Sometimes the selection of a pilot is made according to the mechanics of the season programming environment. These variables may include the time period available, the appeal of talent, the cost of the production, the reputation of the production company, and the program's contribution to the "balance" of the network schedule. With so many possibilities to consider, there is obviously no set formula for success.

Another variable that may influence the network's selection of a program is the "star factor." Well-known television stars, who usually have their own production companies, may pressure their network to select a program that they have developed. This was the case in 1993 when Roseanne Arnold, star of ABC's hit show, *Roseanne*, threatened to leave the network if a sitcom starring her now ex-husband, Tom Arnold, was not selected. ABC purchased the program but cancelled it at the end of the season.

The most successful producers of the 1980s were Marcy Carsey and Tom Werner, of Carsey/Werner Productions. Carsey/Werner struck gold with their prime-time hits *The Cosby Show* and *Roseanne*. Naturally, a successful production team can command higher network license fees and more leverage with network scheduling. Indeed, producers of hit network prime-time television programs have parlayed their success into lucrative network contracts and renewals, which may include bonus payments, two-year commitments, and increased license fees.

With the stakes so high, it is not surprising that talented writers are being wooed into multiyear, multimillion-dollar contracts. For example, Steven Bochco, creator of *L.A. Law* and *NYPD Blue* and one of the most successful writer-producers on television, signed a lucrative contract with CBS.

Promotion

Another factor that can affect the success or failure of a network's programming schedule is the promotional effort made by the company for the new fall season. Elaborate promotional spots featuring network celebrities, glossy production values, and catchy musical slogans all combine to create an enticing image. In a departure from the routine promotional programming campaign, CBS and NBC announced promotional tie-ins with some of the nation's leading retailers for the fall 1989–90 season. CBS joined with K-Mart and NBC with Sears, each focussing on print advertising, direct mail, merchandising, and sweepstakes to lure potential viewers in front of the television set. And NBC's recycling of the 1960s daytime soap opera, *Dark Shadows*, into a prime-time vehicle for the 1991 season involved a multifaceted promotional effort. It included tie-ins with Domino's Pizza, Circuit City Electronic Stores, and United Artist Theaters.[1]

Network Standards and Practices

As a network strives for dominance in ratings and advertising revenue, at the same time it attempts to uphold its public service obligation by providing programming and commercial oversight via its Standards and Practices department. The network Standards and Practices department acts as an internal censor. All scripts for network programs are submitted to this department and evaluated prior to their production. The individuals in the Standards and Practices department watch for potential problems in three major content categories — moral, professional, and commercial. Each of these addresses an ethical agenda that the networks apply to the programs and commercials they distribute.

Each network has defined a moral standard that programming content must adhere to. There are various themes and plots that are avoided in network programming because it is feared that the audience and advertisers may find them offensive. For example, while there are no government regulations that ban nudity from network television, the three networks have themselves censored nude scenes from their made-for-TV movies and television series. Some of the made-for-television movies do contain nude scenes that are included in the movie when it is theatrically released in foreign markets.

There are also sensitive themes that the network Standards and Practices department is concerned about. Incest, homosexuality, interracial marriage, and religious satire are just a few of the areas that networks tend to avoid. While some programs have addressed these matters, they are not a regular feature on network television.[2]

One of the most notable exceptions to this was the CBS network series *All in the Family*, which ran from 1971 to 1991. While its beginnings were shaky—it was rejected by two of the three networks—it went on to become an outstanding success. The series addressed a number of controversial subjects including rape, abortion, infidelity, and religious and racial big-otry. There were, however, certain elements of character and plot that made the program appealing rather than offensive to audiences. Archie Bunker was so stereotypical and his bigotry was so excessive that audiences viewed him as a comic character. Archie's character was also carefully bal-anced by other characters who clearly articulated a more liberal bias.

One of the most controversial programs of the 1989 season was the NBC drama *Roe v. Wade*. Based upon the landmark 1973 Supreme Court abortion case, this program created altercations even before it was broad-cast. Two fundamentalist religious groups, the American Family Association, led by a Southern preacher, Donald Wildmon, and Christian Leaders for Responsible Television, had threatened to boycott products advertised on television shows that they found offensive, which includ-ed *Roe v. Wade*. As a result of public pressure, several advertisers declined sponsorship of the program, and NBC was forced to sell its commercial rates at a significant discount. The script also went through innumerable revisions mandated by Standards and Practices.

Despite the negative publicity surrounding the program, *Roe v. Wade* led its time period for the evening it was broadcast, with a 17.2 rating and a 27 share, providing advertisers with a television bargain. In addition, 210 of NBC's 211 station affiliates cleared the program: this had not been the case for CBS in 1973 when it aired a controversial abortion episode on *Maude* and the network was deserted by 20 percent of its affiliates.

As writers and producers have become valued members of the net-work programming hierarchy, they have also assumed greater editorial control over program content. Because of this, television in the 1990s has had more freedom of expression than ever before. Another factor con-tributing to more programming freedom is competition. Fox Television's attempt to be a legitimate player in the network programming market-place resulted in the production and distribution of such frank and explicit programs as *Married...with Children*, *In Living Color*, and *The Simpsons*. These programs left an indelible mark on the dynamics of net-work programming culture. Indeed, *Married . . . with Children* celebrated its tenth first-run anniversary in 1995.

In addition to programming, the network must also review the con-tent of commercials to assure that claims about their products can be sub-stantiated. The Federal Trade Commission (FTC) is the government agency that has jurisdiction in these matters. Along with the additional responsibilities it carries for regulating hundreds of industries, however, the FTC cannot provide thorough oversight to the thousands of television commercials that are produced each year. Therefore the networks assume responsibility for screening commercials and substantiating claims. This is part of their "nondelegable" obligation as interpreted by the FCC.

INDEPENDENT STATIONS

While network affiliates have maintained a high profile in the broadcast marketplace, there are many stations that are not affiliated with a network. These independent stations also have a formidable presence in many markets and aggressively pursue their local audience.

Independent stations have traditionally had a difficult time competing with the first-run programming of network-affiliated stations. Those independents on a UHF rather than a VHF frequency not only had the network programming to compete against but also the technical bias of the marketplace toward UHF broadcasting. With no network to supply them with programming, independent stations must rely upon themselves and secondary programming suppliers to fill the broadcast schedule. A large percentage of programming appearing on independent stations and cable networks is derived via syndication. More independent stations, however, are joining the ranks of network affiliates. In 1995 two new broadcast networks, United Paramount Network (UPN) and Warner Brothers Television Network, premiered, thus decreasing the universe of purely independent stations.

Syndicated Programs

Syndicated programs are usually off-network reruns or theatrical feature films that are licensed with exclusive multiple broadcast rights to an independent station within a specific market. The price usually depends upon several variables including the size of the market, the popularity of the series, and how recently the series has appeared on network television. In some cases, the original series may still be running on network TV: this of course would be reflected in the price a station pays to license the program.[3]

During the last decade, syndication prices have risen dramatically as a result of competition and the soaring cost of new productions. In 1977 the *Mary Tyler Moore Show* earned an average of $200,000 per episode in nationwide syndication. Lately, however, syndicated programming costs have reached into the stratosphere, with *Cheers* earning $1.4 million per episode, *Magnum P.I.* $1.75 million, *Who's the Boss* $2.5 million, and *The Cosby Show* $4.4 million. (*The Cosby Show's* nationwide syndication sales exceeded $500 million.) Multiply these per-episode costs by a programming inventory of approximately eighty-eight installments (a typical four-year series run), and one can appreciate the enormous financial investment an independent station must make for the right to air a single series.

Although the fees for syndicated comedy series were extraordinarily high during the 1980s, there has been some leveling off in pricing in the

1990s as availability of syndicated programming increases. Over the next few years, a number of sitcoms will have enough programming inventory for domestic syndication. The competition of these programs with each other will ultimately drive prices down. In addition, a significant number of independent stations that were formerly buying syndicated programs are now affiliated with Fox Television and have less need for such programming.

Syndicated series do not always consist of reruns. First-run programs can also be syndicated. For example, Paramount television elected to syndicate its *Star Trek* sequels, *The Next Generation* and *Deep Space Nine*, directly to stations, thus bypassing the networks. These first-run syndicated programs, along with Paramount's *The Untouchables*, cost several million dollars an episode to create. Sometimes producers of network programs that have been cancelled continue production of new material and syndicate the new programs along with the old, as with the series *Fame, Punky Brewster,* and *Baywatch.*

Another type of program that has been successful in syndication and is an important component in the independent station's program schedule is the game show. Programs like *Family Feud, The Newlywed Game,* and *Hollywood Squares* attract a large audience and provide the independent station with a strong revenue base at a reasonable investment.

One of the most successful companies involved in programming syndication is King World Productions. Starting in the 1960s with *The Little Rascals,* King World turned the syndicated hit programs *Wheel of Fortune, Jeopardy,* and *The Oprah Winfrey Show* into the most successful first-run syndicated programs on television. While the syndication programming industry tends to be dominated by large companies like King World, Paramount Television, Twentieth Century Fox, and Warner Brothers Television, smaller companies have also been able to create niche markets for themselves. For example, Worldvision created a first-run syndicated early-morning children's program, *Wake, Rattle, and Roll,* and Republic Pictures Television distribution unit marketed a two-hour weekday movie for late night (11:00 p.m. to 6:00 a.m.) distribution. Small syndication companies usually serve fringe time periods, leaving the prime-time hours to the larger companies.

Other Program Sources

Audience research has continually supported the theory that feature-length films are excellent programs for generating high ratings. Movies have several unique characteristics that make them appealing to independent television stations. They are cost efficient, flexible to program, and adapt easily to various types of promotional campaigns. For exam-

Baywatch, one of the most popular syndicated programs. Courtesy of All American Television Inc. and Richard Mann.

ple, when Fred Silverman, the famous programming executive, started working at his first television station, WGN-TV in Chicago, one of his initial tasks was to take a library of old films and create a new format for them. He accomplished this with a clever new orientation: he created a series called *Family Classics* and hired an attractive host to introduce the "new" films. The technique worked brilliantly. This is a good example of the importance of a successful programmer's ability to creatively recycle old material. Two cable channels, American Movie Classics and Encore, have embraced the same concept and are offering older movies to their audiences.

Another source for an independent television station's programming needs can be found in bartered programs and ad hoc networks. In the barter arrangement, the station agrees to exchange a certain amount of advertising time for program material: no cash payment is made. Some popular bartered programs that have recently appeared on independent television include *Roseanne,* and *The Wonder Years.*

The ad hoc network is similar in technique to the bartered program in that time is exchanged for program material. In addition to the time exchange, however, the ad hoc network also offers a lineup of stations that will broadcast the program at standard times, thus allowing for mass promotion. The ad hoc network is a temporary network that exists for a limited time with a loose coalition of affiliated stations. The Mobil Oil Company created such a network, the Mobil Showcase Network, to broadcast its bartered series *Men Who Dared* and *Edward the King.*

Still another programming variation available to independent stations is cooperative funding of programs. Operation Prime Time, which distributed first-run miniseries including *Testimony of Two Men*, *The Bastard*, and *The Rebel* to affiliated independent television stations, was the first of these ventures. These stations pooled their financial resources to support the series, and each became part of the temporary distribution network.

Thus far all of the programming sources for independent television stations that have been discussed are external. Naturally an independent television station also has the option of producing its own programming: indeed the FCC encourages this and lauds any efforts toward "localism." Nevertheless, the station must weigh several variables, including budget, competition, and talent, before it embarks on a production schedule of its own. News, public affairs, sports, and children's shows tend to be the most successful locally produced programs.

GROUP-OWNED STATIONS

The third category of station ownership is the group-owned station. Group-owned stations are a hybrid of network-affiliated and independent stations. Any corporation, whether it has a media orientation or not, can diversify into group ownership. Within a single group, some of the stations may be network affiliates while others are independents. The stations may be VHF or UHF and may be located in different-sized markets around the country. A large number of these groups are owned by giant corporations that have several cross-media interests—radio, print media, and cable systems. The three networks can also be classified as group owners because their owned and operated stations are administered in a similar fashion, even though all of them are network affiliates. Examples of profitable groups include Group W, Cox Broadcasting, and Storer Broadcasting.

The FCC restricts the number of broadcast television stations that a single licensee may own to twelve. However, maximum ownership also depends upon the percentage of audience already reached by the corporate entity through other media, and no additional licenses can be acquired if it can be shown that undue media concentration has occurred.[4]

Groups generally allow their stations a certain amount of autonomy, but the needs of the group are paramount in the administration of its affairs. Enormous savings can be realized when a group purchases programming for all of its stations. Some groups may also produce original programming and distribute it to the group-owned stations as well as to stations outside the group.

Another advantage of group ownership is the exchange of talent and personnel among the group-owned stations. Personnel with various specializations can be tapped for temporary assignment to other stations within the group. The management style of group-owned stations varies from case to case: some offer a high degree of autonomy to their station executives while others present a more rigid approach. Group ownership provides a flexible approach to management and marketing while achieving substantial economies of scale.

Although there are many similarities between the goals and objectives of networks and station groups, the primary difference is that the networks are a program development and distribution system servicing stations nationwide, while groups consist of a small number of stations that serve discrete parts of the country.

NOTES

1. The combined promotional budgets of CBS, NBC, ABC, and Fox for the 1995 season was estimated at $100 million.

2. In 1968, the first interracial kiss on network prime time television was featured on the *Star Trek* episode titled "Plato's Stepchildren." *All in the Family* in 1971 introduced one of the first homosexual characters to prime time television in the episode titled "Judging Books by Covers."

3. In 1995 Fox began running episodes of the enormously successful series *Home Improvement* while the series continued to run on ABC.

4. As a result of the Telecommunications Act of 1996, restrictions on the number of television stations that companies may own were eliminated, provided the stations do not exceed a reach of more than 35 percent of the United States. The Act also requires the FCC to relax its "duo-poly rule," which limits each broadcaster to one television station per market.

3
The FCC:
The Airwaves and the Public Interest

The Communications Act of 1934 provided for a Federal Communications Commission (FCC), which was to regulate all interstate and foreign communications by wire and radio, including telegraph, telephone, and broadcasting. The seven men who were the first commissioners had no way of knowing that they were poised on the edge of a technological revolution that was about to change the nature of communications in this country and bring about unforeseen results in the politics and culture of the society as well.

Though the FCC was designed to be a watchdog agency, its oversight has been at best inconsistent and somewhat arbitrary. Indeed, the agency's record is more notable for its partisan support of the industries it regulates than for its objectivity. Commissioners frequently accepted gifts and favors from representatives of the broadcast industry and freely engaged in *ex parte* contacts with parties that had petitions before the commission. Or sometimes they formulated policy with an eye toward securing high-paying posts in the industry they were supposed to be regulating.

There have nonetheless been champions among the FCC commissioners, and their contributions to the regulatory process must be acknowledged. The present FCC is charged with a regulatory mandate addressing an overwhelming array of technology that places an enormous administrative burden upon the agency. The FCC had to delay the implementation of the 1992 Cable Television Consumer Protection and Competition Act, which addressed basic service rate regulation, because of inadequate staff and budget. In order to move ahead, Congress had to approve a supplemental budget for the FCC. In an attempt to address the issue of understaffing, FCC Chairman Reed Hundt has lobbied for

Drawn for Broadcasting & Cable by Jack Schmidt
"I think it stands for 'Frequently Conflict-
ing Commissioners!'"

Courtesy of *Broadcasting & Cable.*

increasing the agency's budget and staff. Some Congressional leaders, however, would rather see the FCC eliminated than expanded.

The FCC's oversight of broadcast media has traditionally consisted of a three-phase regulatory procedure that covers allocation of frequency space, assignment of stations, and regulation of existing stations. The commission acts on behalf of the legislature, formulating rules and policy in a quasi-legislative capacity. As it pursues its agenda, the commission publicizes its intention to investigate a matter by issuing a notice of inquiry, and after public hearings it releases a notice of proposed rule making.

The FCC is divided into eight bureaus: the Mass Media Bureau, which addresses over-the-air broadcasting; a Common Carrier Bureau, which provides oversight for telephone and telegraph communications; the Private Radio Bureau, which handles everything from aviation communications to amateur radio; the Field Operations Bureau, which manages the Emergency Broadcast System, enforces regulations, and is involved in inspection and detection of violations; the Cable Services Bureau, which provides oversight for the cable television industry, setting rates and policy, and addresses technological applications of cable; and the two newest bureaus, created in 1994—the Wireless Telecommunications Bureau, which handles the administration of personal communication services (PCS) and frequency auctions, and the International Bureau, which addresses treaty and cross-border issues.

The FCC's regulation of broadcast programming is expressed in a deliberately vague manner because of First Amendment Constitutional guarantees that prohibit prior restraint or censorship of programming content. However, the FCC can take punitive action after a program is broadcast if it can prove that a regulation has been violated.

Section 326 of the Communications Act clearly outlines the

Reed E. Hundt, Chairman of the FCC. Courtesy of the Federal Communications Commission.

Constitutional guarantees of free speech and freedom of the press:

> Nothing in this Act shall be understood or construed to give the Commission the power of censorship over the radio communications or signals transmitted by any radio station, and no regulation or condition shall be promulgated or fixed by the Commission which shall interfere with the right of free speech by means of radio communication.

There are, however, a number of different regulations pertaining to non-program content issues over which the FCC has authority, such as localism, fairness, political broadcasting, programming standards, monopoly, obscenity, and children's television.

LOCALISM

In a 1960 programming policy statement, the FCC served notice to broadcasters about their obligation to serve the needs of their community.

> The principal ingredient of the licensee's obligation to operate in the public interest is the diligent, positive, and continuing effort by the

Figure 3.1
Organizational chart of the Federal Communications Commission (as of January 1995).

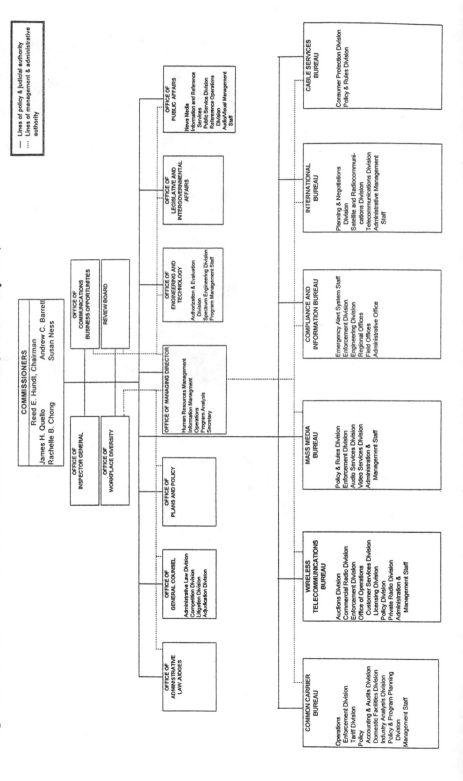

licensee to discover and fulfill the tastes, needs, and desires of his community or service area.

During the 1960s and early 1970s, the FCC made an attempt to encourage more locally produced television programming. In 1971 a new programming policy was initiated by the FCC. Called the Prime Time Access Rule (PTAR), it was an attempt to generate more competition and localism in the nation's top fifty broadcast markets. The PTAR rule required that between the prime-time hours of 7:00 and 11:00 p.m. Eastern time and 6:00 and 10:00 p.m. Central and Mountain times, network affiliated and owned and operated stations surrender an hour of prime time for either first-run nonnetwork syndicated programming or locally produced broadcasts. Traditionally, most local network affiliated stations relied exclusively on network programming to fill their prime-time broadcast day part. The PTAR required them to either produce first-run local programs or acquire nonnetwork first-run syndicated programs.

The rule, however, actually affected only a half-hour of prime time each evening, because most network affiliates already used a half hour of prime time for their own local news shows. There were also several exemptions to the PTAR that applied to network nonentertainment programs and included network programs for young children, public affairs, news, and documentary programs.

Unfortunately, the implementation of the PTAR did little to achieve its goal of encouraging creativity and local production. It did, however, boost a burgeoning new first-run syndicated programming industry that produced network-like programs or retreads of earlier successful network broadcasts.[1]

FAIRNESS

While the FCC encourages the broadcast of local public affairs programs, it also, at one time, required the maintenance of fairness in any programs that addressed controversial issues. The Fairness Doctrine evolved from a 1949 policy statement on editorializing, reinforced by a 1959 amendment to the Communications Act that mandated that broadcasters "afford reasonable opportunity for the discussion of conflicting views of public importance." Under the ruling, stations were obligated to provide balanced viewpoints and to offer air time to responsible spokespersons who wished to express an opposing point of view. The fairness corollaries also outlined detailed procedures to follow if an individual's honesty, character, or integrity had been compromised on the air, as part of the

FCC's personal attack rule. The general Fairness Doctrine provisions were eliminated by the FCC in 1987. However, the political components of the Fairness Doctrine and the personal attack rules continue to prevail under Section 315 of the Communications Act.

POLITICAL BROADCASTING

Fairness rules also still apply to broadcasts made by political candidates. The FCC addressed the rights of political candidates under Sections 312 and 315 of the Communications Act. "Equal time" provisions are the benchmark of the FCC's requirements for political candidates. If a station provides time for a candidate running for elective office, then it must provide equal opportunity for all other legally recognized candidates for that same office. Stations are also obligated to provide candidates with preferential pricing and therefore must provide them with time at their lowest unit charge.

There are several exemptions to the equal time provisions mandated by Section 315. For example, if a candidate appears on a bona fide news program, documentary, talk show, or on-the-spot news coverage, the equal time provisions do not apply. (This policy naturally gives incumbent candidates a considerable advantage.) The FCC has ruled that programs like *Good Morning America, Today, Donahue,* and *Sally Jesse Raphael* are defined as bona fide newscasts and thus not subject to equal time provisions.

SELF-REGULATION AND PROGRAMMING STANDARDS

While the FCC oversees adherence to broadcast regulations, it has always encouraged the industry to also monitor itself. In 1929 the National Association of Broadcasters (NAB), an industry trade organization, developed a voluntary code for its members. Various broadcast issues were addressed in the code, including advertising time standards and programming guidelines. While the code never attempted to dictate program standards to broadcasters, it did offer guidelines for maintaining tasteful programming.

As television matured and audience tastes evolved, the code adapted to the changing mores of American society. Programming themes that were once taboo, such as incest and homosexuality, became acceptable.

In 1982 the NAB Code was declared unconstitutional because of a suit brought by the Justice Department against the advertising time stan-

FCC Commissioner James H. Quello. Courtesy of the Federal Communications Commission.

dards advocated by the NAB.[2] The outcome of this case abrogated the administration of all aspects of the code, including the program standards provision. Although the code was rendered ineffectual by the courts, its programming guidelines, which were always voluntary, are still followed by many television stations.

The seeds for the code's nullification may have been sown as early as 1975. That year marked the beginning of a new programming policy initiated by Congress and the FCC but sponsored by the NAB. Responding to public criticism and Congressional concern, the networks voluntarily initiated a family viewing hour between 7:00 and 9:00 p.m. (Eastern and Pacific times), in which only television programs deemed suitable for viewing by the entire family were to be aired, thus precluding programs with excessive sex and violence. Although this policy was not a regulatory statute, the three networks agreed to its terms in an attempt to quell public criticism of sexually provocative and violent programming formats. In their zeal to enforce the voluntary code, the networks shifted programs around, moving those they deemed unsuitable for family viewing to later time periods. Network censorship also changed language; for example substituting the word "innocent" for "virgin" and urging dress code changes for female artists like Cher.

The family viewing hour raised the ire of many writers and pro-gramming suppliers, including Norman Lear of Tandem Productions, producer of *All in the Family*. They argued that the policy contradicted their First Amendment rights for freedom of speech and that the govern-ment in effect was censoring programming, which it could not do under any legislation or regulation. The courts agreed with the writers and pro-ducers and found that the family viewing hour was an unconstitutional infringement on free speech. In a 1976 decision, Federal Judge Warren J. Ferguson ruled that the family viewing standard constituted a violation of the First Amendment. As a factor in his ruling, Judge Ferguson noted that the FCC had coerced the networks into adopting the voluntary code by informal statements threatening them with sanctions if they didn't comply. Although a United States Court of Appeals overturned Judge Ferguson's ruling in 1979, stating that the Federal District Court had no jurisdiction in the case, the networks declined to reestablish the policy.

While the family viewing hour was an industry attempt at self-regu-lation, recent concerns about the graphic depiction of sex, violence, and illegal drug use on television have led legislators to attempt new statutes designed to address programming of an excessively violent or overtly sexual nature.

MONOPOLY

One area of policy that the FCC has revisited over the years is the station ownership rule. To help guide its judgments in this area, the FCC has established a rationale to control monopoly, promote diversification, and prohibit undue concentration of broadcast properties. In 1940 the Commission established a policy that provided that no single entity could own more than three stations. Responding to industry pressure and a petition by NBC to raise the allotment of owned stations to seven, the commission in 1944 increased the station ownership limit to five. In an effort to promote the growth of UHF television, the FCC in the 1960s expanded television station ownership to seven: five VHF and two UHF.

A change in the economic and competitive climate of the broadcast-ing industry resulting from the forceful confrontation by cable television and VCR technology of television's dominance caused the FCC to once again modify its station ownership rules. Accordingly, in 1991 to 1992 the commission increased the limit of ownership to twelve stations by a sin-gle entity with the proviso that television stations are prohibited from operating in markets that collectively contain more than 25 percent of the nation's television homes. A company may own fourteen television sta-tions if two are UHF, or if two are 50 percent minority owned. The

Telecommunications Act of 1996 removed any limitation on television station ownership, providing the stations owned by a single entity don't reach more than 35 percent of the United States. Also, licenses for television stations were extended to eight years from five.

In 1992 the FCC raised the limit on ownership of AM and FM stations to eighteen each. A single entity could own as many as three AM and three FM stations in the same market, depending upon the size of the community. The FCC also enacted cross-ownership rules that forbid a broadcast licensee to own a newspaper in the same market where they own a radio or television station. Soon after, radio ownership levels were raised to twenty AM and twenty FM stations with no more than two of each in the largest markets. With passage of the 1996 Telecommunications Act, national limits on radio ownership were removed and ownership restrictions in individual markets were relaxed. Licensing terms for radio stations were extended to eight years from the original seven. In addition, the larger the market, the more stations one company may own within it.

Fin/Syn

The commission's efforts to prevent a single network's dominance created a twenty-year conflict pitting the broadcasting and motion picture industries against each other. At issue is the network's proprietary interest in program ownership and distribution. The motion picture industry sees this ownership as a threat to the viability of independent producers. In response to this concern, in 1973 the FCC forbade networks from engaging in syndication and from acquiring any financial interest of any television program produced wholly or in part by an entity other than the network.[3] Under the FCC provisions, networks were allowed to sell and distribute outside the United States only programs for which they were the sole producer. Since the passage of these financial interest/syndication rules—referred to as "Fin/Syn" in the industry—the networks and the film studios have been locked into a perpetual state of confrontation. The FCC's posture on the Fin/Syn rules changed as a result of the competitive realities of the 1990s. Networks could no longer be viewed as the dominant force in television program distribution. As a result the FCC in 1991 and again in 1993 modified the rules, allowing networks to acquire financial interest and syndication rights in any program they distribute. However, networks were still prohibited from domestically syndicating prime-time network and first-run programs.

In November 1995, all Fin/Syn rules were eliminated, allowing the networks to participate in the lucrative domestic syndication marketplace. Preparing for the rules' ultimate demise, CBS, NBC and ABC increased their ownership of prime-time programming. During the

1994–95 season, the three networks combined supplied fourteen hours of prime-time programming. This marked the first time that the network in-house production units became the leading programming suppliers.

OBSCENITY

As the electronic media environment has evolved and regulatory issues have become more complex, one of the most vexing areas that the FCC has had to address is obscenity on the airwaves. In attempting to act as an arbiter of good taste, the FCC must struggle with a contradictory mandate. While it is pledged to uphold the criminal code, which prohibits obscene, indecent, or profane language by wire, radio or television, it must balance those concerns with the Communications Act's clear admonition against the FCC's right to interfere with freedom of speech. The dilemma is this: can the FCC serve as an interpreter of the public's moral standards and define the parameters of good taste without engaging in censorship?

Public morality has long been an element in decisions about content in the media. As early as 1895, with the introduction of the kinetoscope on the boardwalk of Atlantic City, the issue of public decency in the media has been a prominent one. Controversy still prevails today as the public struggles with defining the limits of legitimate artistic expression, from the music videos of Madonna to the erotic photography of Robert Mapplethorpe.

In the 1970s, general permissiveness and increasing explicitness of sexual expression led to a new genre of radio programming. Dubbed "topless" radio by its critics, these programs featured disk jockeys dispensing intimate sexual advice to women callers in a light-hearted and lecherous manner. These radio programs offered little in the way of substantive advice to their callers: instead they were a source of bawdy humor for listeners, based upon innuendo.

As a result of numerous complaints and a review of the programming transcripts, the FCC chose WGLD-FM in Illinois as a target for its scrutiny after it broadcast a call-in program on oral sex. The commission leveled a $2,000 fine against the station for violating the indecency and obscenity clauses of Section 1464 of the Federal Criminal Code. As a result of WGLD's failure to challenge the fine, the other stations broadcasting in the "topless" genre discontinued the format and "topless radio" soon disappeared from the airwaves.

Another case that challenged the FCC's authority to regulate program content occurred in 1973 when New York City's WBAI-FM warned listeners that the language in the George Carlin album they were about to

FCC Commissioner Rachelle B. Chong. Courtesy of the Federal Communications Commission.

broadcast could be deemed offensive. The album, *George Carlin: Occupation Foole*, humorously satirized seven four-letter words that could not be used on radio or television.

After receiving a complaint from a man who had been tuned to the station while driving in a car with his son, the FCC acted.[4] In a declaratory ruling against the station, the commission decided that the language of the album was indecent and that it was broadcast at a time of the day, "where there is a reasonable risk that children may be in the audience." WBAI appealed the ruling and the U.S. Court of Appeals for the District of Columbia struck down the FCC's decision as a violation of Section 326 of the Communications Act, prohibiting the FCC from censoring programming. The court held that the FCC's order was overbroad and vague. In 1979 the case was heard by the United States Supreme Court, which upheld the FCC's ruling.[5] With this decision, the court also established the precedent of creating a "safe harbor" time period in which programming that is unsuitable for children may be broadcast.

The concept of a "safe harbor" as a time during which adult programming could be broadcast on radio and television has generated a great deal of debate. At the time of the WBAI case, the FCC defined "safe harbor" as the hours between 10:00 p.m. and 6:00 a.m.: during that time, programming containing indecent language could be broadcast. In 1987, the FCC moved the concept of safe harbor hours to midnight to 6:00 a.m.

The safe harbor policy came under considerable criticism by Congress as being arbitrary and senseless. Action for Children's Television (ACT) filed a suit in 1988 challenging the safe harbor policy.[6] The court ruled that the FCC had no verifiable evidence that one time was more appropriate than another for broadcasting indecent speech. Indeed, the court stated that perhaps adult programming should be broadcast earlier in the evening, when parents could supervise children's viewing and listening. The court also said that the FCC is not the appointed arbitrator for deciding what children should see and hear.

In 1988, under considerable pressure from Congress and lobbyists, the FCC totally banned the broadcast of indecent programming. But the twenty-four-hour ban didn't last long: in 1991 the U.S. Court of Appeals in the District of Columbia declared it unconstitutional. The court instructed the FCC to establish times of the day or night when adult material could be broadcast based upon verifiable data concerning children's television viewing patterns. In 1992 the FCC asked the U.S. Supreme Court to reverse the ruling, but the court declined. At the present time, the FCC is still struggling with the adult programming and safe harbor issues.[7]

The issue of pornography once again became the focus of debate in 1986 with the release of the Reagan administration's 1,960-page Meese Commission report, which found a causal link between violent pornography and aggressive behavior toward women. The Meese Commission sent a letter to several large retailers around the country, and more than ten thousand stores, including 7-Elevens and Rite Aids, removed *Playboy* and *Penthouse* from their shelves. However, this action was found to be in violation of the First Amendment rights of the magazine publishers and distributors.[8]

In 1987 the FCC decided to broaden enforcement of its indecency standards. This decision was prompted by the proliferation of "shock jocks" on the radio, personalities like New York's Howard Stern who use explicit, suggestive, and often abusive, language. Indeed, Mr. Stern has taken it upon himself to challenge the power of the FCC, pushing his program to the limits of the laws governing indecency in broadcasting. Since 1992, Infinity Broadcasting, which distributes the *Howard Stern Program* has been fined over $2 million for indecent programming. The company is appealing the fines.[9]

Stern, who earns over $4 million a year, is noted for his raunchy humor laced with sexual and racial slurs. His provocative performance style has created difficulties for Infinity Broadcasting's projected growth. Their purchase of KRTH-FM Los Angeles was delayed because of fines for broadcasting various Howard Stern programs. The purchase was challenged by Terry Rakolta's conservative group, Americans for Responsible Television. Although the sale was eventually approved by the FCC, the delay cost Infinity thousands of dollars.

The FCC's actions can seem contradictory at times. In August 1993 the FCC fined Infinity $500,000 for alleged indecency on the *Howard Stern Show* while simultaneously approving its purchase of another radio station in Philadelphia.

A charge of racism did cause Infinity to acquiesce to the terms of the objecting party. The African American Business Association (AABA) of Washington, D.C., sought to block Infinity's $60 million purchase of WPGC-AM/FM, arguing that Stern's program places African Americans in a negative light. In an effort not to further antagonize the FCC, and to expedite the purchase of the station, Infinity reached a financial settlement with the AABA. Under its terms, Infinity agreed to contribute $750,000 to a minority-related business program over the next four years and to provide substantial discounts to minority advertisers.

Advertisers on the Howard Stern Show, which include Snapple, Dial-a-Mattress, and the Nutri-System weight loss program, don't seem to be bothered by Stern's abusive humor. His show reaches 2 million listeners in New York alone and is also heard in nine other large cities. Stern's program is singularly responsible for earning half of the $22 million in annual advertising revenues of the New York station WXRK-FM. His advertising rates are among the highest in radio: a Stern commercial can cost $3,000 for sixty seconds.

Stern's popularity was demonstrated by a 1994 pay-per-view television program, "The Miss Howard Stern New Year's Eve Pageant." The program grossed $16 million, setting a pay-per-view record for event programming. Although critics reviewed the program as vulgar and crude, the cable television audience responded enthusiastically by paying $39.95 to watch the festivities.

The FCC's jurisdiction in this area has not been clearly defined, although the courts, in the WBAI case, sustained the FCC's role in determining the time of day when questionable material could be aired on the radio. Toward the latter part of 1987, the FCC adopted more stringent rules defining programs that include "language or material which depicts or describes in terms patently offensive as measured by contemporary community standards for the broadcast medium, sexual or excretory activities or organs" as indecent.

A case referred by the FCC to the National Obscenity Enforcement Unit of the Justice Department in 1987 concerned the use of questionable language in a radio play about homosexuals and AIDS, *The Jerker*, which was broadcast over the Pacifica Foundation's KPFK-FM, Los Angeles. In referring the case, the FCC noted that the material was not only indecent but might also be obscene. However, the Justice Department did not prosecute, stating that it would have been difficult to prove criminal intent on the part of KPFK. This example illustrates the difficulty of balancing concerns about public morality with Constitutional guarantees of free speech.

The seriousness with which the question of indecency is viewed on Capital Hill was demonstrated in 1988 to 1989 by the Senate confirmation hearings of three FCC commissioners. Al Sikes, the nominee for chairman of the FCC, was opposed by various special interest groups advocating a strong antiobscenity presence on the FCC. He and fellow nominee Andrew Barrett faced intense questioning on obscenity issues by the Senate confirmation committee. After their confirmation, the newly constituted FCC under Chairman Sikes announced a more aggressive campaign against indecent and obscene broadcast programming, naming nineteen radio stations as subjects of the FCC Mass Media Bureau's enforcement division investigation. Sikes resigned shortly after President Bill Clinton's inauguration.

Clearly, broadcasters should be sensitive to sexually explicit programming aired at times when children are apt to be listening. Broadcast licensees are protected by the First Amendment, but Constitutional guarantees do not absolve them from a moral obligation to the communities they serve.

Televised violence has also prompted concern.[10] Legislation passed in 1990 suspended antitrust laws for three years so that broadcasters, cable operators, and the program production industry could establish a joint effort to reduce the amount of violence on television.

Self-regulation can be effective in controlling sex and violence on television. In 1993, the three networks announced that they would voluntarily issue a warning before any television program that was deemed by them to contain excessive violence, sex, or indecent language. Cable television has also responded to the public's concern over violent and indecent programming. In 1990, MTV, which has been a showcase for Madonna videos, refused to broadcast her *Justify My Love*. The 1990 black and white film, with its erotic fantasies featuring scenes of nudity, voyeurism, bisexuality, cross-dressing, and mild sadomasochism, was deemed unfit for MTV. When ABC's *Nightline* broadcast the controversial video, however, the show hit the ratings jackpot; and Warner Brothers decided to release it as a video single.

The issue of television violence has become a focal point for Congressional scrutiny. The two most recent appointments to the FCC, Commissioners Susan Ness and Rachelle Chong, were extensively questioned about their agenda for action on violence and indecency during their 1994 confirmation hearings. As a result of those concerns Congress in 1996 passed the Telecommunictions Act which requires television set manufacturers to include V-chip technology in new sets. The V-chip will enable parents to block programs labelled as violent or otherwise undesirable at specified times of the day on designated channels.[11] In addition the Act requires the industry to develop a rating system to define sexually explicit and violent programming and increases fines for broadcast and cable obscenity from $10,000 to $100,000.

CHILDREN'S TELEVISION

As the FCC has struggled with its role as an arbitrator of broadcast morality, it has also reluctantly become a participant in the public debate over children's television programming. The source of major changes in the children's television environment was an unspectacular group of mothers whose concern for what their kids were seeing on television prompted them to action.

Action for Children's Television (ACT) was formed by a housewife and mother in 1968, and by 1972, four years after its creation, this group had managed to bring about a policy towards children's television where previously none had existed. Their agenda, which they pursued with vigor and determination, led to a legislative assault on the television industry, Congress, the FTC, and the FCC. ACT effectively articulated a sound rationale for a regulatory mandate concerning children's programming. Their goals for regulatory reform on children's television programming included the elimination of sponsorship and commercials, a prohibition against host product endorsements, and the requirement that each station produce a minimum of fourteen hours a week of age-specific programming.

Using skillful promotional tactics that included short-term television boycotts, petition drives, and organized letter-writing campaigns, ACT raised public consciousness, intimidated the industry, and embarrassed the FCC into taking action. In hearings before Congressional committees, the FCC was chided for not having specialists within the commission who could address the substantive issues of children's television. By 1971 the FCC made public a notice of inquiry and proposed rule making concerning the ACT petition; it announced as well the creation of a permanent children's television unit within the FCC. The broadcasting industry was also forced to acknowledge ACT's legitimacy when the FCC received eighty thousand letters responding to its announced notice of inquiry.

Concerned that government interdiction would imperil profitability and compromise their independence, the television networks hoped that a self-regulatory posture would satisfy the parties involved. Led by James Duffy, then head of the ABC Television Network, the networks amended the NAB self-regulatory guidelines for commercial content and program interruption, reducing nonprogram material on network children's programs to nine and a half minutes on weekends and twelve minutes on weekdays, and altered program interruption standards to two in thirty-minute, and four in sixty-minute children's programs. In addition, host or prominent cartoon character product endorsements were forbidden within or adjacent to children's programs.

Marshalling their resources to combat the challenge from ACT, the networks successfully thwarted government intervention by quickly establishing a self-regulatory posture in children's television. The FCC responded by declining to initiate formal rules pertaining to children's programs and endorsing the guidelines formulated by industry associations.

In their 1974 Report and Policy Statement, the FCC reiterated the need to maintain a traditional regulatory approach and "avoid excessive governmental interference with specific program decisions." Disappointed with the FCC's feeble attitude toward a clear-cut policy for children's programming, ACT maintained its vigil. Eventually the FCC did adopt a ban on advertising by hosts of children's programs, and the FTC established a regulation banning vitamin advertisements on programs for children.[12] ACT's extensive lobbying efforts brought about other benefits such as "bumpers" (short segments identifying an upcoming commercial), public-service nutritional messages, and the rule that toy commercials must indicate whether assembly is required or if batteries are included with a product.

Although significant changes have occurred in the regulatory oversight of children's television programming, one of the most difficult areas to address was the time allotment for commercials included in children's shows. In 1990, Congress approved legislation that defined children's television commercial time standards and established a commitment to children's programming as a criterion for station license renewal. The Children's Television Act of 1990 limits advertising on children's shows distributed via broadcast or cable to twelve minutes per hour on weekdays and ten and a half minutes per hour on weekends. In a departure from broadcast policy precedent, the Congress mandated a balance between children's entertainment and educational programming for children, making adherence an issue in license renewal.[13]

One programming policy matter that was not addressed in the legislation but has generated vigorous debate is the issue of program-length commercials. This term refers to children's shows themed to a popular toy, such as G.I. Joe or He-Man. Children's television programming advocates argued that these programs violated the most recent commercial time standards adopted by Congress. The FCC, however, ruled that the toy-based programs could only be in violation of the rules if they included commercials for the toy that the program was themed to. Since networks and independent stations prohibit this practice, the FCC rule effectively allows these programs the same time guidelines as other children's programs under the law.

The FCC has vigorously enforced the limits on children's advertising by selective auditing of television stations and cable systems. When the FCC chooses to fine rather than admonish, it can cost a station up to $25,000 per violation.

Although ACT ceased operation in 1992, their twenty-three-year campaign to improve children's television is a tribute to the dedication, commitment, and perseverance of a group of women who believed that television had more to offer their children than violent cartoons and endless commercials.[14]

THE REGULATORY FUTURE

The FCC faces a number of high-priority issues on its regulatory agenda for the rest of the decade. Its technological oversight will increase proportionally as the tools for access to the "information superhighway" become more readily available. The FCC is using several novel approaches to address these new areas. For example, in the areas of Personal Communications Services (wireless telephones, handheld computers, two-way paging systems, etc.) and Interactive Video and Data Service (IVDS), it organized auctions to award licenses. However, the preliminary auctions, held in July 1994 for IVDS frequencies, proved to be more troublesome than the FCC had anticipated. A number of companies, including two of the largest bidders, defaulted on their down payments and never met the imposed deadline. There was also an alleged attempt by one of the companies to encourage other auction winners to default. In addition to the loss of revenue from defaulting parties, the FCC had to determine whether the companies receiving a 25 percent discount on their winning bids for being women or minority-owned businesses had falsely represented that claim.[15]

Creating a competitive environment in cable television has also been an important item on the FCC's agenda. It has taken an aggressive position on basic cable rate regulation and, by doing so, has expressed its intention of being an active voice in providing oversight for the industry. However, in 1996 Congress passed a Telecommunications Act which phased out cable rate regulation by 1999 for all services except the basic broadcast tier.

In contemplating the future and the investment the FCC must make in overseeing a vast and intricate communications industry, the issue of a self-supporting FCC becomes even more critical. With a yearly budget

approaching $200 million, and regulatory oversight increasing as techno-
logical implementation occurs, the FCC must seek out its own means to
support its regulatory agenda. In this context, user fees can become a
realistic tool in attempting to create self-sufficient funding. Some critics
have expressed concern, however, that the FCC may impose unwarrant-
ed regulation merely to raise money.

One area that the FCC seems ready to act upon is the equal employment opportunity provisions (EEO), which are included in its regulatory
mandate. In 1978 the Commission initiated a two-tiered program that
attempted to increase minority ownership of broadcasting properties. As
part of its policy, the FCC allowed capital gains taxes to be deferred if a
broadcasting station was sold to a minority buyer. This policy, known as
the minority tax certificate, was discontinued in 1994 after Congress
noted widespread abuses of the program.[16]

Although there have been gains in the level of minority ownership of
broadcasting and cable properties, and a modest increase in minority
employment, the commission would like to see greater increases in
minority ownership and employment.

The temptations inherent in overseeing the burgeoning telecommunications industry is likely to challenge the ethical standards established
by the commission for the behavior of its staff. When industry companies
have cases pending before the FCC, FCC officials are forbidden to have
any contact with the petitioners. However, there have been times when
commissioners violated the rules. Though this type of *ex parte* contact is
clearly prohibited by the FCC, when it does occur the problem of regulatory oversight becomes quite complex. While the press may be a natural
agent for the solution of the problem, they are in this case also part of it.
The question then becomes, who oversees the overseers?

NOTES

1. In 1995 the FCC voted to eliminate the PTAR, pending a two-year waiting
period. FCC Chairman Reed E. Hundt declared, "It's high time the Commission
stops this mindless meddling with prime-time programming."

2. In 1982 the U.S. District Court for the District of Columbia ruled that the
NAB's code relating to the number and length of commercials violated the
Sherman Antitrust Act.

3. This was an attempt by the FCC to prevent CBS, NBC, and ABC from
monopolizing entertainment production. The Fin/Syn rules severely limited network ownership in programming and syndication.

4. The man turned out to be a member of the conservative media watchdog

group, Morality in Media.

5. *FCC v. Pacifica Foundation* ,438 U.S. 726 (1978).

6. In 1988, Congress passed legislation for a twenty-four-hour ban on inde-cent programs that the FCC endorsed. In 1989 the U.S. Court of Appeals issued a stay; and in 1990 the U.S. Court of Appeals declared that the twenty-four-hour ban was unconstitutional.

7. In 1995 a federal appeals court upheld restrictions on indecent programs on television and radio, designating a "safe harbor" between 6:00 a.m. and 10:00 p.m. in *Action for Children's Television v. FCC*. There is also a legislative initiative to create safe harbors for violent programming, and to establish ratings for violence and other objectionable content in programming. In January 1996 the Supreme Court refused to hear a challenge to the FCC's indecency rules, thereby uphold-ing the commission's 6:00 a.m. to 10:00 p.m. ban on indecent programming.

8. The report was named for Attorney General Edwin Meese. *Playboy* and *Penthouse* filed suit (*Playboy Enterprises v. Meese*, 1986). The United States district court ruled that the letter sent by the commission threatened the First Amendment rights of the magazine publishers and distributors.

9. In September 1995, Mr. Stern's employer, Infinity Broadcasting, agreed to pay $1,715,000 to settle the indecency charges against Mr. Stern. According to the FCC, the payment was not a fine but a "voluntary contribution" to the U.S. trea-sury.

10. A study conducted by the Center for Communications Policy at the University of California, Los Angeles found that "sinister combat violence" per-vades a significant number of Saturday morning children's cartoons. The study also noted that the 42 percent of theatrical movies aired on ABC, CBS, NBC, and Fox were inappropriately violent. However, researchers did say that network series and made-for-television movies carry little violence.

11. The four networks have each invested $500,000, creating a $2 million fund to investigate alternatives to V-chip technology.

12. In 1974 the National Association of Broadcasters altered its code to elim-inate selling by program hosts. The FTC issued a consent order against a Spiderman vitamin campaign, thus effectively eliminating vitamin commercials from childrens' television programming.

13. While the time standards mandated by Congress were less restrictive than the previously adopted industry limits, the NAB Code, which stipulated the amount of nonprogram material, was declared unconstitutional, effectively negating the voluntary time standard requirement.

14. In 1995 Chairman Hundt attempted to have the FCC endorse a policy requiring a three-hour minimum of educational programming for children on network television. This attempt met with vociferous opposition from commis-sioners Quello, Barrett, and Chong.

15. The FCC's August 1995 auction for PCS services was delayed because of a challenge to the affirmative action preference rates. As a result of a Supreme Court decision relating to affirmative action, the FCC was forced to scrap the spe-cial preference for women and minority bidders.

16. In 1995 the House Ways and Means Committee, citing abuse of the tax certificate policy, voted to repeal the programs. At the center of the debate was Frank Washington, an African American cable entrepreneur and former FCC legal

assistant who helped author the policy. The deal that brought Congressional scrutiny was Washington's planned purchase of Viacom cable systems valued at $2.3 billion. Had the deal been consummated, Viacom would have saved $400 million in taxes for selling to a minority-owned company.

4

A History of Programming: Television's Evolution

The television program is an international ambassador, weaving its electronic images through diverse cultures, evading the frontiers set by politics and government. American television programming is distributed throughout the world, attracting international audiences and amassing billions of dollars in licensing fees. What fuels this vast industry and how it functions is the subject of this chapter.

Most viewers have little interest in the mechanics of programming and are not too concerned with how the program is produced. Indeed, most of them are often unaware of which channel they are watching or which network is delivering the program to them. Television station executives, on the other hand, are most concerned with programming. It is programming that delivers commercials to the viewers, and it is these commercials that provide revenue to the broadcasters. Indeed, the quest for successful, high-rated programs is based on the fact that hit programs attract advertisers and increase the fees broadcasters can charge for advertising on the more popular programs.

EARLY DAYS OF BROADCAST PROGRAMMING: RADIO AND EARLY TELEVISION

There have been quite a few changes in the manner and technique of program policy over the years since the early days of radio. During radio's infancy, hobbyists eagerly turned their homemade wireless receivers to the crackling and cackling transmissions of other eager broadcast hobbyists. Those that listened were delighted to hear any comprehensible sound and were not too concerned with the program format. As radio

technology developed, and microphones and loudspeakers were introduced, programming became more sophisticated. Musical shows became
a mainstay for radio because they were relatively inexpensive and easy to
produce.

As radio became a mass entertainment medium, it began to offer its
audience more diversity in programming. In the late 1920s, variety shows
featuring entertainers and comedians spawned a new format—the comedy variety program. Featured artists included well-known performers like
Al Jolsen, Eddie Cantor, George Burns and Gracie Allen, Ed Wynn, Jack
Benny, and the Marx Brothers. Regional programming, already popular in
the South, also became popular with audiences all over the country.

Dramatic programming on radio developed more slowly than the
other formats. Producers hesitated to attempt drama on the radio because
the tradition of the theater required a visual presentation. Initial efforts at
radio drama involved light-hearted programs devoid of substance or dramatic merit. Soon, however, a new genre developed, the women's series.
The most successful program developed in this format, and indeed one
of the most successful programs in radio history, was *Rise of the Goldbergs*.
In addition to establishing the radio comedy drama as a durable format,
The Goldbergs created new trends in programming, including the use of an
ensemble cast in different situations every week. The program appealed
to radio audiences and television viewers because it portrayed an urban
family led by a dominant female figure struggling to maintain a middle-
class existence amidst the conflicts and tribulations of inner-city life.[1]

By 1933, soap operas, so-called because their commercial sponsors
were soap companies, became an enduring aspect of radio programming
and included the serials *The Romance of Helen Trent* and *Ma Perkins*. These
two serial radio soap operas were among the most successful, with Ma
Perkins dispensing folksy humor and Helen Trent enduring the ups and
downs of romance. The formats of these programs were simple, the characters endearing, and the plots formulaic, but they caught the attention of
devoted radio listeners who tuned in night after night to programs that
lasted in some cases fifteen seasons.

Comedy drama also became a successful format on radio in the late
1920s. One of the most popular comedy drama programs on radio was
Amos 'n Andy, which began on network radio in 1929 and finally concluded on television in 1966. In its heyday, *Amos 'n' Andy's* popularity
even rivalled that of the movie theaters, which would on occasion interrupt the showing of their films for fifteen minutes so that their audiences
could hear the latest episode.

In the 1930s action dramas, including Westerns, thrillers, and sus-
pense, also became a mainstay of radio programming. *Death Valley Days*
(1930) and *The Shadow* (1931) were outstanding examples of popular pro-

grams that captured a mass audience with their dramatic format.

While radio enjoyed exceptional popularity during the war years, its appeal as a mass entertainment medium would eventually be diminished. Although television was not yet readily available during World War II, experimental broadcasts were being conducted. The end of the war signaled a rise in television production and an increase in the manufacture of television sets. CBS and NBC eagerly embraced the new technology and shifted much of their programming production efforts from radio into television.

The 1950s witnessed a surge in the popularity of television, while radio was treated like an overlooked cousin. Most of the popular radio programs and their stars moved to the "electronic canvas." Comedy, drama, variety, news, and music-oriented radio programs became instant successes on television. Milton Berle, "Mr. Television," host of the *Texaco Star Theater*, provided his audience with zany antics and weird character portrayals that made him the most popular television celebrity in the 1950s. What other medium, after all, could provide a program that offered opera, classical drama, and circus acts all in one cohesive show? The program that bridged the culture gap and truly became adored by the masses, however, was the *Ed Sullivan Show*. Its formula endured for more than twenty years and became an important part of American popular culture.

As it had on radio, the situation comedy on television became a significant audience pleaser. *Amos 'n' Andy, The Goldbergs, Life of Riley, Our Miss Brooks, Jack Benny, Burns and Allen*, and, of course, *I Love Lucy* became immediate hits on television in the early 1950s.

Just as television could mix low- and high-brow culture in a single program, it could also provide audiences with a diverse menu of dramatic genres. There were detective dramas, Westerns, soap operas, and serious dramas. Westerns particularly attracted large television audiences. Some were more watched than others, but all of them provided their audiences with the vicarious thrill and excitement of life in the Old West. The Western series, created in the late 1950s included the immensely successful shows *Gunsmoke* and *Bonanza,* among many others.

Police dramas were another variation on the law and order theme that flourished on television in the 1950s, setting a precedent for decades to come. *Dragnet, 77 Sunset Strip, The Untouchables*, and *Perry Mason* were a few of the most successful detective programs on television in the 1950s.

Serious anthology drama also found its place in early television and quickly became acclaimed by both critics and audiences. *Playhouse 90*, which started on CBS in 1956, set a standard of excellence that other anthology series followed. These dramas addressed timely themes and

introduced American audiences to some of the best young writers of that
period, such as Rod Serling, Paddy Chayefsky, Reginald Rose; and actors
like Paul Newman, Robert Redford, and Dustin Hoffman.

Another important development in television programming that
occurred in the 1950s was the television spectacular. Sylvester Weaver, a
programming executive at NBC, devised the format for this programming. The idea of the television special, or spectacular, was to generate
greater interest in a network by altering the traditional programming
schedule. The spectacular would preempt other programming and provide the network with a great deal of publicity. In many ways the philosophy behind the spectacular is the same as that of the miniseries; to draw
attention to a network and attract an audience to a special program.

Generating audience interest in programming is often a challenging
and frustrating task. The programs must attract, stimulate, and excite an
audience; perhaps that is why the networks developed the quiz program.
In 1955, the *$64,000 Question*, sponsored by Revlon, premiered on CBS. It
soon became the most-watched program on television and spawned
numerous clones. What made these quiz programs so popular with television audiences of the 1950s?

They placed average individuals in exciting situations and offered
the thrill of big-money prizes to those who were successful. Audiences
could play along with the contestant and fantasize about winning the
generous jackpots. These programs started to lose their appeal toward
the end of the 1950s, however, when it was discovered that some contestants had been provided with the questions and answers prior to their
appearance on a program.

TELEVISION "GROWS UP"—THE 1960s AND 1970s

In the mid-1960s, the availability of color television sets added a new
dimension to television viewing. In addition the familiar detective/spy
genre was repackaged to reflect the era of the Cold War. Preferred spy
dramas of the 1960s included *The Man from U.N.C.L.E.*, and *Mission
Impossible*. Westerns diminished in popularity during the 1960s, with only
Bonanza, which ran for fourteen seasons, and *Gunsmoke*, which ran for
twenty, maintaining their audience appeal.

Several new programming genres developed during the 1960s.
Comedy took on a more satirical and irreverent tone with programs like
the *Smothers Brothers* and *Laugh-In*. Indeed, the Smothers Brothers'
humor and political satire may have been too controversial for network
executives. In one 1967 program, folksinger Pete Seeger, who had been
blacklisted by the network for seventeen years, taped a segment singing

"Waist Deep in the Big Muddy," a song critical of the war in Vietnam. CBS cut the segment from the tape prior to broadcast, which resulted in a public confrontation between the Smothers Brothers and the network. Although Seeger did return and performed the song in a later broadcast, it was this kind of "antiestablishment" programming that embarrassed CBS and caused the program's eventual cancellation.

Perhaps one of the most unique programs to be introduced was *Star Trek*, in 1966. Gene Roddenberry, the series's producer, conceived the show as a humanistic science-fiction series that would address both classical and modern themes. While it lasted for only three seasons, *Star Trek* generated a phenomenal amount of loyalty among its audience. Fan clubs and conventions were formed, and after the demise of the series, in 1969, Roddenberry pursued the idea of a theatrical movie version. He finally realized his goal in 1980, and to date seven feature-length films have been produced. The first six used most of the original cast from the television series, while the seventh film, *Star Trek: Generations* featured actors from the syndicated series *Star Trek: The Next Generation*. In 1992, Paramount introduced *Star Trek: Deep Space Nine,* another first-run syndicated series, and in 1995, *Star Trek:Voyager* made its debut as the first program offering on the new United Paramount Network (UPN). Naturally, with the enormous success of *Star Trek,* several other space-oriented series were introduced. None of them, however, were able to generate the appeal *Star Trek* had, and they were soon cancelled.

As the appeal of the Western diminished in the 1960s and 1970s, the police drama, in a more realistic form, became very popular. Most of the police shows were much like their Western predecessors, addressing similar themes and using similar characters. *Kojak, Police Story,* and *Ironsides* were all designed to provide the audience with a graphic view of police work.

Several attempts at issue-oriented social drama series, while receiving critical acclaim, did not capture audience interest. In the 1960s two series in this category, *The Defenders*, about a father/son lawyer team, and *East Side, West Side*, starring George C. Scott as a New York City social worker, failed to generate large audiences.

One programming genre that did maintain its appeal through the 1960s and 1970s was the medical show. These dramas could provide viewers with romance, excitement, practical information, and entertainment. The 1960s produced *Dr. Kildare* and *Ben Casey*, the two most notable examples of this genre. In the 1970s, medical shows continued their appeal with programs like *Marcus Welby, M.D.*

While specials and spectaculars were the audience pleasers of the 1950s, the feature-length film proved to be one of the most popular programming formats of the 1960s. In 1961, NBC pioneered the regularly scheduled prime-time movie with *Saturday Night at the Movies*. This format became so successful that by 1967, the combined network prime-time allocation to theatrical features increased to twelve hours. The popularity of prime-time movies created an unusual demand on Hollywood feature films for prime time broadcasting. Soon demand surpassed supply, and the networks had to look elsewhere for feature-length films. In 1966, NBC introduced *World Premiere*, a prime-time series that featured made-for-television movies. Once again, this concept proved successful, and by 1972 nearly one hundred made-for-television movies had been shown on the three networks.

With the accomplishment of theatrical features and made-for-television movies, the networks continued to develop entertaining long-format programs. Faced with a dwindling supply of feature films, the networks introduced the miniseries.

Actually the miniseries concept was first brought to the United States via public television. In the 1960s, public television introduced *The Forsyte Saga*, a series of twenty-six programs based upon the Victorian-Edwardian novels of John Galsworthy. The success of this British import prompted public television to create a permanent berth for British series and miniseries entitled *Masterpiece Theater*. American networks were impressed with the audience interest generated by these series and soon created their own limited-run series. The first major miniseries event was ABC's twelve-part adaptation of Irwin Shaw's novel *Rich Man, Poor Man*, in 1973. Of course the most phenomenal miniseries event in television history was the 1977 ABC broadcast of *Roots*, which broke all audience rating records with an average rating of forty-five during its eight-night run.

Another program genre introduced in the 1970s was the "docudrama." This programming format portrays actual events and real people with a fictional slant. Because it mixes fact with fiction, critics have maintained that the docudrama is intentionally misleading and inaccurate. A number of docudramas have stimulated debate over matters of authenticity and accuracy.[2] While the docudrama builds the substance of its program from fact, it weaves a dramatic web that freely mixes fact with fiction. However, very often, through program publicity, television audiences are led to believe that the docudrama is an accurate portrayal of actual events. As news and information programming, the docudrama is a fraud.

TELEVISION IN THE 1980s

The decade of the 1980s ushered in revised programming orientations and an increased emphasis on fiscal restraint. The "new kid on the block" of network television, the Fox Broadcasting Company, which began in 1986, and aggressive challenges from cable and home video made broadcasters more sensitive to competition and the reality of a shrinking audience. A number of other factors, such as the stock market crash of 1987 and various corporate realignments at major studios and television networks, also contrived to place new priorities upon programming development. As the 1980s evolved, original programming genres were developed, some of them controversial.

The decade began with an auspicious programming event, the debut of NBC's twelve-part miniseries, *Shogun*, based on the James Clavell novel and filmed entirely on location in Japan. Starring Richard Chamberlain, *Shogun*, although conceived in the prescribed miniseries format, departed from tradition by casting Japanese actors for twenty-eight principal roles and the two leads. Toshiro Mifune, a famous Japanese leading man, and Yoko Shimada, a young, relatively unknown actress, took the two starring roles.

The miniseries proved to be an important programming strategy, although a number of questions were raised about its versatility and economic return. While miniseries like *Shogun*, the *Winds of War* (1983), *Massada* (1981), and *The Thornbirds* (1986) generated respectable audience ratings, concerns were raised about their long-term worth. As miniseries production costs escalated into the megamillion-dollar range, production executives began to reassess their value: research revealed that miniseries did poorly in the rerun and syndicated programming marketplace.

One miniseries that seemed to exemplify all of the industry concerns with the genre was *War and Remembrance*. Based on Herman Wouk's novel and conceived as a sequel to the *Winds of War*, ABC broadcast the initial eighteen hours of the projected thirty-hour miniseries in November 1988. Everything associated with the production of *War and Remembrance* was on a monumental scale: a 1492-page script, 757 sets, 2070 scenes, two years of preproduction, twenty-one months on location, one year of postproduction, 358 speaking parts, 30,310 extras, 2 million feet of film, and production costs of close to $100 million. Most industry programming executives agreed that the staggering expenditures associated with the production made it virtually impossible for ABC to realize a profit even if it sold out all the time on the series. Adding to the profit and loss problem was the unheard-of control given the author to limit the kinds of advertisers associated with the program.

In May of 1989 ABC broadcast the final installments of *War and Remembrance*. The average ratings fell significantly below the network's advertiser guarantee, prompting Capital Cities/ABC Chairman Thomas Murphy to raise the loss projection of the miniseries to between $30 and 40 million.

One miniseries that helped to renew confidence in network programming and audience loyalty was CBS's production of *Lonesome Dove*. Broadcast during the first week of the February 1989 "sweep" period, *Lonesome Dove* earned high ratings/shares, generating a three-network combined 80 percent share of available audience. The increase was noteworthy because the previous record had been established a year and a half earlier, and until *Lonesome Dove*, network audience shares had been in a slump. Although CBS officials had expressed confidence in the miniseries, their ratings projections of 17.6 to 18.6 during the four-part miniseries were considerably below its actual achievement.

Lonesome Dove was definitely a coup for CBS, which had been running last in the three-network ratings race. Its success also revived interest in the miniseries as a programming genre capable of generating considerable audience interest. However, most industry observers agree that shorter miniseries are more attractive to viewers, and the trend is toward series lasting between four and six hours.

The sitcom continued to be an important programming staple of the 1980s. In response to the newly defined trends in audience demographics, 1980s sitcoms identified a changing American family. The junk man from *Sanford and Son* evolved into the successful African American professional in *The Cosby Show*, while the liberated woman professional of the *Mary Tyler Moore Show* became more sophisticated and successful in *Murphy Brown*, starring Candice Bergen. Indeed, this television character became something of a cause célèbre in 1992, when she was criticized by Vice President Dan Quayle for having a baby out of wedlock. The vice president said, "It doesn't help matters when prime time TV has Murphy Brown . . . mocking the importance of fathers and bearing a child and calling it 'just another lifestyle choice.'" The Murphy Brown morality debate became a national news item when the issue was raised at a White House press conference.

A national debate inspired by a fictional television character delighted the broadcast networks, who viewed this as an opportunity for them to assert their dominance as the preferred entertainment medium. No one was happier than CBS, who saw its highest-rated show generate even more publicity. Indeed, *Murphy Brown* charged advertisers an average of $310,000 for a thirty-second commercial during the 1992–93 season, making it the most expensive prime-time spot on network television during the year. CBS and the producers of *Murphy Brown* couldn't have done a better job of promoting the show if they had planned it themselves.

Despite the vice president's concern, families were still in fashion in the 1980s, although their foundations were a bit shaky. *Family Ties* was the network's answer to the maintenance of the family unit. The working class ethic was also represented with the wisecracking factory worker,

Roseanne, of the *Roseanne Barr Show. Roseanne* is a humorous treatment of working class realities as she and her husband struggle to maintain the all-American household.

A NEW DECADE: THE 1990s

As the 1990s began, the broadcasting industry came face to face with the harsh realities of declining audience shares, decreasing revenues, competition from cable television, and the depletion of programming resources resulting from the coverage of the war in the Persian Gulf. These factors led to a rethinking of priorities and to a restructuring of corporate assets. Network programming came under close scrutiny as executives redoubled their efforts to maintain a dominant edge in daytime and prime-time programming. As Brandon Tartikoff, former president of NBC's programming division, succinctly stated, "Tried and true is dead and buried."

While the beginning of the 1990s did reflect a trend toward innovation, much of the new programming was associated with previously familiar formats and themes. Made-for-television movies made an auspicious debut in 1990 with solidly written and well-acted programs, among them *The Incident*, with Walter Matthau, and *Decoration Day*, starring James Garner. ABC revisited the Battle of the Big Horn with its movie *Son of the Morning Star*, a probing look into the personality of General George Armstrong Custer.

During the early 1990s, network television clearly became enamored of the gritty reality of "true story" adaptations, grounding 35 to 40 percent of television movie productions in reality-based themes. Made-for-television movies became sensational as producers plucked their story lines from screaming newspaper headlines. This trend was exemplified by the case of Amy Fisher, the Long Island teenager convicted of shooting the wife of her lover, Joey Buttafuoco, in the head. Eventually the case produced no less than three Amy Fisher television movies—one each for CBS, NBC, and ABC.

The miniseries offered at the start of the 1990s addressed political and celebrity themes: *Family of Spies* was about the John Walker case, and *The Kennedys of Massachusetts* dramatized the rise to power of this political dynasty. As for docudramas, *The Tragedy of Flight 103: The Inside Story*, a coproduction between pay cable's HBO and Britain's Granada Television, offered a vivid and dramatic theory of the events that might have led up to the tragic Pan Am flight.

At ABC, Robert Iger, former president of ABC Entertainment and current President and COO of Capital Cities/ABC, acted on Tartikoff's statement about burying the "tried and true." The network attempted a dramatic innovation with David Lynch's *Twin Peaks*, a 1990 miniseries that piqued the viewing audience's interest with its unusual plot and odd characters. Although the series developed a cult following, it eventually settled into the prime-time soap opera routine and was cancelled.

Undaunted, Iger tried again in 1993 with *Wild Palms*, a television miniseries directed by filmmaker Oliver Stone. The series, a futuristic look at a world based upon a culture of technology, with holograms and virtual reality used as tools of subversion, received praise for its production values, story line, and acting. Although it was a ratings flop, it generated a great deal of publicity for ABC.

At the beginning of the 1990s, several network dramatic series distinguished themselves by addressing social themes in a mature and sophisticated way. *Law & Order*, *Shannon's Deal*, and *The Trials of Rosie O'Neill* departed from the ordinary by endeavoring to treat issues of the inequities of American society. There was also an attempt at dramatic innovation. Steven Bochco's *Cop Rock* combined elements of drama and song in a highly stylized presentation of urban law enforcement. Unfortunately, the sight of cops, attorneys, jurors, and judges spontaneously breaking into song was too much of a stretch for American audiences, and the show was cancelled.

Bochco's accomplishments in network television exemplifies the roller-coaster relationship of failure and success that network television has with its producers and writers. With hits like *Hill Street Blues*, *L.A. Law*, *Civil Wars*, and *Doogie Howser, M.D.*, Bochco became a valuable "property," and in 1987 ABC signed him to an exclusive deal estimated at about $50 million. The terms were very attractive and included a guarantee that Bochco's next ten series would make the ABC schedule.

But failure on network television can be expensive and sobering. *Cop Rock* cost $1.8 million for each program hour, and the show was cancelled after eleven episodes, with two segments never broadcast. Bochco's *NYPD Blue*, which premiered on ABC in the fall of the 1993–94 season, was the subject of controversy because of its gritty reality, violence, and sex. Indeed, the network's concern over the propriety of the program led Bochco to edit fifteen seconds from a love scene in the premiere episode.

ABC, clearly concerned about the response to *NYPD Blue*, used a cautionary statement prior to its premiere, stating "This police drama contains adult language and scenes with partial nudity. Viewer discretion is advised." In 1993 ABC also introduced an 800 number for viewers to call and inquire about which ABC programs carry warnings about violence.

If anyone understands the ups and downs of producing programs for network television, it is Aaron Spelling, acknowledged in the *Guinness*

Book of World Records as the world's most prolific television producer, with twenty-seven hundred hours of programming. Spelling knows what it means to descend from the heights: The man who produced such familiar hit television shows as *Charlie's Angels, The Love Boat,* and *Mod Squad* in 1989 had to face the reality of not having a single program on a network prime-time schedule after ABC cancelled *Dynasty.* After being shunned for several years, Spelling beat the odds by returning to prime-time network television in an industry that usually offers few second chances. His vehicle for re-ascension was a program about Beverly Hills teens called *Bevery Hills 90210* for the Fox Broadcasting Network. The program was a hit, and soon Spelling Productions was once again on a roll, spinning off another popular program for Fox, *Melrose Place.* Spelling's success a second time around is rare in television, but it illustrates the importance of identifying new trends in programming.[3]

Brooklyn Bridge and *I'll Fly Away,* two dramatic television series that premiered in 1991, attempted to revisit history and focus on the values of the American family. Both series were produced by experienced professionals: Gary David Goldberg, whose previous credits included *Family Ties,* and Joshua Brand and John Falsey, who had also produced the quirky hit *Northern Exposure.* Although both programs received enthusiastic support from the critics and attracted loyal audiences, their ratings were judged as failures, and the programs were both cancelled in 1992. One of the reasons for the cancellations may have been that both programs tended to appeal to a more mature audience, while most network programming is targeted toward the eighteen-to-forty-nine-year age group.

Another producer who has tried to break the mold of formulaic television programming is Jay Tarses. He created, produced, and directed *Buffalo Bill* and *The Slap Maxwell Story.* Tarses is somewhat of an iconoclast in the television industry, tending to disregard convention and ignore traditional boundaries of form and taste. His NBC series, *The Days and Nights of Molly Dodd,* which premiered in 1987, lasted one season on the network and then moved to the Lifetime cable channel, where it ran until 1991. The series, which starred Blair Brown, was an irreverent look at the life-style of a single, liberal Manhattan woman whose romantic involvements included some interracial relationships.

During the 1992–93 season, a number of dramatic network program series premiered and established themselves as successful programs. Perhaps the most unexpected success of the season was CBS's *Dr. Quinn, Medicine Woman.* Another well-received series, *Young Indiana Jones Chronicles,* also attempted to mix fiction with history in an entertaining format. The series, produced by noted filmmaker George Lucas, had excellent production values and foreign settings, which made it costly to produce. This, along with lackluster ratings, forced ABC to cancel the series.

Another dramatic series, *seaQuest DSV*, produced by filmmaker Steven Spielberg and Universal Pictures, made its debut in the fall of 1993. Like Lucas's *Young Indiana Jones Chronicles*, this was an expensive, colorful television series, concerning a high-tech submarine exploring the uncharted seas. Its theme was very much like that of *Star Trek*, except that the ocean replaced space as "the new frontier."

The situation comedy, long a mainstay of American television, got off to a shaky start in 1990. The awkward pairing of comedian Jackie Mason with actress Lynn Redgrave, along with its forced ethnic humor, quickly turned American audiences off to *Chicken Soup*.

While, as always, some of the new sitcoms were cancelled, several venerable favorites including *Golden Girls* and *The Cosby Show* also disappeared from first-run network television in 1992. *The Cosby Show* was one of the most popular sitcoms in the history of television. It earned its star and principal owner, Bill Cosby, millions of dollars in program licensing revenues.[4] And in 1993, after eleven years and 271 episodes, *Cheers*, one of America's most beloved sitcoms, went off the air. Its star, Ted Danson, reportedly earned $12 million a season, and the production companies, Paramount and CBC, received more than $2 million an episode in license fees from NBC. The sitcom, however, is an integral component of American television, and those that end are replaced by others.

Comedy took a creative turn in 1990 with the appearance of *In Living Color*. Produced by Keenan Ivory Wayans and appearing on the Fox network, the program, which featured African-American talent and writers, specialized in irreverent humor and pointed satire.

Another program distributed by Fox that became an instant hit was the animated series *The Simpsons*. Initially appearing as an animated short on Fox's *Tracey Ullman Show*, cartoonist Matt Groening's off-beat characters quickly became America's best-loved family. As is often the case, success invites imitation, and CBS, NBC, and ABC quickly rushed into animated prime-time program development for the 1991 season. Several of the animated programs had big-name talent associations: Steven Spielberg and *Batman Forever* director Tim Burton coproduced CBS's *Family Dog*, Steven Bochco produced ABC's *Capital Critters*, and the veteran animation studio of Hanna-Barbera Productions, Inc., handled two animated series, *Fish Police* for CBS and *The Terrible Tunes* for NBC.

One of the most enduring television formats is the daytime soap opera. The longevity of the "soaps" is unmatched by any other television program format. In 1992, CBS's *Guiding Light* celebrated its fortieth anniversary—and soap opera runs of twenty or thirty years are not uncommon.

Present-day soap operas owe their debt to a handful of writers and producers: Irna Phillips for *As the World Turns*, Agnes Nixon for *One Life to Live* and *All My Children*, and William J. Bell, who made the genre even more daring with *The Young and the Restless* and *The Bold and the Beautiful*.

While dealing with the traditional soap opera plots of infidelity and jealousy, the 1990s have seen a more socially conscious awareness in these programs. The themes addressed in today's soaps range from interracial love affairs to late-in-life pregnancies and domestic violence. In attempting to bring more realism to their characters and story line, soap opera producers are also using their programs as vehicles for enlightenment.

As television programming evolves to act in concert with interactive and digital technology, it will expand the limits of viewer participation. In many respects the audience will be able to control the destiny of the characters and the action. In effect, viewers will become programmers, creating their own agenda for performance, information, and entertainment.

NOTES

1. In some respects, producer Gary David Goldberg later attempted to dramatize the same values as *The Goldbergs* with the television network series *Brooklyn Bridge*. Interestingly, both series appeared on CBS: *The Goldbergs* from 1949–53, and *Brooklyn Bridge* 1992–93.

2. See, for example, the discussion of the controversy surrounding *Death of a Princess* in Chapter 9.

3. In August 1995, Viacom announced that it was selling its 78 percent interest in the Spelling Entertainment Group. Viacom had acquired Spelling in September 1994 when it purchased Blockbuster Entertainment Corporation.

4. Mr. Cosby agreed to another situation comedy series for CBS in the fall of 1996. The program, based on the successful British sitcom *One Foot in the Grave*, will be produced by Carsey-Werner Productions. During the 1995–96 season, Carsey-Werner had four successful half-hour sitcoms on network television, including their latest hit, *Third Rock from the Sun*, on NBC.

5
Programming Staples: Enduring Genres

Although there is no certain formula for success, there have been a number of programming genres that have sustained their interest and popularity over the years. These program formats have become an integral part of American culture, reflecting the concerns and aspirations of television viewers.

THE TALK SHOW

One of the most enduring programming formats has been the late-night talk show. The *Tonight Show* was introduced in 1954, with host Steve Allen. From 1957 to 1960 Jack Paar hosted the show, and in 1962 Johnny Carson began his thirty-year "reign" over late-night television. Carson's inimitable style and wit inspired a generation of comics. In 1992, after thirty years, Carson retired from the *Tonight Show*. His last week as host of the *Tonight Show* proved to be a bonanza for NBC, with thirty-second commercial spots increasing to $200,000, five times the regular price. The week-long farewell culminated with a bravura performance by Bette Midler, who sang Johnny her own rendition of "You Made Me Love You." Carson's last program earned the highest ratings in the *Tonight Show's* history, with a national ratings of 27.9 and an audience estimated at 50 million.

A week after Carson's retirement, NBC introduced the *Tonight Show with Jay Leno*. Leno did well his first night out, attracting 25 million viewers with an overnight ratings of 13.9, besting Carson's average year-long rating of 5.2. His ratings lagged behind David Letterman's, however, until 1995, when his show began to edge out the competition.

The talk show format remains an enticing vehicle for networks and performers because of its potential for generating vast sums of money. It is estimated that the *Tonight Show* generates $100 million in annual advertising revenues. Therefore it is not surprising that others make the effort to succeed with this late-night format. In 1993, CBS made the bold move of enticing David Letterman, host of NBC's *Late Night with David Letterman*, to its 11:30 p.m. time slot. Letterman, annoyed at being passed over by NBC for host of the *Tonight Show*, accepted the $16 million annual salary offered by CBS.

The late-night talk show programming landscape has become a lot more cluttered in recent years. In 1989 Arsenio Hall made his debut with the *Arsenio Hall Show*, syndicated by Paramount. After an initially strong showing, however, the program declined in popularity and suffered a mortal blow when many CBS affiliates who were distributing the program switched to the *Late Show with David Letterman* in 1993. Although celebrities like Whoopie Goldberg and Chevy Chase also entered the syndicated talk show marketplace, they soon realized that achieving success was more difficult than anticipated.

Television has in recent years also become inundated with talk/interview programs that fall into a number of different genres. Along with the traditional entertainment-oriented programs, beginning with the requisite host monologue, there are the more intense intimate interview formats like *Larry King Live*, the gossipy format of *Oprah Winfrey* and *Joan Rivers*, and the tabloid television genre exemplified by *Geraldo*.

One of the most enduring and successful talk/interview programs is *Larry King Live*, on CNN. King started his career in radio, and in 1978 the *Larry King Show* became the first national radio talk show. In 1985, *Larry King Live* began broadcasting from Washington, D.C., on CNN. Since then King's program has become a television phenomenon, earning the highest ratings of any program on CNN, seen in 130 countries.

One of the most notable broadcasts on the *Larry King Live* television program was the February 20, 1992 appearance of Ross Perot. On that program Mr. Perot announced that he would consider running for president if his supporters would register him and get his name on the ballot in fifty states. Thus, overnight Larry King became a part of the American political process.

Indeed, talk shows played an important role in the political process during the 1992 presidential campaign. Many applauded the ability of the candidates to talk directly to the electorate via interview and call-in programs. Some critics, however, expressed their disdain for this "direct access media," pointing out that candidate Bill Clinton's playing the saxophone on *Arsenio Hall* or George Bush's fielding questions on *Larry King Live* did not answer the need for serious comment and debate.

Nevertheless, talk show politics took their place in the presidential campaign of 1992, circumventing the traditional fifteen-second news "sound bite" and making Larry King, Phil Donahue, Arsenio Hall, and David Frost important players in the political process.

One controversial programming genre that developed during the 1980s was "tabloid television." Using a traditional interview/discussion format, these programs provided a forum for confrontation between representatives of disparate political and ideological groups. The concept of this programming type was not new: Allan Burke had pioneered the reality-oriented, hostility-prone confrontational interview program in the 1960s. The shows of the 1980s, however, seemed more determined to incite raucous behavior and provide a platform for inflammatory debate. The programs began modestly enough with the *Phil Donahue Show*, in 1970, and gradually evolved into the more hard-edged, incendiary tone that became the hallmark of the *Oprah Winfrey Show* and the *Sally Jesse Raphael* program.[1] Two programs that brought criticism and concern about the tabloid program format into focus were the *Morton Downey Jr. Show* and *Geraldo*, starring Geraldo Rivera. The adversarial style of these two hosts and their proclivity toward sensationalism and muckraking made them popular with some of the more rebellious and antagonistic elements of our society. These programs offer little in the way of substance and appeal to the viewer's emotions and instincts, not to the mind. The hosts freely engage in verbal abuse directed toward guests and audience members, and occasionally the participants are whipped up into such a frenzy that physical violence occurs. The appeal of these shows is in their circus-like atmosphere.

Advertisers have also expressed their concern about the hostile nature of the tabloid programs, and stations and networks have responded by not airing certain segments. The *Morton Downey Jr.* program was cancelled in 1989 in response to complaints from viewers and advertisers alike that the program was too provocative.

Indeed, when the confrontational nature of these talk programs evolved into "ambush" encounters, the potential for active or delayed hostility increased. This reputedly happened in 1995 when the *Jenny Jones Show* taped a segment called "Secret Crushes on People of the Same Sex." The program featured Scott Amedure, a gay man who was the secret admirer of Jon Schmitz, a professed heterosexual. During the taping of the show, Schmitz met his "secret admirer" amidst the snickers and giggles of the studio audience. Three days later, Scott Amedure was allegedly murdered by Jon Schmitz. While sympathizing with the families of both parties, Jones denied that the tragedy had anything to do with her show. The producers and hosts of these talk shows have displayed little concern for or knowledge of the frailties of the human psyche and the degree of humiliation and pain that their guests endure.[2]

GAME SHOWS

Another programming format that has enjoyed a long run on network and syndicated stations is the game show. While the concept of the big money giveaway program suffered from the quiz show scandals of 1959, game shows have nevertheless evolved into an integral component of the programming marketplace. The 1960s generated more benign game show concepts like *I've Got a Secret, What's My Line,* and *Concentration.* In the 1970s, game shows became more daring, offering more grandiose prizes and catering to the greediest instincts in audience participants. Popular game shows of the 1970s included *The Dating Game, The Newlywed Game,* and *Let's Make a Deal.* During the 1980s, game shows continued their popular appeal, and several new programs attracted a wide audience. One of the most successful game shows of the 1980s was *Family Feud.* This program created competition between families for generous gifts and cash prizes. Two other game shows that became successful in the 1980s were *Jeopardy* and *Wheel of Fortune,* emceed by Alex Trebek and Pat Sajak respectively.

The relatively modest production costs of these syndicated quiz programs make them a favored programming choice for the 1990s. Additional entries into the syndicated game show arena in the 1990s included *The Challengers,* hosted by veteran television personality Dick Clark; *Jokers Wild; Instant Recall;* and *Tic Tac Dough.* One of the more unique syndicated contestant game shows that generated audience interest when introduced in the 1989–90 season, was *American Gladiators.* The program, which arranges competitive events between its ten co-ed muscular resident gladiators and screened audience contestants, slowly built a loyal audience.

A new style of syndicated game shows of the 1990s have taken a daring step toward sexual permissiveness, suggestion, and innuendo. The programs, called "relationship" shows, usually feature attractive young men and women who make provocative comments about each other's appearance and sexual prowess. The first of these programs, *Studs,* produced by Twentieth Television, premiered on the Fox Broadcasting network during the 1992–93 season. *Studs* featured three young women and two young men, along with host Mark DeCarlo, who made ribald remarks about each other in an attempt to win their "dream date."

While *Studs* introduced frank talk about sex to the game show genre, it is not the first time that sex was an integral component of a television game show format. In the early 1980s, *Everything Goes* premiered on cable television. The program reconceptualized the game of "strip poker" for television: each time the male or female contestant got a question wrong they had to remove an article of clothing. *Everything*

Goes lasted only one season because of reluctant advertisers and concerns about negative audience reaction.[3]

REALITY-BASED PROGRAMMING

In addition to the tabloid talk shows, another new genre of reality-based programming has captured the interest of American audiences and advertisers. These programs present dramatic re-creations of unsolved crimes and include Fox's *America's Most Wanted* and NBC's *Unsolved Mysteries*. Since their introduction in the 1987–88 season, these two programs have been instrumental in bringing about the apprehension of many criminals: *America's Most Wanted* has led law enforcement officials to over 240 suspects, and *Unsolved Mysteries* led to the capture of 80 more. However, a number of concerns have been raised about the impact and value of such programming. Some critics argue that these programs are unabashedly biased toward law enforcement professionals and that the "re-creations" of crimes featured in the program are melodramatic and misleading. Others point out that at times these programs portray relatively minor offenders as big-time criminals.

The competition for ratings and stories can also lead to mistaken identities. That's what happened to Robin John Delgado, a Los Angeles bartender who was arrested after being incorrectly identified as a fugitive profiled on *America's Most Wanted*. Delgado filed a libel suit against the program and also sued the Los Angeles police and the FBI.

The success of the reality crime programs led to the development of rescue programs. *Rescue 911* is one of the most successful of this genre: this program dramatizes medical emergencies by recreating actual events from 911 logs. This program also has its critics, especially since 13 percent of its audience is children. Some psychologists have expressed the concern that children watching life-threatening situations on a regular basis may view them as normal occurrences of daily living. The program attracts a large audience, and the producers of *Rescue 911* have shown some sensitivity toward their young audience by selecting stories that are less intimidating to children.

The success of these programs has given reality-based crime and rescue programs a priority position in syndication and network distribution. These programs are cost effective: about $150,000 per segment for *America's Most Wanted* and $500,000 per episode for *Unsolved Mysteries*, as compared to the $1 million needed to produce a prime-time drama of the same length. This factor has encouraged the production of other, similar "reality programs" such as *Crime Watch Tonight, Cops, Code 3*, and *American Detective*.

CHILDREN'S PROGRAMMING

Once the neglected stepchild of television, broadcasters and producers have in recent years taken on a new initiative in the development of children's programming. The reasons for this change have to do with the realities of business and government regulation.

With a population of about 40 million, American children are a formidable force in the television and video entertainment marketplace. Children ages two to five watch an average of about 28 hours a week (almost 4 hours daily), and those in the six to eleven age group, almost 24 hours (3.4 hours per day). Children are also responsible for either spending or influencing the spending of $100 billion annually.[4]

Attempts to legislate oversight of children's programming were repeatedly defeated by the aggressive lobbying efforts of broadcasters and program producers over the years. And in 1984, FCC regulations pertaining to commercial time standards—9.5 minutes on weekends, and 12 minutes on weekdays in children's programming—were dropped.

While the 1980s witnessed the demise of children's programming time standards, it also became the decade when networks returned to live-action children's programming. After the discontinuation of *Captain Kangaroo*, which stopped airing in 1984, for years there were no live-action children's programs on weekend morning network television. In 1987, CBS took a bold step and scheduled the live action *Pee Wee's Playhouse*, starring Pee Wee Herman, on Saturday mornings. The program proved to be a refreshing configuration for children's television which integrated conventional themes into a rather irreverent format.

The passage of the Children's Television Act of 1990 has set a new agenda for children's programming in the 1990s. The law, which became effective in 1992, stipulates commercial time standards for hourly children's programming for audiences aged twelve and under at 10.5 minutes on weekends and 12 minutes on weekdays. In addition, the law requires children's television programming to serve the educational, informational, and social needs of children, furthering their intellectual and cognitive development.

The FCC has made enforcement of the Children's Television Act a priority and has fined stations for violating its commercial time standards. One of the problems of the act, however, is its vague language, which allows broadcasters to define programs like *The Flintstones*, *G.I. Joe*, and *Yo Yogi* as informational and educational. As a result, the FCC is considering articulating clearer compliance guidelines and setting a children's television programming quota standard.

The four broadcast television networks have responded to the legislative mandate by scheduling educationally entertaining children's programs, many of which are live action. ABC continued with its successful, award-winning *ABC After-School Special* (started in 1972) and *ABC Weekend Specials* (since 1977), along with new programs like *Cro and City Kids*. CBS acquired the rights to *Beakman's World*, a zany syndicated science program that now appears both on CBS and on cable's the Learning Channel. CBS also broadcasts a program called *Storybreak*, which features animated adaptations of children's books and encourages its audience to read. NBC has a number of live-action children's programs, including *Name Your Adventure*, which combines entertainment and education in a challenging format. And Fox, which has been a ratings leader in children's television programming, is broadcasting a televised version of the popular computer game *Where on Earth Is Carmen Sandiego?* and *Bobby's World*. Naturally, the networks also continue to broadcast other programs, including cartoons, which are still an important component of their children's programming.[5]

Independent production companies have responded to the Children's Television Act by producing syndicated children's programming that enables stations to fulfill their educational mandate. These programs include *Disney Presents Bill Nye, the Science Guy*; Zodiac Entertainment's *Twinkle, the Dream Being*; Pandora International's *Scramble*; and Tribune Entertainment's *Energy Express*.

Cable television has become an important distribution source for children's programming. There are two cable networks specifically designed to cater exclusively to children, Nickelodeon, founded in 1979, and The Disney Channel, which became operational in 1982. Nickelodeon has achieved a great deal of success by combining original programs with prepackaged material targeted toward preschoolers to teenagers. Nickelodeon programs appealing to the teenage audience include *Double Dare, Kids Writes*, and *Mr. Wizard's World*, which are both intellectually challenging and entertaining. The cable network also distributes several animated programs that appeal to younger children. These programs distinguish themselves from traditional cartoons with their creative plots and serial story lines. Examples of this genre include *Papa Beaver, Doug*, and *Rocco's Modern Life*.

Other cable networks have blocks of time that are dedicated to children's programming. Turner Broadcasting's Cartoon Network offers viewers a steady diet of cartoons and features cartoon-character festivals like the twenty-four-hour *Huckleberry Hound Labor Day Marathon* it held in 1993. And the Family Channel, which delegates daily morning and afternoon blocks of time to children's programming, offers familiar cartoons like *Popeye, Supermario Brothers*, and *Inspector Gadget*.

Preschool programming is a also strong component of the Learning Channel, which offers a block of daytime programming including *Ready,*

Set, Learn, The Magic Box, and *The Happy Professor,* aimed at two-to-five-year-olds.

With children's programming having become a strong profit center, cable networks have made considerable investments in acquiring children's programming from both domestic and foreign production sources. Along with familiar titles like *Star Trek* and *Return to the Planet of the Apes,* the Sci-Fi Channel turned to Japan's Shinsha Company Ltd. for fifty-one half-hour episodes of the animated series *The New Adventures of Gigantor.*

The network that distributed the most innovative children's programming during the 1970s and 1980s was PBS, however, and the company responsible for the production of these programs was Children's Television Workshop (CTW). CTW was able to successfully integrate instructional objectives into an entertaining format, with programs like *Sesame Street, Electric Company, Reading Rainbow,* and *Shining Time Station.* In 1991, PBS announced a long-term children's initiative plan to expand its inventory of children's programming and develop more substantive educational themes in their series.

Three PBS programs that were tremendously successful in the 1990s were *Barney and Friends, Lamb Chop's Play-Along,* and *Ghost Writer.* Barney, the silly but loveable dinosaur, became an instant hit with the preschool audience. Originally produced as a home video, Barney's success on public television has created a bonanza in licensing fees for the Lyon's Group, creator of the Barney character. Barney-related retail merchandise earned about $200 million in 1993.

For a performer who hadn't had a national television series since 1963, Shari Lewis proved that quality children's television programming is always in demand. In 1992, PBS began regular broadcasts of *Lamb Chop's Play Along.* Ms. Lewis, who had an NBC Saturday morning program from 1960 to 1963, has once again integrated her skills in puppetry, music, and magic to produce an Emmy-award-winning children's program.

Ghostwriter, another program produced by CTW, became a hit of the 1993 season. The program, which is targeted toward six-to-eleven-year-olds, teaches writing skills and raises social issues in an entertaining, nonintimidating format. Another popular program was *Mr. Rogers' Neighborhood,* featuring the soft-spoken Fred Rogers who presided over a small world of fantasy and reality.

BROADCAST SPORTS COVERAGE

Another type of "reality" programming that has been a mainstay of television culture is broadcast sports coverage. The broadcasting of sporting events has a rich tradition in American entertainment. From the shortwave transmissions of the Shmeling/Lewis prizefight in 1938 to the satellite coverage of the Summer and Winter Olympics, television has made sports one of the most lucrative industries in America. Indeed, sports-related advertising on the three commercial television networks (ABC, CBS, NBC) increased from $50 million in 1960 to $190 million in 1970, $813 million in 1980, and up to a $1.5 billion in 1987. Over the years television has increased its coverage of American sports and as a result alternative distribution channels were needed to accommodate the volume. Cable television has also become an important competitor in the sports arena, vying for the broadcasting rights of various events.

For network television, the right to broadcast the Olympic games has become the holy grail of sports programming. As athletes compete for the gold, silver, and bronze medals, network executives engage in nervous fingernail biting, trying to determine the magnitude of their losses. Ironically, the Games have generated an inverse proportion in value: ratings have declined for almost every Olympic telecast since 1972, while broadcast rights have increased to almost $500 million.

The allure of the right to broadcast the Olympic Games, especially the summer competition, is inexplicable. Each time the International Olympic Committee (IOC) opens negotiations for exclusive broadcast rights, at least three of the networks (ABC, NBC, CBS), pledge restraint, and yet one of them always manages to "break the bank."

One of the biggest losers in Olympic broadcast history is NBC. When the network broadcast the Summer Games from Seoul in 1988, for which it paid $300 million, ratings for the Games suffered their biggest decline in Olympic broadcasting history, forcing NBC to provide advertisers with free time to make up for the loss. Undaunted, NBC once again pursued the Olympic grail and paid the IOC $401 million for the right to broadcast the 1992 Games from Barcelona. Encouraged by CBS's favorable ratings from the broadcast of the 1992 Winter Games in Albertville, France, NBC felt confident that it could achieve a ratings victory with the Summer Games. In fact, NBC joined forces with Cablevision Systems Corporation to offer the first pay-per-view Olympic television coverage in broadcast history. The attempt proved to be disastrous for both companies, with losses estimated between $100 to 150 million.

Hoping to attract 2 million pay-per-view homes to "Triplecast" (the marketing name for the Olympic pay-per-view), the venture only signed about 250,000 subscribers, and those were at heavily discounted prices. The pay-per-view package was initially priced at $125 for fifteen days of coverage and $29.95 for individual daily orders: however, this was too expensive for most viewers. In addition to the overpricing, the time-delay dilemma from Barcelona presented another problem. The primary incentive for purchasing "Triplecast" was to see the Olympics live: however, the live broadcasts started at 5:00 a.m. on the East Coast, and 2:00 a.m. on the West. With viewers nationwide still asleep, the appeal of live programming was lost, and anyone interested in taped highlights of the events could easily turn to NBC and watch them free of charge.

Amazingly, NBC decided to try again and won the right to broadcast the 1996 Summer Olympics from Atlanta for $456 million. In August 1995 they won the rights to the 2002 Winter Games in Salt Lake City for $555 million and the 2000 Summer Games in Australia for $715 million.[6] NBC hopes to use the games as a vehicle to move it into a more competitive ranking among the four television networks. To promote the Atlanta Games, the network provided at least $6 million in advertising time on other sports events. In addition, NBC provided the IOC with nine half-hour weekend daytime slots that the IOC programmed and sold advertising for. As a preview to the 1996 Games in Atlanta, NBC produced a program on the 1996 Olympics that aired just before the 1994 Super Bowl pre-game show, which was also in Atlanta.

One component of NBC's winning bid for the Games is revenue sharing. NBC offered the IOC a share in gross network ad sales when NBC reaches a threshold of $615 million. With the Games being expanded from sixteen to seventeen days, starting on a Friday night, and offering 168 hours of coverage, NBC may reach its threshold. By the summer of 1995, NBC had already sold $600 million in Olympic advertising.[7]

The Winter Olympic Games of 1994 may have heralded a turning point in broadcast coverage of the event. The Games from Lillehammer, Norway, were the highest-rated Olympic winter event on broadcast television since the 1980 Winter Games in Lake Placid. In addition to the inherent interest of the event, there was the dramatic rivalry between two of the American figure skaters, Nancy Kerrigan and Tonya Harding, which was complicated by a bizarre attack on Kerrigan as she was leaving a practice session shortly before the Olympics. The element of human drama also played a role for speed skaters Dan Jansen and Bonnie Blair, each trying to overcome personal tragedy to achieve their "individual best." While some of the ratings success of the Games from Lillehammer can be attributed to the unfolding of these human dramas, NBC is hedging its bets that the thrill of competition, and the power of Olympic achievement, will also bring about record ratings for its future Olympic coverage.

One area of sports coverage that cable television has excelled in is the exhibition of special sporting events. HBO, the pay-cable network, has specialized in covering major boxing matches and featuring them on their service, often on a delayed basis. Cable pay-per-view channels cover these events live and offer them to subscribing households on a per-viewing basis. Most pay-per-view sporting events cost between $3 and $4 per person: however, a well-publicized match can cost as much as $32.

Sporting events and concerts have had the most success on cable pay-per-view, while revenues from movies have been disappointing.

While only about 20 percent of the nation's cable homes are equipped for pay-per-view, sporting events like the 1991 Evander Holyfield-George Foreman "Battle of the Ages" boxing match have proven to be audience pleasers. Distributed by TVKO, Time Warner's sports pay-per-view network, this event earned $60 million in pay-per-view revenue and was purchased by 1.4 million cable subscribers. In contrast, *Fatal Attraction*, the most successful movie in pay-per-view history, earned only $1.2 million. Most industry observers agree that pay-per-view television will become an important component in the sporting marketplace because of its ability to provide a more profitable margin than the sixty-four cents per television household that broadcast networks can pay.

As sporting events have become an important programming genre for cable television, concerns have been raised about the declining availability of free sports programming.[8] As a result, legislators, sports fans, and leading industry representatives are discussing plans for limiting cable's role in the sports marketplace. A reaction to cable's aggressiveness in the televised sporting event arena occurred in the 1989 contracts that CBS negotiated with the National Collegiate Athletic Association (NCAA), and NBC with the National Basketball Association (NBA). CBS agreed to an exclusive seven-year package that included a $1 billion payment for sole broadcast rights for the NCAA basketball tournament. Significantly, the arrangement forbid the broadcast of any NCAA events on cable or independent television. The deal, which became effective in 1991, required CBS to cover the sixty-three-game basketball tournament and removed another sixteen NCAA sports championships from cable television. The CBS arrangement effectively freezes out the Entertainment and Sports Programming Network (ESPN) from telecasting NCAA games and ended that network's eleven-year relationship with the NCAA. CBS's previous contract with the NCAA cost it $55.3 million, while the new contract has a price tag of $143 million annually, a high price to pay for exclusivity.

NBC was equally anxious to get its hands on an exclusive sports franchise. In 1989, after CBS had allowed its seventeen-year NBA option to expire, NBC accepted the same deal CBS had rejected. NBC agreed to pay the NBA $600 million over four years to broadcast NBA games. Included in the agreement is a $40-million commitment by NBC to air NBA on-air commercials, 60 percent of which must be in prime time, and an additional $4 million paid by NBC to cover the NBA-sponsored McDonald's Open. NBC's arrangement with the NBA was for exclusive over-the-air broadcast rights. The NBA earned themselves an additional $275 million by selling the cable rights to TNT. In 1993, NBC extended its exclusive NBA broadcast rights through 1998 (an addition of four years), for $750 million.

The aggressive nature of NBC's pursuit of exclusive sports franchises resulted in a splintering of the unified collective bargaining stance of the College Football Association (CFA). ABC had signed a $210 million, five-year contract with the CFA to broadcast the football games of the sixty-four universities participating in the television pool. However, Notre Dame, a member of the CFA television broadcast pool and usually the college team that attracts the largest television audience, had negotiated its own five-year, $75 million deal with NBC. To ABC's chagrin, the separate deal meant that the network that spent $210 million for CFA football rights could not broadcast the six home games played by Notre Dame in South Bend, Indiana. The FTC took a dim view of the CFA/ABC contract, charging that the terms restricted competition, violated antitrust laws, and reduced the selection of games for consumers.

Notre Dame's defection and the FTC's scrutiny eventually led to a disintegration of the CFA's ability to represent the six major football conferences and several dozen independent schools. As of 1995, when ABC's agreement with the CFA ended, there was no longer any centralized organization negotiating for college football television rights. For example, CBS signed both the Southeastern Conference and the Big East to multiyear, multimillion-dollar television deals for football and basketball rights. ABC soon followed with a five-year extension (to the year 2000) of its Big Ten and Pacific 10 television deal and negotiated a multimillion dollar deal with the Atlantic Coast Conference.

This newly created competitive marketplace for college football is due in part to the increased independence of college teams and conferences and also to the escalating value that the networks have placed on professional football.[9] When the NFL television rights package expired in 1994, the networks were determined to play hardball with the football league in a concerted effort to lower license fees. The three networks had paid a combined sum of $1.67 billion for NFL football and had experienced heavy losses from the deal. CBS had lost $100 million a year and was eager to reach equitable terms without sacrificing its forty-year relationship with the NFL.

But the Fox Network's successful bid for a televised NFL franchise foiled this plan and led to even more outrageous licensing fees. Fox changed the negotiating climate when it offered a staggering $1.58 billion to the NFL for the NFC package. (Some analysts project a $600 million loss for Fox over the four-year contract.) Shortly after this bid, NBC ponied up $868 million for the AFC games, and ABC followed with a $920 million bid. ESPN and TNT paid $524 and $496 million respectively for their football packages. There weren't even any crumbs left for CBS to nibble on, as they were effectively frozen out of football until 1998.

One of the most attractive components of the NFL agreement with the networks are the Super Bowl games. These games generate blockbuster ratings and are consistently the most-watched sports programs on television. Indeed, of the ten most-watched programs in television history (measured in total viewers), the Super Bowl takes nine of the positions, while the final 1983 episode of *M*A*S*H* ranks fourth. A new licensing package assigned the games to ABC, NBC, and Fox.

The prominent issue facing all televised sporting event distributors, of course, is the ability to earn a profit after paying hundreds of millions of dollars for broadcasting rights. This issue becomes even more crucial when the sports franchise places restrictions on the distributor. For example, the CBS agreement with the NCAA required the network to reduce beer commercials by one-third, and NBC's deal with the NBA limited the network to forty-six to forty-eight thirty-second commercials per game, with no option to earn extra revenue by adding commercials.

Certainly network and cable distributors realize that these huge investments will not return a proportional profit. Instead they view their expenditure as part of a comprehensive strategy to make their company a more viable competitor in a fiercely competitive marketplace. For example, the CBS strategy was to build a powerful sports franchise into its programming schedule in an effort to reverse its downward audience trend. Fox is using the same strategy for its investment in the NFL games, hoping that these games will provide it with the visibility it needs to be a competitive force in American network television. Noting CBS's losses of hundreds of millions of dollars for its baseball and football packages, one can only guess that Fox has pockets deep enough to absorb the potentially heavy expense.

Like the other sports, baseball has become more diversified in its distribution. This diversification is a result of the increased costs of exclusive broadcast rights and an extended season with more games. While the networks continue to provide World Series coverage, many regular season games now appear on cable television. In 1988 CBS completed an agreement with the baseball commissioner's office, securing the exclusive broadcast rights to the league championship play-offs, the All-Star game, the World Series, and twelve games a season, for a cost of $1.06 billion and a term of four years beginning in 1990. Unfortunately, the CBS baseball contract generated considerable losses for the network, based upon a 1990 four-game World Series sweep and a 20 percent decline in advertising rates from the previous year. However, CBS did better during the 1991 and 1992 World Series games.

That same year, ESPN negotiated a $400 million deal with major league baseball to obtain the exclusive television rights to 175 baseball games annually for four years beginning in 1990. ESPN is 80 percent owned by Capital Cities/ABC, with the remaining 20 percent held by RJR Nabisco. However, ESPN is not the only cable network to acquire rights to the distribution of baseball games. Most of the Yankee's baseball games were seen on the Madison Square Garden cable network beginning in 1991, and half of the Mets games were seen on the Sports Channel.

Well aware of to CBS's $500 million loss on its baseball contract, other networks have been hesitant to pursue costly exclusive television rights for baseball games. Instead, in 1993 ABC and NBC reached an agreement with Major League Baseball (MLB) to form a new joint venture, the Baseball Network. For the first time, MLB produced and distributed its own games for network television. The networks paid no rights fees, and MLB sold most of the advertising time. Unfortunately, MLB's first season as a baseball program producer was curtailed by the 1994 players' strike. ABC and NBC terminated their participation in the Baseball Network in August 1995, after failing to negotiate a contract with MLB.[10]

Televised coverage of sporting events remains a basic feature of television programming. If anything, sports coverage is expanding, from World Cup Soccer to the Gay Games, making athletic competition an essential component of a balanced programming schedule.

RELIGIOUS BROADCASTING

The arrival of television ushered in a new era in religious broadcasting for both traditional faiths and for the spectacle of television evangelism and Christian fundamentalism. One of the longest-running network television religious programs was *Lamp unto My Feet*, which premiered on CBS in 1948. This program, which was presented on CBS as part of the Protestant Radio Commission, was eclectic in its choice of religious themes, addressing ecumenical issues and exploring connections between the world's major faiths. *Lamp unto My Feet* was a prominent fixture of the CBS network programming schedule for over three decades, until it was taken off the air in 1979. Other religious network programs that were broadcast during the 1950s included *Directions* (ABC), *Frontiers of Faith* (NBC), and *Look Up and Live* (CBS). None of these programs attempted to proselytize to their audiences, but instead focussed on the universal need for faith in God.

Network television produced its first celebrity preacher in 1952 with the premiere of *Life Is Worth Living*, hosted by Catholic bishop Fulton J. Sheen. Known as the "Angel of the Airwaves," Sheen had a formidable presence. Draped in a cape and wearing a large crucifix, his subdued delivery made an eloquent statement on the importance of allegiance to the faith. His unique style and his devotion to questions of spiritual matters rather than the rhetoric of retribution made his program a popular prime-time event.

The bishop was not a newcomer to broadcasting, having preached a number of radio sermons in 1928 on WLWL in New York and having hosted a regular spot on the National Catholic Hour. Sheen was a master of language, and he enraptured his audience with his dynamism and eloquence. Although Sheen was paid $26,000 for each program, the money was donated to the Society of the Propagation of the Faith, of which he was the director.

Tele-Evangelism

Television became the savior of evangelism, turning itinerant self-proclaimed nickel-and-dime ministers into powerful preachers from electronic pulpits, able to earn millions of dollars on demand. Billy Graham was the first to use broadcast media to carefully stage his evangelical crusades. This obscure rural preacher created an image for himself, in the style of William Randolph Hearst or Henry Luce, and it made him an international celebrity.

Several events served as catalysts for the movement toward evangelical broadcasting. Certainly the Civil Rights movement and the African-American community's association with evangelism helped to popularize the practice of a religious faith that previously had not been particularly attractive to Northern European audiences. Other factors contributing to the rise of electronic evangelism were the unsettled political climate of the 1960s and the social unrest that brought the country to the brink of revolution. Indeed, after a period of stabilization, there were sudden revelations by some of those associated with these troubled times that they had become born-again Christians.

Another event that helped to legitimize the evangelical movement in America was the election in 1976 of Jimmy Carter as president. Carter was a self-proclaimed born-again Southern evangelical who gave national prominence and credence to evangelism and helped to popularize the movement in the United States.

The growth of cable television also helped to sustain and extend the reach of electronic evangelism.[11] Cable offered evangelists an opportunity to realize more for their television dollars by disseminating their message to a wider audience with a greater potential for donations. With the advent of cable television, evangelical broadcasters could attain a penetration level similar to that of network television at a much lower cost.[12] Many of the most successful evangelical broadcasters had humble beginnings in their quest for a devoted flock. Oral Roberts, who was one of the first television evangelists, came from a destitute family and suffered from a severe stutter. He achieved a great deal of notoriety as an itinerant faith healer, travelling rural America and conducting revival meetings in his canvas "cathedral." Seeing the potential of television to spread the good news, Roberts packed away his tent and turned to the electronic pulpit. Since 1954, when Roberts produced his first television program, he has created a multi million-dollar empire including the program production facility that produces his Sunday program.

One of the most astute and politically seasoned of broadcast evangelists is Pat Robertson. Robertson's family had a political orientation: his father was a senator from Virginia, and Robertson himself attended Yale Law School. With his business acumen, political savvy and connections, and pleasant personality, Robertson built a multi billion-dollar enterprise, the Christian Broadcasting Network (CBN). Starting with the purchase in 1960 of a bankrupt Virginia Beach television station, Robertson has, over the past thirty years, engineered an evangelical empire. He is the founder and chairman of CBN and International Family Entertainment, the parent company of the Family Channel and MTM Entertainment, the company founded by Mary Tyler Moore and her ex-husband, Grant Tinker. The Family Channel, created in 1977, specializes in wholesome entertainment and distributes Robertson's popular program, *The 700 Club*, twice daily. It has an ample program library for television syndication and is an active television production company.

As chairman of the U.S. Media Corporation and Broadcast Equities, Inc., Robertson also oversees Standard News, a radio news network with 272 affiliated stations, and Zapnews, a Fox news service with over 300 broadcast affiliates. Another broadcast enterprise is North Star Entertainment, which produces and distributes programs for family audiences.

After the Bakker and Swaggert sex scandals of the 1980s, Robertson's keen business astuteness and political instincts led him to renounce his ordination. This allowed him to build a profitable business empire while continuing his political and humanitarian efforts. Although Robertson failed in his bid for the Republican presidential nomination in 1988, he has maintained a high visibility supporting conservative causes and candidates. The Christian Coalition, of which he is the founder and president, is one of the most active political lobbying groups in the country. In 1993 the coalition forged an unprecedented cooperative political effort with the Catholic Church in two states—for school board elections in New York City and a school voucher initiative in California. Cardinal John J. O'Connor of New York agreed to the distribution of ten thousand voter guides in New York City churches, supporting school board candidates opposed to the distribution of condoms. And in California, 2 million coalition voter guides were mailed, with several hundred targeted at Catholic priests, in an effort to have Proposition 174 (concerning school vouchers), passed. Although neither effort was victorious, the power of the Christian Coalition, with its 850 chapters and 450,000 members, to influence voters was clear. Indeed, it was the coalition's support of Mike Huckabee, a Republican Baptist preacher, that helped to elect him lieutenant governor of Arkansas in 1993.

A part of the Christian Coalition's political agenda for the 1990s is to forge a "rainbow coalition"—European Americans as well as people of other descents—to consolidate its power and support of conservative legislators. In this way they hope to rally constituents around the coalition's opposition to abortion, homosexuality, pornography, and support of school prayer.

Supporting the political efforts of the Christian Coalition are the American Center for Law and Justice (ACLJ) and Regent University. The ACLJ, which operates on an annual budget of $9 million, defends conservative causes and opposes the liberal legal agenda of the American Civil Liberties Union (ACLU). Regent University, of which Robertson is chancellor, provides graduate education and prepares students for careers in law and public service. The university has a $200 million endowment, most of it in the form of International Family Entertainment Stock.

In 1992, Robertson offered shares in Family Entertainment, Inc. to the public, making millionaires of Robertson and his son, Timothy, who is president of the Family Channel. Robertson and his son together own approximately $40 million of Family Entertainment Class B stock, which carry a single vote. Class A stock, which has ten votes a share, is exclusively owned by Robertson and his son. As chairman of International Family Entertainment, Robertson earns in excess of $300,000 a year, while his son Timothy earns more than $400,000 as the company's chief executive.

Timothy Robertson is credited with turning the Family Channel into a secular entertainment company, making it the tenth-largest cable television company, with an audience close to that of MTV (over 54 million households).

The Robertsons also have the distinction of being one of the first American media companies to invest in Vietnam after the U.S. trade embargo was removed in 1994. Entering a partnership with Hanoi Television and his International Family Entertainment, Robertson plans a twenty-eight-channel cable television system that has the potential of reaching 10 million Vietnamese viewers with family-oriented programs.

For Pat Robertson, the scandals of the 1980s that rocked the foundation of tele-evangelism proved to be a harbinger of good fortune. He is now positioned as a leading figure in conservative politics and as a broadcasting executive with a large and powerful constituency.

One characteristic of the electronic evangelistic pulpit is the grandiose theatrical design that is employed to thrill and titillate audi-

ences. One of the leading stars of religious televised theatrics is Robert
Schuller. Dr. Schuller has come a long way from his humble beginnings
in 1955, preaching the drive-in theater circuit in Orange County,
California. He was raised in the stern Dutch Reform tradition in Iowa
farm country, and received an ordination in the Reformed Church of
America. Eventually, Schuller turned away from the dogmatic teachings
of John Calvin and instead embraced the "positive thinking" approach of
Norman Vincent Peale.

Schuller's eloquence as a master orator has made his program, *Hour
of Power*, the most popular religious television program on television.
After twenty-five years, *Hour of Power* is broadcast in fifty countries and
is translated into seven languages. In the United States it has the largest
audience of any religious program, with over 1.5 million viewers. The
program originates from Schuller's "Crystal Cathedral" in Garden
Grove, California, a $15 million glass cathedral that provides an appro-
priate stage for Schuller's grandiose rhetoric.

As television evangelism evolved into a billion-dollar industry, there
were some preachers who could not resist the temptations of sin and
there were others who, guided by greed and jealousy, attempted to
manipulate this theater of theology. Two of the most spectacular abuses
occurred within the Pentecostal parish of Jim and Tammy Bakker and the
PTL (Praise the Lord) ministries and with the Jimmy Swaggert Ministries.
Both men were accused of sexual misconduct and were eventually
defrocked. Bakker was sentenced to forty-five years in prison for wire
fraud and was released in 1994 after a successful appeal.

The tele-evangelical flock, once considered the prize of electronic
preachers, has rejected the hypocrisy of their clerics and abandoned their
video pews. Their devotion has been betrayed by the dalliances of their
leaders and the arrogance of their behavior. Bakker's imprisonment,
Swaggart's dramatic fall from grace, and Roberts' manipulation of "faith"
for the dollar have contrived to alienate the audience and compromise
their trust. As a result, the broadcast audience for the top twenty syndicated religious programs has declined.

Not surprisingly, one of the reactions to the scandals has been heightened scrutiny by the government agencies that provide oversight to religious broadcasters. According to the IRS Tax Code, it is a felony to use
tax-free donations for personal or political causes. In 1987 the House
Ways and Means Committee's Oversight Subcommittee held hearings on
the tax-exempt status of television evangelists. The critical issue
addressed by the committee was the role of government in policing the
financial affairs of evangelical broadcast ministries and their tax-exempt
status. Naturally the issue of government oversight as it pertains to religious broadcasters is a sensitive one because of the Constitutional guar-

antee of separation of church and state. Nevertheless, the IRS did conduct investigations into religious broadcasting, concerning itself with unreported income.

Membership within the National Religious Broadcasters (NRB) numbers about twelve hundred, all of whom subscribe to the NRB Code of Ethics. The code prescribes various forms of accountability and obligations that religious broadcasters must meet, some of which include production, advertising, finance, and financial accountability.

Among the membership services that the NRB makes available is an active publications division that provides members with a monthly magazine, *Religious Broadcasting*, circulation of about ten thousand, and various directories and professional articles. The NRB also organizes regional and national conventions, conducting seminars and workshops. Their annual meeting in the nation's capitol is viewed as an important event and usually attracts a leading Republican as a keynote speaker. At the 1989 convention, the NRB adopted a permanent Ethics and Financial Integrity Commission (EFICOM), which would require all members to submit annual independent audit reports. The bylaws of EFICOM address a wide range of rules governing fundraising and accounting practices. It sets ethical and professional guidelines for financial activities of the ministries and provides oversight in the management and disbursement of these funds. All ministries subscribing to the EFICOM code are required to pay an annual membership fee from $175 to $5,000, depending upon their contribution income.

Obviously the move toward a more rigorous self-regulatory posture is designed to avoid further government scrutiny and regulation. The effectiveness of this body will depend upon the members' willingness to abide by its principals and enforce its own provisions.

As television moves toward the next generation of technology and evolves into an interactive information and entertainment medium, there is a great deal of speculation as to what shape programming will take. No doubt television programming will become more than just a reflection of cultural norms, parodying the American life-style. More channels to choose from and the merging of computer software with television hardware can transform television into a medium of substance that can do more than just entertain. However, the entertainment component of television programming will probably continue to be the strongest revenue base of the business. Then, are we to look forward to more of the same sitcoms, made-for-television movies, miniseries, and sporting events? Certainly some future television programming will be business as usual, but another part of it will be new and inventive, stimulating and, yes, maybe even enriching.

NOTES

1. In 1995 Multimedia, the company that syndicates *Donahue* and the *Sally Jesse Raphael* programs, was sold to the Gannett Company for $1.7 billion. Gannett is the largest newspaper publisher in the United States. After twenty-nine years on television, Phil Donahue taped his last program on May 2, 1996.

2. In 1995 tabloid television programs were attacked by former education secretary William Bennett (leader of the advocacy group "Empower America") and Senator Lieberman, a Democrat from Connecticut. As a result, a number of companies—including Sears & Roebuck, Kraft, and M&M/Mars—reduced their advertising on these programs. Geraldo Rivera announced that he will change the format of "Geraldo" beginning in September 1996 and change the name to "The Geraldo Rivera Show." The new format will be more news-oriented and less sensational.

3. *Everything Goes* debuted on the Playboy Channel on September 12, 1981. It was produced by Scott Sternberg Productions.

4. This includes $2.4 billion in 1992 sales of children's videos, $800 million spent on advertising in children's programs, and billions spent on licensed merchandise sales.

5. In 1995 Time Warner's WB Network and its Saturday morning lineup kids' WB! became fourth in children's programming among the networks. Two of its most popular programs are Steven Spielberg's "Pinky & The Brain" and "Animaniacs."

6. Once again NBC stunned the broadcasting industry with its December 1995 announcement that it had secured exclusive U.S. rights to the 2004, 2006 and 2008 games for $2.3 billion.

7. One hundred sixty-one hours of programming were broadcast from Barcelona, from which NBC generated approximately $520 million in advertising sales.

8. In an unusual turn of events, boxer Mike Tyson's second fight since being released from prison was shown on the Fox Television Network in 1995. Viacom Inc.'s Showtime Networks sold the rights to Fox for $10 million. It was the first time in a decade that a professional boxing match was seen on prime-time broadcast television.

9. CBS paid $150 million to broadcast Fiesta and Orange Bowls through 2001.

10. In 1995 major league baseball negotiated a five-year package of national television deals with Fox, NBC, ESPN, and Liberty Sports worth $1.68 billion through the year 2000.

11. As of this writing, there are 23 religious cable networks.

12. Those religious cable networks with the greatest reach include: Eternal Word Television Network, Trinity Broadcasting Network, Faith & Values and the Inspirational Network (formerly Praise the Lord Network).

6
Merchants of News

Broadcasting's journalistic imperative was created by visionary individuals who understood the drama and pathos inherent in a medium that could touch the soul of its public. Television was quick to capitalize on the value of moving pictures as a tool that could capture with immediacy and emotional impact breaking news stories. With remarkable success, television has felt the pulse of its audience.

For forty years, the three broadcast television networks dominated the dissemination of national and foreign television news. Their predominance, however, has been challenged in recent years by new technologies that threaten to undermine the historical hegemony of the networks.

Television news has undergone quite a metamorphosis since the early 1950s. In early television, news programming was presented as an afterthought and produced on a minimal scale with a modest budget. Over the past two decades, however, news programming has become a priority for both the networks and local television stations. Television news has evolved from the single fifteen-minute nightly newscast of the 1950s to a twenty-four-hour cable television service.

The reality of competition in a fragmented television news environment has made the drive for ratings an ever greater determinant in the success or failure of a television news program. Ratings translate into revenue earned from the advertising placed on news programs, which turns into profits for the company. The competition for high ratings has affected the nature of the news reported and has helped to set both the tone and the journalistic agenda of the newscast. Lead stories are chosen for their ratings appeal, and local news stories, which may continue for several nights, are selected to coincide with major network theatrical programming events. For example, stories about domestic brutality appeared on local news programs during the network premiere of *The Burning Bed*. Quite often local news stories are chosen more for their ability to titillate audiences than to inform them.

LOCAL TELEVISION NEWS

As news has evolved into a valuable commodity, local stations have embraced it as a profit center and promotional tool. With their striking visuals, prominent personalities, and "beat" specialists, local news programs have become the cultural symbols for the stations they serve. In some markets local news has been positioned as a conspicuous programming feature and is designed to provide an alternative to regular programs. Since 1990, Los Angeles station KCAL-TV has been broadcasting five local news programs each night.[1]

Both network affiliates and independent stations are also attempting to maximize distribution of their news programs by creating unique business alliances. Although it has discontinued the relationship, at one time NBC-owned WRC-TV in Washington, D.C., extended its news programming schedule by producing a 7:30 weeknight newscast carried on a rival station.[2]

Indeed, local television has expanded its "beat" by including coverage of national and international events with a local angle. Local stations have availed themselves of satellite technology to bring national and international stories covered by local anchors to their viewers.

The news story that served as a catalyst to this trend and helped to give local news an international agenda was the drama of Americans held hostage in Iran in the late 1970s. When the hostages were released in 1981, hundreds of local reporters were dispatched to Wiesbaden, West Germany, to record the event, providing a local spin to the international drama. Regional audiences have also seen local coverage of riots, natural disasters, spectacular criminal trials, visits by the pope, the caning of an American citizen in Singapore, the destruction of a religious cult in Waco, Texas, and a tragic terrorist bombing in Oklahoma City. Local television journalists have also distinguished themselves by providing national news coverage of local events for network broadcast.

Sometimes a local station will gain the advantage on a network to a story with national significance. The 1988 Summer Olympic games in Seoul, South Korea, provided numerous opportunities for local correspondents to test their mettle against their seasoned network colleagues. It was KRON-TV of San Francisco that obtained an exclusive interview with a Korean student activist and later, from his tip, got the first pictures of a massive antigovernment student demonstration. At the 1994 Winter

Olympic Games in Norway, a gaggle of local television correspondents were on hand to cover the performances of ice skaters Tonya Harding and Nancy Kerrigan. While most Olympic games attract a modest contingent of local reporters to provide local coverage of hometown athletes, the assault on ice skater Nancy Kerrigan just before the Olympics added to the drama of the event and increased the number of local reporters on the scene.

Occasionally local correspondents evolve from being mere observers to active participants in a story. It should be noted, however, that only under the most extreme circumstances do journalists become involved. Such a case presented itself in 1988, when a helicopter pilot and photographer from KCNC-TV, Denver, were covering a high-speed police chase. They saw the suspect's car run down a police officer; as the suspect eluded police, the helicopter continued to pursue him, finally maneuvering itself above the hood of the suspect's car and hitting its windshield. As a result of the reporters' aggressive actions, the suspect was apprehended by the police.

While some reporters may become dramatically involved in a story, there are also more detached forms of involvement. For example, in 1988 KRON-TV, San Francisco, covered a demonstration by the United Farm Workers against George Bush in which a police officer beat a female farm labor leader. The police denied the allegation, but producers at KRON-TV viewed the taped coverage on a slow-frame replay and offered conclusive evidence of police brutality and identified the officer involved.

In general, however, local news has been criticized for its tendency to emphasize sensational crime stories and to neglect more substantive stories that require analysis and investigation. Edward R. Murrow was the first one to create a stir within the broadcast news industry when he spoke before the Radio, Television News Directors Association (RTNDA) in 1958. At that time Murrow criticized his colleagues for their lack of substance and for the overcommercialization of television. He characterized television as a medium with great potential for the dissemination of information and enlightenment but cautioned his colleagues that its pursuit of the almighty dollar might turn it into nothing more than "wires and lights . . . in a box."[3]

In 1993, in a speech before the same organization entitled "Call It Courage," Dan Rather, the veteran CBS news anchor, referred to Murrow as "a commander in the battle against ignorance, intolerance, and indifference." Rather expressed some of the same concerns as his predecessor, decrying television news' focus on tabloid-style sensationalism and its failure to spend more time on substantial issues or to provoke thoughtful analysis. He concluded that there was a shortage of courage and the trend was toward, "Make nice, not news."

Some thought Rather's speech was a rather self-serving critique of the industry to which he owes his success. But his comments should be viewed and weighed in the context of the larger issue of professionalism.

Rather's call for accountability in the industry, while a noble gesture, must be examined realistically. Should television news organizations presume to know what's best for their viewers and focus on stories of greater import and substance? A 1994 study by the *Times Mirror* Center for the People and the Press found that fewer than 40 percent of Americans are aware of or interested in stories related to health care reform or President Clinton's Whitewater investments. While ultimately the audience chooses what to watch, it should be possible for television journalists to provide at least some balance between substance and sensationalism.

Sometimes a news organization gets caught up in the drama and emotion of a story, and is subverted by its own hype. In 1989 one of the most bizarre and terrifying news stories ever to be covered by local television began to unfold. A young Boston couple, having just left a childbirth class, were allegedly accosted in their car by an African-American man who shot the pregnant woman in the head, wounded her husband, and fled. The husband, Charles Stuart, managed to dial 911 from his car phone, and his dramatic conversation with the dispatcher was heard on radio and television stations around the country. Dan Rather, on CBS News, was in the enviable position of having exclusive video of the gruesome murder scene because a CBS crew from the program *Rescue 911* happened to be travelling with the local emergency squad when they responded to the call.

It was a tragic story of dreams shattered by the specter of inner-city crime. The media was seduced into the frantic search to find the African-American man described by Stuart as the gunman. In the meantime the drama continued to unfold as an attempt was made to save the life of the unborn child. The governor of Massachusetts, Michael Dukakis, along with other dignitaries, attended Carol Stuart's funeral. During this time the police scoured Boston's African-American neighborhoods for the man believed to have committed the crime. A suspect was found, but soon after, various inconsistencies in the story began to surface and pointed to Charles Stuart as the murderer. In January he committed suicide, leaving to his survivors the problem of healing the wounds between the black and white communities of Boston and the need for the news media to examine its handling of the story.

Few events in the history of television news could equal the pathos, tragedy, and drama of the O. J. Simpson story. It became a road show for television when Simpson, apparently attempted to flee the country. Local news organizations provided hours of live helicopter coverage of Simpson's white Ford Bronco meandering along California freeways until it finally returned to his Brentwood home, where he gave himself up to the authorities. The pictures of this odyssey were distributed live to 95 million television viewers who witnessed a real-life saga that seemed staged for television. This included a phalanx of pursuing police cars and crowds of spectators along the way, some of whom shouted words of encouragement to the suspect as the Bronco passed by.

Local television has the ability to distinguish itself while covering sensational stories, by providing viewers interpretations that can put what they are seeing into context. The savage beatings of Rodney King by Los Angeles policemen and Reginald Denny, a victim in the riot that ensued when the police were acquitted, were signs of an urban culture gone amok, but local and network television reporters attempted to provide a perspective on the events so that viewers could make some sense of what they were seeing. There are times, however, when local television simply abandons its ethics and professional responsibilities.

The reality of competition in local television journalism sometimes conflicts with the responsibility to present an accurate portrayal of events. Occasionally, in the frenzy for getting an "exclusive," stations may sacrifice their obligation to carefully research stories and verify the facts. Under these circumstances stations become vulnerable to the temptation to manipulate events.

In 1990 when the New York State Lottery Commission announced a single winner for its $35 million jackpot, a young, attractive, single woman claimed to hold the winning ticket. Two local stations in New York, WWOR-TV and WNBC-TV, along with the newspapers the *New York Post* and the *Daily News*, announced that the young woman was the winner without attempting to confirm the identity with the Lottery Commission. It turned out this was all a trick played on the media by veteran hoaxer, Alan Abel. The real winner was a diminutive, middle-aged, immigrant autoworker from Westchester County who was neither glamorous nor exciting. The media bias for choosing glamorous characters to star in its stories is often apparent.

THE NEWS SHOWCASE

The stakes are high in the television news business, especially in a major market like New York City. Annual major market local news budgets range from $30 to 40 million and generate revenues of about $220 million a year. Millions of dollars are spent every year by television news organizations on the design of sleek sets, striking graphics, and colorful logos. Every effort is made to create the illusion of "high-tech" professionalism. Careful attention is paid to color balance and lighting. The design of the set also includes the attire of the newscasters and anchors. What they wear has to coordinate with the overall "look" of the program.

The quest for dominance of the local market and the need to create a visually attractive presentation has led stations to engage the services of television news consultants. These specialists assess the visual appearance of the program and identify its perceived weaknesses. They evaluate sets, format, talent, and even wardrobe. Al Primo, a former station manager and news consultant, helped to create the "Eyewitness News" format, which premiered in 1965 at Philadelphia station KYW and quickly moved to other television markets, including WABC-TV, New York. The "Eyewitness" approach to news coverage was marked by informal chatter between newscasters and was perfected by Frank Magid Associates, one of the leading consultants in the industry.

The newscasters also come under close scrutiny during a consultant's visit. The consultant recommends changes in hairstyle, wardrobe, and makeup. Sometimes an attempt is made to change the overall image of the newscaster. In one city a local television station embarked on a major publicity campaign to present their anchor as a "family man." Commercials for the news program included shots of him at home with his family and doing various chores around the house.4

On-air television news anchors are often selected more for their physical appearance than their professional journalistic credentials. They must look, sound, and act like actor/entertainers rather than journalists. Most are carefully made up and costumed to maintain an image of sophistication. In New York City, at the insistence of station executives, popular anchor Roland Smith of superstation WWOR-TV regrew a mustache that he had sported a decade earlier as local anchor of WCBS-TV.

Consultants sometimes recommend that the news talent be replaced. Quite often the decision to terminate a newscaster is based more on rating concerns than on journalistic ideals. Christine Craft, a television news anchor at KMBC-TV, Kansas City, created quite a stir in the industry in 1983 when she sued her former employers for terminating her because of age and sexual bias. Craft maintained that she had been hired as a news anchor for her journalistic abilities. Although the station brought in an image consultant that worked on Craft's hair, makeup, and wardrobe, she nevertheless was dismissed on the grounds that she was "too old, unattractive and not deferential enough to men." A jury concluded that sexual discrimination had occurred and awarded her $500,000. The amount of the settlement was reduced in later trials and the charge of sexual discrimination was dismissed. However, Craft's public condemnation revealed a widespread acknowledgement by many leaders in the television industry that the appearance of a female newscaster was an important criterion for employment. Her case exposed the practice of sex and age discrimination in the television news industry.[5] On the other hand, sometimes female journalists themselves complicate the issue and contribute to the problem: When Diane Sawyer posed for a photo layout in a 1987 issue of *Vanity Fair*, she validated an image of herself as vamp. No doubt the sensual photographs of such a beautiful woman pleased many, but the issue highlighted the ambiguity of her status: is she a sex symbol or a journalist?

Indeed, television news has a rather shameful record in the area of equal employment opportunity. Women and minorities have been historically excluded from on-air and managerial positions. A handful of women who, in the early days of radio persisted in distinguishing themselves as broadcast journalists, were the exception to this rule.

Although women managed to gain a small presence on radio news in the 1930s and 1940s, their entree into television journalism was met with resistance. They started out as weather "girls" and commercial spokespersons. Betty Furness became famous in the 1950s for demonstrating refrigerators by opening and closing their doors hundreds of times. Eventually, she became a consumer affairs reporter for NBC.

The first on-air network female television correspondent was Pauline Frederick. Frederick started her broadcasting career in 1953 at NBC and proved to be an astute observer of the international scene. Eventually she became NBC's chief United Nations correspondent, a post she held for twenty-one years. After her retirement from television, she worked for National Public Radio, and in 1976 she was chosen as the first woman to moderate a presidential debate.

In the 1960s, Nancy Dickerson became CBS's first woman White House correspondent. Also in the 1960s, Liz Trotta was assigned as network television's first foreign correspondent, serving three tours in Vietnam for NBC. Another milestone in network television news was achieved by Marlene Sanders of ABC, who became the first female correspondent to be appointed vice president at a network news organization.

As women gained prominence as television correspondents, minorities also began moving into the industry, but at a much slower pace. One of the first African-American women to work for a network news organization was Charlayne Hunter-Gault, who began as a local reporter and then moved to the MacNeil-Lehrer News Hour on PBS. Asian-American women comprise a smaller share of the talent pool for television news, with Connie Chung being one of the most well-known female Asian-American news anchors.[6]

For minority men, the pursuit of a television news post has also been frustrating. The first network to hire an African-American male reporter was ABC, when in 1962 it named Mal Goode, a reporter for the *Pittsburgh Courier*, as correspondent. (Goode, however, was not the first African-

American male to deliver news on a network. William Worthy, a newspaper reporter for the *Baltimore Afro-American*, had worked free-lance for CBS and reported from Moscow and Communist China in 1954.) In the 1960s Bob Teague, the first African-American correspondent to be hired by NBC, made his mark as a respected network and later local television reporter. He started at NBC in 1963 after having been a reporter at the *New York Times*.

The first African-American men to become anchors on network television were Ed Bradley, Max Robinson, and Bernard Shaw. Bradley's association with *60 Minutes* made him one of the most popular journalists on television. In 1976 he anchored the *CBS Sunday Night News*, providing him with the distinction of being the first African-American male anchor on network television. Two years later, Max Robinson became the first African-American male anchor to present nightly news at the ABC network. Robinson, reporting from Chicago, was part of a "troika" that also included Frank Reynolds in Washington and Peter Jennings in London. Bernard Shaw had worked at CBS and ABC before he became the anchorman for CNN in 1980. He helped to establish the cable network as an able competitor in the field of broadcast journalism.

Part of the reason minorities and women began to appear as anchors on local and network television had to do with the advice of news consultants. Putting it simply, they recognized the need to be sensitive to the significant number of minority television households who view the news, watch the commercials, and are prospective buyers for the products advertised on the program.

During the 1980s another new player emerged in network newsrooms, taking its place along with media consultants as a force for dictating change. As the number of news hours increased on network, local, and syndicated television, the need for talent to support the myriad of magazine and tabloid programs became necessary. Talent agents have become particularly adept at negotiating substantial salaries for their clients, along with various "performance" criteria associated with their employment. One of the most visible agents is Richard Leibner of the N. S. Bienstock agency. The benchmark year for Leibner and his clients came in 1980 when he negotiated Dan Rather's $1.6 million deal at CBS. Leibner has become a skillful power broker in the business of television news. He has mastered the technique of "shopping" his talent to competing news organizations, winning them enormous salaries, coveted air time, and high-profile network exposure. In doing so, he has also helped to perpetuate the celebrity culture over which many critics have expressed concern, and which many celebrities have found to be extremely invasive.

One of the best "products" of agency-driven manipulation is Diane Sawyer. A former Junior Miss, weather girl, and aide to Richard Nixon,

Sawyer has become an icon symbolizing the frenzy of competition, greed, and posturing inherent within the news industry. In 1989, Leibner negotiated her first million-dollar contract, moving her from CBS's *60 Minutes* to ABC where she coanchored *Prime Time Live* with Sam Donaldson. When Sawyer's contract expired in 1994, Leibner again put up a "for sale" sign that created a stampede of million-dollar offers from the four broadcast networks. Fox, high on the excitement from its acquisition of the NFL rights, offered Sawyer a bank-busting $7 million deal to jump ship. Leibner, however, negotiated a $6 million deal with ABC, which caused a reorganization of the network's prime-time news magazine division and the creation of another prime-time network news program for Sawyer to anchor.

The irony of the multimillion-dollar anchor and network television's showcasing of news talent is the compromise in independence the network news divisions must pay for it. Traditionally television news organizations have insisted upon their autonomy and have avoided any external influence on their operations by advertisers, government, or company management. That ethic now seems to have been sacrificed to the priorities of celebrity demands and entertainment programming values. Commenting on the use of women broadcast journalists in the mix of substance and entertainment the news has become, *New York Times* critic Walter Goodman wrote, "female television personalities are judged by the same standards as men. . . but showboats are still wanted for display. All television, including news programs, is entertainment packaged with an eye to decor."[7]

GETTING THE NEWS

The way talent is used to gather and report the news is another area of concern. While undercover journalism can be a valuable tool for television news, it should be used responsibly. Using covert methods, many reporters have gone undercover to research stories on crime, welfare, and misconduct in government agencies. Television correspondents have posed as drug dealers, homeless people, municipal workers, and welfare clients, using hidden cameras and microphones to record their stories. Most states have no statutes prohibiting news reporters from taping in public with concealed equipment, nor is it a crime for a reporter to misrepresent himself or create a fictional scenario for the purpose of entrapment. Nevertheless there are many media observers who feel that covert newsgathering threatens basic principles of privacy and infringes on the rights of unsuspecting individuals.[8]

Many reporters and news producers defend undercover journalism and take the position that the pursuit of some stories requires them to misrepresent themselves or conceal their identity. They argue that the presence of a camera crew and a well-known correspondent can inhibit their search for truth and candor. Unfortunately, too often undercover television journalism is caught up in its own hype and publicity. Local stations may use this kind of story during the rating "sweeps" period and tantalize the public with sensational and suggestive advertising. The subject matter for the undercover stories may not be chosen for its newsworthiness but for its ability to arouse the voyeuristic impulses of the audience. Clearly there should be a great deal of thought and deliberation before a television station approves an undercover story. Those making the decision must weigh the invasion of privacy against the audience's "right to know" and determine if the clandestine behavior is really in the public interest.[9]

An interesting case involving a hidden camera in a doctor's office addressed the issues of privacy and prior restraint. In 1990, *Inside Edition*, a reality-based syndicated television program produced by King World Productions, secretly taped a "diet doctor" who was under investigation by the New York State Department of Health's Office of Professional Medical Conduct. A producer of the show posed as a patient and secretly videotaped the doctor's consultation with her. Attorneys for the doctor were successful in obtaining a temporary restraining order against release of the video from a U.S. district judge in Detroit, but the U.S. Court of Appeals for the Sixth Circuit overturned the ruling, citing that the order constituted an unconstitutional "prior restraint" of free speech. The Supreme Court upheld the decision of the Court of Appeals, allowing *Inside Edition* its First Amendment right to broadcast the hidden camera segments.[10]

The privacy issue was a key determinant in a California jury's award of $1 million to two plaintiffs depicted in 1993 *Prime Time Live* story entitled "Hello, Telepsychic." In the report, a 900 telephone number offering psychic advice was revealed as a sham. The jury decided that the use of hidden cameras showing the two plaintiffs giving readings violated their privacy.

The popularity of the use of hidden cameras in investigative reporting has resulted in the Society for Professional Journalists creating a checklist for the use of concealed cameras. Foremost on the list is whether or not the information acquired is of "profound importance" and "vital public interest."

CAMERAS IN THE COURTROOM

The issues of the preservation of an individual's constitutional right to privacy and to a fair and speedy trial have created a dilemma for local television news coverage of judicial proceedings. The coverage of courtroom trials by journalists has always been a sensitive issue within the legal community; the first live radio coverage of an historic trial occurred in 1925. Known as the "Monkey Trial," the Scopes trial pitted two of America's most distinguished lawyers, William Jennings Bryan and Clarence Darrow, against each other. The issue was whether John Scopes had violated Tennessee state law by teaching his high school students about Charles Darwin's theory of evolution. Darrow was from Chicago, and interest in the case was high there, so radio station WGN, owned by the *Chicago Tribune*, used a telephone line, at a cost of $1,000 a day, to broadcast live commentary from the courtroom.

The first murder trial to be covered by radio, although microphones were not directly present in the courtroom, was in 1935, in the case of Richard Bruno Hauptmann, the accused kidnapper and murderer of Charles Lindbergh's son. Lindbergh was a national hero, and because of his fame, the case attracted worldwide attention. Unfortunately for Hauptmann, the courtroom became a media circus, with photographers and radio commentators disregarding the basic rules of courtroom behavior. Even the judge in the case gave in to the mood of the day when he arranged for his wife to be seated next to a well-known radio commentator. The case became a *cause celebre* and provided intimate glimpses of all the principals in the case. As a result, the American Bar Association adopted a new rule that forbade photographic or broadcast coverage of a trial.

For more than five decades, the prohibition against broadcast and photographic coverage of courtroom trials has been a hotly contested issue, with some critics claiming that it violates the First and Sixth amendments. The question arises, whose rights take priority, the defendant's right to a fair trial or the public's "right to know"?[11] In the early 1960s a Texas case addressed the issue of televised courtroom coverage. The defendant in the case was Billie Sol Estes, a noted swindler and confidence man who was convicted by a jury of his peers. However, the judge in the case had allowed two television cameras into the court over the objections of the defendant. Estes appealed his conviction, claiming that the presence of the television cameras had denied him due process, and the Supreme Court ruled in his favor, noting that the rights of journalists must be subordinate to the right of the defendant to receive a fair trial.[12]

In the 1970s a number of states began experimenting with cameras in the courtroom. In 1977, Florida allowed television coverage of the murder trial of Ron Zamora, whose defense for murdering an elderly woman was based upon the argument that excessive viewing of violent television programs had served as the impetus for his crime. After the trial, Florida became one of the first states to allow permanent television coverage of courtroom proceedings.[13]

As technology improved, television cameras became less cumbersome and intrusive. In 1972 the American Bar Association updated its rules to provide more flexibility for judges in considering broadcast coverage of a trial. During the 1980s, television cameras gained wide access to courtroom trials. A Supreme Court ruling in 1981 helped to set a precedent for broadcast access to legal proceedings.[14] As of 1995, forty-seven states have allowed cameras into their courtrooms.

A chink in the armor of the rule excluding federal courtroom proceedings from live television coverage occurred when the Cable Satellite Public Affairs Network (CSPAN) was allowed to cover live oral arguments on the constitutionality of a death sentence passed on a Marine lance corporal. In 1991 a three-year experiment allowing cameras in selected federal courtrooms covering civil cases began. In 1994, however, the Judicial Conference of the United States, headed by Chief Justice William H. Rehnquist, declined to continue the experiment. Commenting on the proliferation of frivolous "soundbite" reporting, and posturing by dubious "expert" analysts, the federal judges chose to close their courtrooms to television coverage. The Judicial Conference, by a vote of 14–12, reversed themselves in 1996, deciding to allow cameras in federal appeals courts. Each of the thirteen federal circuits will decide whether to allow cameras into courtrooms.

Court TV, a twenty-four-hour cable channel launched in 1991, has been successful, covering such high-profile and sensational cases as the William Kennedy Smith, Menendez brothers, and O. J. Simpson trials. Reporting on celebrity trials can, whether intentionally or not, create a tawdry tabloid atmosphere. Steve Dunleavy, the acerbic host of *A Current Affair* described the William Kennedy Smith trial as "the biggest circus since Ringling Brothers, which is a sad commentary on all of us, but nonetheless it is gigantic news."[15]

CAMERAS IN THE LOCKER ROOM

While the question of televised access to courtroom proceedings remains a lively controversy in broadcast policy, another question of access has also generated debate. Usually, a reporter's gender has no bearing on the issue of access, yet gender became a controversial subject at the beginning of the 1990s over two female newspaper reporters and the issue of their admittance to the lockerrooms of football players after the games. While these cases involved reporters from the print media, the dilemma applies to female broadcasting correspondents as well. In the first instance, *Boston Herald* reporter Lisa Olson claimed that she had to endure verbal sexual abuse from New England Patriot players during her postgame lockerroom interviews. Another case concerning locker room privileges occurred when Denise Tom, a *USA Today* reporter, was barred from the Cincinnati Bengels' locker room by Coach Sam Wyche.

These incidents raise thorny questions pertaining to the Constitutional issues of freedom of the press on the one hand and the right to privacy on the other.[16] In an effort to resolve the dispute, some officials of the NFL have recommended that separate interview areas be designated for postgame coverage or that all reporters, both men and women, be denied access to the locker room until all players are showered and dressed. Neither of these proposals is perfect, as they produce deadline delays that create even more pressure for reporters.

NEWS AS ENTERTAINMENT

Competition from cable television and the broadening horizons of local news stations made possible by technological advancements have threatened the networks' former dominance in news distribution. In this climate, in an effort to sustain its hold on its audience, the networks have tapped their vast resources of creative talent and personalities and have begun to pursue a more entertainment-oriented format.

Defining news as entertainment is not a new concept in television. Even in the 1950s, Ed Murrow's fame as a journalist brought success to *Person to Person*, a celebrity interview program on CBS. Many local stations have developed entertainment-oriented news magazine programs such as *P.M. Magazine* and *Live at Five* in New York City. These "magazine" programs have little substantive news, but they use familiar news correspondents and a news-oriented format to suggest a journalistic orientation. The resultant blurring of news and entertainment programming at the networks and local stations is an issue of concern to media critics.

The networks, in seeking to improve their prime-time ratings, began to concentrate on elements of personality and style, production values more appropriate for entertainment programming than for the presentation of hard news. In an effort to carve a profitable prime-time news niche for their networks, ABC, NBC, and CBS have all experimented with news "magazine" programming that offer news in an entertainment format. Various factors make these programs attractive to network television executives. News magazine programs can be produced for about two-thirds the cost of a traditional prime-time entertainment hour. And advertising revenues for the ten prime-time news magazine hours on network television in 1993 reached $1.1 billion, making up 15 percent of the sixty-six combined hours of prime-time programming each week.[17] Since they are less expensive, magazine programs also offer the opportunity to show more first-run hours during the glut of summer reruns; and since most news programs, unlike most entertainment programs, are owned by the network, the network has a greater interest in their success.

The program that set the standard and created a modern genre of prime-time network news magazine programming was *60 Minutes*, which premiered in 1968. With this program, Don Hewitt devised a new format for news, making it personality driven, and highly entertaining. Once *60 Minutes* reached its stride and became one of the most popular shows on prime-time television, the other networks were quick to attempt their own versions of the successful format.[18]

While imitation may be the most sincere form of flattery, both ABC and NBC found that there was more to creating their own magazines than merely plugging into the *60 Minutes* formula. Ten years after the premiere of *60 Minutes* on CBS, ABC tried its own version with the debut of *20/20*. (The title proved to be prophetic, as it took some time for *20/20* to achieve its focus.) The premiere for *20/20* featured two male anchors, both new to television: one was an Australian with a pronounced Australian accent. It was a disaster, and the following week both hosts were gone, replaced by veteran anchor Hugh Downs, who was eventually joined by Barbara Walters.

Of all the broadcast networks, NBC had the most difficulty in establishing a presence in the production of a prime-time magazine news program. Their beginning effort, *First Tuesday*, which premiered a few weeks after *60 Minutes* in 1969, lasted only a couple of seasons. It was later resurrected as *Special Edition*. NBC continued to pursue success in this format, although it remained elusive, with a series of programs including *Weekend*, *NBC Magazine*, *Prime Time Sunday*, and *Real Life with Jane Pauley*.

In its desperation to find a working news magazine format, NBC experimented with a number of different approaches, *Yesterday, Today and Tomorrow* was a program initially developed by the network's entertainment division and later controlled by the news division. It presented news stories through dramatic re-creations, and it featured three hosts, popular New York City local anchor Chuck Scarborough, Mary Alice Williams (formerly of CNN), and NBC correspondent Maria Shriver. The program lacked sophistication, smacked of sensationalism, and eventually was cancelled by the network for failing to attract a significant audience.

Finally, in 1993, NBC introduced *Dateline NBC*, hosted by Jane Pauley and Stone Phillips. *Dateline* became a success in its time period, but its ethics came under attack as a result of several stories it covered. It managed to survive the criticism and remain a contender in the high-stakes prime-time news magazine marketplace. In fact, *Dateline* has become one of the most visible news magazine programs on network television. For the 1994–95 television season, it was scheduled for three prime-time hours each week on Tuesday, Wednesday, and Friday.[19]

When Roone Arledge, then head of ABC News and Sports, managed to win his "prize," Diane Sawyer, from CBS in 1989, he needed a regularly-scheduled prime-time news magazine hour for her to star in: thus *Prime Time Live* was born. Sawyer was joined by Sam Donaldson, and the "glitz" and show-biz hype of the program was readily apparent. The set included a $400,000 video wall, a live audience, and coverage of a potpourri of events ranging from interviews with newsmakers to tours of the White House and the Kremlin. The program, which premiered in 1989, has been criticized for its lack of substance and the awkward relationship between its two star anchors. Sawyer herself has described her relationship with Donaldson as "fire and ice," and their pairing as cohosts as "a date between Emily Dickinson and the Terminator."[20]

This was not the first time ABC had missed the mark at matchmaking; they had also wooed Barbara Walters away from NBC to join ABC and Harry Reasoner as a coanchor for the evening news in 1976. Walters wanted more visibility and her million-dollar salary helped to set a benchmark for other celebrity journalists. This on-air relationship was so bad that the director had to avoid showing the two together in the same shot (a "two-shot") because their facial expressions revealed their obvious contempt for each other. One executive familiar with the on-air relationship between Reasoner and Walters described a visit to the news set as being like walking into a couple's home just after they have had a terrible argument.

The relationship between Sawyer and Donaldson on *Prime Time Live* didn't fare much better. Eventually, the live audience component of the program was jettisoned, and the anchors were split, with Sawyer staying in New York and Donaldson going back to Washington, where he had served as ABC's White House correspondent.

Not to be outdone in the pursuit of high-profile female television journalists, after losing Diane Sawyer, CBS recruited popular anchor Connie Chung. CBS, with its tradition of solid broadcast journalism going back to Edward R. Murrow, tarnished that heritage with its prime-time news magazine entry *Saturday Night with Connie Chung*, introduced in 1990. The program was a slick pastiche of celebrity interviews and dramatic reenactments that did little to enlighten viewers. Chung played the role of deferential interviewer well, with feigned modesty and superficial interest. One segment in particular, which featured an overdrawn interview with an overweight Marlon Brando, was notable only for its exceptional boredom and banality.

Connie Chung's talent as a celebrity interviewer became the focal point of another personality-driven program, *Eye to Eye with Connie Chung*. The program was an updated version of Edward R. Murrow's

Person to Person. Chung's February 1994 interview with iceskater Tonya Harding earned it one of its highest ratings and outflanked ABC's *Prime Time Live* for the time period. Diane Sawyer called in sick for that evening's *Prime Time Live* segment, presumably sensing defeat and not wanting to associate herself with the program's one-time decline in ratings, especially during her sensitive contract negotiations with ABC. Chung had another ratings blockbuster in 1995, when she interviewed the mother of Speaker of the House Newt Gingrich. With some gentle prodding, Chung persuaded Gingrich's mother to reveal that her son referred to Hillary Clinton as a "bitch" on prime-time network television. The interview did little to support the seriousness of CBS News' stance against the encroachment of tabloid values into news programming.[21]

The debate over whether entertainment values have compromised the agenda of broadcast journalists has focused mostly on female television anchors. Perhaps the blame for turning television news into a superficial beauty contest can be attributed to American culture and the value it places on physical appearance rather than substance. Television, however, helps to set the public agenda and has a great influence on the evolution of American culture. National television anchors can either validate the myths of pop culture by playing up their celebrity roles or attempt to divorce themselves from the glitter and tinsel of fame. The choice, however, can be a difficult one especially for female television personalities who are more often hired in part for their looks. As Walter Goodman of the *New York Times* noted, female journalists "are paid by the standards of entertainment, not journalism."[22] Therefore, the question is whether to succumb to the temptation of fame and fortune, setting aside the traditional values of journalism.

One of the difficulties in broadcast news is that the public has come to perceive those personalities associated with it as larger-than-life figures. Broadcast journalists must face the dilemma of having to deal with human emotions that might seem to contradict their public persona. It can be especially difficult for female correspondents who are attempting to fulfill their roles as both professionals and mothers. When Connie Chung announced publicly that she was cutting back her schedule because at her age she needed "to take a very aggressive approach to having a baby," the comment brought snickers to the lips of many; one more indication of the underlying bias against women within the industry. And Meredith Vieira was fired from her position as a *60 Minutes* correspondent because executive producer Don Hewitt decided not to agree to her request for a part-time assignment. Vieira had arranged with Hewitt to work part time so she could care for her young son. When she became pregnant again, she asked to continue that arrangement, but Hewitt refused. After he fired her, Hewitt implied that her work had not lived up to the standards of the show. To take her place Hewitt hired Lesley Stahl, a veteran correspondent who was a coanchor, with Richard Threlkeld, on the *CBS Morning News*, a White House correspondent, and the host of *Face the Nation*. Although Hewitt replaced Vieira with another woman, the incident once again speaks to the conflicting roles women must play as they attempt to satisfy both their professional and maternal obligations.

The television networks seem to have supported the ethics of glamour by pursuing attractive talent vigorously. In 1973, CBS teamed a totally inexperienced Sally Quinn with Hughes Rudd to coanchor the *CBS Morning News*. Quinn was an attractive, talented writer for the *Washington Post* but had absolutely no experience in television. She lasted only four months before returning to the *Washington Post*.[23]

Seemingly none the wiser from its mistakes, CBS made news once again when it chose former Miss America Phyllis George as a coanchor for the *CBS Morning News*. George's only prior experience was as host of the *NFL Today* pregame show and of the short-lived *People* series. She had little experience as a journalist, and her ability was clearly taxed on the *CBS Morning News*. When CBS terminated George, they had to pay her $1 million, honoring the terms of her contract. Although Quinn and George were seriously out of place as on-air anchors, the fault was not theirs. Unfortunately they were caught up in network television's pursuit of glamour and entertainment priorities, things that should never have been associated with television news in the first place.

It can also be difficult for people who work behind the scenes in television news. If they let down their professional guard and express a personal opinion, they can be pilloried for what they say. When Jeff Gralnick, executive producer of *NBC Nightly News*, referred to Somali faction leader General Mohammed Farah Adid as an "educated jungle bunny," his remarks were taken out of context and he was forced into a position of trying to explain what he meant.[24] Similarly, when Emily Rooney, formerly executive producer of *World News Tonight*, commented that the stereotype of liberal bias in the news media "happens to be true" and that she would be taking a closer look at conservative views, she caused an outburst of concern within her own news organization and among the television news industry in general.[25]

In another twist on the "news as entertainment" phenomenon, well-known female anchors and correspondents played themselves on the popular *Murphy Brown* series, as guests at the newswoman's baby shower. Seeing the likes of Mary Alice Williams, Katie Couric, Faith Daniels, Joan Lunden, and Paula Zahn gushing over Murphy's pregnancy once again raised the questions about the wisdom of presenting reporters as entertainers.

A related concern has to do with the use of national personalities as celebrity endorsers. The advertising industry has a long-established tradition of using entertainers and athletes to serve as spokespersons pitching products to the public. Most news organizations forbid their talent to make commercial endorsements while under contract; however the issue becomes relevant when either the talent is terminated or exceptions are made. In one case Kathleen Sullivan, a host of *CBS This Morning*, became a spokesperson for Weight Watchers International after she left the network in 1990. Apparently, her "weigh-ins" were so impressive that during the period of time her commercials ran on television, Weight Watchers International experienced a significant increase in sales and popularity. While one cannot blame Sullivan for pursuing a lucrative source of income, her image as host on a network news program clearly enhanced her credibility as a celebrity endorser.

A similar situation arose when Charles Osgood, a popular radio and television news personality, was given a new television assignment in 1994, replacing Charles Kuralt as host of CBS's *Sunday Morning*. Osgood accepted the assignment only on the condition that he would continue his three-minute "Osgood File" commentaries on CBS radio, where he also wrote and read commercials. Although CBS has a long-standing rule prohibiting broadcast personnel, especially news division employees, from doing commercials, an exception was made for Osgood so he could continue collecting the substantial talent fees for his endorsements. While Osgood proclaimed that he never had a problem with his dual role as news commentator and commercial pitchman, the conflict-of-interest issue strikes at the very heart of journalistic ethics.

As television news becomes more competitive, the need to provide an entertaining format intensifies; it is in this context that tabloid news has surfaced. Network news divisions have traditionally rejected any drift toward tabloid values, but in recent years these values have encroached upon the traditional news programs nonetheless.

Naturally, certain stories lend themselves more toward sensational coverage that are typical of tabloid news coverage. There is of course a difference between traditional journalistic narrative and tabloid reporting. And although the networks condemn tabloid news as irresponsible, too often they have chosen stories that embrace the same sensational values as centerpieces for their magazine news programs. ABC's *20/20* took its cameras to a church- approved exorcism and did an extensive "report" on life after death. And *Prime Time Live* covered a story alleging that Martin Luther King was assassinated by the mob and not by convicted killer James Earl Ray. Although Donaldson openly admitted that the story did not have much credence, they decided to cover it anyway because, as he said, "the story was there, it was hot."[26]

No doubt stories like the O. J. Simpson murder trial, the caning of teenager Michael Fay in Singapore, and the criminal conspiracy of Tonya

Harding against Nancy Kerrigan are all newsworthy and deserve some television coverage. However, it is important for traditional broadcast journalists to uphold the values of responsible reporting in their role as "gatekeepers" of the public good. A. M. Rosenthal of the *New York Times* expressed his concern about the changing ethics of modern journalism: "If some other journal or broadcast distributes unverified rumors—the equivalent of journalistic garbage—do we just pick it up and peddle it ourselves? . . . Aren't we obliged to exercise some restraint, forgive the word, before printing damaging information that we say we know but really don't? My concern is for journalism whose cleanliness and ethics are important to the country."[27]

While the recent trend has been toward the presentation of news as a circus, with celebrity anchors filling the role of ringmaster, it is important for those in positions of responsibility within the networks to reexamine their agenda and to consider the long-term implications of a superficial and perhaps ultimately quite damaging approach to the dissemination of news in a democracy.

A longstanding principle of the journalistic tradition has been the idea that journalists act as surrogates of the citizenry and as such should maintain a close watch on government and business. Indeed, the dogged persistence of journalistic inquiry has provided the public with startling revelations of official improprieties ranging from the Watergate and Whitewater scandals to the Iran/Contra affair. There has been some concern, however, that journalistic privilege has no legal boundaries. Should news organizations be allowed to deliberately violate the law, becoming principals in a case and a threat to its appropriate resolution?

An illustration of the contradictions that can arise when a news organization is implicated in a judicial proceeding occurred when CNN acquired taped telephone conversations between incarcerated former Panamanian dictator General Noriega and his legal defense team. CNN's possession of the tapes, which contained privileged client-lawyer information, demonstrated the delicate balance between the conflicting demands of Constitutional rights. In this case, a defendant's Sixth Amendment right to legal counsel came into conflict with the First Amendment right of a free press.[28]

ACCURACY IN THE NEWS

When the United States landed a man on the moon, there were a substantial number of Americans who viewed the event with skepticism and even disbelief. Some thought that what they saw was a fiction, staged for television. Was this skepticism the product of a widespread suspicion that the ethics of television news had been compromised to the extent that a major event such as this might have been "faked"? The findings of many studies confirm television's high credibility rating. However, there have been lapses in judgment that have conspired to undermine the plausibility of televised news.

The manipulation of reality to suit broadcasters' needs has raised serious questions of journalistic integrity. In 1989, Felix Bloch, the beleaguered government attaché who was rumored to be a traitor was shown on the ABC network newscast *World News Tonight* passing a briefcase to a Soviet KGB agent. Unfortunately, ABC News did not bother to identify the videotape as a dramatic re-creation. During a broadcast of the same videotape that evening, the network finally deemed it necessary to label the events depicted on the tape as a simulation. After a shower of criticism, four days later on his evening newscast, Peter Jennings apologized for the lapse in judgment.

Poor judgment was also used in a 1993 *Dateline NBC* report on exploding gas tanks in General Motors CK trucks. *Dateline* no doubt hoped to create a big splash similar to the one that CBS's *60 Minutes* had made with its damaging reports on Ford Pintos and Volkswagon Audis.[29] Instead, GM filed a multimillion dollar damage suit against the network that resulted in the most comprehensive on-air broadcast apology in the history of network television news.

In attempting to prove that GM trucks with "sidesaddle" mounted gas tanks were unsafe, *Dateline* staged a collision. The contractor hired to stage the event had informed NBC that tiny sparking devices, or rockets, were strapped to the underside of one of the trucks to insure an explosion if the gas tank leaked after a collision. Under pressure of the lawsuit, NBC admitted that the public should have been informed about the presence of the igniters. "What we characterized in the November *Dateline* as an unscientific demonstration was inappropriate and does not support the position that GM CK trucks are defective," the network conceded. "Specifically, NBC's contractors did put incendiary devices under the trucks to insure there would be a fire if gasoline were released from the gas tank. NBC personnel knew this before we aired the program, but the public was not informed because consultants at the scene told us the devices did not start the fire. We agree with GM that we should have told the viewer about these devices."[30]

The apology was read by coanchors Jane Pauley and Stone Phillips, and NBC consented to reimburse GM for the cost of its investigation. As a result of the report, Michael Gartner, vice president of NBC News, along with three producers, were forced to resign their positions.

Some argue that reenactments and dramatic re-creations of news events can be a valuable tool, helping viewers to understand a news story. In the interest of sustaining the ethical posture of the news organization, however, it is crucial that reenactments be clearly identified as such. Television critic Walter Goodman has written in the *New York Times*: "The re-creations, however fastidiously undertaken, cannot be entirely accurate, and for anyone who wants accuracy, they set off warning bells that reality is being massaged for viewer stimulation. You just can't trust them."[31]

Indeed, the credibility of a news organization can be rendered suspect by even a hint of impropriety. When Dan Rather decided to seek out an intimate look at the Afghan/Soviet conflict in 1988, he arranged to be surreptitiously smuggled into an Afghan rebel camp. Accompanying the rebels on several raids, Rather and his crew shot some vivid videotape of the Afghans in action. After the material was broadcast on the CBS television network, questions were raised about its authenticity. Although Rather vehemently denied any allegations pertaining to the reliability of the tapes, lingering suspicions remained.

While television's stated purpose is to report the facts, at times accuracy may be sacrificed in the network's search for dominance of their time period. Frequently, television news divisions, caught up in the frenzied race of deadlines and ratings, jettison sound journalistic judgment. During one week in May 1986, the networks showed how vulnerable they could be to journalistic fraud. The news divisions of NBC and ABC agreed to pay $11,000 to a Rome-based photo agency for a video of the damaged Soviet Chernobyl nuclear plant, supposedly secretly shot by a Yugoslavian tourist. The video was broadcast on the two networks and also on Italian television network, RAI. Soon after the broadcast on Italian television, viewers telephoned RAI and informed them that the video shown was not of the Chernobyl nuclear facility but was in fact a cement factory in Trieste. After further investigation, the hoax was confirmed, and the American networks were alerted. Both Tom Brokaw of NBC and Peter Jennings of ABC acknowledged their mistakes on the air. Nevertheless, the incident serves as a sobering reminder of how the most sophisticated news-gathering organizations in the world can be manipulated and duped by news-pandering charlatans.

The issue of accuracy was prominent once again at ABC when a 1990 *20/20* broadcast purportedly tracked down the original "Buckwheat" character from the celebrated *Our Gang* comedy series. Unfortunately, the man interviewed in the *20/20* piece was an imposter. Had the producers bothered to do their research, they would have learned that the original Buckwheat, William "Billy" Thomas, died in 1980. This embarrassing lapse in basic factchecking brought about the producer's resignation and once again raised serious questions about television's commitment to providing viewers with reliable information.

The reliability of a network is measured not only by the trust viewers place in the substance of a particular program but also by the level of confidence they have concerning the news organization's professionalism in general. Any deviation from that professionalism, whether accidental or deliberate, can compromise the faith of the viewer. In November of 1991, thirty ABC affiliates mistakenly broadcast an ABC News Special Report by Peter Jennings, disclosing that war had erupted in the Persian Gulf. The material was part of a closed-circuit videotaped feed by *News One*, the ABC affiliate news service which was providing library material to WTUR in Utica, New York, for a retrospective program on prominent news stories of 1991. Although the feed was preceded by a verbal warning, the logo identifying it as a special report confused many affiliates in the Northeast, who proceeded to broadcast the video. Alarmed viewers called their local stations for verification, and on-air announcers quickly notified their audiences of the error.

If television news is to act in the public interest, it must take risks in attempting to reveal violations of the public's trust. When ABC's *Day One* did a report on the tobacco industry and made claims that manufacturers like Philip Morris artificially spiked its cigarettes with nicotine, the network was slapped with a $10 billion defamation suit from Phillip Morris, the largest libel suit in the history of litigation. The claim, however, was supported by sound research and solid reporting, and producers of the story did not resort to the gimmickry of dramatic re-creations, slow motion, or distorted sounds to make their case. Nevertheless, in 1995 ABC was forced to settle the case out of court, agreeing to read public apologies on the air—once on the *ABC Evening News* and once on *Day One*, the program where the assertion was originally made.[32]

In another case involving *60 Minutes* and the Brown and Williamson Tobacco Corporation (B&W), attorneys for CBS advised that a report featuring an interview with Jeffrey Wigand, a former B&W head of research, be pulled from broadcast. Fearing reprisals from B&W on Wigand's claim that the tobacco company had deliberately abandoned its efforts on the development of a "firesafe" cigarette, and concerned about Wigand's nondisclosure contract with B&W, CBS killed the story. Attorneys for CBS cited the legal precedent of "tortious interference"' as a reason for refusing to broadcast the investigative piece. Although rarely used, the most prominent tortious interference case was brought by the Pennzoil Company against Texaco for breaking up Pennzoil's planned merger with Getty Oil. Pennzoil received a $10.5 billion judgement which placed Texaco into bankruptcy in 1987. Clearly then, CBS was not willing to "bet the company" to ensure its journalistic integrity. However, in January 1996 portions of Wigand's interview were aired on the *CBS Evening News* and on *60 Minutes*. This change of heart occurred when the *Wall Street Journal* published an article about Wigand's sealed November deposition and its dissemination by the *Journal* over its Internet and WorldWideWeb site.

International politics and organized terrorism have produced new ethical and moral enigmas for television journalists. Issues of security and appeasement can involve critical life and death decisions upon which television journalists may have an impact. The important role television may play in these events and whether broadcast journalists should be active or passive participants in an unfolding crisis situation are issues that need serious examination. In certain instances, either deliberately or inadvertently, television journalists have assumed the role of intermediary, transmitting information back and forth between the parties involved in a confrontation. When the role of the journalist begins to border on that of a diplomat, weighty questions can be raised about the propriety or wisdom of allowing television to be used as a political tool.

Occasionally, the emotional drama surrounding a hostage situation can cause television journalists to lapse into a haze of righteousness and self-importance. During one of these episodes, former *Good Morning America* host David Hartman was thrown into the role of diplomat when he conducted a live interview with Nabi Beri, who was serving as an intermediary between the American government and the kidnappers holding Americans hostage in the Middle East. The televised forum for such a meeting was inappropriate, and Hartman's credentials as a negotiator were clearly suspect.

In another instance, NBC gave in to temptation when, in 1986, it shot an exclusive interview with Abu Nidal, the leading terrorist figure in the Middle East, and NBC agreed not to reveal the location of the interview. It was obvious from the nature of the interview that NBC was fishing for rating points and had snared a big catch for their evening news program. The interview itself presented no new information and merely provided an excellent forum for this terrorist leader to threaten the West. In addition, some critics communicated concerns about the network's compromising its credibility by agreeing to terms set by Nidal.

While television correspondents have at times sacrificed dignity and risked their integrity while covering terrorism, they have also provided astute commentary on unfolding events. In 1972, during the Munich Olympic games, Jim McKay, a sports commentator, provided outstanding coverage of the kidnapping and subsequent murder of the Israeli athletes. Though he was not trained as a news reporter, he did a first-rate job. And during the Iranian hostage crisis, ABC Television News initiated a nightly in-depth series, *America Held Hostage*, hosted by Ted Koppel, which was by far the most intelligent, probing, and comprehensive series ever produced to cover a hostage situation. After the resolution of the crisis, the program was retitled *Nightline* and continues as one of the most respected news programs on network television.

There are times when a hostage situation may provoke a conflict between law enforcement officials and journalists. While everyone involved agrees that the safety of the hostages was the number-one priority, the agenda of the journalists and police may differ widely. This can create mutual mistrust between reporters and police. A hostage incident in 1991 in Berkeley, California, provides a good example. An emotionally deranged man held thirty-three people hostage in a hotel bar. As the police moved their SWAT team into position, the gunman was able to follow their moves by watching live local coverage of the situation on the barroom television set. One of the hostages had already been murdered, and the police were concerned that live television coverage would compromise their ability to subdue the criminal. As Walter Goodman of the *New York Times* wrote, "Would viewers have been unduly deprived if the channel to which they were tuned did not transmit descriptions of police tactics that might have put the hostages in greater danger?"[33] At issue here is a moral and ethical question pertaining to the sanctity of human life, and journalists' responsibility both to the public and to their own consciences.

Television has been an extraordinary tool in reporting emergencies, disasters, and international events. During times of crisis, television can be an important resource for a public eager to know the most up-to-date and accurate information available on a situation. At times like this, television can provide the instantaneous coverage necessary to calm a nation and dispel fear.

The 1994 Los Angeles earthquake was a natural for coverage by television. It had all the ingredients for successful programming: bold visual images of dramatic heroism and tragic death. All three major broadcast networks, as well as CNN, committed vast resources toward coverage of the disaster. Network as well as local station coverage of the earthquake was controlled and somber. Attempts were made to confirm information as it came in, and any statements not verifiable were identified as such. In 1995, the worst incident of domestic terrorism in America's history, when the Federal Building in Oklahoma City was bombed, was also marked by responsible and fairly restrained reporting.

From China and the Persian Gulf to Oklahoma City, television has been a witness to history in the making, training its unblinking eye on the popular and unpopular alike. It has distinguished itself in the field of popular rebellion and the theater of war. In 1989, CBS and CNN dispatched correspondents and crews to China to cover the first summit between the leaders of the Soviet Union and the People's Republic of China in thirty years. Dan Rather headed the CBS delegation, while correspondent Bernard Shaw led the CNN contingent. The other two major

American broadcast networks, ABC and NBC, judged the event a low-priority item on their news agenda, declined to send staff to China, and relied upon secondary news sources for their coverage. The summit was eclipsed by an unexpected mass protest demonstration for a more responsive, democratic government by a million students and workers gathered in Beijing's Tienanmen Square. As Chinese troops assembled to crush the rebellion, the government moved to stifle satellite television transmissions and jam *Voice of America* broadcasts, which reach about 100 million listeners. (This was the first time since 1978 that the Chinese had interfered with *Voice of America* broadcasts.)

At great risk to themselves and their colleagues, American broadcast journalists devised ingenious methods of improvising audio and video coverage of the demonstration's bloody aftermath. Using rickshaws, walkie-talkies, cellular telephones, and clandestine camera coverage, American journalists reported on the devastating carnage resulting from the army's attack on the civilians. Frequently a single picture can provide a dramatic symbol of unfolding events. In Beijing this image was of a solitary young man with one arm raised in a halting gesture, facing—and heading off—the lead tank in an armored column.

"HISTORY'S FIRST ROUGH DRAFT"

Philip Graham, the late publisher of the *Washington Post*, once said that "journalism is the first rough draft of history." If that is the case, then television is history's picture archive, burdened with storing the images of war and peace, achievement and decline.

Television's ability to offer riveting coverage of historic events as they unfold was clearly demonstrated several times during the 1990s. Keeping abreast of the swiftly changing events in the Soviet Union in 1991 provided an invigorating challenge for American broadcasters and cablecasters, who furnished American audiences with a first-person view of a crumbling regime. It was a staggering display of rebellion and glee that Americans saw, as the Soviet Union witnessed a monumental political change. And the emotion and drama of the moment were available to Americans with the great immediacy of live television news coverage.

A few months later, on Capitol Hill, live television coverage of the Senate confirmation hearings for Supreme Court nominee Clarence Thomas had the nation transfixed as a cool Anita Hill explicitly articulated her charges of sexual harassment, while the close-ups of Clarence Thomas revealed his defiant attitude.

In Washington, television once again may have been a catalyst to history, by prompting dramatic posturing between the PLO and the Israelis in their historic peace accord of 1993. The medium presented an electronic proscenium for their political maneuvering, creating an intimate world theater for the expression of their mission and goals.

California was much in the news with the 1992 Los Angeles riots and the beatings of Rodney King and Reginald Denny. These events helped to solidify television's role as an objective observer, sometimes able to provide evidence that can bridge the gap between hearsay and truth. The viciousness of the attacks on King and Denny, both of which were clearly documented on videotape, brought the horror of violence home to Americans in terrifying detail.

Another compelling drama covered live by television news was the 1993 fifty-one-day siege by federal law enforcement officials of a religious sect known as the Branch Davidians near Waco, Texas. The government agents, after a failed initial raid, waited around the perimeter of the compound trying to negotiate with the heavily armed cult. Finally their patience wore thin, and they stormed the compound. The result was a nightmare of destruction fueled by a devastating fire that left most of the sect members— men, women, and children—dead. The images of the carnage were reminiscent of the tragedy in Jonestown, Guyana, in 1978. Some media observers posed questions about the presence of television cameras in Waco. Had the government viewed the perpetual delay in negotiations with Koresh as an embarrassment to their stature? Did they fear that their prestige was being compromised by television portraying them as passive negotiators? Would they have waited longer to raid the compound if the cameras had not been present? These are difficult questions, ultimately unanswerable. However, there is little doubt that television news had an obligation to cover the tragedy in Waco and provide some kind of analysis and commentary on its aftermath.

Delay and frustration were also critical variables in the 1994 story in Haiti when dramatic negotiations between the Clinton administration; Lieutenant General Raoul Cedras; the exiled president, the Rev. Jean-Bertrand Aristide; and former president Jimmy Carter averted a hostile invasion. The first American troops to land in Port-au-Prince were greeted by reporters eager to document their arrival. On the second day of the occupation, cameras were there to capture the brutal beating by club-wielding Haitian police of a pro-Aristide coconut vendor. The vivid images of the dead vendor demonstrate the power television has to circumvent conventional political rhetoric and tell a story from the peoples' point of view.

While these events all generated drama and spectacle, the essence of television's journalistic imperative was most clearly manifested by the events in the 1991 Persian Gulf War. At no other time in its history has television played such a pivotal role in disseminating information, analysis, and interpretation of a conflict unfolding. To some the immediacy of the coverage brought comfort and insight, while others felt that it compromised the quality of the analysis, and that the presentation was often sensationalized.

In the months leading up to the war, Iraq's aggressive stance toward Kuwait was monitored by the American television networks. Images of Iraq's "guest" hostages were mixed with commentary and interviews as the networks provided coverage of the global reaction to events in the gulf. CBS claimed the first broadcast "scoop" from the region when Dan Rather secured an exclusive interview with Saddam Hussein. For CBS this interview proved to be the highlight of an otherwise dismal performance in covering the conflict.

Where CBS faltered, ABC excelled, showing an expertise and professionalism that capitalized on the strength of its talent. Peter Jennings quickly demonstrated a command of the issues that generated a sense of confidence in his reporting. Jennings was joined by Ted Koppel, the first Western journalist in Baghdad after the invasion of Kuwait, whose perseverance and persistence brought him an exclusive interview with Iraqi foreign minister Tariq Aziz. Under Jennings's leadership, ABC produced a provocative special, "A Line in the Sand," which used an elaborate map set design to explain the politics and geography of the region to American viewers unfamiliar with that part of the world.

As the bombs and missiles began to fall on Iraq, American networks and local stations scrambled to obtain the best possible competitive posture. Their ability to report on the drama of the armed conflict was hampered by the Pentagon's efforts at containment. The military organized press pools for select journalists, who were taken to "newsworthy" areas and briefed under escort. As might be expected, the military was manipulating the press, and journalists fought against the censorship and delay that these tactics created.

The Pentagon, however, was not the only censor. Reporters in Baghdad felt the scrutiny of Iraqi "minders," who intently watched and listened to what was said and shown. As Americans viewed the bombing of Iraq, surprise Scud attacks on Israel, and Patriot missile defenses in Saudi Arabia, the everpresent reminder of the "minder" was vividly displayed on the screen. Could journalism flourish in such a controlled environment?

It was CNN that set the tone for coverage of war news from the gulf. As their exclusive report of the first bombs to fall on Baghdad came in, reporters Shaw, Arnett, and Holliman deserved credit, but the accomplishment was really Ted Turner's. His quest for establishing global legitimacy for CNN had by now transformed what was once considered an upstart network into a worldwide news organization that had built its credentials with solid reporting and earned the respect of politicians, the public, and its competitors in the press.

As CNN and Peter Arnett became the most visible link to Baghdad, his presence there became the subject of controversy and debate. He was accused of complicity with the enemy and of providing them with a propagandistic forum. These accusations came not from hysterical jingoists but from a senator and thirty-nine members of the House of Representatives. In addition, Accuracy in Media, a conservative lobbying organization, formed the "Victory Committee" and pledged to boycott CNN until Arnett left Baghdad.

The unsubstantiated assailments upon Arnett's loyalty and professionalism were largely due to CNN's preferred status as "network in residence." The maintenance of CNN's four-wire telephone line that sustained operation while others were terminated, Arnett's wartime interview with Saddam Hussein, seen and heard in 105 countries, his report on the alleged bombing of a baby formula factory, and his presence as the only Western journalist left in Baghdad were all factors that contributed to the attacks on his loyalty and character. Arnett's visibility as Baghdad's resident correspondent aroused resentment on the part of some politicians and broadcasters, who challenged his objectivity and criticized his intimacy with the enemy.

Competitive forces also contrived to compromise the credibility of CNN. The broadcast networks, already reeling from accumulated audience erosion and declining revenue, were faced with the alarming prospect of drastically reduced income resulting from preemptive war news programming. Many advertisers were reluctant to continue aggressive television campaigns targeted at a sensitive audience that they feared might view their huckstering in the middle of a war as unpatriotic and unseemly.

The three broadcast networks were losing their competitive edge to CNN and viewed the cable service's incursion into their war coverage as an affront and a threat to their autonomy. Some of the networks' own pool reporters were appearing on CNN before being seen on their own networks; and affiliated stations were dropping network news feeds in favor of picking up CNN at an alarming rate. As CNN's ratings soared and surpassed broadcast levels in certain time periods, the networks scurried to prevent further affiliate defections and to avoid having their correspondents appear on CNN.

The government viewed CNN's presence with mixed feelings, alternatively praising and questioning the accuracy of its coverage. Managing the media became a priority for the government, which wanted to place its own spin on reporting events in the gulf. Pool reporters were photographed, fingerprinted, and warned about what not to show—for example, unmonitored interviews, severely wounded soldiers, and body bags. As the indoctrination proceeded, journalists raised a universal cry of protest against what they viewed as excessive restraint by the military and attempted to rally viewers to their cause.

The audience, however, didn't respond. Some viewers were mesmerized into a hypnotic state by the portrait of battle. Others became isolated and withdrawn, while "Stress Hotline" numbers reached their threshold of service. Mothers complained of childrens' frightened reactions to planes flying overhead, while others demonstrated their fears by purchasing gas masks and planning bomb shelters. Employers reported a decline in productivity, and medical professionals referred to the heightened stress experienced from prolonged exposure to televised war coverage as the "CNN complex."

The competitive race for exclusive war video, while hindered by the Pentagon's strict control of the media, nevertheless became the goal for news teams as the ground war in the gulf commenced. The success of the coalition force's rapid deployment and the confusion that prevailed provided broadcast journalists with the opportunity to form technological support caravans for live coverage from the field of battle. Fly-away portable dish antennas, with their requisite hardware, were loaded onto trucks and dispatched to newsworthy locales. Reports made by television correspondents gave American audiences some of the most vivid and descriptive commentary on the war. The liberation of Kuwait demonstrated the ability of network correspondents to report live from the scene with integrity and professionalism. As U.S. and UN troops exhibited their superiority, broadcast journalists provided American audiences with a close-up view of the painfulness of defeat and the euphoria of victory.

The Persian Gulf War supplied drama, heroism, and conflict in abundance. Television's first "real-time" war made heroes of our generals and villains of the enemy. It served as an electronic canvas, portraying vivid scenes of battle, military briefings, and capture of the enemy. With its technological ability for spontaneity, television also created a resonant platform upon which negotiation, diplomacy, and propaganda unfolded. The world did seem to become McLuhan's "global village," and television played a crucial role in creating it.

As television broadcast the "war" story, it set new records in ratings, broke the bank in production costs, and lost revenue in preempted advertising time. Ironically, the medium demonstrated its evolving posture toward women from a location in a culture in which women have little independence. Female television correspondents were for the first time given equal time as witnesses of battle and distinguished themselves, demonstrating both knowledge and fortitude.[34]

Television had succeeded in showing the world the might of America and the fortitude of its troops. It also provided an electronic proscenium for glamorous celebrities like Barbara Walters to interview heroic figures like General Norman Schwarzkopf. As usual, television was able to rationalize the marriage of culture and kitsch.

DOCUMENTARY TELEVISION

The television documentary has evolved from the straightforward factual analysis of a subject to a hybrid vehicle of both entertainment and information. As television journalism matured, it redefined the objective of the documentary to suit the needs of business and competition.

The documentary format had its start in the photographic essay that later developed into the creative manipulation of news via radio's *March of Time* program. This radio series, which debuted March 6, 1931, used actors to dramatize real events and evolved into a theatrically distributed newsreel utilizing actual news film footage that would cover two to four stories in twenty-two minutes.[35] The format and design of both these series helped to set the tone and style of television news and documentary when the new medium came along.

The small screen of television and the intimacy it could project became a creative element in *See It Now*, television's first regularly scheduled documentary series. Under Edward R. Murrow and Fred Friendly's creative guidance, the series developed from a compilation of disparate news items to the more thorough coverage of a single story in each broadcast. The result was compelling television that used the visual capabilities of the medium to powerfully explore the conflict of life.

Network television eventually embraced the documentary format as a regularly scheduled programming component and distinguished itself with continuing series such as *CBS Reports*, *NBC White Paper*, and *ABC Close-Up*. *CBS Reports*, conceived by Frank Stanton, premiered in 1959 with "Biography of a Missile," and it soon became apparent that the show would address contemporary themes in a confrontational manner.[36] One of its most outstanding efforts was "Harvest of Shame," an exposé on the plight of America's migrant workers.[37] The series matured during the 1960s and 1970s and became a forum for serious analysis of matters in the public interest. Some of its more notable efforts included "The Selling of the Pentagon," "The CIA's Secret Army," and the five-part series "The Defense of the United States." Meanwhile, NBC's *White Paper* raised the consciousness of Americans with documentaries on civil rights and the plight of the poor, and *ABC Close-Up* experimented with cinema verité, exploring topics as diverse as anti-American sentiment abroad and domestic political turmoil.

In the 1980s the networks largely abandoned the traditional documentary. In 1970 the three commercial networks broadcast a total of seventy-nine documentaries: in 1986 the three-network total had fallen to fifteen; and by 1991 it had decreased to only a handful. There are a number of reasons for this decline in documentary production. Compared to other programming formats, the documentary has a fairly low profitability. Regulatory neglect in the 1980s, followed by the austere fiscal climate of the late 1980s and early 1990s also made for a fairly inhospitable environment for documentaries.

Under the eight years of the Reagan administration, the FCC adopted a laissez-faire policy toward broadcasters, leaving the marketplace to provide industry guidance. Many broadcasters interpreted the policy of "deregulation" as a divestiture of their proprietorship of the public interest. This led to an abandonment of a commitment to produce documentaries and other public affairs programs.

While the networks have reneged on their obligation to traditional documentary, PBS has remained a resolute patron of the genre. Public television has aired excellent documentaries on subjects as diverse as the Civil War, the American family, and AIDS. It has encouraged independent production and provided a viable forum for documentary distribution.

The news magazine programs, which are less expensive to produce than documentaries, are also immensely popular with audiences and highly profitable as well. *60 Minutes* earns a profit of about $70 million a year. Producer Don Hewitt claims that "there is no story you can do in an hour documentary that we couldn't do in a *60 Minutes* segment. And nobody looks at [documentaries] when they're on the air."[38]

Many news producers also argue that television must adjust to a new generation of viewers who, raised with the staccato visual style of *Sesame Street* and MTV, are unable to focus their attention on a single story lasting more than ten minutes. A. V. Westin, formerly executive producer of ABC's *20/20*, ABC's answer to *60 Minutes*, said flatly "The word [documentary] has become deadly."[38] And Richard Salant, former President of CBS News, summed up the industry's position when he said, "It's time to write the obituary. The decline and fall of the hard news documentary is the price we must pay for television coming of age as a business guided by considerations other than just those journalistic."[39]

Indeed, these considerations are inherent in network television's manipulation of news to force it into the demands of an entertainment agenda. Rather than explore the substance of the bizarre and exploitive relationship between Amy Fisher and Joey Buttafuoco, and its implications upon the themes of marital infidelity, child abuse, and teenage prostitution, the networks preferred to reap the profits available to them by fanning the flames of sensational gossip and making a personal tragedy into a pop culture event. Instead of offering viewers insight and analysis, they served up tasteless programming produced by their entertainment divisions. The competition for viewers was heated, with CBS and ABC going head to head, broadcasting their movies on the same night. Unfortunately, cheap docudramas of this nature have edged out more responsible and mature forms of programming, in seeking to meet the "lowest common denominator" in the mass market audience.

Although the arguments for elimination of the traditional documentary may sound credible, they mask underlying motives that may be addressing very different priorities. News magazine programs tend to present issues that seem to have a clear delineation between right and wrong. They rarely discuss substantive issues where there is no easy answer or quick fix. While a documentary may not solve a particular problem, it can provide an audience with important information and help them to formulate their own opinions. American broadcasters have a documentary tradition to sustain, one that has distinguished the role of journalists as gatekeepers of democracy. Occasionally, however, their mission has become blurred by "considerations, other than just those journalistic."

In 1983, CBS broadcast a program entitled "The Uncounted Enemy: A Vietnam Deception." The documentary, reported by the acerbic correspondent Mike Wallace and producer George Crile, raised serious allegations that General William Westmoreland and his staff had deliberately distorted enemy troop strength during the Vietnam War. According to the program, the general had estimated Viet Cong troop strength at 285,000 and enemy casualties and deserters at 250,000, which ostensibly left 35,000 Viet Cong troops, a figure that was grossly underestimated. After the broadcast of the program, the general filed a widely publicized million-dollar libel suit, claiming that CBS had deliberately defamed him, misrepresented his position, and alleged a conspiracy where none existed. CBS appointed a distinguished veteran documentarist, Burton Benjamin, to head an investigation into the production of the documentary.

Benjamin's task was not an easy one and was made more difficult by the severity of the allegations, which included the claim of conspiracy; CBS's payment of $25,000 to a consultant and rehearsals of the consultant prior to filming; the screening of prerecorded interviews to sympathetic witnesses; harsh treatment of unfriendly witnesses; and quoting out of context. The Benjamin report was critical of various techniques employed in the production of the documentary. Benjamin found that the program was unbalanced and that those who disagreed with the show's premise had not been fairly represented. In addition he concluded that a conspiracy had never been proved, certain witnesses had been treated harshly by the producers, double interviews and screening had been used with certain key individuals, and the producers had failed to identify the consultant as a paid participant. The matter was settled out of court.[40]

Although this case shows that documentarists can be vulnerable to bias and breaches of ethical conduct, the importance of the documentary tradition for an informed and enlightened public remains. As the *Columbia Journalism Review* noted, the "viewing of history in terms of conspiracy and betrayal invites the presumption that journalism is seeking its own kind of retribution and is encouraging the public to seek revenge as well. Good journalism should place itself above and beyond such presumptions."

The news has become a profitable industry for television: there is more of it than ever before. In addition to the myriad of magazine shows, CBS, ABC, and NBC are all using news to fill their early morning hours (2:00–6:00 a.m.). The early morning news programs include CBS's *Up to the Minute*, ABC's *World News Now*, and NBC's *Nightside*.

Local television stations are also caught up in the frenzy of reporting and merchandising the news. As local news becomes more competitive, the stations search for formats that will distinguish them from other local television stations in the same market. Some have turned to a format known as the "environmental newscast," where the anchor strolls behind the scenes of the newsroom, stopping along the way to chat at the desks of various reporters. Other local formats include "Action News"—the cramming of multiple grisly stories into a half hour featuring the "murder du jour."

The competitive nature of television news has produced many concerns about its ethics and values. Critics have decried its lack of substance and its fascination with reporting the "doom and gloom" of society. Osborn Elliott, former editor of *Newsweek* and dean emeritus of the Columbia School of Journalism, refers to this type of communication as the "curled lip school of journalism." While competition can serve to enhance the stature of reporting, thus far television news organizations have been followers, rather than leaders.

NOTES

1. In 1996, after petitioning the FCC for an eighteen-month waiver of the one VHF to a market rule (Disney Capital Cities ABC would own KCAL and KABC-TV) Disney decided to sell KCAL rather than jeopardize its $19 billion merger with Capital Cities.

2. In a similar venture, Channel 16 in Wilkes-Barre, Pennsylvania, expanded its newsday with a half-hour newscast disseminated on rival Channel 38.

3. This speech was given October 15, 1958.

4. John O'Connor, "Onscreen Journalism: Show Biz or News?" *New York*

Times, May 14, 1992, C17, C20.

5. In 1983 Craft sued station KMBC-TV, Kansas City. A jury awarded her $500,000 in damages, but a judge later overturned the award. In a second trial, Craft was awarded $325,000. She now works in local radio news.

6. Chung was forced out as coanchor of the *CBS Evening News* in May 1995.

7. Walter Goodman, "Beauty and the Broadcast," *New York Times,* January 26, 1992, 29.

8. In *Dietemann v. Time, Inc.,* a court ruled that "the First Amendment is not a license to trespass, to steal, or to intrude by electronic means into the precincts of another's home or office." In Alabama, Delaware, Georgia, Hawaii, Maine, Michigan, New Hampshire, South Dakota, and Utah it is illegal to use a hidden video or still camera to record an individual without their consent.

9. In a 1992 case involving Food Lion Inc., a grocery chain headquartered in Winston–Salem, North Carolina, and ABC's Prime Time Live, the grocery chain won court approval to conduct discovery on about five years' worth of ABC News undercover investigations. They accused ABC of staging, fraudulent editing, and concealing unaired video. In March 1995 a court ruled that Food Lion could not recover damages for injury to reputation.

10. Steve McClellan, "Tabloids Pull Out the Checkbook, Proudly," *Broadcasting & Cable,* May 9, 1994, 42.

11. See Don Hewitt's Op-Ed in the *New York Times,* June 20, 1995.

12. *Estes v. Texas,* 1381 U.S. 532 (1965).

13. "Florida Trial of 'TV Addict' Goes on the Air," *Broadcasting,* October 3, 1977.

14. *Chandler v. Florida,* 449 U.S. 560 (1981).

15. David Margolick, "A Peek under the Tent of the West Palm Beach Media Circus," *New York Times,* December 15, 1991, 2.

16. The results of a CBS/*New York Times* poll released shortly after these events revealed that of 960 adults interviewed, 27 percent approved of access by both men and women reporters to lockerrooms, 21 percent said only men should be allowed in, and 4 percent would bar all reporters regardless of gender. The remainder expressed no opinion.

17. Steve McClellan, "Magazines Prime Earners in Prime Time," *Broadcasting & Cable,* May 9, 1994, p. 40.

18. In February 1996 Don Hewitt announced a change in format for *60 Minutes.* The program includes additional commentary from three newspaper columnists and coverage of a topical news story each week. *60 Minutes* will eliminate reruns and offer new stories fifty-two weeks a year.

19. *Dateline* expanded to four nights a week, including Sunday, in March 1996. For 1995 it is estimated that *Dateline* generated 40 percent of the NBC News Division's earnings in excess of $100 million.

20. Walter Goodman, "Beauty and the Broadcast," *New York Times,* January 26, 1992, p. 29.

21. Chung left CBS, however, in May 1995. She had been criticized for her coverage of the Oklahoma City bombing and her tabloid-style interview with Newt Gingrich's mother.

22. Walter Goodman, "Beauty and the Broadcast," *New York Times,* January 26, 1992, 26.

23. See Sally Quinn, *We're Going to Make You a Star*, (New York: Simon and Schuster, 1975).

24. Elizabeth Kolbert, "When News Producers Become Part of the News There's Bound to Be Tension at the Network," *New York Times*, October, 18, 1993, D7.

25. Ibid.

26. Edward Felesenthal, "The Torturous Story Behind a *Prime Time* Story," *Wall Street Journal*, July 27, 1993, 9.

27. A. M. Rosenthal, "The Press and Simpson," *New York Times*, June 24, 1994, A27.

28. *Cable News Network v. Noriega*, 917 Fad 1543 (1990); 111 SAT 451 (1990). Judge Hoeveler eventually lifted the ban against airing the audiotapes.

29. "Is Your Car Safe?" on the Pinto, was broadcast on June 11, 1978. "Out of Control," the Audi story, was originally broadcast on November 23, 1986, and rebroadcast on September 13, 1987.

30. Another point that escaped public disclosure was that Bruce Enz, the individual who headed the Institute for Safety Analysis, which was responsible for conducting the *Dateline* demonstrations, appeared to have a conflict of interest. Enz was also known as a professional expert witness testifying against General Motors and other automakers. See Elizabeth Kolbert, "NBC Settles Truck Crash Lawsuit, Saying Test Was 'Inappropriate,' " *New York Times*, February 10, 1993, A1, A16.

31. Walter Goodman, "Television, Meet Life. Life, Meet TV," *New York Times*, June 19, 1994, sec. 4, 1.

32. The settlement also held ABC liable for Philip Morris's legal expenses, estimated at about $2.5 to $3 million. See Mark Landler, "ABC News Settles Suits on Tobacco," *New York Times*, 22 August 1995, A1, D6.

33. Walter Goodman, "How Much Should TV Tell, and When?" *New York Times*, October 29, 1990, C20.

34. John Burns, "Day and Nights in Baghdad," *New York Times*, November 11, 1990, sec. 6, 54.

35. The American newsreels included Pathé News (later Warner–Pathé News), Fox Movietone News, Universal News, Hearst International Newsreel (later, Hearst Metrotone News, then News of the Day), and Paramount News. The first installment of *March of Time* appeared on February 1, 1935, at the Capital Theater in New York City.

36. *CBS Reports* returned to the CBS television network in 1993. From 1993-1995 it produced nine documentaries, substantially less than the fifteen per year quota it had produced in the 1960s.

37. On July 20, 1995, Dan Rather hosted a documentary special, "Legacy of Shame," an update of "Harvest of Shame."

38. Burton Benjamin, "The Documentary: An Endangered Species." Gannett Center for Media Studies, Occasional Paper No. 6, October 1987.

39. Ibid.

40. Burton Benjamin, *Fair Play: CBS, General Westmoreland and How a Television Documentary Went Wrong* (New York: Harper & Row, 1988).

7

Electronic Currency:
The Bottom Line of Television

The concept behind advertising is as old as humankind itself. Prehistoric men and women advertised their exploits with drawings on the walls of caves. As they became more civilized and educated, the process of advertising became more sophisticated. Town criers were used in Babylon, and with the Egyptian discovery of papyrus, advertisements were set to paper. In Greece and Rome advertising proliferated, with outdoor signs announcing sporting events and shows. The printing press revolutionized communications and made way for the mass distribution of advertising messages, which now could be disseminated to thousands of people.

While the general concept of advertising has its roots in ancient civilizations, the creation of modern advertising agencies is a uniquely American phenomenon. One American entrepreneur, Volney Palmer, founded what could be considered the first advertising agency in 1842. Palmer sold newspaper space, earning a 25 percent commission on each sale. After six years in business, Palmer had offices in Baltimore, Boston, Philadelphia, and New York—and numerous competitors.

Some of Palmer's competitors became institutions in American advertising. F. Wayland Ayer founded N. W. Ayer and Son in 1869. In 1887, J. Walter Thompson started what was to become one of the most influential, productive, and respected agencies in the business. Thompson offered advertisers an exclusive list of thirty magazines and used his business savvy to create a highly successful advertising agency.

Many of the agencies that pioneered the technique and philosophy of American advertising became leaders in radio and television merchandising. They helped to set a creative universal standard that enabled them to assume a global presence in marketing and sales. It started in 1922, when the Queensboro Corporation paid $50 to radio station WEAF in New York to announce the virtues of suburban apartment living in Jackson Heights, Long Island. Since then, advertising has been the driving force of radio and television in America. The advertising industry has been criticized, satirized, ridiculed, and maligned. Yet it remains the primary economic support of television in the United States.

Early radio advertising was quite different from the advertising audiences are accustomed to seeing and hearing today. While many programs included the sponsor's name in their title, outright product pitching and sales talks were limited. The National Association of Broadcasters (NAB), which was created in 1923 and has over the years formulated voluntary codes of behavior for broadcasters, addressed the question of advertising in its first code, published in 1928. The NAB discouraged radio advertising between the hours of 7:00 and 11:00 p.m., as that period was considered to be family oriented. With the creation of a second network, CBS, in 1927, advertising was given more latitude on radio. Announcers began to mention the virtues of the product, along with the name and the price. Advertising thus began the long road toward the brazen and aggressive form we know today.

Although there has always been dissatisfaction with the manner in which radio and television advertising has developed in the United States, no legislation ever came so close to changing the status of the industry as the Wagner-Hatfield amendment to the Communications Act of 1934. The Roosevelt administration had proposed new legislation to replace the Federal Radio Act of 1927 and had created the FCC, which would regulate not only radio but telephone and television as well. Distressed with the growing commercialization of the airwaves, critics of advertising seized this opportunity to restructure the rules concerning radio broadcasting. The Wagner-Hatfield Amendment proposed to nullify all existing station licenses and reallocate channels so that one-quarter of all frequencies would be assigned to educational, religious, and various other nonprofit organizations. It was, however, defeated in Congress after extensive lobbying by the broadcasting industry.

When television arrived, advertisers were quick to embrace it, seeing its great potential for sales promotion. Corporate America was stunned by the power of television: a small cosmetics company, Hazel Bishop, which was earning $50,000 a year before television advertising, grew to $4.5 million after only two years of television sponsorship. From the beginning it was clear that television could indeed provide a fertile ground for corporate propaganda and image building.

In the 1950s, many television programs were produced by advertising agencies for their clients. These agencies often censored programming on their clients' behalf. For example, in a *Playhouse 90* drama about the Nuremberg trials and death chambers, sponsored by the natural gas industry, the word "gas" was removed at the request of the agency. Procter and Gamble, the largest advertiser on television, also issued program content guidelines but of a more general nature. They expected themes in their programming to avoid any negative reference to business and to pay particular attention to the mention of businesses that used Procter and Gamble products.

Perhaps the most insidious example of an industry's manipulation of television occurred with the tobacco companies. While the dangers of smoking had been known since the 1930s, it wasn't until the 1970s that the public became fully aware of them. Over the years the powerful tobacco lobby did everything within its power to deny or discount any negative findings concerning its product. In the early 1950s, Camel cigarettes sponsored the *Camel News Caravan* on NBC and censored all news that took place where a "No Smoking" sign appeared in the background. The tobacco industry was also sensitive to the manner in which their product was depicted on television. The Brown and Williamson Tobacco Corporation issued guidelines concerning the use of cigarettes as props in television programs, which stated that cigarettes should never be ground out violently or referred to in disgust, associated with villains, or treated in a disrespectful manner. And network documentaries that attempted to address the question of tobacco and its connection with various illnesses were too heavily "balanced" to be meaningful.

In 1970, with the medical evidence mounting and the dangers of smoking becoming increasingly clear, Congress banned cigarette advertising from radio and television. Prior to the ban, cigarette advertising on television had been a multimillion-dollar industry. Indeed, tobacco had played an important role in the growth and success of advertising in the United States.

ISSUES AND TRENDS IN CONTEMPORARY ADVERTISING

One of the most interesting ad campaigns of the 1990s was created for the Infiniti, the Japanese Nissan Motor Company's luxury import. The advertisements used a series of natural visual images—fields of pussy willows and rain falling on a pond—with a voice-over script that spoke of humanity's harmony with nature. In a revolutionary departure from traditional automobile advertising, the car itself was not displayed. Hill, Holliday, Connors, Cosmopulous, the agency that created the $60 million campaign, took the risk that this novel approach would pique the interest of the American public. Apparently it didn't: it is now known, disparagingly, as the "rocks and trees" campaign that has become a symbol of what not to do in car advertising.

However, some agencies still think a nonconformist approach like the Infiniti campaign is worth trying. In 1995 Saab initiated a $40 million advertising campaign featuring sophisticated animations and focusing on the theme of defying convention. In a nod to the Infiniti campaign, the Saab automobile is never seen nor are any of its attributes mentioned. Apparently, Angotti, Thomas, Hedge, the New York agency that created the commercial, felt that their nonconformist approach would prove more successful than the Infiniti commercial.

Occasionally even the most carefully planned automobile advertising campaigns can stumble and generate negative publicity and embarrassment. For twenty years the American advertising agency Scali, McCabe, Sloves had been emphasizing the safety and durability of Sweden's Volvo automobiles. During the 1970s and 1980s, Volvo North America entered the luxury American automobile market and became the car of choice among upwardly mobile "yuppies" and their families. This carefully cultivated image was compromised, however, when a 1990 television commercial, which depicted a "monster truck" with oversized tires driving over a row of cars, and crushing all the roofs except the Volvo's, was exposed as having been rigged. Not only had the Volvo's roof been reinforced with wood and steel, but the roofs of the other vehicles had also been weakened prior to shooting. Vehicle tampering was not unique to this particular Volvo commercial: during the 1970s and 1980s, Volvo's advertising campaign included television commercials and print advertisements depicting the automobile's strength that showed how it could support the weight of other vehicles stacked on its roof. It was later discovered that to accomplish this feat, several jacks had been placed between the tires to prevent the car from sagging.

Volvo attempted to quell criticism of its manipulative advertising by a public admission of guilt and an apology for the misrepresentation. And although the advertising agency responsible for the ads resigned the account, the negative publicity may have adversely affected sales of the automobile.

Of course, Volvo is not the only automobile manufacturer to have created commercials that were misleading. In a General Motors commercial for Oldsmobile, an Oldsmobile 98 was dropped from the underside of an in-flight cargo plane via parachute, and then driven away after it hit the ground. In reality, the car dropped was only a shell, and a different car was driven away.

While automobile manufacturers defend their commercials, insisting that sometimes viewers assume claims that have not actually been made, critics counter that viewers can be manipulated by claims that are implied visually but not stated. Although some viewers may have a fairly healthy skepticism about advertising claims, many less sophisticated viewers believe in its truthfulness.

Contemporary cultural themes are also important in planning an advertising campaign. Like other product manufacturers, automobile makers have been sensitive to consumer concerns about environmental issues. Toyota and General Motors created "green" ads that stress their product's contribution to a better environment.

Another technique that automobile manufacturers use in their advertising strategies is called product exclusivity. A company may make a contractual agreement with a network that theirs will be the only product advertised within a certain specified time on the network. For example, the General Motors Corporation entered into a $400 million, seven-year agreement with CBS establishing General Motors as the exclusive domestic automobile advertiser to appear on the network's NCAA basketball broadcasts. In a similar deal, General Motors arranged the same advertising status on the CBS network major league baseball broadcasts. This practice maximizes advertising effectiveness, since advertisements by competitors will not be seen by the viewer, at least not one after the other.

The high visibility of automobile advertising on American television shows how important the automobile manufacturing industry has become in determining the survival of agencies that serve these multi-million-dollar accounts. In 1991, Mercedes Benz of North America, faced with four years of declining sales, decided to place its $88 million account with McCaffrey and McCall up for review. The Mercedes account represented nearly a third of McCaffrey and McCall's total annual billings, and its loss was a devastating financial blow to the small agency. A similar defection compromised the ability of Levine, Huntley, Vick & Beaver to survive, when in 1991 the agency lost a lucrative account with Subaru. As the economy continues to contract and automobile sales decline, automobile manufacturers have had little patience with ad failure and, instead of recognizing the realities of a depressed market, have been inclined to blame the advertising agencies for sluggish sales.

Competition is, of course, an important element in a capitalistic society. The essence of competitive television merchandising is embodied in the athletic shoe television commercials of Nike, Reebok, and L.A. Gear. Rival claims, visual dramatizations, celebrity endorsements, and corporate debunking are all common weapons in the arsenal of sneaker advertising. The $5.5 billion sneaker industry increased its advertising expenditures from $70 million in 1989 to $115 million in 1991. Most of the money is spent in television, with ads that reflect the intense competitive positioning between the various sneaker brands.

In 1990, a commercial made by Chiat/Day/Mojo, Inc. for Reebok pump sneakers was denied distribution on NBC and had only limited broadcast on ABC and CBS. The commercial showed two men—one wearing Nike sneakers, and the other Reeboks—preparing to jump off a bridge to which they were tethered with elastic bungee cords. Only the bungee jumper wearing the Reeboks bounced back into view, the implication being that the Nike man, whose empty sneakers appeared onscreen, might not have survived. In its attempt to overtake Nike as the industry leader, Reebok has pursued an aggressive, sometimes even abrasive, television advertising campaign. Starting in 1991, Reebok's advertising campaign had its own celebrity endorsers ridicule Nike's star athletic spokesmen, Michael Jordan and Bo Jackson, referring to the two by name in the Reebok commercial. The practice of mentioning the names of star endorsers from a competing commercial set off a round of debate concerning the legality and propriety of the tactic.

Another sneaker company, L.A. Gear, also nurtured a stable of big-name endorsers and initiated an aggressive television campaign whose spots premiered on Super Bowl 1991. The L.A. Gear commercial raised the ire of competitors and television networks with a tag line that referred to its competitors' products as "just hot air." Although ABC broadcast the commercial on the Super Bowl, both NBC and CBS declined to follow suit, stating that the L.A. Gear commercial made an unsubstantiated assertion.

Television commercials are composed of a number of variables that work together to achieve the ultimate audience impact for the product. The design of the commercial must consider all of these in order to maximize a commercial's reach and effectiveness.

For television commercials, the "vehicle," or program, that the message is adjacent to is an important element in terms of advertising exposure. The annual Super Bowl football game usually draws the largest television audience of the year. Television advertisers are attracted to the Super Bowl as an advertising vehicle because of its large reach and broad demographic base. Super Bowl advertisers also enjoy the advantage of having their commercials viewed by the audience in "real time," since viewers rarely tape this event for playback at a later time: this minimizes the chance that they will skip over, or "zap" the commercials. Advertising rates for television spots on the Super Bowl reflect the great value placed on the event: NBC charged $1.2 million, or $40,000 a minute for fifty-eight thirty-second units in the 1996 Super Bowl XXX.

One of the most daring and innovative commercials produced for the Super Bowl was Apple Computer's spot, which appeared on the 1984 Super Bowl. Some 38.9 million viewers watched as Apple introduced the Macintosh line of computers in a highly stylized commercial that cleverly played on the theme of Orwell's Big Brother.

The lure of Super Bowl advertising is not limited to giant corporations. One of the most consistent Super Bowl advertisers has been the Master Lock Company. Its clever commercials, which show one of its locks still working after being pierced by a bullet, have been associated with the game since 1974. Some industry analysts estimate that the Master Lock Company spends nearly its entire annual advertising budget for the one-time exposure on the Super Bowl.

Corporate America flocks to the Super Bowl hoping to make a shopping impact on the millions of households tuned to the event. But are these advertisers getting the "biggest bang for the buck?" Historically it was felt that Super Bowl viewers had a higher commercial retention rate as compared to viewers in other prime-time categories. However, the findings of a study conducted in 1994 by Creative Marketing Consultants appeared to dispute that theory. Immediately following the 1994 game, 373 Super Bowl viewers were interviewed. In almost every case, the vast majority could not recall which products had been advertised. The inventory of commercial time for the 1994 game included fifty-six thirty-second spots. The most memorable ad was a Frito-Lay commercial, which had a 38 percent viewer recall. It is important to note that the study also found a significant drop-off in retention after only one day.

Some advertisers create promotional campaigns that offer prizes in an attempt to entice consumers to purchase their products. The complexity of an ambitious promotional campaign such as this can be illustrated by examining the competitive confrontation between America's two leading cola manufacturers, Coca-Cola and Pepsico, who used Super Bowl 1991 as the ideal time to challenge each other's promotional and marketing skills. The lure of big money was used by both cola manufacturers: Coca-Cola had its million-dollar "Crack the Code for Diet Coke," and Pepsico had an interactive toll-free Super Bowl number offering million-dollar annuity prizes. The competition became so heated that Pepsi threatened to produce its own half-time show on a competing network in order to thwart Coca-Cola's Super Bowl half-time promotion. External factors, however, altered the advertising strategy of both rivals. Pepsico could not line up the necessary stations for its alternative half-time show, nor was it able to deliver on its annuity contest. And as a patriotic gesture to the troops in the Persian Gulf, the Coca-Cola Company altered its campaign, pulled humorous commercials, and promoted its contest with little fanfare. These circumstances, of course, compromised the effectiveness of both the Diet Coke and Diet Pepsi campaigns.

Unfortunately, sometimes even the best ideas and advertising efforts are jeopardized by external circumstances. When Pepsico Inc. enlisted the rock star Madonna for a soda pop commercial, Pepsico executives thought they had a sure thing. Their expectations, however, were foiled when an unrelated rock video featuring Madonna dancing around several burning crosses was released. Responding to pressure from religious groups, Pepsico agreed to withdraw their commercial. In another soft drink endorsement, Michael Jackson's relationship with Coca-Cola was strained after he was accused of sexually abusing a minor. An out-of-court settlement with his accuser did not alleviate suspicions about his guilt.[1]

Some competitive sports provide advertisers with unique advertising opportunities. Football, baseball, and basketball contain an inherent structure that make them well-suited for commercial interruption. Other sports, such as soccer, with its continuous action, pose problems in broadcasting. The World Cup soccer match of 1994 was the first time the event had been played in America. ABC and ESPN took their coverage cues from Univision, the Spanish-language network. Rather than interrupt the fast action of the game, since 1982 Univision had used ten-second "crawls" at the bottom of the screen to advertise various products. Instead of the crawls, ABC and ESPN placed the sponsors' logos on a clock and superimposed it on the upper left-hand corner of the screen during play.

Celebrity Endorsers

Advertisers must be receptive to changing trends in audience taste. For example, for many years celebrity endorsements were a reliable technique for selling selected products and services even though American television audiences seemed to be fickle when it came to the popularity of celebrity endorsers. A market research company, Video Storyboard Tests, has tried for years to measure the effectiveness of this advertising technique. At the end of the 1980s and in the beginning of the 1990s, Video Storyboard Tests declared that audiences were bored with celebrity hucksters. At that time the most popular commercials featured animation or animals. Indeed, one of the favorite commercial campaigns of the 1980s was for California raisins which featured animated clay figures.

However, when in 1995 Video Storyboard Tests conducted its eighteenth annual survey of the year's most popular celebrity endorsers, all but two of the top ten were female. It included Candice Bergen, Elizabeth Taylor, Kathi Lee Gifford, and Whitney Houston. While the trend may have shifted back toward celebrity endorsers, there are still risks associated with this advertising technique. A number of embarrassing incidents have occurred in connection with some commercials featuring celebrities. For example, during the time Cybil Shepherd was acting as television spokesperson for the National Beef Council, she stated in an interview that she rarely ate meat. Her former costar on *Moonlighting*, Bruce Willis, was appearing in ads for Seagram's wine coolers when a story broke alleging that he had a drinking problem.

A landmark court case settled in January 1990 addressed the area of substantiation of claims made by celebrity endorsers. The case involved a Midwest mortgage brokering company that had defrauded its investors. Two celebrity endorsers, George Hamilton and Lloyd Bridges, had pitched the merits of the company to the public. The celebrities, who were named in the suit, pleaded ignorance of the fraudulent investment scheme. The judge in the case rendered a far-reaching decision when he found that celebrity endorsers must independently verify that the claims they make in ads are true and that actors can be held liable for fraudulent claims.[2]

Other risks inherent in building an advertising campaign around a celebrity were also illustrated when O. J. Simpson, a familiar figure to television audiences through his endorsements for Hertz, Chevrolet, Royal Crown Cola, and Wilson Sporting Goods, was charged with the murder of his former wife and a friend of hers. As circumstances of the case unfolded and the public heard a desperate Nicole Brown Simpson pleading for police assistance on a 1989 911 emergency call, questions were raised about Hertz's continued affiliation with Simpson. Some critics charged that Hertz should have dropped Simpson back in 1989 after he pleaded "no contest" to wife-beating charges. Clearly, while the client advertiser bears no guilt for the actions of the celebrity endorsers they hire, their product, which has become closely associated with the celebrity, could be tainted in the public mind.

Advertising Copy and "Political Correctness"

The 1990s have posed several other new challenges to advertisers. In addition to the difficulties inherent in a sluggish economy, there is also a new awareness of the need to be more conscious of what is "politically correct." The 1991 television campaign for Old Milwaukee Beer, manufactured by Stroh Brewery, managed to insult several segments of its audience. The campaign, which featured the antics of the "Swedish Bikini Team" frolicking with male beer drinkers, generated a swell of protest and charges of blatant sexism. Several female employees of Strohs and Hal Riney and Partners, its advertising agency, accused both the brewery and the advertising agency of sexual harassment. In response to the controversy, Stroh's quickly withdrew a commercial for its Augsburg beer that displayed the bikini-clad bottoms of three women, along with the slogan, "Why the average beer commercial has more cans than bottles."

In adopting a more inclusive policy toward physically and mentally challenged individuals, advertisers have had mixed success. Grand Metropolitan PLC, parent company of Burger King, ran a commercial in Chicago that featured an adult male with Down's Syndrome who had difficulty remembering and repeating a special slogan for a discounted meal. The ad was taken off the air after parents of children with Down's Syndrome complained.

Two other campaigns seemed to successfully integrate individuals with Down's Syndrome into their commercials. McDonald's, in what was more of a corporate image ad than a product pitch, featured a student with Down's Syndrome working at a McDonald's restaurant, mopping the floor and cleaning up. And Dow Chemical's Dow Brands featured a mother and her eight-year-old daughter, who has Down's Syndrome. Dow's commercial showed mother and daughter using Dow's Stain Stick product: the tag line for the commercial was, "because the last place we need another challenge is in the laundry room." Both commercials were greeted positively by the National Down's Syndrome Congress. Sometimes what appears to be an innocent advertising reference can be offensive. The Black Flag insecticide company had to alter a commercial when a veterans' group protested the playing of "Taps" over an image of dead insects.

Advertisers have become concerned about special interest groups that may boycott their products in response to offensive commercials. A number of organizations representing special interest groups have been formed who can assist advertisers in the assessment of commercial propriety when dealing with sensitive matters.

Creative Merchandising Strategies

As promotional efforts become more competitive and costly, advertisers continue to seek out new merchandising strategies.[3] One area being pursued is the visible placement of products into the context of a television program. Long a practice in theatrical feature-length films, this technique, referred to in the industry as "product placement," can either be passive or active. In the passive version, the product becomes part of the set and is visually prominent during a particular shot or scene; in an active placement, the product may play an integral role in the plot or may be referred to verbally by one of the characters. FCC regulations require that there be disclosure for any advertiser who has paid to have a product included on a television show: production credits at the end of a program must identify donor companies. Since the networks generally disapprove of commercial product placement, advertisers may circumvent the rules by providing their product free to television producers. These free endorsements may range from the simple—like a box of Quaker Oats Squares on an episode of *Roseanne*—to the more elaborate—free IBM computers for the sets of *Murphy Brown* and *L.A. Law*.[4]

Aggressive posturing by advertisers to place brand name products and services on television programs has prompted the networks to design exclusive programming packages for clients. Cooperative promotional efforts, coproductions, and product exclusivity have become profitable tools in the network's array of advertising opportunities.

Another attractive network advertising venue is the theme week. Creating a five-part series centering on a single theme may attract advertisers whose products relate well to the theme. Advertisers attempting to break through the clutter of televised product pitching are also receptive to exclusive promotional arrangements initiated by the television network. For example, in return for doubling its advertising expenditures on NBC's Saturday morning children's programming lineup, Toys "R" Us became the focus of a four-week network promotional campaign. In a similar arrangement the Coca-Cola Company agreed to exceed the normal purchase acquisition of commercial prime time in the defunct CBS series *TV 101* in return for the placement of a Coke machine in episodes of the program.

Designing creative programming techniques that increase client visibility has become the key to success in the 1990s. In a departure from traditional network practice, NBC created an advertising vehicle for clients in the guise of a sports program. *Jock Spots*, which featured superstars Jimmy Connors and Michael Jordan making commercials, included scheduled advertisements for the same products that were featured in the program. Critics of this practice complained about the blurring of the lines between program and commercial content that has resulted from the introduction of these "advertorials" and "infomercials," contributing to what some feel is an atmosphere of deceptive merchandising.

Commercial Clutter

The evolution of advertising in television programming has further focussed attention on the issue of "creeping clutter," the increase in non-program material aired in prime-time and other time periods.[5] Over the past few years the broadcast networks have expanded their prime-time allotment of non program material significantly.[6]

Critics of commercial clutter come from both the business and public sectors. A number of consumer groups, including the Center for the Study of Commercialism, the Center for Media Education, the Consumer Federation of America, and the United Church of Christ, have expressed their opposition to the increasing frequency of commercials. Industry concern has also been voiced by the Association of National Advertisers. For the networks, however, increased commercial time has meant record revenues. For 1995, the networks (ABC, CBS, Fox, and NBC), broadcasting cable revenue was $15.4 billion, with operating profits in excess of $2.5 billion.

While not exactly attempting to contain clutter, three of the networks (ABC, NBC, CBS), did implement a policy of "seamless" programming for the 1994–95 prime-time season. "Seamless" programming called for eliminating commercials and promotional announcements between prime-time programs. During these transitions it is estimated that 15 to18 percent of the audience changes channels or leaves the television viewing area.

The networks are also urging producers to shorten opening and closing titles and credits and to begin programs with "cold" openings; that is, going immediately to the opening scene of a program. Some of these techniques may cut down on nonprogram clutter, although the networks plan to place the commercials that were previously seen between programs into the body of the shows.[7]

In their quest to attain product exclusivity and achieve merchandising prominence, advertisers are entering the field of production. In exchange for providing a customized programming vehicle for the advertiser, the network delegates a considerable portion of production expenses to the advertiser. For example, CBS sold a minority ownership in the prime-time series *Northern Exposure* to Procter and Gamble, which agreed to buy half the commercial time on the series as part of its investment.

The presence of advertisers in the television program production process does have a precedent. In the 1950s, many network television programs were produced by advertising agencies for their clients. After the quiz show scandals in the late 1950s, however, the networks assumed exclusive control over program selection and production. Although they did not produce most of their programming, they took over the responsibility for oversight.

Over the years advertisers like Hallmark, AT&T, General Motors, and General Foods have produced their own specials and movies for network television. Although networks have traditionally resisted advertiser production and program equity, the strain of a shrinking revenue base and competition are forcing the networks to be more receptive to such arrangements. Critics of advertiser programming support object that content censorship by the advertisers is always a concern in this kind of situation. While advertisers that fund programming for television can exercise a degree of content control, audience taste and programming trends will probably prevail over censorship.

ADVERTISING OVERSIGHT

Although misuse of the airwaves and violation of the public trust may seem clear cut in some cases, there have been other circumstances where the legitimacy of commercials is more ambiguous and complex. Some of these cases will be discussed later, but first a review of government policy toward advertising regulation is in order.

The regulation of truth in advertising is provided by a joint effort at the state and federal levels of government. In 1911 a regulatory trends publication called *Printer's Ink* devised a model statute for statewide adoption that addressed the problem of untrue, deceptive, and misleading advertising. Today many states have adopted truth-in-advertising laws patterned after the 1911 *Printer's Ink* model.

The concern for honest advertising at the turn of the twentieth century led to the creation of a number of advertising clubs that in turn stimulated the formation of the American Advertising Federation and the development of Better Business Bureaus. The increasing concern for truthful advertising led President Woodrow Wilson to sponsor the Federal Trade Commission Act, which was passed by Congress in 1914. This act created a Federal Trade Commission (FTC), consisting of five members who were appointed by the president and confirmed by vote of the Senate. Each commissioner could serve no more than seven years, and a maximum of three members could be from the same political party. The commission's mandate was to regulate unfair competition and assure the maintenance of a free and competitive marketplace.

In 1938 the FTC's authority to control the truthfulness of advertising claims became law. The Wheeler Lea Act amended the Federal Trade Commission Act to include within the commission's jurisdiction the determination of untruthful or deceptive advertising. During the next twenty-five years, state governments worked in partnership with the federal government to codify a cohesive advertising regulatory policy.

In 1966 the Fair Packaging and Labeling Act attempted to legislate standards for the textual content of package labels. The FTC and the Food and Drug Administration (FDA) work together to enforce this law: the FDA sets the standards for food, cosmetics, and nonprescription drugs, while the FTC regulates other merchandise, from cleaning products to electrical equipment. Unfortunately, the lobbying of special interest groups have compromised the law's effectiveness and made it ambivalent and confusing.

During the 1970s, consumerism once again became a prominent issue, when the Magnuson-Moss Warranty Federal Trade Commission Improvement Act was passed in 1975. This act defined new regulatory areas and created more stringent standards in the determination of fair advertising practices, which included disclosure and content guidelines for warranties, a regulatory precedent for the FTC to define what is "fair" and what is not, and a consumer redress provision.

While networks try to accommodate the needs of their advertisers, advertisers do not have a free hand in placing commercials on the network. The propriety and claims of all commercials are examined by the network's Standards and Practices department. Scripts may be accepted, rejected, or sent back for a rewrite, depending upon the network's findings. Usually the advertising agency that handles the account for the advertiser first submits a storyboard of the proposed commercial to the network for review. The storyboard consists of a series of drawings with captions that resemble the film or video version of the commercial. By submitting the storyboard, advertisers and agencies can avoid the costly effort of reshooting material to conform to network objections: changes can easily be made on paper prior to shooting the commercial.

Decisions concerning the propriety of commercials can at times be arbitrary and even hypocritical. For example, previously, networks did not allow commercials that depicted live models presenting women's lingerie. However, at the same time, in their daytime soap operas and prime-time entertainment programs, the networks allowed a great deal of sexually suggestive material.

While birth control products had always been denied access to the airwaves, the Surgeon General's 1987 report recommending the use of condoms as a means for preventing the spread of AIDS brought pressure to bear on the networks, who now had a public health obligation in conflict with their traditional puritanical policies. In 1993 Fox Broadcasting was the first of the broadcast networks to initiate a policy of accepting condom advertising within the context of disease prevention, with no reference to its usefulness as a birth control method. In 1994, CBS, ABC, and NBC followed Fox's lead. Along with Fox, they agreed to donate television air time to broadcast condom ads sponsored by the Center for Disease Control. A total of six commercial spots were produced by the Ogilvy and Mather advertising agency. NBC and Fox broadcast all six without alterations. ABC added a qualifying tag line to two of the commercials, which read: "Abstinence is the safest, but if you do have sex, latex condoms can protect you." CBS broadcast all of the commercial spots except for one that featured an HIV-infected counselor and an 800 telephone number.

Substantiation

Substantiation of advertising claims is a sensitive issue for both advertisers and consumers. The public expects advertisements to be legitimate: the advertisers are concerned with presenting their products in the most favorable light possible. Quite often the purpose of the advertiser conflicts with the interests of the consumer. In 1971 the FTC adopted a resolution requiring advertisers to substantiate claims relating to product performance, quality, effectiveness, safety, and price. Claims by manufacturers need not be completely false to be judged as needing substantiation. If the advertisement has a tendency to deceive or mislead, that is enough to warrant closer scrutiny.

There are a number of actions the FTC can pursue in its effort to insure the integrity of advertisements. If an advertiser agrees to voluntarily discontinue a questionable advertising campaign, it may file an "assurance of voluntary compliance" with the FTC. Although this has no legal standing, it will satisfy the requirements of the FTC if it is honored by the party involved. When an advertiser clearly violates an FTC ruling, it may enter into a consent agreement with the commission. In a consent agreement, the parties negotiate a nonadjudicated settlement that is binding on the advertiser.

In adjudicated cases, an advertiser challenges the FTC complaints and the case is heard before a commission hearing examiner. The procedure is similar to that in a federal district court. Evidence is presented, witnesses are called, and oral arguments are heard. An administrative law judge files an opinion within ninety days after the hearing. The judge has the option of dismissing all or part of the charges, implementing a cease-and-desist order, or ordering a corrective advertising campaign.

The complexities involved in the determination of the validity of an advertisement are staggering. Claims must be examined and carefully reviewed. The slightest nuance in language may be sufficient to charge an advertiser with wrongdoing. Many advertising claims by the manufacturers of cold remedies, for example, can be deliberately vague and confusing to consumers. For years Dristan touted its "fever reducer," which was nothing more than aspirin, to a gullible public. Congespirin, which led the public to believe that its children's aspirin was a special product, was marketing a medicine that was merely a smaller dosage of aspirin. Sometimes it is not even what is said or written, but what is seen that is questionable. In 1956 the television advertisements for Rolaids featured an actor dressed in a white coat pitching the virtues of Rolaids. Although nothing was said about the medical community's approval of the product, the white coat was a subtle attempt to imply endorsement by that profession.

A product, however, does not need to have been sanctioned by the medical community in order to suggest medicinal value. A single word in the product's name may be sufficient to convince the public that a product has medical virtues. Such was the case of Carters Little Liver Pills, a product advertised in print and on radio and television for decades. The pills that Carters advertised had absolutely no effect upon the liver. Yet it took the FTC sixteen years of litigation to have the word "liver" removed from the product's name. In a similar case, the manufacturers of Geritol were ordered by the FTC to stop claiming that the product would cure "tired blood" due to iron deficiency. The case lingered in the courts for eleven years before it was finally settled in 1976 with the payment of a $125,000 fine by the J. B. Williams Company, a subsidiary of Nabisco. Geritol was then repositioned in the marketplace and given a more youthful orientation, making it even more successful than its "tired blood" predecessor.

In 1971 the FTC introduced a new idea: corrective advertising. If all the parties agreed, then the advertiser whose claims were considered specious could make amends by initiating an advertising campaign that would correct any misleading information that had previously been communicated to the public. The first company to use this technique was ITT's Continental Baking Company, makers of Profile bread. In their corrective commercial, the manufacturer explained that Profile bread was sliced thinner than other bread, and this is why it had "less calories per slice." The manufacturer did not admit to any wrongdoing and in fact implied that the audience had misunderstood the message of the original commercial. In another case the manufacturers of Ocean Spray Cranberry Juice agreed to run a corrective ad that explained a confusing term previously used in its advertising. In addition they agreed not to advertise their product as being nutritious, because the claims lacked merit.[8]

Health and nutrition claims made by television advertisers have become a particularly troublesome and vexing issue during the last decade. As an explosion of health consciousness gripped American consumers in the 1980s, manufacturers rushed to capitalize on the fitness craze by incorporating nutritional hype into their advertising campaigns. The carnival of claims made by advertisers concerning the virtues of oat bran, fiber, and other "healthful" diet supplements caused the FTC to launch a new initiative in the area of commercial health claims.

Policing the airwaves for false claims can be a daunting task. Fortunately, the competitive marketplace of a capitalistic society can provide self-regulatory oversight of suspect commercials. In *The Gillette Company v. Wilkinson Sword, Inc. and Friedman Benjamin, Inc.*, Gillette petitioned the U.S. District Court for an injunction against Wilkinson Sword. At issue were claims made by Wilkinson in their television commercials pertaining to Gillette's Atra Plus system. In its advertising, Wilkinson attempted to position its Ultra Glide razor as superior to Gillette's Atra Plus system by asserting that eight out of ten Atra Plus consumers would purchase Ultra Glide. Wilkinson also stated that the lubrication strips on the Gillette Atra Plus would "melt and become messy."

This case was adjudicated under the Lanham Act, which applies mostly to trademark infringements. There is, however, Section 43(a) of the act that addresses unfair competition caused by false or misleading advertising. The court agreed with Gillette that the claims made by

Wilkinson were deceptive and misleading, and enjoined Wilkinson to immediately desist from disseminating those claims.

Another part of the court's decision had more extensive implications. In assessing the scope of Wilkinson's liability, the court found that the advertising agency that had created the commercial, Friedman Benjamin, had knowingly participated in the creation and dissemination of a false advertising campaign. As a result the court found that the agency was also liable for the damages caused by the false advertising. This decision had a far-reaching impact on the advertising industry; agencies will be much more sensitive to the validity of product claims made by their clients if they are to be held liable in court.[9]

Another case involving two large gasoline distributors revealed how industry mediation can resolve advertising disputes. In 1994 Texaco began a $40 million advertising campaign for its new gasoline product, Clean System 3. Chevron spent $500,000 testing the Texaco product and found that Texaco's claims pertaining to "breakthrough technology" and "highest performance" were specious. It petitioned the three major television networks, and they consented to stop running some of the commercials. The National Advertising Division, a subsidiary of the Council of Better Business Bureaus, agreed to arbitrate the dispute, and Texaco submitted to its recommendations.

This case illustrates how the nuance of advertising language can mislead. In justifying its claims, Texaco noted that when it advertised "the highest performance," it meant "the highest performance the engine was designed to provide," not the highest performance of any gasoline. Similarly, its claim of "best mileage" according to Texaco meant "the best mileage an engine can achieve when it's clean." From this case, as well as others, it is apparent that consumers are in the difficult position of attempting to understand advertising language, which is deliberately vague and misleading.

Another area that the FTC has identified as potentially deceptive is the televised infomercial. The infomercial, introduced in 1985, quickly showed itself to be a valuable advertising tool. Disguised as an informative television program, the infomercial has a hidden agenda with a singular purpose: sales. Some of the products advertised in infomercials have included personal care products—such as remedies for male baldness, nutritional supplements like bee pollen, and curatives for male impotence. The infomercial projects a spurious air of authenticity by providing viewers with "scientific data," investigative reports, and celebrity endorsements, and presents a commercial message using the format of television talk shows.

To establish oversight for infomercials, the FTC chose a unique regulatory posture. Instead of prosecuting the manufacturers of the advertised product, the FTC pursued the production companies responsible for creating the infomercials. In a landmark decision, the FTC brought a case against Twin Star Productions of Scottsdale, Arizona, which had produced three thirty-minute infomercials hawking diet, impotency, and baldness cures. The FTC found that the product claims were false and unsubstantiated and that the thirty-minute programs were presented as regular programs and not as paid advertisements. Pursuant to its prosecution of Twin Star, the FTC established guidelines for infomercial production that include standards for the documentation of reliable scientific data and require disclosure for sales presentations lasting more than fifteen minutes clearly labelling the show as an advertisement.[10]

The FTC's tactic of going after the producer of the commercial instead of the product manufacturer has recently been expanded to include advertising agencies. In 1990 a toy manufacturer and its New York advertising agency were both cited for misleading television advertising and agreed to desist from making similar future claims.[11]

Substantiation of medical claims by infomercial producers, including on-camera endorsements by a medical professional, present another challenge to FTC oversight. In 1991 the FTC charged Synchronal Corporation, one of the largest infomercial producers, with making false and unconfirmed claims related to the Omexin system for hair growth, "a baldness remedy." The FTC disputed the claims made by a physician that this product was scientifically proven to stop hair loss and promote growth for a majority of balding men and women. In addition, Synchronal was charged with automatically shipping unordered merchandise to viewers without their consent.

While the FTC has been diligent in its efforts to govern the truthfulness of advertising claims, it has been less than successful in its attempt to provide oversight in the area of children's television advertising. Historically, children's television advertising has been an unregulated area in which advertisers can aggressively push their wares on the children of America. As one advertising executive pointed out, "when you sell a kid on your product, if he can't get it he will throw himself on the floor, stomp his feet and cry. You can't get a reaction like that out of an adult."[12]

Even such revered personalities as Captain Kangaroo were not above selling to the kiddies. In an early promotional photograph, Captain Kangaroo is seen kneeling and embracing two of his tiny fans while behind them we see boxes of Jets, Cheerios, and Trix cereals stacked in a commercial backdrop display.

Children's advertising has since become sophisticated and although program hosts are no longer used to sell products, various other sales techniques are employed quite successfully. Critics of children's television advertising have expressed their concerns about the effects of advertising on children. They argue that preschoolers don't have the sophistication necessary to understand the objective of commercials and, in their innocence, assume that commercials are part of the program. Most children are susceptible to the manipulative tools of television that include animation, bright colors, catchy music, and child actors. These elements are effective in transmitting commercial messages to youngsters.

Many in the advertising industry defend their right to produce such commercials: they claim that the advertisements are harmless and that they provide valuable information to the consumer. Unfortunately, some commercials can have a detrimental effect on children and their families. Medical practitioners, for example, are concerned about advertising that promotes candy and sugared cereals. In a country where 98 percent of the children suffer from tooth decay, commercials promoting the consumption of sweets are clearly undesirable.

High-fat foods advertised on children's television programs also create a dietary problem that is difficult for any parent to combat. Research has shown that 41 percent of the foods advertised on Saturday morning children's television programs contain one-third or more of their calories in fat. A viewing survey conducted in 1993 found that during fifteen hours of children's programming there were 423 commercials on the stations sampled: 47 percent were for foods, while 16 percent advertised toys. The food commercials broke down as: 38 percent cereals, 38 percent fast food chains, and the remainder taken up by cookies, candy, and high-fat snack products.

While regulatory efforts have been somewhat successful in tempering the excesses of the broadcast industry and protecting children's welfare, much more must be done to create a healthier television environment for children. Some critics argue that neither government nor industry should take the role of monitor and that parents should assume that role. Yet most parents have neither the sophistication nor the inclination to monitor the viewing habits of their children. (And those who do may not have the time or the ability to control it.) Many parents today were raised in homes with television where little effort was made to control their viewing habits. Unfortunately, in many homes television was an ever present entity surrounding the family from early morning to late evening and interrupting the normal flow of family interaction.[13] Many parents, having been television "abusers" themselves, simply fail to recognize the harmful effects television can have on their children. Therefore it is necessary to have policies and legislation that protect the interests of the child television viewer.

Parents have at times banded together and assumed an aggressive posture toward advertisers by announcing boycotts of products and programs deemed unsuitable for children. Terry Rakolta, a Michigan housewife, became a national celebrity in 1989 when she complained about the sexual innuendos that were a regular part of Fox Television's series *Married . . . with Children*. Protests like Rakolta's have led important national advertisers like Coca-Cola, McDonald's, General Mills, Campbell Soup, Ralston-Purina, and Sears to cancel advertisements during programs that viewers find objectionable.[14]

MERGERS AND ACQUISITIONS

While the early development of American advertising and the agency system was the product of ambitious individuals and their entrepreneurial efforts, the industry has recently assumed a different profile more in consonance with modern business trends. The 1980s proved to be a definitive decade for the merger of advertising agencies: vast holding companies that offered access to an abundant talent pool, enormous financial resources, and an impressive array of clients were created. These agencies created advertising campaigns that were the envy of the world, with innovative production techniques, creative scripts, catchy slogans, and lively jingles.

One of the first mergers to shake the foundations of the advertising industry was the combination of three of America's largest and most successful shops. In 1986, Batten, Barton, Durstine, and Osborne (BBDO), an agency that was founded in 1891, announced that it would merge with Doyle, Dane, Bernbach (founded 1949) and Needham, Harper, Steers (founded 1965) to create a holding company with a multinational scope. The new agency had a combined workforce of 10,221 and annual billings of $5 billion.

During the 1980s there were more than forty agency mergers, creating an environment of consolidation that completely changed the character of the advertising industry. The rationale for this trend toward consolidation has been based upon a view of the industry as serving a worldwide market with the opportunity to extend the traditional boundaries of the business far beyond American borders.

One acquisition that reflected the move toward the development of an international market was the 1986 $450 million purchase of Ted Bates agency, an icon of American advertising, by Saatchi and Saatchi of London, creating one of the world's largest advertising agencies. As a result of this agency consolidation, Saatchi and Saatchi was provided with a firm foothold in the American marketplace, enhancing its international presence in over sixty-five countries.[15]

The French are also aggressive acquisition artists in the American advertising arena. In 1990, the BDDP Group (Boulet, Dru, Dupuy, Petit), one of France's most successful advertising agencies, became a large minority investor in Wells, Rich and Greene. This American agency has a distinguished client list including companies like IBM, Procter & Gamble, and Hertz, which have global business interests. And this was not the first French incursion into American advertising: in 1988 the French company Publicis and the American agency Foote, Cone and Belding, (now known as True North Communications) traded equity shares, creating one of the top five largest advertising agencies in the world.[16] The alliance became strained, however, when in 1995, Publicis petitioned the Securities and Exchange Commission with a list of grievances charged to True North Communications.

The JWT Group's acquisition by yet another British company was the showstopper agency buyout of 1987. The initial attempt to acquire the 123-year-old J. Walter Thompson Agency by the WPP Group, a London-based marketing services company that was one-eighteenth the size of the JWT Group, was met with hostility and suspicion. JWT, which had revenues of $649 million in 1986, was a paragon of American business and a highly respected ad agency. Initially the move by the British company was viewed as a hostile takeover; however, after lengthy deliberations and written assurances, the purchase was consummated for $566 million, or $50.50 a share. Included in the acquisition were the JWT subsidiaries Hill and Knowlton, a public relations firm, and Lord, Geller, Federico and Einstein, a blue chip ad agency.

In 1989, Martin Sorrell, the head of the WPP Group, created another flurry when he announced a hostile bid of $45 a share for the Ogilvy Group Inc., parent company of Ogilvy and Mather, one of America's most venerable advertising agencies. Sorrell had been a key player while working for Saatchi and Saatchi and is credited with laying the foundations for Saatchi's acquisition strategy. In May 1989, Sorrell closed the $864 million deal to acquire the Ogilvy Group, thus placing himself within reach of his former employers, the Saatchi brothers, and creating the world's second largest advertising agency. In 1990 the WPP Group eclipsed Saatchi and Saatchi and became the world's biggest marketing communications company, followed by Interpublic Group and Omnicom.

The foundation of any agency is the clients it serves. Many agencies provide exclusive service to their clients and protect good accounts by not serving competitors. Agency clients have come to expect the exclusive nature of this arrangement, and both parties seem to respect its implications. A problem may arise, however, when a merger produces competing agency clients both served by the newly formed agency. Most often these conflicts are resolved by the resignation of one of the clients.

Agency mergers have also raised concerns about the trend toward the consolidation of American business. Critics argue that the immense resources of the huge mega-agency will effectively freeze out smaller

Betsy Frank, executive vice president at Zenith Media Services. Courtesy of Betsy Frank.

companies, making it more difficult for independent entrepreneurs to succeed. Indeed, as we approach merchandising on a global scale, agencies like the WPP Group, Interpublic, and Omnicom will become the norm rather than the exception.[17]

There are, however, those in advertising who are willing to buck the trend of large agencies by streamlining and specializing their services. This has led to the development of "boutique shops" that focus on the creative aspect of advertising, eliminating the overhead for research and media buying by not providing those services. Although small, these agencies have put a unique spin on some advertising campaigns with their creative writing and imagery.

Part of a large multiservice agency's responsibility is to provide advice to clients on the suitability of buying time on a particular network and television program. To that end, some advertising executives have become "programming gurus," predicting the success or failure of new programs on a network's schedule. One of the most visible and outspoken advertising executives is Betsy Frank, former executive vice president of Saatchi and Saatchi.[18] Frank headed a twenty-person staff in charge of media buying and supervised the spending of hundreds of millions of dollars of clients' money. During the month of June 1994, Frank, along with her colleagues at other agencies, purchased up to 75 percent of the air time for their clients, during what is known as the up-front period. For example, in June 1994, advertising agencies collectively spent $4 billion in less than ten days. By acting before the season begins, Frank receives deep discounts for purchasing advertising time on programs whose success or failure has yet to be determined. Her public pronouncements on a new program's likelihood of success or failure are uncannily accurate. Naturally network programming executives bristle when Frank identifies one of their new programs as a potential failure. Indeed, some have accused her of deliberately criticizing shows in an effort to negotiate better deals for her clients. None of the network executives, however, wants to admit that an advertising agency executive may have better programming instincts than they do.

The most formidable challenge to television advertisers in 1991 was how to present their messages in the context of war news. During the first days of the Persian Gulf conflict, the three networks and CNN either eliminated or drastically cut advertising time in order to cover late-breaking developments in the Gulf. Advertisers, notoriously concerned about their public image, feared that their messages would not fare well sandwiched in between the horror and tragedy of war.

Some companies did maintain television advertising during the Persian Gulf War. Of those that stayed the course, some simply maintained their commercial messages without changes: others assumed a patriotic posture in their television advertisements.

Several days after the conflict began, the networks returned to a seminormal schedule, with program preemptions as the exception rather than the rule. The networks hoped to lure advertisers back to news as well as entertainment and to recoup revenues lost during the start of television coverage. The daily advertising income generated by ABC, CBS, and NBC averages approximately $26 million. During the first twenty-four hours of the war, preemptions may have cost the networks close to $15 million.

As the war continued, networks, ad agencies, and trade organizations worked together to persuade advertisers that running commercials during a war was not distasteful. CBS, the Television Bureau of Advertising, and the Network Television Association all publicized research data that basically concluded that viewers did not find commercials offensive during war coverage.[19]

BROADCAST MARKET RESEARCH

An important component of the relationship between advertiser and broadcaster is market research. The television audience is one of the most scrutinized populations in the country. Broadcasters need to know what kind of people are watching their programs so that they can describe them to advertisers. Advertisers are especially interested in audience demographics so that they can choose the most effective programming vehicle to deliver their messages to their targeted audiences. The reason that televised sporting events are sponsored by beer and shaving cream companies is that most of the audience is male. It would be foolish to place advertisements appealing to women in these programs unless they are positioned so as to convince men that they should buy the product for a woman.

The number of broadcast households tuned to a particular program is an important factor in the success or failure of the program. Audience volume is measured by a standard developed by the broadcast industry and known as "ratings." In the early days of radio several attempts were made to define the extent of radio listening and ownership via costly, time-consuming interviews. Another way to determine the size of the radio audience was by measuring the volume of fan mail for radio stars. Neither of these methods was very accurate, and the Association of National Advertisers (ANA) was concerned about the inadequate data available to advertisers when they expressed interest in buying time on radio.

The need to establish a systematic approach to audience data collection was prompted by the needs of two major corporate advertisers in the early days of radio. The Davis Baking Powder Company wanted to find out how many stations in the network in which it bought advertising time actually carried its show, and Eastman Kodak wanted to learn the percentage of families with radios that heard its program. Both companies turned to Archibald M. Crossley, the man who developed the first rating system for network broadcasting. Started in 1929 and called the Cooperative Analysis of Broadcasting (CAB), the service used the telephone to identify listeners of CBS or NBC radio programs: potential listeners were called the morning after a broadcast and asked if they had heard it. This method, of course, relied heavily upon the accurate recall of the interviewee, as well as the interviewer's ability to reach the listener.

In 1934 another broadcast rating service was established. Clark-Hooper Inc. began by selling advertisers audience data concerning magazines and radio. Hooper was the first broadcast rating service to use a national "coincidental" telephone method of collecting listener information, which involves the calling of radio listeners as they are engaged in hearing a radio program. The Hooper methodology was considered more accurate than the CAB system because it did not rely upon listener recall. Hooper's service was very successful; it became known as the Hooper ratings, and networks and advertisers soon embraced it as a decision-making tool. Eventually, the Hooper organization was assimilated by the A. C. Nielsen Company.

The most familiar broadcast research firm, A. C. Nielsen, introduced a novel electronic audience data collection device in 1942. Known as the Audimeter, the device was connected to a radio receiver and automatically recorded whether a set was on and which channel it was tuned to. Although the Audimeter was not the major measuring device used in radio, Nielsen's methodology became the standard for television audience measurement and was for almost four decades the undisputed authority in television ratings.

Arthur Charles Nielsen was an electrical engineer with keen accounting skills. Shortly after graduating from the University of Wisconsin, Nielsen discerned a need to generate sales data for consumer goods manufacturers. During the Depression, he used customer interviews to track retail sales of grocery and drugstore products. He soon realized, however, that the customer interview did not accurately reflect retail sales, so he switched to another method: analysis of merchant ledgers and receipts. In 1936 Nielsen purchased the rights to the Audimeter, a device developed by an MIT professor that mechanically kept a record of programs received on the radio. By 1950, Nielsen had adapted his Audimeter technology to television.

The Nielsen ratings methodology was based upon statistical sampling techniques, reports from households using audimeters, and diary entries made by viewers in the households sampled. The audience data compiled by Nielsen was summarized in three reports: the Nielsen Television Index (NTI), the Nielsen Station Index (NSI), and the National Audience Composition (NAC). The NTI used a sample of approximately seventeen hundred television homes to estimate the viewing patterns of the households in the television population at large. The results were then used to predict the national audience for various network television programs. The NSI report measured about 220 television markets three times a year—in November, February, and May "sweep" periods—and analyzed the responses made in ninety thousand diaries. Nielsen oversampled the market to factor in the percentage of diaries not returned or incorrectly filled out. The NAC survey was started by Nielsen in 1954 to provide additional demographic data not available through the audimeter.

While other companies like Arbitron, Pulse, and Trendex also provide audience data, the Nielsen Rating Service has remained the most prominent television research company. Over the years, however, a number of criticisms concerning Nielsen's research methodology—concerning sampling error, demographics, measuring techniques, and household bias—have been raised.

In order for Nielsen to accurately project the nation's television viewing habits from a sample of several thousand families, it is essential that they include representative households from all the various demographic groups within the entire population. Some critics have argued that the Nielsen sample is skewed in favor of the middle class and neglects the poor and wealthy. Indeed, in 1962 Congress held an investigation into the Nielsen households and found that minorities and some income groups were underrepresented, and some families had remained in the sample too long to be considered statistically valid. The Harris Committee, a congressional committee empaneled to investigate research abuses in ratings methodology, issued a report in 1966, making a number of recommendations concerning the professionalism and controls necessary to improve the viability of audience research. In response to these findings, Nielsen reconfigured its sample to become more representative of the population and instituted a mandatory turnover rate of 20 percent a year, which would mean that at the end of a five-year cycle, the entire sample would have been replaced. In addition, it was deemed necessary for the sample in the NAC panel to be replaced every three years.

Another component that compromises the value of the Nielsen sample is the manner in which its households are selected. Nielsen's primary source of household information is the U.S. Bureau of Census records. These records provide the most comprehensive data about households in America, but they may undercount certain populations, such as non-English-speaking and single-parent households. In an effort to address the problem of inadequate ethnic inclusion in audience measurement, Nielsen and other ratings organizations have tried a number of techniques to insure cooperation by minorities. These include allowing Spanish-language diaries and hiring Spanish-speaking field workers, special mailings directed at non-English speakers, added incentives, and midweek interview calls on minority households. Nielsen also tried defining hard-core poverty areas as separate geographical cells and weighting diaries returned from African-American households.

The research design of both the Nielsen Station Index and the Nielsen Television Index present other flaws that can cause sampling error. In the Station Index, diaries must be completed to reflect quarterly-hour viewing, even though television viewing patterns do not conform to this pattern. This methodology also fails to address the "grazing" or "surfing" phenomenon—the frequent switching of stations via remote control tuning.

Diary entries made by participants are also subject to a high degree of error because of the level of functional illiteracy that exists among certain segments of the population. Consequently, the targeted population must be oversampled to adjust for the high percentage of unusable diaries (54 percent).[20] Another factor that may affect the reliability of the data is the truthfulness of the viewer: some participants may deliberately falsify their reports in order to make it appear that they watch more sophisticated programs than they really do.

The most glaring structural flaw in the methodology of the Nielsen Television Index was the use of a passive electronic measuring device. Nielsen used the Audimeter to electronically record the time of day, channel, and length of viewing in selected households. Initially, Audimeters had a mechanical design and used a 16-mm film cartridge and a beam of light that recorded viewing patterns and cumulative set usage onto the film cartridge. Over the years Audimeter design evolved as new developments in electronic technology became available.

The weakness in the Audimeter method was that the device recorded when the television set was turned on, but it could not count the number of people viewing or even ascertain whether or not anyone was watching at all. To help bolster data collected by the Audimeter, Nielsen asked subjects in sample households to complete diaries whose entries theoretically would correspond to Audimeter surveys. However, respondents may have felt an obligation to keep the television set on even when they were not viewing and falsify diary entries to match the information on the meter.

Nielsen and other rating companies take extraordinary precautions to secure the integrity of their measurements. The identity of Nielsen families is kept strictly confidential, although there have been attempts to compromise their security. One of the most notable of these occurred in 1966, when a former congressional staff investigator, who had been involved in the Harris Committee ratings investigation, tried to manipulate the data for a particular network television program. Through surreptitious means, he acquired the identities of fifty-eight Nielsen households and contacted the producer of the network evening program *An Evening with Carol Channing* in an effort to manipulate the ratings for that time period. Nielsen's security department discovered the plot, excluded those homes from its sample for the evening, and prosecuted the staffer. While this was not the only attempt to break through Nielsen's security system and alter ratings, none have ever been successful in breaching the validity of Nielsen's measurements.

People Meters: Fact or Fantasy

As the competitive landscape for distribution technologies became more complex with the emergence of cable television, VCRs, and pay-per-view programming, the television industry became increasingly dissatisfied with the Nielsen methodology. The People Meter is similar to the Audimeter in design: it differs in the method of data collection. Unlike the Audimeter, People Meters are active measuring devices that rely upon participatory responses by the subject. The participant is required to hold a microprocessing terminal, similar to a calculator, and press various buttons corresponding to coded reactions while he is actually viewing a program. This methodology generates both quantitative and qualitative data, including the respondent's opinion of the program being watched. Nielsen had experimented with "People Meters" in 1974, when it held trials of the new technology in Tampa, Florida. But the company failed to implement a People Meter national sample until 1983, when it was forced to by the appearance of a competitor.

In 1987 Audience of Great Britain (AGB) introduced its People Meter rating technology in the United States. Having successfully used People Meters in Great Britain, the company was encouraged by America's broadcasting industry to enter the U.S. market. Nielsen quickly followed suit and after huge operating losses, AGB eventually abandoned the American television ratings marketplace.

From the moment it was introduced, the People Meter created a great deal of controversy and debate among scholars, industry professionals, and advertisers. First of all, almost immediately the People Meter measured a sharp decline (9 percent) in the three-network share of audience. This of course created a vigorous protest from network representatives, who could translate the decline into millions of dollars of lost advertising revenue. The People Meters numbers also revealed a significant drop in the viewing patterns of men and women of certain age groups but did not show a decline in the total television audience. Audience data generated by Nielsen's People Meter methodology also proved to be inconsistent with audience figures pertaining to local television markets.

As questions about the People Meter continued and the network broadcast audience reported by People Meter homes plunged, the industry closely examined Nielsen's research design. The advertising and broadcasting industries questioned the accuracy of Nielsen's sample design of 4,093 homes, which is supposed to reflect the viewing habits of millions of television households. Critics also cited viewer fatigue as a variable that could produce a bias in the ratings. Since the People Meter relies upon viewer participation, these critics contended, viewer fatigue, carelessness, or just plain boredom might affect the results by undercounting the audience. In addition critics of the technology argue that People Meters undercount viewing by children because children are less likely to punch in their responses on the handheld computer console.

The networks responded to the Nielsen findings by placing their own spin on the figures and working together to coordinate damage control. NBC took the lead by announcing that it would address the decline in people using television (PUT) numbers by integrating their findings into audience viewing trends established over the past eight years. The advertising community looked with disdain on the network plan, claimed they were simply rearranging the numbers to suit their needs, and diverted up to $200 million into advertising in other media. Responding to a precipitous loss in revenue, in 1991 the three networks announced that they would abandon their audience averaging plan and return to the traditional audience measurement system.

As the television and advertising industries attempt to adjust to the People Meter and the deviation it reports in audience trends, critics continue to raise serious questions about the technology and its methodology. Industry critics have charged that Nielsen's People Meter technology may have been introduced too hastily: however, the company denies any fault with its operational design.

Other problems found with the design of the People Meter technology include the undercounting of visiting and vacationing families, especially during the summer months. A 1990 study conducted by Bruskin Associates for ABC discovered that 62 million adults on vacation were not being counted, at a cost to the networks of between $90 and 180 million. A related study conducted by Statistical Research found that Nielsen underrepresented viewing in other people's homes by 52 percent, and also pointed out the substantial viewing in bars, hotels, and other public places that does not show up in the Nielsen numbers.[21]

In response to industry concerns about the reliability of the People Meter data, Nielsen is considering diversifying its research design so that the People Meter would be used along with other audience measuring methodologies. These concerns also led Nielsen toward the development of a passive people meter system. In June 1989, Nielsen Media Research announced a joint effort with the David Sarnoff Research Center at Princeton to develop a passive television measurement device that would use an image recognition sensor to scan the facial features of family members watching television. This system's sophistication would even enable it to note when a viewer's eyes are averted or turned away from the television screen. With the aid of a small computer and a camera, the "smart sensing" system would store the facial features of family members and record their viewing habits, while ignoring those of outside viewers identified as guests.[22] Many concerns have already been raised about issues of privacy in connection with the use of this device.

Another effort to connect actual behavior with television viewing habits was announced in 1991 by Arbitron, a Nielsen competitor, and its Scan America ratings service. The Arbitron methodology attempted to measure the correlation between product purchases and the viewing of television commercials by the buyer. Arbitron used People Meter technology in their sample homes and also provided households in the sample with a scanning wand to record the Universal Product Code (UPCs) from goods purchased. By using this methodology, Aribtron hoped to provide an integrated approach to data collection and behavior.

However, competition from the Nielsen People Meter Service and the expenses associated with implementation of the Scan America operation eventually forced Arbitron to discontinue it. In 1994 Arbitron returned to household audience surveys when it began testing its local motion qualitative television measurement service in Montgomery, Alabama, and Fort Wayne, Indiana.

Clearly the television industry is not at all satisfied with Nielsen's People Meter methodology. In 1994 the three major networks underwrote a three-year, $30 million effort for an alternative rating system. They commissioned Statistical Research Inc., a respected marketing firm, to conduct the study.[23] With advertising revenues reaching into the billions of dollars (the 1993 combined three-network revenue was $7.86 billion), the need to have a reliable research audience methodology becomes critical for the industry.[24] More than one exasperated network executive has surely felt that the spending of billions of dollars based on the research from such a fragile system is, simply put, insane.

Television advertising is in a dynamic state of flux, responding to a myriad of variables, from geopolitical realignments to revolutionary technological advances. As the world moves toward a global economy, television advertising will assume greater visibility as a disseminator of information. Advertisers will design their advertising campaigns to reflect more universal themes and will require greater visual sophistication in the merchandising of their products and services. As advertisers embrace the changing televisual environment, their need for accurate measurement of audience behavior is becoming an essential factor in the determination of marketing trends and viewing habits. The television industry's ability to provide both interactive and passive audience measurements will furnish advertisers with important comprehensive data; no doubt it will also generate debate concerning its encroaching intrusion into households and the potential compromising of individual privacy. Indeed, as we evolve into members of McLuhan's "global village," the essence of his axiom "the medium is the message" will take on new meaning in the advertising marketplace.

NOTES

1. Jackson's viability as a celebrity endorser was further compromised by anti-Semitic lyrics featured in his 1995 two-disk compilation album, *History*. Jackson yielded to the critics and rerecorded the offensive segments.
2. Joanne Lipman, "FTC Is Cracking Down on Misleading Ads," *Wall Street Journal*, February 4, 1991, B6.

3. The Chrysler Corporation is one of the most active of the automobile companies in courting African-American and minority buyers. In 1995 Chrysler underwrote the presentation of *Hoop Dreams* on the Public Broadcasting Service.

4. The ultimate "product placement" on regularly scheduled prime-time network series programming occurred on February 26, 1996, when CBS featured Elizabeth Taylor in four back-to-back sitcoms. Taylor was starring to promote her Black Pearls perfume by Elizabeth Arden. The four sitcoms were *The Nanny, Can't Hurry Love, Murphy Brown,* and *High Society.*

5. In 1994 there were 731 advertisers and 3,303 brands that appeared on network television. On spot television there were 2089 advertisers and 11, 945 brands. The 15-second commercial accounted for 30.2 percent of all network activity, and the 30-second commercial for 65.6 percent of network use. Off network, the 30-second commercial represented 84.3 percent of non-network activity.

6. Nonprogram material includes production credits, public service announcements, promotional segments, and product commercials, which account for the bulk of time allocated to nonprogram material. In 1994, Fox Broadcasting led the pack with twelve minutes, three seconds per hour. CBS followed with eleven minutes, six seconds, NBC with eleven minutes, and ABC was the lowest, with ten minutes and sixteen seconds. All represented an increase over previous figures except for Fox, which declined by twenty seconds.

7. Another means to controlling commercial clutter is the use of "sectionals." This procedure splits a nationally broadcast commercial into different versions for different parts of the country. Local stations have been critical of this technique because of the potential loss of revenue that it poses. In 1994 McDonalds Corp. moved approximately $100 million of its advertising budget out of local stations and into network "sectionals."

8. The confusing term was "food energy." In their correction, Ocean Spray explained that "food energy" meant calories, not vitamins and minerals.

9. Christopher D'Orta, "Advertising Agencies Face Stricter Scrutiny for Their Ads," *Media Law and Policy,* vol. II, no. 1, Spring 1993, 10.

10. Joanne Lipman, "'Infomercial Makers Try to Clean up Act," *Wall Street Journal,* March 4, 1991, B3.

11. Joanne Lipman, "FTC Is Cracking Down on Misleading Ads," *Wall Street Journal,* February 4, 1991, B6.

12. Erik Barnouw, *The Sponsor: Notes on a Modern Potentate,* (New York: Oxford University Press, 1978), 93.

13. In 1994 a typical U. S. household viewed seven hours, sixteen minutes of television per day.

14. The Harlan Page Hubbard Lemon Awards presented by the Center for Science in the Public Interest publicize misleading claims by advertisers.

15. In 1995, Saatchi and Saatchi changed its name to Cordiant P.L.C., after Maurice and Charles Saatchi left to form a new advertising agency, M. & C. Saatchi.

16. In 1996 True North agreed to acquire Bayer, Bess Vanderwarker, a Chicago agency. Also in 1996, Marcel Bleustein-Blanchet, who founded Publicis as a teenager in 1926 and eventually became its Chairman, died at the age of 89.

17. In 1996 the Omnicom Group acquired Ketchum Communications, the 25th-largest American agency with more than $1 billion in billings. In 1995

Omnicom purchased Ross Roy Communications and Chiat/Day.

18. Frank is now executive vice president and director of strategic media services at Zenith Media Services.

19. Thomas R. King, "Agencies Scramble to Prove Ads Aren't Hurt by TV War Coverage," *Wall Street Journal*, February 21, 1991, B7.

20. Nielsen Media Research expanded local market diary samples by 15 percent in the Fall of 1996. Nielsen hopes to expand its local market diary base by 50 percent (one million diaries) from 1996 to 1998.

21. A 1995 study conducted by Nielsen Media Research revealed that each week 23 million adults watch an average of five-and-a-half hours of television in out-of-home locations.

22. In August 1995, Nielsen Media Research initiated a service measuring usage on the Internet's World Wide Web, thus providing legitimacy to using the Internet as a commercially viable medium. However, Professor Donna L. Hoffman of Vanderbilt University challenged Nielsen's findings, claiming their estimates on World Wide Web usage was too high.

23. Frustration with the lack of consistency in Nielsen's ratings led NBC Television Network President Neil Braun to announce in early 1996 an arrangement with Statistical Research Inc. to produce a business plan for a measurement system providing an alternative to Nielsen Media Research. In 1996, CBS announced that KDKA-TV, its owned-and-operated station in Pittsburgh, was being dropped from Nielsen Media Research coverage. At the heart of the dispute was the use of contests to manipulate the ratings.

24. Total advertising volume in 1994 was $150 billion, with television accounting for 22.8 percent of the total.

8
Technology and Change

Miniaturization, laser technology, rocket mobility, and portability—these technological advances have made ordinary Americans into operative technocrats. With our cellular telephones, portable CD players, and notebook computers, we are becoming an extended electronic "family." As a result of recent technological developments, many individuals have more control over their work and home environments than ever before. Technology has changed leisure time patterns and created new industries while permanently altering the structure of traditional media. It has also raised complicated issues of privacy and access and has upset the equilibrium of public policy and government regulations concerning communications. Indeed, the rapid pace of technological development has created new gray areas of regulation and enforcement that are continually rendered obsolete by further developments. Therefore any discussion of communications technology must deal not only with the "nuts and bolts" of technological advances but also with the attendant social implications.

ELECTRONIC ROOTS

While one could choose any one of a number of historical junctures at which to begin a discussion of the development of modern communication technologies, for the purposes of this discussion we will start with the introduction of communication by wire, or the telegraph. Samuel F. B. Morse is recognized as the inventor of the telegraph, in 1844. Morse perfected a system for recording intermittent electronic signals coded to the letters of the alphabet. The telegraph was an important development because it created a precedent for the use of electrical energy to transmit information. In fact, some of the techniques developed by Morse for the telegraph are still employed in facsimile data transmissions—more commonly known as fax machines.

As America progressed from a rural into an industrial society, the need for more effective point-to-point communication became paramount. Voice communication by wire was the next frontier, and it was Alexander Graham Bell who, in 1876, filed the first telephone patent. The telephone was the precursor of all modern communication technologies because it demonstrated the technique of electronic modulation and applied voice transmission over long distances with a minimum of interference and degradation in the quality of the sound.[1]

Both the telegraph and the telephone were significant technological achievements because they made it possible to communicate speech and writing through modern electronic technology. It is important to note that each new technological advancement has been built upon a predecessor that has been incorporated into the new technology. For example, when Marconi began experimenting with wireless telegraphy in 1897, he adapted telegraphic receiving equipment to record wireless messages, creating the technology needed for radio. Indeed, while a number of scientists and inventors were experimenting with wireless telegraphy, it was Marconi's genius and shrewd business acumen that led to the popularization of the fledgling technology and its use in a new medium.

Although Marconi never transmitted the human voice over his wireless, he did demonstrate the feasibility of broadcasting wireless signals over long distances. The next step was voice transmission. Reginald Fessenden, using a G. E.-designed high-speed alternating current generator, was the first to send voice and music by "wireless" (radio) from Brant Rock, Massachusetts, on Christmas Eve 1906. Another important development in the evolution of radio and television was the invention of the vacuum tube. Thomas Edison and Ambrose Fleming contributed to the refinement of this tube, but it was Lee DeForest who perfected the vacuum tube for use as an amplifier, called an Audion tube, in 1912.

Television's prehistory includes the discovery by Joseph May and Willoughby Smith in 1873 that the element selenium could produce small amounts of electricity in response to the amount of light falling on it. The next crucial development, scanning, was discovered by French scientist Maurice Leblanc in 1880. Then, in 1883, Paul Nipkow of Germany invented the first scanning disk that was the basis for all mechanical television disk-scanning systems.

Working for Bell Telephone Laboratories in the 1920s, Herbert E. Ives was able to transmit still and moving pictures over telephone lines. John

Logie Baird, an Englishman, conducted the first public demonstration of television in London in 1926. In 1928, Baird televised the image of a woman, using shortwave, from London to Hartsdale, New York. In the United States, Charles Francis Jenkins transmitted both still and moving pictures by wireless during various experiments from 1923 to 1925.

The two individuals who invented and helped to implement an all-electronic design for television were a Russian emigré working for RCA, Vladimir K. Zworykin, with his iconoscope camera tube, and a young inventor from Rigby, Idaho, Philo T. Farnsworth, whose high school notes later became important evidence in patent litigation. With the invention of the vacuum tube and the iconoscope camera tube, the age of modern communications had begun.

Of all the electronic technological innovations, television has probably had the greatest impact upon American society. It has provided information, entertainment, comfort, and company to millions of Americans while becoming the first piece of "high-tech" equipment in almost all American homes. It has changed the life-styles and leisure time patterns for millions of American households. In doing so, it also affected other media, radio, and film, at times decreasing their popularity.

As Americans watched the flickering phosphorescent images on their television sets, they became aware of the world of new technology now available to them—electric toasters, washing machines, electric coffee pots, automobiles. Industry responded by manufacturing attractive merchandise at competitive prices. The age of conspicuous consumption began, and manufacturers rushed to answer the demand.

As American audiences were settling in with their television sets, scientists, corporate America, and the military were working together and aspiring to even greater technological heights. Bell Labs developed the transistor in 1948, introducing solid-state technology and miniaturization to the field of electronics. Meanwhile, computer technology was developed at the University of Pennsylvania, while the army worked on rocket technology, assisted by the German scientists who had pioneered rocket design.

In the 1950s new technological developments created two great breakthroughs for industry and consumerism: the satellite and the transistor radio.

SATELLITES

Although the Soviet Union was the first to successfully launch a satellite—Sputnik, in 1956—the United States quickly responded by developing a sophisticated space program based upon scientific achievements in both the private and public sectors. The first generation of satellites were passive: that is, they served as reflectors for signals from earth. In 1960 the United States launched its first active satellite: this satellite had the ability to transmit signals from one earth station to another.

Before 1963, satellites were put into fast-moving, low elliptical orbit. These satellites required close monitoring, and even with sophisticated tracking their low elliptical orbit would cause them to disappear from sight for long periods of time. In 1963 this problem was resolved with the launching of the first geosynchronous satellite 22,300 miles above the earth, which travelled at a speed of 6,875 miles per hour. At this distance and speed, the satellite's orbit is in phase with the earth's rotation: it takes twenty-four hours to circle the globe and remains in line of sight for signal reception.

Both regulatory and technological developments led to the stimulation and growth of the satellite industry. In 1972 the FCC announced an "open sky" policy, which liberalized satellite regulation and encouraged development by the private sector. Rocket design improved, allowing for the launching of heavier, more powerful, and more efficient satellites that could transmit signals more directly to smaller receiving antennas.

Satellites became the industry buzzword of the 1970s and 1980s. The new technology was embraced by both cable operators and broadcasters. For the cable television industry, the liberalized regulatory climate and technological accessibility meant a renewed vitalization of a stagnating marketplace. Satellites provided cable operators with a networking facility for the distribution of pay and basic cable television programming services. Interfacing with cable, satellites created alternative networks and established national distribution patterns for what were previously local television stations. Although broadcasters have used satellite technology for their international news coverage, their network communications have traditionally been via AT&T telephone long-distance lines. More recently, however, the networks have used satellites for program distribution and regional feeds.

As satellite transmission technology improved and components decreased in cost, the technology became more accessible to consumers. For an investment of a couple of thousand dollars, individuals could build their own satellite earth stations. This would allow them to receive signals directly from designated satellites. Another new development was the creation of direct broadcast satellite (DBS) programming services. DBS program suppliers would install the necessary satellite technology in the subscriber's home and for a monthly fee provide programming via satellite. Although several companies entered the DBS market in the late 1980s and early 1990s, the reaction from consumers was lukewarm. Apparently the competition from cable, network television, and videocassettes was sufficient to make consumers skeptical about embracing one more programming delivery system.

In 1990 several companies announced a renewed commitment to the development of DBS technology. SkyCable, a joint partnership of NBC, Cablevision Systems Corporation, Rupert Murdoch's News Corporation, and Hughes Communications Inc., hoped to develop a 108-channel digital satellite transmission service that would be sent to homes equipped with small flat antennas. Each of the companies made a $75 million commitment to the project, which required $1 billion in start-up capital. As of this writing, however, SkyCable has not yet entered the domestic DBS marketplace.[2]

Not to be outdone by their rivals, in 1990 a group of cable television companies announced the formation of Primestar, another DBS programming delivery system. The principals partnered in Primestar include TCI, GE American Communications, Continental, Comcast, Cox Cable, Newhouse, and Time Warner. The company began national distribution in July 1991. Subscribers don't own the receiving equipment, but they do pay an installation charge of between $100 and $200. Monthly subscription fees for the Primestar DBS programming service range from $25 to $35 a month. Most recently Primestar petitioned the FCC for high-power DBS channels that would give it greater flexibility in programming and distribution.

One of the most ambitious DBS satellite ventures made its debut in 1994. DIRECTV Inc., a subsidiary of GM Hughes Electronics, is targeting approximately 3 percent of U.S. television homes and eventually hopes to have 10 million subscribers.[3] The company has invested $100 million in building the first fully digital broadcast facility in the United States: the Castle Rock Broadcast Center in Castle Rock, Colorado. Subscribers must purchase a $700 eighteen-inch home dish DBS satellite receiver: monthly subscription fees range from $21.95 to $29.95. United States Satellite Broadcasting, a pioneer in DBS satellite distribution, is also associated with the venture.

Presently, the domestic DBS industry is only a small part of the U.S. telecommunications marketplace. About 3.6 million households receive television programming using seven-to-ten-foot-wide C-band satellite receiving dishes. Of those 3.6 million households, 1.7 million of them have decoders to receive pay TV program services. Even with the competing technologies of fiber optics and cable television, DBS is poised for significant growth in the United States.

DBS programming services have been moderately successful, especially in rural areas not served by cable television. DBS technology has also been implemented in Europe, the United Kingdom, and Japan. Japan has the largest market, with approximately 2.5 million subscribers tuned into a two-channel DBS service. The DBS subscriber base in the United Kingdom is approaching 1 million, while in Germany and France the numbers are below 100,000.

Satellite technology has created a complex web of political, international, and industrial concerns. There are domestic satellites that are part of Comsat, the Communications Satellite Corporation that is a 50 percent public, 50 percent government agency. The Western Hemisphere has its own international satellite organization called Intelsat that owns and operates fifteen satellites worldwide and has 119 member countries, including the United States. Huge corporations like GTE, GE American, Hughes Communications, and AT&T also own and operate satellites. In 1988, a small private company, Pan American Satellite, (PanamSat) invested $85 million to launch the first privately owned satellite. Although the company had difficulty securing international landing rights because of its competition with Intelsat, more than seventy countries honored its request. Founded by Renee Anselmo, a flamboyant, shrewd entrepreneur, the company turned a $17 million profit in 1993 and announced an aggressive multimillion-dollar recapitalization plan to expand its satellite service to Asia, Africa, and the Indian Ocean. The satellite industry has also, as part of its component businesses, companies that subcontract or broker satellite time. These satellite brokers lease time in volume and resell it to users. A satellite brokerage company like Bright Star Communications Ltd., a London-based organization, leases time on Intelsat Satellites and resells it to customers. The Bright Star rate for a signal going from New York to London ranges from $1700 to $2250 per hour.

The Persian Gulf conflict illustrated the critical role of satellites in the communications process. Live television pictures of coalition forces bombing Baghdad offered viewers a dazzling display of "the War show." Instant images of the destruction in Iraq and Israel gave American viewers an intimate view of the horrors of war. Just as the United States-led coalition war machine was heralded for its high-tech arsenal, so too could the media be praised for its high-tech hardware, including portable satellite earth stations and compact satellite telephones. The satellites provided an electronic canvas on which television cameras painted a grand spectacle of personalities and events—an intimate portrait of power and submission.

As satellite technology has become more accessible to consumers, new questions about copyright liability have been raised. Earth station owners can easily aim their backyard dish antennas to receive signals from satellites distributing pay cable networks. In addition to theft of service by individuals, pay cable programmers like HBO have also been sidestepped by foreign countries who happily receive their programming without bearing the expense for it. Although the pay cable programmers have attempted regulatory redress, there is little they can do to thwart these modern day pirates through the courts. In 1986 the pay cable industry initiated an aggressive new technological assault on signal theft— they began a sophisticated program of scrambling signals that requires the interface of a highly specialized descrambler.

FIBER OPTICS

While some look toward the heavens for high-tech communications, others have sought to develop more sophisticated earthbound technology. For that they returned to the traditional concept of communication by wire but added new dimensions made possible by advances in twentieth-century electronics.

In the 1870s a British physicist, John Tyndall, first discovered that light can bend: and in the 1880s Alexander Graham Bell demonstrated that a light beam could carry voice signals. It was not until 1970, however, that this technology was applied, by Corning Glassworks, to signal transmission.

In fiber optics all electrical energy is converted into light via a laser (light amplification by simulated emission of radiation), or light-emitting diode. These concentrated beams of light travel through the glass fibers in straight lines or around curves and are less subject to fatigue and electrical interference than with copper cable. Digital applications of fiber optic cable can be realized by converting the light into pulses of equal intensity rather than a continuous beam of varying intensity. These pulses are analogous to the turning on and off of a flashlight, with each pulse being assigned a value — for example, "on" would equal one, "off," zero. In essence, all information is converted to a string of pulsating light, which is assigned numerical values. This is the same kind of code or language that a computer uses. One of the first applications of digital technology was in the music industry, when analog records and tapes were replaced by digital compact disks.

Fiber optic technology uses narrow glass fibers, each no larger than a strand of hair in diameter and each having the capacity to transmit over a hundred television signals or sixteen thousand telephone conversations. When the fibers are clustered into a cable, their signal capacity can reach into the thousands. These optical fibers do not use electrical current for transmission but instead rely upon light as the information carrier. The ability of light to bend makes fiber optic technology superior to other means of carrying information. And the speed and capacity of fiber optic cable makes it a most suitable tool for modern communications—the entire text of the Encyclopedia Britannica and the Bible can travel around the earth via fiber optic cable in less than two seconds!

At the present time there are approximately 4 million miles of fiber optic cable in the United States, and cost estimates for a nationwide fiber-based broadband network range upward of $250 billion. The high cost, however, has not deterred American companies from investing in and testing the technology. An important regulatory initiative that spurred investment in fiber optic technology was the implementation by the FCC of a "video dial tone" service. This ruling effectively allowed local telephone companies to establish broadband networks for delivering video, information, and telephone services. The decision also allowed long-distance telephone companies like AT&T, MCI, and Sprint, to enter the cable business. Prior to this ruling, a federal appeals court supported the right of the local Bell telephone companies to distribute information services. Telephone companies like New Jersey Bell (a Bell Atlantic company) viewed this decision as affirming their right to invest in the "new age" of information technology. They were one of the first of the regional Bell operating companies to announce a $1 billion plan to replace 56.3 million miles of copper wire with fiber optic cable for their 3.2 million customers.[4] One of the most comprehensive application models is being conducted by the GTE corporation in conjunction with the local cable operator in Cerritos, California. The test involves seven hundred households that are receiving both telephone and television signals over the same fiber optic line. Another application is being tested by Time Warner in its Queens, New York 150-channel Quantum System, which uses a combination of fiber optic lines and conventional cable.

OVER-THE-AIR DISTRIBUTION SYSTEMS

A number of other distribution systems are classified as "over-the-air" because they transmit microwave signals in a variety of different formats. These systems include subscription television (STV), multipoint multichannel distribution service (MMDS), instructional television fixed service (ITFS), and low power television (LPTV).

Subscription Television

STV provides subscription television service from a local station that scrambles its signals. Subscribers who pay a monthly fee for the service are equipped with specialized receiving equipment, including an antenna and descrambler. One company that pioneered in STV was Wometco Home Theater, which offered recently released movies over its channel. As cable television penetrated the marketplace, STV lost its hold on the market because it could not compete with the multichannel capacity and programming tiers that cable television offered its subscribers.

Multipoint Multichannel Distribution Service

MMDS, also known as wireless cable, is a more sophisticated version of STV. Using line-of-sight microwave frequencies, MMDS can offer in excess of four channels from a single transmitter to paying subscribers. The technology is not new; the concept of multiple channel subscription television was introduced by the Microband Corporation of America in the early 1980s. MMDS companies lease or buy microwave licenses from existing companies and use them for their pay television services. In some cases these frequencies might be licensed to school systems as instructional television fixed service (ITFS) frequencies and are then sublet to the MMDS provider.

Although one could not describe the MMDS industry as a burgeoning field, it is poised for growth in the 1990s. Indeed, telephone companies have embraced wireless technology as a transitional tool for their entry into the video distribution business. In 1995, regional Bell operating company Pacific Telesis purchased Cross County Wireless of Southern California for $175 million, while Bell Atlantic and Nynex invested $100 million in CAI Wireless Systems Inc., a Northeast wireless concern. These regional Bell operating companies plan to upgrade wireless service to digital capacity, thus expanding the number of channel options available to subscribers. By investing in wireless cable, the regional Bell operating companies can assure their position as "servers" on the information highway while upgrading their wired telephony to fiber optic capacity.

With lower subscriber costs—$600 per subscriber for wireless, as compared to $1,000 per subscriber for cable—wireless services could present stiff competition for cable operators in the same market.

Low Power Television

LPTV, a delivery system that was envisioned as a community-oriented service, has not fared as well as some of the other innovative over-the-air technologies. Low-power stations are licensed by the FCC to serve small areas with low transmission power that will not interfere with the signals of full power, over-the-air broadcast stations. In 1982, when the FCC first invited low-power applications, they were flooded with applicants, some from large corporations interested in creating low-power pay-television networks. In 1983 the FCC instituted a freeze on the granting of new LPTV applications. That freeze was lifted in the summer of 1987, when the FCC decided to award an additional 483 licenses.

LPTV operators face many of the same obstacles as other entertainment entrepreneurs: competition from mainstream broadcasting stations and other delivery systems, and the struggle to obtain programming for their stations. In an effort to address these problems, the LPTV industry created the Community Broadcasters Association, a trade organization, to assist them in coordinating their interests and lobbying activities. The association has organized the CBA Programming Cooperative to assist stations in acquiring programming that they could not individually afford.

While the industry is still in its infancy, its proponents are enthusiastic and optimistic about its future. Indeed, in several smaller communities in parts of Ohio and the Shenandoah Valley, the LPTV station is the only signal serving the area.

VIDEO TECHNOLOGY

Video Cassette Recorders

One programming delivery system that has had an astounding impact upon the entertainment industry and consumers is the videocassette recorder (VCR). Video technology was introduced in 1956 by the Ampex Corporation. However, it took twenty years for the technology to become widely available to the public.

Although the first half-inch VCR, the Beta Max, was not introduced by Sony until 1975, the company had pioneered the development of half-inch tape in the 1960s, with the introduction of the first low-cost, portable black-and-white television camera and recorder, the Sony Portapack, or Rover.

Initially the motion picture industry was not at all thrilled about the development of video technology: they were concerned about the impact that VCRs would have upon theatrical box office sales. In 1979 Universal City Studios, Walt Disney Productions, and other program production companies sued the Sony Corporation of America, claiming that VCR owners who taped movies from their television sets were assuming copyright liability for those recordings.[5]

The trial court ruled in favor of Sony, but the decision was later reversed by the United States Court of Appeals for the Ninth Circuit, which ruled against Sony.[6] Each side of the controversy then marshalled their forces for a hearing before the Supreme Court. In 1984 Justice John Paul Stevens wrote the majority opinion reversing the ruling by the Court of Appeals and affirming the right of consumers to make home recordings for their own noncommercial, nonprofit use.[7]

With the affirmation of home recording rights and the enthusiastic reception from consumers, the sales of VCRs increased, despite a period of confusion in the market regarding the standard format. Sony attempted to make its Beta format the industry standard but was sidestepped by JVC when it introduced the lower-cost VHS technology. This led to a problem in the prerecorded videotape sales and rental market: tapes now had to be produced in both formats. Responding to market pressure, in 1988 Sony introduced its first VHS machine, acknowledging consumer preference for VHS technology. (Sony's Beta standard is still widely used in industry.)

The most dramatic rise in VCR sales occurred in 1984 to 1985, when sales rose by 4.5 million; a levelling off in retail prices and the introduction of improved picture resolution were no doubt largely responsible for the significant increase in sales. In 1985 Sony introduced Super Beta and Beta II, which extended the video frequency response, improving picture resolution by 20 percent. JVC responded with an upgraded VHS system referred to as HQ ("High Quality"). The HQ system reduced graininess and improved the video brightness range. By 1995 more than 80 percent of all American television households had at least one VCR, and the percentage of multiple-VCR households is increasing.[8] Most of the sales are of VHS recorders, with the Sony Beta models accounting for only 1 percent of annual sales.

One thing that VCR manufacturers are attempting to improve is the ease of programming the VCR for recording off-air television shows. Recent studies indicate that VCR owners spend only twelve hours a week, or 3 percent of total television viewing time, watching recorded programs. One reason for this low percentage may be the frustration most consumers encounter in programming their VCRs. A number of electronic tools have been developed to help the consumer with this task: one device requires only that the code corresponding to the program to be taped, which is listed in the television program guide, be keyed in.[9]

Another issue plaguing broadcasters and television advertisers is the ability of viewers to skip over commercials from recorded programs by activating the fast-forward control. Studies have shown that the television viewer's disenchantment with commercials has increased since 1985. According to one study conducted by Video Storyboard Tests, two-thirds of one thousand viewers surveyed expressed irritation with the frequency of television commercials.

In 1995 RCA responded to this dissatisfaction by introducing a VCR (VR678HF and VR542) with "commercial advance" technology. By detecting the brief silent fades broadcast before and after commercial breaks, the RCA VCR speeds up the commercials and can mask the picture with a blue screen.

For the time being, broadcasters and television advertisers will have to cope with the public's ability to speed through commercials, ignoring their content. Advertising executives are considering creating shorter commercials, (about four seconds), using slow motion formats, (which would play at normal speed when fast-forwarded), and more visually striking video, in their attempt to combat viewer "zapping."

Super VHS

In 1987 JVC once again pioneered a new VCR format whose impact upon the industry has yet to be measured. The technology, known as Super VHS (SVHS) has a higher picture resolution than either present VHS video or broadcast and cable television. A number of features associated with SVHS technology make it superior to regular VHS or Beta.

The bandwidth of the SVHS system is supplemented, so it can yield up to 400 lines of picture resolution as opposed to 240 lines in the regular VHS mode. Another important technological factor concerns the separation of the chrominance and luminance signals. In standard VHS the two signals are blended together into a composite video output, creating crosstalk or picture noise and distortion. While the chrominance and luminance signals are recorded together on the videotape in an SVHS recorder, they are not mixed into a composite video signal. Instead, they are separated by a special four-pin "S" connector so that they travel as discrete signals from one component to another. This technique expands the luminance signal and results in 50 percent more picture detail recorded onto the tape.

While one can use an SVHS tape deck with any television monitor, superior resolution standards can only be realized with a specially designed monitor to separate the chrominance and luminance signals. Also complementing the system is a specially designed videotape that has smaller tape particles and a smoother tape surface, achieved by coating the densely configured ferric oxide particles with cobalt. The videotape heads on the recording deck are tooled with narrower gaps so that they can "read" the smaller tape particles. These heads are more sensitive and can expand the frequency response range of the video signal.

Super VHS is "backward compatible," meaning that standard VHS tapes can be played on a SVHS deck, but SVHS tapes cannot be viewed on standard VHS. While SVHS improves picture brightness and resolution, it has no effect on color fidelity. In fact, SVHS uses standard VHS technology to record color. The superior quality achieved by SVHS comes at a high price: the tape decks sell for about $1000.

Of all the new technologies introduced within the last decade, the VCR has had the most profound impact upon the structure of the entertainment industry. Prior to the VCR there was a systematic release pattern of Hollywood feature films designed to generate the most profit for the Hollywood studios. Films were usually simultaneously released in domestic and foreign markets and then, after a prescribed period of time (depending upon the success or failure of the film), a release window was established for the lucrative first-run domestic network television rights. For a popular theatrical feature, the networks would bid against each other for the film's exclusive run, thus driving up the cost of acquiring the rights for broadcast.

Cable television and VCRs have dramatically altered the traditional distribution pattern of films. Now Hollywood has turned to video as the first stop after theatrical exhibition in the domestic distribution chain. The time selected for release to the videocassette industry still varies according to the success of the film— usually from three to nine months after theatrical release. Some films are simultaneously released to videocassette and pay cable networks; however, there is usually a delay in the window of release to pay cable television.

In 1994 a new ripple occurred in theatrical feature film release patterns. The feature film sequels to *Aladdin* and *Darkman* bypassed theatrical release entirely and went directly to the videocassette sales and rental market. In another twist, the film version of James Michener's bestselling novel *Texas* also went directly to video, though it was eventually broadcast on the ABC television network, which contributed 40 percent to its production.

As a result of these new technologies, network television is now third in the distribution chain: this has created a rethinking of acquisition priorities at the three networks. Naturally, with significant prenetwork exposure, network television executives are no longer willing to pay astronomical licensing fees for already released movies. Part of their solution to this problem has been to produce more made-for-television movies and miniseries. Although the cost of these television films are high, the networks can at least recoup a percentage of production costs on foreign theatrical and television release.

As mentioned earlier, Hollywood's first reaction to the videocassette was one of fear: they envisioned another depression within their industry similar to the one that occurred with the introduction of television. In fact just the opposite happened. In 1988 there were more movie theaters with more screens than there have been since 1948, when movie theater census records were started: 22,721 screens, with the bulk of them accounted for by the multiplex theater, which has a minimum of two screens and as many as eighteen. With multiscreen theaters, exhibitors are able to offer the movie audience greater choice, and ideally this brings them increased repeat admissions. Even the less popular films are guaranteed theatrical exhibition space to legitimize the title in the home video marketplace. Videocassettes and home video rentals and sales have become a profitable ancillary business for the Hollywood studios, with many of them involved in prerecorded videocassette distribution.

Videodisks

There is little doubt in the entertainment industry that videocassettes are a dominant force in delivering home entertainment to the American public. However, there is a competing technology that is even more sophisticated and offers greater potential. Videodisks were developed at about the same time as videocassettes. Initially, as with video cassettes, there were two competing standards, the optical or laser format and the stylus/groove standard. N. V. Phillips, the Dutch electronic firm, pioneered the development of the laser disk, while RCA invested heavily in the stylus/groove standard.

The difference between the two standards offers a lesson for technological developments of the future. RCA, looking backward rather than forward, developed a video technology that was similar to that used in record players. Its videodisk used a stylus or needle which, like that of a record player, travelled over the grooves of the disk and decoded the electrical impulses into video images. The design of the Phillips optical disk, on the other hand, was a complete departure from traditional electronics, using a laser beam to "read" the information on the disk and decode it into video pictures. The laser system was more in tune with the times and quickly became the standard for videodisks. After a couple of years and millions of dollars in losses, RCA realized the inferiority of its system and ceased manufacturing and distribution.

It is important to note, however, that the laser disk has not captured a significant percentage of the home video entertainment market. There are both technological and marketing reasons for this: videocassettes reached the consumer before videodisks, and few expected the home viewer to reinvest in a new home video standard. There were also fewer titles available for home viewing in the videodisk library, thereby offering consumers little incentive to purchase the new technology. In addition, the videocassette offered a unique option that was unavailable on the videodisk, the ability for home video recording. Although there have been attempts to adapt videodisk technology for home recording, no recording option is presently available to the consumer videodisk market. There are industrial digital-disk-based recording systems that can store one hundred hours of uncompressed video. However, these machines are very expensive, and it will be years before they are available to the public.

There are, nevertheless, several advantages inherent in videodisk technology that may eventually make it the more preferred home video recording option. Unlike videotapes, videodisks can be pressed just like records, which can lower manufacturing costs to as little as $1.25 a unit.[10] Also, the longevity of the disk surpasses that of videocassette tape, because unlike videocassettes, where the tape is subject to wear and tear as it travels across the tape heads and is coiled on the cassette, the optical laser doesn't physically touch the disk. Therefore there is no degradation over time in the components of the disk.

Recently consumers have expressed more interest in the videodisk. One reason for its renewed popularity is the CD, or audio compact disk. These five-inch disks, which totalled over $100 million in sales in 1994, have generated increased revenues in the audio recording market. With the addition of digital audio recording, the CDs have become a hot item for audiophiles.

Digitization standards for videodisks became a critical issue of the 1990s. A new generation of videodisks, digital disks or DVDs, and new players with the potential of storing far more data than traditional CDs and CD-ROMs were developed by separate consortia with conflicting standards. The Sony Corporation and Phillips Electronics supported a 3.7 billion byte system with a 135-minute capacity of high-resolution digital video, stereo sound, and three-language dialogue. Time Warner and Toshiba created a competing technology with a capacity of 4.8 billion bytes and 180 minutes of high-resolution digital video, and two-sided disks with optimum storage potential of 9.6 billion bytes. Toshiba/Time Warner's super–compact disk has been embraced by Hollywood and video player manufacturers, while the computer industry has endorsed the Sony/Phillips Multimedia CD (MMCD) format. In 1995 a unified DVD standard was agreed upon by Toshiba/Time Warner and Sony/Phillips. The compromise involved a one-or-two-layer single-sided disk with either 4.7 gigabytes of memory (single) or 8.5 gigabytes (double).[11]

Although consumer-oriented digital-disk recording technology is still several years away, professional applications are already revolutionizing the broadcasting industry. Whereas videotape recorders gather television information (digital or analogue) serially as pictures (first picture first, last picture last), digital disk recorders do not capture pictures but instead scatter information making up the picture throughout the disk in a sequence that is deciphered at the direction of a software routine. This nonlinear recording has a number of superior aspects compared to videotape, including ease of distribution and postproduction.

Another significant advantage of the compact videodisk is its interactive capabilities. Interactive systems allow the viewer to retrieve and access information on demand. The technology has created a revolution in the video game industry, which has applied digital CD technology to video games. Companies like Sega, Nintendo, and 3DO have all introduced CD video-based digital hardware for the new generation of interactive video game software.

Several electronic giants contributed to the development of digital interactive CD video technology. Of course Phillips Electronics, which pioneered the development of the laser CD, was a leader in developing prototypes for interactive digital CD-based video games. Phillips, working with Sony, developed a compact disk player for their CD-interactive system. Intel has also designed a digital interactive video (DVI) system that utilizes video compression technology to generate stable, full-screen video images.

A critical factor in making videodisks a viable competitor in the home entertainment marketplace is the availability, of software. Addressing this need, Sony and Pioneer Electronics have created Sony Classics and Pioneer Artists respectively to generate a library of programs available for videodisk playback. With three thousand titles now available on videodisks and several hundred thousand disk players sold since 1987, the videodisk could be a prominent feature of home entertainment by the year 2000.

Camcorders

Just as the VCR revolutionized home entertainment, the video camcorder has created a new genre of motion photography that has changed both professional and amateur filmmaking. Introduced in the early 1980s, the camcorder is a portable video camera that integrates the video recording mechanism into the body of the camera. Prior to this marriage of two technologies, video cameras were joined to separate portable recording decks via a power cord, an arrangement that was at best cumbersome and awkward.

The first generation of camcorders available to consumers were large, heavy, and expensive. By 1987 the camcorder had become much smaller and was available in a variety of sizes, shapes, and formats. Today there are more than thirty different brands of camcorders sold in the United States, with Panasonic and RCA capturing more than 30 percent of the market. Sales of camcorders have reached 3 million a year, generating $2.3 billion of yearly revenue.[12] With the advent of Super VHS, 8-mm., and Hi-8, a new generation of camcorders with greater video definition is now available to the public.

The 8-mm and Hi-8 formats, introduced in the late 1980s, were developed by Sony. Their design allowed for the use of smaller cassettes and brought about the smallest mass market video cameras manufactured to date. The Hi-8 camera is a sophisticated electronic tool that offers over four hundred lines of resolution, separate luminance and chrominance video output, a high zoom ratio, and stereophonic sound. Its level of sophistication has made the Hi-8 camcorder a competitor in the professional marketplace.

In an effort to create a wider demographic base for their product, camcorder manufacturers designed more user-friendly models. They also repositioned their product to appeal to retirees, singles, and business. One thing camcorder manufacturers have been reluctant to do is lower their price: most camcorders still cost around $700. Many industry observers believe that if camcorders are to achieve the same market penetration as VCRs, their pricing will have to come down.

In 1995 videodisk technology was married with the camcorder when Avid Technology introduced a digital-disk-based camera. Although this technology was primarily aimed at the professional market, disk-based digital camcorders will eventually become affordable for the consumer electronics marketplace.[13]

EXHIBITION AND TRANSMISSION TECHNOLOGY

While the focus of this chapter has been on delivery systems, it is also important to consider exhibition and transmission technology. American television design has progressed rather slowly in the area of technological innovation. With the ever increasing array of technological wizardry available, it is not at all surprising that there have been numerous attempts to create large screen television sets that provide enhanced picture resolution. These sets fall into three classifications: rear screen projection, direct view, and liquid crystal display (LCD).

Rear Screen Projection

Projection television sets were the first attempt to provide a large picture format—up to fifty inches—using existing television technology. At first these sets produced less than state-of-the-art pictures, with dark and excessively grainy images. Today, however, a new generation of rear projection televisions has circumvented these problems and is displaying clear, sharp, crisp images and achieving annual sales approaching three hundred thousand units.[14]

Direct View

Direct view television sets, unlike those that use rear projection, can provide enhanced resolution by increasing the number of lines contained within the image. These sets provide up to 500 to 600 lines of resolution compared to traditional sets, which usually have a minimum of at least 230 lines of horizontal resolution. Although these direct view sets do have enhanced picture quality, with extralarge picture tubes, their worth is questionable because broadcast reception is limited to about 330 lines of horizontal resolution. If the goal is to create sophisticated, enhanced television picture standards, a new transmission system must prevail. It is toward this goal that high definition television (HDTV) was developed.

Liquid Crystal Displays

The most significant development in the technological evolution of television sets was the interface of active matrix liquid crystal display (LCD) into set design. The organic substance that forms the liquid crystal has been known to researchers for one hundred years and is produced in nature by octopi and squid. In 1964 George H. Heilmeier, an RCA researcher, began to experiment with liquid crystals. He discovered that with the application of an electronic current, liquid crystal could generate a molecular configuration that would enable the crystals to either block light or allow it to pass, somewhat analogous to a camera's shutter. RCA declined to pursue LCD research, and although IBM, GE, AT&T, and ITT at one time all committed resources to LCD, they too eventually abandoned their efforts.

While the American electronics industry chose to ignore the possibility of flat, lightweight LCD video screens, the Japanese eagerly explored it. Companies like Sharp, Hitachi, and NEC are each spending about $100 million a year on making the flat-panel screens.

The reason the production cost for flat glass LCD panels is very high is that transistors must be embedded next to the liquid crystal solution so that each picture element can provide the liquid crystals with either a positive or negative charge.

In the United States about a dozen small companies are attempting to manufacture flat-panel LCD screens, but they are woefully underfinanced. The development of HDTV, and its logical interface with flat-panel technology, however, has rekindled a cautious interest in some large American manufacturers. In 1990, IBM announced a rare joint venture with Toshiba to manufacture large color flat-screen panels. Xerox has also been experimenting with LCD and flat-panel technology. They developed sophisticated LCD matrix display systems, and in 1993, in a joint venture with AT&T, announced a major breakthrough in combining computer and television technology into a flat-panel video screen no thicker than a pad of paper. The Japanese, nevertheless, still maintain the lead in research and development of LCD flat-screen technology and as a result are well positioned to control this new and important market.

High Definition Television

Before beginning a discussion of HDTV, it is important to first have a rudimentary understanding of how the present American system of television technology operates. America's broadcast standards were adopted in 1941 by the National Television System Committee (NTSC). The standard set, which received unanimous approval from the electronics industry, was a 525-line, thirty-picture format.

The 525 horizontal lines on American television actually generate sixty pictures, or fields, per second. First the odd-numbered lines and then the even-numbered lines are scanned, transmitting 262.5 lines for each field: this is known as interlaced scanning. In the American system, the scanning of two consecutive fields (both odd- and even-numbered lines), makes up a television frame that represents the smallest complete picture unit. Thus a frame or picture consists of 525 (262.5 odd, 262.5 even) numbered lines, which generates sixty fields or thirty frames (pictures) per second.

Another technological aspect of the American system is the size of the bandwidth for transmission of the television signal. (A bandwidth is the amount of electromagnetic spectrum space that is occupied by a channel.) The size of the bandwidth is determined by the amount of information to be transmitted. In the NTSC standard, the bandwidth is 6 MHz. The video portion of the picture takes up 4.5 MHz, while the remaining 1.5 MHz is taken up by the audio component and other transmission information.

Two other variables concerning the NTSC standard that impact upon HDTV are aspect ratio and picture resolution. Aspect ratio refers to the size of the television screen and picture, which in the American standard is three units high (vertical) and four units wide (horizontal). Picture resolution is determined by picture elements also known as pixels and is multiplied by the number of horizontal lines scanned for each picture by the number of complete pictures.

In 1981 the Japanese Broadcasting Corporation, NHK, introduced the first operational HDTV system in the world. Called MUSE E, the NHK technology compressed a 1,124-line image at sixty cycles into an electronic bandwidth of 8.1 MHz with an aspect ratio of sixteen-to-one. Eight years later, in 1989, the David Sarnoff Research Center publicly demonstrated the first HDTV system compatible with NTSC transmission standards. (The MUSE E NHK system is not compatible with the American technology, as the bandwidth differs by 2.1 MHz.) If the MUSE E system were to be adopted in the United States, it would render immediately obsolescent approximately 130 million television sets, worth about $80 billion. Obviously, then, either a technological compromise will have to be reached or an HDTV system such as the one demonstrated by Sarnoff Labs, with compatible bandwidths, will have to be adopted.

In an effort to achieve technical consensus and to insure a move toward standardization, the FCC announced that proposed HDTV systems must have the ability to be simulcast. That is, any land-based terrestrial HDTV system must accommodate its transmission technology to that of standard television sets, making it compatible with existing transmission design. The industry has responded to the HDTV compatibility problem with some innovative and creative technological designs.

The first HDTV submissions made by major American electronic manufacturers relied upon traditional analog technology and interfaced image compression and channel augmentation into the HDTV design. (Image compression and channel augmentation relate to the need for HDTV to squeeze one hundred times more information into the broadcast spectrum bandwidth allocated for television by the FCC.) Analog technology relies on the translation of images from variations in electronic current, whereas digital technology reduces all information to coded numbers of zero and one, allowing for more precise imaging with little distortion.)

In 1990, General Instruments Corporation turned the FCC submission process upside down when it announced its proposal for Digicipher, an all-digital HDTV transmission system using image compression techniques to construct high-definition television pictures. In 1992, Digital Instruments Videocipher exhibited the first demonstration of digital HDTV. It was disseminated from the Bethesda, Maryland TV tower of PBS-affiliate WETA, to the Thomas P. O'Neill Room on Capitol Hill, before an audience of senators and congressmen. The first image was of an American flag fluttering in the breeze.

On the heels of General Instruments' announcement, several of America's largest and most powerful electronic manufacturers abandoned their original analog proposals and created joint ventures for the development of all-digital HDTV. In 1993 a compromise was reached among the electronic companies vying for acceptance of their digital HDTV proposals. The system designs had been undergoing testing from 1991 to 1993 by a special FCC advisory committee. The compromise created an alliance between three consortia that had previously been competitors.[15]

Perhaps the most important achievement of the alliance is a recognition that digital HDTV technology has entered the realm of information processing and the computer age. Digital HDTV sets will be more than repositories of entertainment for "couch potatoes": they will also offer interactive video services. To establish a synergy between entertainment and interactive video, a technological design had to be created, and digital HDTV is it.

To achieve a multimedia dimension for digital HDTV, traditional television technology had to be re-examined. The interlaced scanning process, which scans every other line on the television screen thirty times a second, was deemed inferior for computing needs because of its susceptibility to image flickering. An alternative scanning design was advanced by Zenith Electronics and the Massachusetts Institute of Technology. The technique, known as progressive scanning, does not skip rows and instead scans every line on the screen in sequence, sixty times a second. This technology eliminates the flicker associated with interlaced scanning.

Proponents of the interlaced scanning system argue that it is less expensive to manufacture and more suitable for depicting moving images. Those supporting progressive scanning argue that it is more compatible with the needs of computing technology because it provides sharper resolution of graphics and is free from flickering.

The accommodation reached by the companies calls for a hybrid system that combines the interlaced and progressive scanning designs in a single standard. Television stations would have the option to transmit programs in five different formats of progressive scanning and one format of interlaced. This would afford a flexibility in program transmission, allowing a station to select the best transmission technique for the program being broadcast—for example, a major movie event would use the high-end progressive format, while a news program would likely use the less sophisticated interlaced scanning process.

Some critics have raised concerns that the single standard comprising both formats does not address consumer expectations concerning mass-marketed television sets. Television sets have come to be seen as necessary items offered to the public at a low price, while home computers are still viewed by many as extravagances. The composite HDTV technology agreed upon by the alliance will mean that consumers will have to pay between $1000 to $2000 more for each television set, which will make them once again something of a luxury.[16]

The sale of HDTV sets in Japan shows how a market can stabilize and offer economies of scale to the consumer. When they first went on sale in 1991, Sony's complete HDTV system cost $32,000 (4.1 million yen). By 1992, Sony, Sharp, and Matsushita Electric Industrial Company had lowered prices by 70 percent, with sets being priced below the $8,000 range. In the United States by the end of the 1990s, HDTV receivers should stabilize in the $2000 price range.[17]

Another doubt expressed by some industry observers relates to the amount of latitude television equipment manufacturers have. According to the terms of the alliance, HDTV sets smaller than thirty-four inches can be manufactured using the interlaced scanning process and be offered to the consumer at a lower cost than the hybrid interlaced/progressive television receivers. However, there was a consensus among members of the alliance that television sets with screens larger than thirty-four inches must offer progressive scanning.

Some of the concerns expressed by the merging of progressive and interlaced scanning are reminiscent of the rivalry between the VHS and Beta video technologies. Marketplace forces will be a critical determinant in providing a rationale for stations and set manufacturers as they choose their HDTV technological options.

The need to define regulatory oversight for HDTV digital technology has been a daunting task for the FCC. In its quest to move the United States into the twenty-first century, the FCC has had to deal with numerous imperatives, including a transition timetable and the allocation of additional channels. The FCC estimates that the shift to digital HDTV will take about fifteen years, during which time television signals will be broadcast in both the old and new standards. To provide for this, in 1992 the FCC authorized the assignment of a second channel to all television licensees. This channel would be utilized by broadcasters as a conversion channel and could not be used to augment programming, as some broadcasters had hoped. With increased competition from cable television and its myriad channel offerings, some broadcasters do not feel the need to duplicate programming on both channels. Indeed, they view the second channel as a means for offering digital services that would allow them to reap financial benefits from the information superhighway. In February 1996, congress passed the long-awaited Telecommunications Act, awarding the digital spectrum to the television stations. However, the FCC agreed not to award any licenses until Congress decided whether or not to auction off the spectrum.

The policy of allocating a second channel free to broadcasters became a political issue in 1995. After raising $9 billion through FCC spectrum auctions, the Republican-controlled Congress took a decidedly lukewarm position on handing over a second television channel to broadcasters free of charge.[18]

The evolution of FM radio offers another interesting example of the FCC's regulatory oversight of a developing technology. At one point in FM's history, there were more stations going off the air than on. In an effort to promote FM broadcasting, the FCC allowed stations to duplicate their AM radio programming on the FM band. Then in 1963 the commission changed its regulatory posture and required that AM/FM radio stations operating under the same ownership in the same market program the stations separately at least some of the time. This eventually led to a complete divorce of FM from AM radio and the growth of a new and vital technology.

Over the last forty years, American manufacturers have experienced a decline in domestic market share of electronics manufacturing from 100 percent to 15 percent. American companies forfeited their dominance because of their inability to compete with Japanese competitors who had wider profit margins and lower production costs. In addition, Japanese manufacturers enjoyed government assistance through protected domestic markets that allowed Japanese manufacturers to set prices on some consumer products that were almost twice as high as those in the United States.

Many scientists believe that America's development of digital HDTV technology will provide an opportunity for the United States to regain a competitive lead and eventually take back the business lost to the Japanese and Europeans in recent decades. They cite the Japanese dependence on analog technology and satellite delivery as inherent impediments to their system design. Another advantage to the U. S. design is its terrestrial HDTV distribution system: the Japanese and European systems use satellite distribution, which serves smaller populations than the land-based terrestrial system. Indeed, in 1994, both the Japanese and Europeans tacitly admitted the probable superiority of the American digital HDTV system. In Japan a public call by the government to abandon the analog MUSE E system caused a political uproar. Japanese electronic manufacturers had invested twenty years and $1 billion in the technology and weren't about to turn their backs on it. However, they did accept a rationale for the gradual phase-in of digital HDTV. And in Europe, where the Japanese had been lobbying extensively for the adoption of MUSE E, France announced the creation of Le Très Grand Alliance, between Japan, Europe, and the United States. This is the first international effort to create a universal digital HDTV broadcast standard.

The rewards of digital HDTV could be bountiful, with estimates reaching as high as $250 billion in revenues generated from the sales of advanced design television systems and their ancillary industries.

INTERACTIVE TELEVISION

Since the early 1980s there have been attempts to conceptualize interactive technology within the framework of television. One of the most ambitious pioneering interactive cable television efforts was implemented by Warner Amex Cable Communications in the early 1980s. Their Qube system, tested in Columbus, Ohio, was the precursor of the interactive technologies that are being pursued today. Qube offered interactive home shopping, education, game shows, and even voting on its service. Although it was terminated in 1984, it helped to establish a rationale for the creation of programs and services for interactive television.

In 1992 the FCC, acting on a successful test application of T.V. Answer, an over-the-air interactive television system, authorized the reservation of special radio frequencies for over-the-air interactive television services. T.V. Answer, which was founded by Fernando Morales, has already invested close to $100 million in the technology and has several former Reagan administration officials on its board of directors.

Interest in interactive television has motivated some of the biggest players in entertainment to invest in research and development. In 1991, NBC, A. C. Nielsen, and Cablevision Systems invested in Interactive Network, an interactive television start-up company based in California. However, the company failed to secure enough of a customer base to make it economically viable.

The interactive television industry has been associated with a lot of hype that does not always translate well into the dollars-and-cents reality of the marketplace. One company called 3DO (for "three-dimensional optics") attracted major corporate investors like Time Warner, Matsushita, MCA, Kleiner Perkins, and AT&T. The technology used CD-ROMs that can store substantial amounts of data. 3DO positioned their product to compete with video games like Nintendo and Sega. Even with their substantial corporate backing, however, 3DO sold only forty thousand units of its hardware in the United States and generated a loss of $51.4 million. An important determinant for the company's success was the support of an extensive software library to interface with its hardware. With 3DO's failure to mass market its hardware, software companies were reluctant to make the considerable commitment to develop a library for hardware that could quickly become obsolete. This is one dilemma that 3DO and other companies face in the competitive world of interactive television.

Two of the largest, most visible, and dominant companies in the cable television industry have also been aggressively diversifying into interactive technology. Time Warner and US West have announced an alliance, and TCI is involved in a number of technological applications of interactive technology, including data compression, fiber optic upgrading of its cable holdings, and investment in two interactive home shopping networks: Home Shopping Network and, through TCI's spin-off company Liberty Media, the QVC Shopping Channel.

TCI and Time Warner collectively control over 17 million of the 60 million universe of cable television subscribers. In an effort to establish a compatible interactive cable standard for equipment and technology, the two companies in 1993 announced a joint venture to create an "open architecture" for their competing interactive technology. This would produce compatible hardware so that subscribers of either company could communicate with each other.

The issue of universal standards is also a critical component for the interface of technology on the "information superhighway." The American National Standards Institute (ANSI) and the Digital Audio Visual Council (DAVIC) are attempting to establish a protocol for interactive video technology. Indeed, one of the most important pieces of hardware associated with interactive technology is the set-top box that will serve as a gateway between the interactive information superhighway and the consumer. General Instrument, a leader in the manufacturing of set-top converter boxes, along with other companies like Microsoft and Intel are attempting to position themselves in this potentially lucrative market. Thus far, the companies involved have yet to agree upon any comprehensive standards.

While many companies have issued glowing proclamations of their investment in the information superhighway, in reality there are still a great many detours and traffic jams that must be overcome. The myriad of interactive test demonstrations by high-powered companies like Time Warner, AT&T, US West, Viacom, and TCI have yielded data that cannot necessarily be projected to the population at large. Frequently, these interactive video trials have had inherent biases built into their testing design. In some cases the television households chosen to participate were decidedly upscale, yielding data that would be useful only to that population sample. Another area for concern was the expense associated with creating these test environments. For example, Time Warner, in its video-on-demand Orlando test spent $7,000 per home to wire four thousand households. That kind of expenditure would be totally impractical on a large-scale basis.

The hype that has been associated with interactivity on the information superhighway has clouded the reality of its implementation. There are some extremely complex technological hurdles that must be surmounted before any homes will be able to interface with the highway for interactive data services and video-on-demand.

Two of the most important of these technological problems are the storage and distribution of information. If video-on-demand is to be a practical option, then local providers must be able to store as many movies as are presently available in the local video store. Current estimates suggest that eighty thousand gigabytes of disk space and the capacity of four hundred thousand medium-sized personal computers would be needed to accomplish this.

In order for video storage to become a practical reality, all information must be digitized and compressed. For example, the movie *Jurassic Park*, which has 100 billion bytes of data, could be compressed into 4 billion bytes by temporarily eliminating redundant information.

At the present time, the Motion Picture Expert Group (MPEG-2) standard for digital compression appears to offer the most viable universal technique. It relies upon algorithms to compress functions that can be applied to a digital signal representing picture, sound, and control data. This information would be embedded in a data stream that would provide the needed information to break down the encoded signal and reassemble it.

Another standard for video compression is the Joint Photographic Experts Group (JPEG) standard. The JPEG standard is best suited for the digital compression and recovery of still images, as in postproduction video editing.

After enabling a system to store the great amounts of information necessary to provide an interactive data stream, the next problem that must be addressed is the dissemination of the signal to thousands of viewers. This is accomplished through video server technology. In developing a video-on-demand viewing system, an accommodation must be made to provide simultaneous transmission of popular titles to thousands of viewers during high-peak viewing times.

One company, the Oracle Corporation, is working on a three-tiered video server that stores information either on hard disk or eight-millimeter video tape. Programming would be arranged into categories by popularity, the more popular programming stored on hard disk, the less popular on eight-millimeter videotape.

Video server technology need not be limited by geographical boundaries. Two companies, AT&T and NCR, developed a long distance video networking system for their interactive video trial in Castro Valley, California. A central video digital archive was built in lower Manhattan, and requests for programming were sent electronically to a video server near Castro Valley.[19]

Two techniques that are being tested to serve large numbers of people with the same on-demand programming are memory striping and disk striping. In memory striping, a computer grabs a movie running at 30 frames a second and boosts its framing capacity to 240. By doing this, eight viewers can have access to the same portion of the disk at one time.

With disk striping technology, each movie is chopped into tiny portions and automatically placed on a separate disk. This technology would enable about eight thousand viewers to simultaneously watch a small segment of a movie. Essential to the successful implementation of disk striping technology is the ability to maintain proper chronological order of the small programming segments.

Although the theatrical feature film industry has had its share of failures with new technology, it is viewing interactive television optimistically as a means to greater profitability. Having missed out on the $5 billion home video game bonanza, Hollywood is now positioning itself for a bigger stake in the interactive video industry. Hollywood's technological wizards George Lucas and James Cameron are using computer technology that they pioneered for application in interactive video. Cameron's company, Digital Domain, has attracted IBM as an investor.

More and more of the Hollywood studios are attempting to create a synergy between their theatrical feature films and interactive technology. Sony USA, which owns Columbia Pictures, created an electronic publishing unit: one of their first products was a CD-ROM video game of Francis Ford Coppola's movie *Bram Stoker's Dracula*. Sony's Japanese rival, the Matsushita Electric Industrial Company, which owned Universal Pictures before selling 80 percent of the company to Seagrams in 1995, invested in 3DO, which released an interactive video game based upon Steven Spielberg's movie *Jurassic Park*.

Paramount Communications has created a software development company and is working on establishing virtual reality entertainment centers based upon the television series *Star Trek: The Next Generation*. Their movie *Addams Family Values* was simultaneously released as a theatrical feature and as an interactive video game.

Interactive films in theatrical release is another area of interest for some Hollywood studios. In 1995 Sony and Interfilm released *Mr. Payback*, an interactive feature film, to thirty-seven specially equipped theaters. Audiences in those theaters could select among twelve different options for changing the action in the film.

Major publishers like the Hearst Corporation are also attempting to diversify into interactive media. Hearst created HomeNet, a network of CD-ROMs interfaced with on-line computer services. The programming is themed to various Hearst publications, including *Popular Mechanics* and *Good Housekeeping*, with interactive programs on home renovation, decorating, and entertaining.

THE INFORMATION SUPERHIGHWAY

In a global economy that requires the dissemination and assimilation of large volumes of data, the information superhighway is a necessity, not a luxury. In addition to the need for continued technological advances, however, there are also a number of policy issues associated with its implementation and design.

The availability of the technology is a critical issue that policymakers must face. The expense of services on the superhighway may effectively block access by those who cannot afford to pay. As it becomes an essential tool, the difficulty of access to the interactive data stream could perpetuate a culture of poverty and ignorance, especially among minority groups. When John Malone, CEO of TCI, the largest cable company in the United States, and a leader in the development of interactive television said, "If you don't pay your bill, we'll turn off your television," the words cast an ominous chill on the issue of control over the information superhighway.[20] Who will levy the tolls, and whether they will be too high for some people to pay, is a matter of critical importance.

Another area of concern is the level of sophistication of the software that allows consumers access to the superhighway. If the software is not user friendly and is biased toward those with a relatively high level of technological knowledge, it could block access by those who are not technologically literate.

VIRTUAL REALITY

The most creative application of linking the computer to the television set is virtual reality (VR), the ultimate in high-definition interactive television. Virtual reality is a term coined in 1989 by Jaron Zepel Lanier, former CEO of VPL Research Inc., and presently associated with New Leaf, a Silicon valley company, and Original Ventures in New York City.

A virtual reality application would allow the user to enter a computer-mediated environment that sustains the illusion of physical reality by achieving vivid depictions of space via sophisticated graphic software technology, creating an immersion in a "virtual" environment for the user. With virtual reality, an individual can become surrounded by an artificial environment while experiencing the visual, tactile, and auditory sensations of presence that VR technology provides. Thus, the individual achieves a "telepresence," perceiving the virtual environment via the mediated feedback of a computer.

To create an authentic virtual environment, an array of hardware peripherals have been developed. An integral component of VR technology is the head-mounted display (HMD). This device allows the user to view the virtual landscape with stereoscopic vision, achieving binocular parallax. In conventional television and motion pictures, each eye sees the same scene as it was recorded from the point of view of the camera. The HMD provides the VR user with a realistic construction of perspective coordinated with his or her own head movements that reflect upon the virtual reality objects in the VR landscape. This is achieved by the placement of small cathode ray tubes (CRTs), or liquid crystal displays (LCDs), in front of each eye.

The HMDs, which are presently a necessity for most VR systems, are at times cumbersome and uncomfortable. But this technology is only the first generation of VR hardware. In an effort to make the technology more user friendly, experimentation with laser-based retinal scanning systems has been demonstrated. With this type of application, the image is assembled line by line on the retina and appears to float in space two feet in front of the user. The retinal scanning systems replace the HMD with a much smaller and lighter head-mounted light-emitting diode (LED) display.

In 1995 a new generation of VR hardware was introduced to the consumer marketplace. The technology signaled a move from a helmet-driven orientation to lower-cost VR glasses. An added advantage was the reduction of motion sickness resulting from the lighter-weight gear.

Another component of VR technology is the acoustic sensation associated with the VR environment. To achieve auditory authenticity, the VR landscape must alter its variables to the changing properties of acoustic space. Unlike traditional stereo, which creates an auditory perspective determined at the time of the recording, sound for VR application must be dynamic and interactive, changing its acoustic properties in relation to the VR sound source and in coordination with the movements of the user. So, for example, if the user turns his head to the right, objects to the right of the user will be proportionately louder, and objects to the left will fade in intensity of sound.

Of all the peripherals associated with the human/computer interface of VR technology, one of the most challenging is the creation of tactile sensory perception. To achieve a total illusion of physical reality in a VR environment, the user must be able to interact with VR objects and sense the manifestations of texture and touch.

A number of technological applications have been designed to generate the illusory sensation of touch—these are known as haptic interfaces. The sensation of touch is achieved through a data glove that can deliver electrotactile and vibrotactile impulses through the glove to the user. Electrotactile stimulation relies upon the transmission of electric currents, while vibrotactile surface illusions are created by vibrating mechanical prods, also known as piezoelectric vibrotactile actuators.

To effect an even greater sensory immersion, a data suit can be worn. In addition to the component of touch, the use of the suit can provide the sensation of resistance and pressure. Thus, a user can experience the "reality" of a VR car crash without actually being injured, yet enduring the physical and emotional impact of the event.

Motion is another important variable within the VR landscape. The simulation of motion, even in its simplest form, has held great fascination for consumers. From the rudimentary twenty-five-cent rocking-horse ride to the motion platforms of Disney's Star Tours, the illusion of motion coupled with a coordinated visual display has thrilled young and old alike. In the VR landscape, movement can be simulated by motion platforms and treadmills that can provide the user with the perspective of either retreating from or moving toward a VR object or scene.

To complete the VR sensory cycle, illusions of smell and taste could also be programmed into the VR experience. While there have been experiments in olfactory stimulation, most notably in the 1960s with Sensorama and at Disney's Epcot Center, its use in VR simulations has been limited. Some purists argue that the manufactured aromas that use derivatives from the actual physical scents blur the line between physical and virtual reality. Another obstacle is the lingering quality of olfactory stimuli, which makes it difficult to quickly change from one aroma to another. The same limitations apply to the sense of taste, which at the present time is difficult to reconstruct in the virtual landscape.

Certainly virtual reality and its expansion of electronic perception can provide unique opportunities in both education and entertainment. VR simulations have already been used by NASA, the armed forces, and in industry. The handling of hazardous wastes and toxic chemicals has benefitted from VR simulations. In the field of medicine, VR has been used in the teaching of surgical procedure, while architectural applications have used the three-dimensional landscape to "build" structures and "walk through" them, examining their strengths and deficiencies before actual physical construction takes place.

The potential applications for VR technology are vast and project possibilities for education and entertainment that have unlimited boundaries. There are, however, concerns about the human/computer interface and how that will impact the welfare of society. Researchers speculate that the average person already spends about seven years of their life watching television. It is conceivable that individuals could spend twenty years immersed in a VR environment.

Other lingering questions to consider are the effect that continued VR immersion will have on an individual's perception of physical reality and how such exposure will influence their judgment about reality. Will the VR experiences have the capability of overwhelming the intellectual capacities of individuals? The Orson Welles radio broadcast of *War of the Worlds* in 1938 demonstrated the dangers of blurring the line between illusion and reality, when thousands of listeners took to the streets, trying to escape a gas attack from Mars that they believed to be factual. How peoples' judgments of reality will be mediated by VR exposure will be an issue of concern as virtual reality becomes more readily available to the public.

In the 1991 film *Lawnmower Man*, an adaptation of a Stephen King short story, two characters enter a virtual environment and engage in "cybersex," a simulated physical and emotional union. Will virtual reality provide an emotional release for men and women who are physically attracted to one another but bound by the covenants of marriage or com-

mitment to someone else? If such a liaison takes place in a VR environment, would it be subject to the current laws governing sexual conduct?

Although at the present time the simulation of sexual contact via VR
technology is unavailable, the ability to achieve the experience is a matter of technological advancement and desire. When such applications are
available, will it create a new industry of cyberporn? Looking toward that
time, a magazine entitled *Future Sex* instructs its readers to "Strap in,
tweak out, turn on!"

The term "virtual reality" was popularized by the 1993 six-hour ABC
miniseries *Wild Palms*. Conceived by Bruce Wagner and directed by
Oliver Stone, this series focused on the essence of virtual reality by creating a world where patriarchal totalitarianism existed as a function of
three-dimensional holographs, creating a confusion between fact and
fantasy. The series was helpful in making viewers understand the creative possibilities of VR, while also pointing to its conceivable misuse.
The entertainment application of virtual reality seems to be one of the
most desirable areas for development. The Edison Brothers, a St.
Louis–based operator of twenty-eight hundred specialty shops has set up
ten "virtuality" centers and is in the process of licensing Star Trek virtual
reality centers in shopping malls across the country. For larger applications, the company is planning Star Bases, while smaller ones will be
called Star Posts.

While the potential of virtual reality as a tool for learning and recre-
ation is great, there is also a responsibility associated with this new technology that requires its intelligent and careful application as a medium
whose boundaries are as yet unknown.

INDIVIDUAL PRIVACY IN THE INFORMATION AGE

While much has been written about the electronic superhighway and the
vast array of interactive services it will supply, little attention has been
paid to the potential abuses of individual privacy this technology could
lead to. Fiber optic cable, coaxial cable, computers, telephones, and television sets are all converging to supply an endless stream of data to
American households: movies, home shopping, banking, games, and
travel services. These services are tremendously convenient, but is there
a price to pay for the deluge of information entering our homes? What is
the fate of individual privacy in today's sophisticated electronic marketplace? Will Orwell's science-fiction fantasy evolve into fact as the privacy of Americans is invaded by silicon chips, microcomputers, and interactive cable television, each with the capacity to store limitless data on
individuals?

Since the invention of the computer, there has been a great deal of concern about its ability to store large amounts of personal information retrievable within an instant and the potential abuses to individual privacy that this access implies.[21] Within the last few years, however, the technology has taken a dramatic turn and, because of miniaturization, a blending of computers, television, and telephones has been consummated: one that has moved even Orwell's harshest critics to be concerned.

Through this new technology, television viewers, transformed from passive to active participants, are sending an abundant amount of information about themselves and their families into computer memory banks.[22] With about 70 percent of all American television households already wired for cable, and with an ambitious program underway to upgrade coaxial cable to fiber optic systems, interactive cable will reach a significant number of viewers by the end of the 1990s, making the maintenance of individual privacy a critical concern of the new century.

At issue is the proper and legal use of information obtained from subscribers through their interactions with cable television systems. Whether or not individual data collected by the cable television operator should be made available to third parties is at the heart of the problem. Before discussing the propriety of sharing subscriber data, however, it is appropriate to define the term "privacy." Legal scholars have devised a concise definition: "the claim of individuals, groups, or institutions to determine for themselves when, how, and to what extent information about them is communicated to others."[23] Justice William O. Douglas described privacy as the "right to be let alone" and Justice Louis Brandeis called it "the most comprehensive of rights and the right most valued by civilized men."[24]

Legislation dealing with privacy issues can be divided into four categories: *appropriation*—the unauthorized use of a person's picture or likeness for a commercial purpose; *intrusion*—the acquisition of personal information by surreptitious surveillance techniques; *private information*—confidential information made public via newspaper, television, or radio; and *"false light"*—private information made public with malicious intent.

Legislating Privacy: A Historical Perspective

During the last two decades, the courts and the federal government have considered various privacy issues with contradictory and ambivalent results. As of this writing there is no federal statute sensitive to the potential abuses to individual privacy that interactive television may afford.[25] There is, however, legislation that touches the periphery of this debate.

In 1968 the federal government passed the Omnibus Crime Control and Safe Streets Act. Title III of the act concerns itself with wiretapping and the interception of verbal messages. The act implies, however, that textual or video messages may be excluded from the law's purview and indeed restricts its jurisdiction to common carriers like telephone services, a classification that does not include cable television.

Perhaps the most potent catalyst in provoking legislative concern about individual privacy was the threat posed by the centralization of credit data banks and their abusive policies concerning the dissemination of credit information. This concern resulted in the 1970 Fair Credit Reporting Act that, while far from generating comprehensive protection to consumers, did provide them with the right to learn the "nature and substance" of their records.

In 1971 the Supreme Court, in declining to review a State of Washington court opinion, let stand a decision that an individual may not correct a false and damaging record until he discovers that actual harm occurred as a result of the misleading information.

The debate over individual access to personal data files continued throughout the 1970s. In 1974 a federal privacy law was passed that addressed the misuse of personal data compiled by the federal government. This act was designed to regulate the collection, storage, and dissemination of personal information by federal agencies. It also established a precedent by allowing individuals access to personal data along with the ability to correct any false information. As well, the law developed rigid guidelines concerning the sharing of information among various federal agencies.

By 1980, Congress became concerned with the privacy of professionals working in the mass media. This concern culminated in the Privacy Protection Act of 1980. This act addressed the manner in which law officers and government officials could seize materials pertaining to people working in the mass media. It placed limitations on the acquisition of recorded information, including reporters' notes and undeveloped film. It should be noted, however, that these laws protect an individual's right to privacy only where the federal government is concerned: they do not include other levels of government or the private sector. And a 1976 Supreme Court decision held that absent a specific law or contract, personal data records are the sole property of the system operator holding them and that subscribers have no legal interest in them.[26]

The need for a comprehensive privacy policy is increasing, along with the growing number of abuses of individual privacy now possible with the new technology of interactive television. Compiling aggregate data and cross-referencing it with other information sources can provide detailed consumer profiles on cable-subscribing households. The sharing of cable-monitored information concerning a user's buying patterns, political beliefs, and program choices with third parties is another avenue of potential abuse. A third, and probably the most threatening, form of potential misuse is interception or eavesdropping: that is, the unauthorized access to a subscriber's transmission, or electronic mail (e-mail).27

While the potential for abuse clearly exists, critics opposed to a legislated privacy standard argue that an industry-wide sensitivity to this issue is sufficient to thwart any wrongdoing. But industry-sponsored codes, while laudable for their intent, may be inadequate in their design. Two incidents illustrate the complex nature of the privacy question: both occurred in Columbus, Ohio, home of the nation's first consumer-oriented interactive cable system, Qube, which was owned and operated by Warner Amex Cable Communications from 1977 to 1984.

The first case involved a theater owner who was being prosecuted on obscenity charges. As part of his defense, his counsel attempted to subpoena the names of Qube system subscribers who had viewed a certain X-rated film on the Qube adult pay channel. The defense strategy was to identify several prominent Columbus citizens who had watched the same film that the theater owner was being prosecuted for showing. Fortunately the judge was sensitive to what an affront to individual privacy this would be: he approved only the transfer of the *number* of viewers watching the film and not their names.

In another Columbus case, a mayoral election was influenced by confidential data inappropriately leaked to the public. The incumbent had apparently viewed several sexually explicit films on the Qube adult channel. This information was released to the press without authorization and became a prominent election issue.

Another troubling case, this one involving the scrutiny of a family's video rental records, occurred in 1987. The incident involved Judge Bork, who had been nominated by President Ronald Reagan to a seat on the Supreme Court. A weekly Washington newspaper did a profile on the judge based upon 146 films that his family had rented from a video store. Although there were no sexually explicit videos in the records, and no embarrassing revelations, concerns were raised about the privacy of an individual's video rentals and purchases. As a result Congress passed the Video Privacy Protection Act in 1988, which prevents retailers from selling or revealing video rental records without the customer's consent or a court order. At the present time, the privacy of records held by government agencies are protected by the 1974 Privacy Act, but there is still no comprehensive law that protects records collected by private institutions and business.

Another concern related to the right to privacy is raised when the government attempts to obtain information deemed necessary for the preservation of national security. In 1987 the FBI asked libraries to supply them with a list of people who had borrowed books on subjects that might aid terrorists. The libraries refused to produce the lists, arguing that their borrowing records are private: nevertheless, the agency's request raised serious concerns about government access to private individual records. In the wake of the Oklahoma City bombing, such FBI requests might well become routine.

The privacy debate has touched every corner of our lives, from the living room to the garbage dump. Indeed, in 1988 the Supreme Court ruled that an individual's right to privacy does not extend to preventing the police from searching through garbage. This may seem a rather remote problem for most people, but it can be a very real one for celebrities: former Secretary of State Henry Kissinger once attempted to restrain a reporter from going through his garbage on the grounds that his privacy was being invaded.

State and Municipal Privacy Legislation

Absent a federal privacy statute, states and municipalities are assuming more of a role in creating legislation for interactive television. Although several states have adopted or introduced cable television privacy legislation, their intent has sometimes been weakened by the political fallout of the regulatory process. The first state to translate its expression of concern about privacy into statutory rule was Minnesota. In 1975 an administrative agency of the state, the Minnesota Cable Television Commission, was granted legislative jurisdiction for formulating rules addressing the privacy issue. These regulations must be incorporated into all cable television franchises negotiated by the various municipalities within the state. They include strict prohibitions against unauthorized monitoring and sharing of subscriber information without prior written consent from the subscriber. An increasing number of municipalities across the country have become sensitive to the cable television privacy issue and are using the Minnesota Privacy Rule as a model for enacting similar legislation.

In 1981, Illinois became the first state to enact comprehensive statewide privacy legislation. The basic components of the Illinois Cable Television Privacy Act include provisions prohibiting the unauthorized monitoring of subscriber services and the sharing of information with third parties. Other states that have either enacted or introduced privacy legislation include Maryland, California, Massachusetts, New York, and New Jersey. While most state bills address the critical areas of monitoring, access, and subscriber confidentiality, they are often inadequate in their enforcement and procedural design.

While the federal government has not as yet acted on providing Americans with a universal privacy protection standard, it has passed legislation providing access to court-authorized wiretaps and traced calls. In a bill passed by Congress in 1994, $500 million in federal money was provided to communications companies to allow for the development and installation of surveillance software.

The legislation, which was strongly lobbied for by the FBI, authorizes the monitoring of public communications networks but excludes conventional cable television services and private corporate telephone and computer networks. However, the legislation does apply to two-way communications, which is a function of both cable television and telephony. It also provides limited access to billing data associated with interactive communications.

The Cable Communications Policy Act of 1984 established an important precedent concerning a cable operator's use of personal subscriber information. The 1984 act states that a cable company can collect "personally identifiable" information for only two purposes: information to serve the subscriber or for the investigation of unauthorized reception of a cable signal. Any information gathered must be destroyed once it is used. Such information cannot even be disclosed to the government unless there is a compelling reason that outweighs the subscriber's right to privacy.

As our society evolves toward an electronic "information highway," rules governing the collection of personal data about individuals will define a critical dimension of the right to privacy. The need to create safeguards against the potential abuse of this data is paramount to the protection of the Constitutional rights of all Americans. Mechanisms must be established to address the accuracy, currency, and relevance of data collection and the way it is applied and manipulated. As we develop a "womb-to-tomb" electronic dossier, the need for a comprehensive privacy policy is not a luxury but a necessity.

NOTES

1. See Peter Huber, "Loose Ends," *Media Law & Policy*, vol. IV, no. I (November, 1995), 1–9.

2. In 1996 Rupert Murdoch's News Corporation announced an agreement with MCI to launch a joint DBS effort by 1997. In a 1996 FCC auction, MCI purchased the last available orbital DBS slot for $682.5 million. TCI, having lost the orbital slot to MCI, in 1996 announced a joint venture with Telsat Canada to launch a U.S. DBS service.

3. In January 1996 AT&T announced that it would purchase 2.5 percent of Direct TV for $137.5 million. This purchase represents AT&T's first investment in television during its 111-year history.

4. Bell Atlantic has estimated that it may cost as much as $17,000 per household for a fully interactive video and telephone system.

5. *Universal City Studios v. Sony* (1979).

6. *Universal City Studios v. Sony* (1981).

7. *Sony Corporation v. Universal Studios* (1984).

8. According to marketing statistics, it is estimated that consumer product revolutions in the United States average a ten-to-fifteen year time frame before taking hold. Various technological improvements over existing technologies, like FM radio and color television, took about five years to reach 1 percent of the population and ten years to penetrate another 50 percent of households. About 13 million VCRs were sold in 1995.

9. This system is known as VCR-Plus. In 1995, StarSight, an on-screen programming grid, was introduced. Developed by StarSight Telecast Inc., the service is keyed to a local cable system and costs about $4.00 a month. Index Plus, another on-screen programming device, offers free listings with its signal carried over the ABC television network.

10. It costs ten-to-fifteen cents to manufacture a Lexan (clear plastic polycarbonate) audio compact disk.

11. Digital videodisk players became available to the public in the fall of 1996, and recordable DVD machines are scheduled for introduction by 1998.

12. Patrick M. Reilly, "Camcorder Makers, with Growth Easing, Try to Bring New Markets into the Picture," *Wall Street Journal*, December 26, 1991, B1.

13. In 1996 RCA and Sharp introduced consumer compact digital camcorders, the RCA CC900D and Sharp's Digital Viewcam.

14. Anthony Ramirez, "New Video Previewed by Makers," *New York Times*, June 3, 1993, D5.

15. The consortia are: General Instrument Corporation, Massachusetts Institute of Technology, and Zenith Electronics Inc.; American Telephone and Telegraph Co., David Sarnoff Research Center, U.S. units of Thomson SA of France, Phillips Electronics, NV of the Netherlands, General Electric Company's subsidiary NBC, and Compression Labs, Inc.

16. The cost of early television sets in 1948 are roughly analogous to that of the HDTV sets of the 1990s. In 1948, a five-to-seven inch television receiver cost between $375-500, which represented several weeks' pay for the average U.S. worker.

17. However, none of the sets will be manufactured by U.S. companies. In July 1995, the Zenith Electronics Corporation, the last American-owned television manufacturer, sold 57.7 percent of its company (valued at $350 million) to L. G. Electronics, Inc., a South Korean company that markets equipment under the Goldstar name.

18. Current estimates projected by the government call for a total income of $32.3 billion generated from spectrum auctions over the next seven years.

19. AT&T is no longer associated with the Castro Valley test.

20. Geraldine Fabrikant, "The King of Cable Reaches for More," *New York Times*, May 30, 1993, sec. 3-1, G.

21. A 1995 Louis Harris & Associates poll found that 80 percent of Americans agree that "consumers have lost control over how personal information about them is circulated and used by companies."

22. In 1995 Paul C. Kocher, a researcher and security consultant, discovered a vulnerability in "public-key encryption," a technology used in electronic bank-

ing and shopping. He found that the mathematical security codes could be compromised.

23. *U.S. v. Miller* (1976).

24. See Don R. Pember, *Mass Media Law, 7th edition.* Dubuque: Brown & Benchmark, 1996.

25. In 1996 Congress passed Public Law 104-104, the Telecommunications Act of 1996. Section 222 of the Act addresses "Privacy of Customer Information." Included in the Act are subsections (b) and (c) which address Confidentiality of Carrier Information and Confidentiality of Customer Proprietary Network Information, respectively.

26. *U.S. v. Miller* (1976).

27. *Shoars v. Epson Am. Inc.,* No. SWC 112749 (Cal. Super. Ct., December 8, 1992).

9
Public Broadcasting:
Its Dwindling Account

The history of educational broadcasting—now called public broadcasting—is a story of idealism, greed, ignorance, and broken promises. While one must respect the lofty intentions of those who created public broadcasting's original design, the scheme was inherently flawed by the expectation that the system could function effectively as a partnership between the federal government and the private sector.

That broadcasting should have an educational orientation is not surprising, since some of the first experimental radio broadcasts were done under the auspices of colleges and universities. By the end of 1922, of the five hundred radio stations on the air, seventy-four were operated by colleges and universities.

During these early years, educators attempted to reserve radio frequencies for educational use, but their efforts were met with great resistance from commercial broadcasters. An amendment to the Communications Act of 1934 was proposed by two senators, Wagner from New York and Hatfield from West Virginia. It recommended that all current broadcasting licenses be cancelled and then reassigned, with 25 percent of all frequencies going to nonprofit organizations.

The Wagner-Hatfield amendment met with vigorous opposition from commercial broadcasters who focused their attack on a funding provision that would have allowed educational broadcasters to sell advertising to defray operating costs but not to earn a profit. Commercial broadcasters argued that if the purpose for assigning more radio frequencies to educational broadcasters was to decrease advertising, then this provision made no sense. The Communications Act of 1934 became law without the Wagner-Hatfield amendment.

In 1939 the FCC allocated the first FM channels for educational use, and in 1945 the FCC rearranged the FM band, allocating twenty out of a hundred channels for noncommercial or educational programming. To understand the low priority the FCC gave to educational and noncommercial broadcasters, however one need only look at the 1948 FCC allocation of FM stations. These stations had ten-watt power and so could not broadcast further than two miles. So they were doomed to fail even before they started.

The fate of noncommercial educational broadcasting in the United States was determined by a set of coincidences that would have a dramatic impact upon its future. In 1948 President Harry F. Truman was elected by a narrow margin over his opponent, Thomas E. Dewey. Coincidentally, in 1948 the FCC, after having issued approximately one hundred television licenses, announced a freeze on any new allocations. The rationale for the freeze was that the FCC needed time to study interference problems between stations and to create some equity in the national distribution of television stations.

During the freeze, which lasted three and a half years, some of the most important decisions concerning noncommercial television were made. Among other things, public broadcasting gained a great champion in Frieda Hennock, Truman's appointee to the FCC and the first woman to hold the post.[1] Hennock campaigned vigorously for the reservation of television frequencies to noncommercial educational broadcasters. With the aid of private funding, the Joint Council on Educational Television (JCET) was formed, with the mission of lobbying for television frequencies.

The freeze ended in 1952, and a new table of frequency allocations that included noncommercial television was assigned. For educational use, 242 television channels were now reserved, and eventually the number was increased to 655. This victory, however, was compromised by the fact that only 127 of the channels were in the VHF band, while the other 528 were in the difficult-to-receive UHF spectrum. Nevertheless, a precedent had been established for the importance of educational television in broadcast media.

While the allocation of frequencies was a significant first step in the evolution of educational television, the funding support of an educational television system was also of importance. Initially the federal government did not furnish any funds for the development of educational television (ETV). The first coordinated support for ETV was generated from the private sector and came from the Ford Foundation. For two and a half decades, from the 1950s to the early 1970s, the Ford Foundation provided funding for program production, distribution, and system development.

In 1962 the federal government allocated its first funding for ETV via the Educational Television Facilities Act. This legislation provided

$32 million over five years to assist in the construction and development of educational television stations. By the end of 1966, 126 stations were on the air. As the construction of new stations proceeded, programming considerations became the next priority for ETV. The Ford Foundation addressed this issue in 1952 when it established the Educational Radio and Television Center (ERTC), which moved to New York City in 1959 and became National Educational Television (NET). In 1960 the first of the regional networks, the Eastern Educational Network (EEN), was founded to share programs with other networks and stations. Another important programming development occurred in 1962 when by some slick maneuvering and political pressuring, a New York City commercial station, WNDT, was purchased by a nonprofit organization and became WNET, the largest noncommercial station in the country and one of the most productive.

THE CARNEGIE COMMISSION

Educational television has generated a number of commissions and reports over the years which have addressed a myriad of issues pertinent to noncommercial broadcasters. By far the most important of these was the 1965 Carnegie Commission on Educational Television, which was sponsored by the Carnegie Corporation and financed by the Carnegie Foundation. Many of its recommendations were included in the landmark Public Broadcasting Act of 1967, which codified and designed the first national public broadcasting service in the nation. Key recommendations of the Carnegie Commission included a Corporation of Public Television to "receive and disburse private and federal funds," an excise tax on the sale of television sets to generate funds for noncommercial broadcasting, and for the creation of interconnection networking facilities by the Corporation for Public Television, and federal funding from the Department of Health, Education, and Welfare (HEW).

PUBLIC BROADCASTING ACT

Although many of the commission's provisions were integrated into the Public Broadcasting Act, several alterations and omissions have created perpetual problems for public broadcasting. In the legislation, the Corporation for Public Broadcasting (CPB) (so named to also include radio) was to provide station operating support directly and not via the

Department of HEW. This arrangement proved to be extremely disadvantageous for public broadcasting since Congress rejected the excise tax on television sets as a means of funding and instead adopted the annual budgetary appropriation scheme used for other government agencies. This increased the corporation's vulnerability to political pressures that could affect the funding of projects at various stations. Although the legislation made an attempt to "insulate" public broadcasting from outside interference, this effort was rendered useless by two other provisions.[2]

In its recommendations, the Carnegie Commission had proposed a twelve-member board for the CPB and had urged that six members be appointed by the president and the remaining six selected by the board. By proposing this arrangement, the Commission had hoped to protect the CPB board from political pressures. The Public Broadcasting Act, however, created a fifteen-member board, all to be appointed by the president and confirmed by the Senate. Although Section 396B of the Public Broadcasting Act clearly states that the CPB would not be "an agency or establishment of the United States Government," it effectively became such as a result of the provisions in the Public Broadcasting Act.

Just as the Public Broadcasting Act compromised the funding and operational elements of the CPB, it addressed programming priorities in a similar manner. Whereas the Carnegie Commission felt that public television was capable of "becoming the clearest expression of American diversity and of excellence within diversity,"[3] wording that left plenty of room for interference by disgruntled politicians or offended business interests. The act stipulated that programs and series must provide "objectivity and balance" on any subject of a controversial nature. In addition, Section 399 of the act forbids any noncommercial educational broadcasting station to engage in editorializing or to support or oppose any candidate for political office. Politicians were obviously more concerned about protecting their own interests than in guaranteeing programming freedom to public broadcasting.

The act also prohibited the CPB from operating any networking facilities, and in 1969 the Public Broadcasting Service (PBS), a station membership organization, was created to manage the interconnection of stations.

As early as 1967, when public broadcasting was still in its infancy, it became apparent that the spheres of influence that dominated the system would eventually clash. These included CPB, PBS, local stations, corporate underwriters, and the White House. Most of these conflicts concerned programming accountability and control. During the Nixon administration, public broadcasting's vulnerability to political pressures became painfully apparent. By 1969, public television was distributing programs that demonstrated the diversity and creativity that was supposed to be an important part of its mission. Some of these programs, however, raised the ire of conservative politicians, and they responded with attempts to restrain public television's programming freedom. The programs that created the most controversy were *The Great American Dream Machine* (1970–71), an irreverent satirical series, and *Banks and the Poor* (1972), a probing documentary about the banking system and its discrimination against the poor, which also named 133 legislators and government officials who had connections in the banking industry. In addition, various news commentators, including Sander Vanocur, Robin MacNeil, Elizabeth Drew, and Bill Moyers, were all perceived as liberals holding a negative bias against the Nixon administration. Many of the public affairs programs featuring these commentators were produced at the National Public Affairs Center in Washington (NPACT), which was funded by the CPB and the Ford Foundation. NPACT became a target for attack by Nixon administration supporters.

In 1972 President Nixon used his veto power to defeat legislation passed by both houses of Congress that would have provided a $155 million funding authorization for CPB. Nixon cited both a lack of localism within the system and fiscal prudence as the rationale for his veto. His action, however, could also be seen as an obvious attempt to suppress the "liberal" orientation of public television programming. Despite the Nixon veto, a bill to support public broadcasting was finally passed in 1973.

FUND-RAISING

One of the most persistent problems facing public broadcasting is financing. Producing high-quality television programs is expensive even in the best of times, and the costs are not nearly covered by federal or state station appropriations. Therefore, public television stations around the country have turned to a number of alternative fund-raising schemes including auctions, membership drives, and corporate underwriting.

Membership drives have also long been a cornerstone of public television station fund-raising efforts. The money generated from viewers represents a significant portion of public television's funding: in 1989, 22 percent of public television's revenues came from direct viewer support. Unfortunately, although viewer financing is an integral component of public television's revenue base, there has been a declining trend in viewer contributions.[4] This may be attributed to audience dissatisfaction with the increased frequency of the membership drives. Also, competition from cable stations and the home video market have cut into PBS's audience support.[5] Further declines in membership contributions occurred into the 1990s as the recession took hold. In addition, many parents of preschool children were appalled at the perceived manipulation of children with fund-raising messages aired adjacent to the *Barney and Friends* preschool television program. Indeed, the offering of *Barney*-related premiums for specified donations placed many parents in the awkward position of attempting to explain economic realities to whining preschoolers, an unpleasant task to say the least. Stations responded to viewer complaints by decreasing the number of pledge weeks, using alternative membership recruitment schemes, and devising a national programming schedule that responds to audience needs and tastes.

During the last two decades, public television stations have also cultivated a continuous source of funding from the private sector: this is known as "enhanced corporate underwriting." However, cable television, which offers programming similar to that of public television, has siphoned away some of the corporate underwriting dollars to advertising on cable channels. And while the money allocated to public television stations by corporations has alleviated some of the financial stress upon the system, concerns have been expressed about some of the negative effects corporate money can have upon programming.

Although the dangers of corporate underwriting are perhaps more covert than overt, there have been notable abuses by corporate underwriters. One of the most flagrant of these occurred in 1977, when PBS announced that it had acquired the license to broadcast a British-produced docudrama entitled *Death of a Princess.* The program dramatized an actual event involving a young Saudi Arabian princess who had committed adultery, and was publicly executed along with her lover. The program had caused such a stir in England that the Saudis recalled their ambassador: they threatened similar action if PBS broadcast the program in the United States. Mobil, the corporate underwriter, led a print advertising campaign by the oil interests to squelch the program, while the Saudis hired an influential Washington law firm that attempted to win a restraining order. Although the program was distributed by PBS, a number of affiliated stations chose not to broadcast it. This was an outrageous attempt by the corporate sector and a foreign power to censor American public television: unfortunately, their efforts did have an impact on the number of stations that carried the program.

A corporate underwriter may also use its presence in public television to manipulate public opinion. In 1987, the Mobil Corporation provided $300,000, or 80 percent, of the funding for a documentary critical of prime-time television's treatment of businessmen. The program, "Hollywood's Favorite Heavy: Businessmen on Prime Time TV," criticized programs like *Dallas, Dynasty,* and *Falcon Crest* for their negative treatment of the business community.

While at times the objectives of corporate underwriters may conflict with those of public television, their support in other cases has yielded distinguished results. After the successful distribution of the BBC's *Forsyte Saga* on public television in 1970, Mobil was approached by Boston public television station WGBH to underwrite a series featuring both literary adaptations and original programming. Selecting Anglophile and former British subject Alistair Cooke as host, Masterpiece Theater made its debut in 1971 with a historical-costume drama, *The First Churchills*. Distinguishing itself with original scripts, high-quality literary adaptations, and provocative dramas, Masterpiece Theater legitimized the miniseries as a standard format for American television.

Masterpiece Theater provided Mobil with an excellent vehicle to cultivate and nurture its corporate image. At times criticized for featuring British programs exclusively and for addressing themes removed from American culture, Masterpiece Theater nevertheless set a standard of excellence that served as a model for American commercial television.

Although British programming has been a visible component of public television, marketplace economics and a new competitive agenda have conspired to force a reevaluation of programming priorities. The competitive realities of audience dispersal to cable television and video rentals has made PBS more receptive to commercial television formats and themes. Cable television especially has challenged PBS's traditional niche in science, nature, and foreign programming. The rivalry between cable and PBS in this area is evidenced in the change in programming and acquisition patterns at PBS. At one time Lionheart Television, the BBC-owned distribution company in the United States, earned 80 percent of its income from public television: however, cable has opened new markets for its product, and the BBC has entered into some exclusive relationships with cable networks.

These factors have prompted PBS to aggressively pursue commercially oriented imperatives. Starting with the fall 1990 season, PBS launched a "Showcase Week" designed to promote returning series and urging viewers to tune in. Creating viewer awareness of their programming schedule has become a priority at PBS, with an increased allocation to promotional budgets, national advertising on commercial television, and miniseries "stripping" (scheduling segments on consecutive nights).

For the fall 1994 season, PBS launched an ambitious schedule dubbed the "children's initiative." "PTV, The Ready to Learn Service," featured a nine-hour block of children's programming with extensive community outreach services. Featuring the first wholly owned, copyrighted PBS characters, known as the P-Pals, new programs included in the schedule were *The Puzzleworks*, *Storytime*, and *The Magic School Bus*, the first fully animated program on the PBS schedule. As part of this outreach effort, PBS also created a new magazine, activity guides, a program calendar, and on-line services that provide direct access to PTV materials. Initially premiering in ten television markets, the Ready-to-Learn Service is now scheduled on all of the 346 PBS stations.

Recognizing the need for a stronger national PBS programming service, a 1993 report issued by the Twentieth Century Fund Task Force on Public Television recommended that about half of the $250 million appropriated annually to public television be allocated to national programming.[6] The task force also proposed that the government generate income for public television funds from spectrum auctions (a way of charging broadcasters for using valuable television and radio frequencies) and from surcharges on the sale of broadcast stations and other FCC-licensed facilities. In addition, the task force urged private partnerships between public television stations and business.[7]

One funding recommendation that appears to be popular is the creation of an endowment or trust that would earn money from spectrum auction fees and transfer fees on commercial broadcast licenses. It is estimated that billions of dollars could be raised through such a mechanism.[8]

Facing declining corporate support and the specter of decreased government funding, public television stations have had to establish an agenda of fiscal austerity to survive. In this new climate, stations have been forced to lay off personnel and consolidate operations. For example, New York's station, WNET, and Connecticut Public Broadcasting merged their back-office operations in order to effect significant savings. Other stations are leasing out their production facilities and forming joint ventures with domestic and foreign producers.

Programming for public television emanates from a number of sources including public television stations, independent production companies, joint productions of public television and independent companies, and foreign acquisitions. Independent producers contribute the largest share of programming, followed by the public television stations.

One of the most valued and respected television components of the PBS schedule is its children's programming. Although funding of children's programs is modest by commercial standards ($16.3 million in 1993, while a network might spent that amount on a single program), the ratings for children's public television programming are the envy of the industry. Preschool programming is particularly strong, with 65 percent of the nation's 15.2 million children tuning into PBS each week.

In an effort to tap new sources of funding for their children's television schedule, PBS, along with the respective production companies, are licensing popular program characters to the retail marketplace. One of the most successful of these endeavors is the Barney dinosaur character from *Barney and Friends*. Indeed, Barney has come to symbolize the issue of mass merchandising that has raised the ire of many lawmakers and caused Senator Robert Dole (Republican, Kansas), to refer to the popular character as a "cash cow."[9]

Why would the endearing, loveable characters of some of television's most popular children's programs bring a scowl to the faces of legislators? The answer, of course, is money. *Sesame Street* has generated a billion-dollar industry in licensed product merchandise, and its parent company, Children's Television Workshop (CTW), has an investment portfolio with an estimated worth of $58 million. In 1995 CTW signed an exclusive agreement with Sony for distribution of *Sesame Street* theatrical films, home video, audio tapes, and book publishing.[10] The deal with Sony expires in the year 2000. In addition, CTW is hoping to launch its own cable channel by 1997.[11] With the commercial success of Barney, who alone generates several hundred million dollars annually in merchandise sales, legislators question the need to provide funding for public television programs, claiming it could be self-sufficient.

The question of ancillary revenue has become even more critical as legislators struggle with a huge budget deficit. Legislators have protested the meager amount of money the CPB received as a share of these earnings. (Of the millions of dollars generated from character merchandising sales, the CPB's share of revenue reached an all-time high of $317,000 in 1991!) Ervin Duggan, the former FCC commissioner who assumed the office of president and CEO of PBS in 1994, has made the issue of merchandising revenue a priority. New contractual terms have been negotiated, with some producers requiring PBS to use the money within ten years for new national public broadcasting programming.

The PBS network distributes about fifteen hundred hours of programming a year to its affiliated stations. One of the most respected programs on the network was the *MacNeil-Lehrer News Hour*, which began in 1983. This program has received the most corporate support of any program on public television. In 1995, three underwriters—Archer Daniels Midland Company, New York Life Insurance, and Pepsi Cola Incorporated—each provided grants of $4.4 million, with the balance of its $26 million budget coming from the CPB. Robert MacNeil left the program in 1995 to pursue other interests. Other programs in the public television public affairs genre include *Frontline* and *Wall Street Week*.

An important factor in PBS programming has been the maintenance of a "core" programming schedule by all PBS member stations. Unlike the commercial networks, PBS affiliated stations can choose to broadcast PBS programming at times that are best suited for them. For the core schedule, which includes some of PBS's most popular programming, stations are urged, but not required, to broadcast on the same night.

Broadcasting the national PBS core programs on a common time schedule allows for more effective national promotion and is more attractive to national program corporate underwriters.

Defining the public television audience can be difficult. Research has revealed that this audience is more selective, better educated, and watches less television than their commercial television audience counterparts. Income levels of public television households also tend to be higher than their commercial television counterparts.[12]

The public television audience is quite small when compared to that of the commercial networks, independent stations, and all of basic cable programming. PBS's share of audience falls significantly below the commercial broadcasters. Indeed, recent estimates have indicated that the PBS audience has declined in excess of 10 percent over the last five years.

These relatively small audiences, along with competition from cable and the occasional controversy generated by PBS programming, have caused some critics to charge public television with being elitist. In 1992 Dr. Laurence Jarvik, a Heritage Foundation scholar, wrote a paper entitled "Making Public Television Public," in which he described public television as "a solution in search of a problem" and called it "unnecessary and wasteful." His recommendation was to end public funding and to turn the CPB into a private company.[13] And Dr. Neil Postman, a communications scholar and professor at New York University, has charged that the children's programming on public television does not inspire ghetto children, and that the programming causes children to love the activity of watching television rather than the characters depicted on the programs.[14]

One characteristic that has distinguished public television programming from programs on cable or broadcast television is the controversy and debate that it sometimes generates. While this could be viewed as a healthy sign of independence in programming, it also places public television in the awkward position of constantly having to defend itself.

One program about being black and gay, "Tongues Untied," broadcast on PBS in 1991, generated a substantial amount of protest. As part of a series titled POV (for "Point of View"), the program outraged some legislators and prompted Senator Jesse Helms (Republican, North Carolina), to publicly condemn it. The Christian right used the program as a rallying cry for its cause, and Pat Robertson of the Christian Coalition produced a seven-minute tape of highlights of the program for distribution to members of Congress.

Interestingly, the POV series, which is produced by WNET in New York, derived a substantial amount of its support from private funding, including a three-year, $1.65 million grant from the MacArthur Foundation. However, it had also received a grant from the National

Endowment for the Arts (NEA).

While public television has adopted some commercial priorities in response to marketplace realities, it nevertheless has sustained an impressive and unwavering commitment to excellence in programming. It has attempted to present diversity in its programming while addressing cultural and societal issues that are at the heart of American society. The themes it focusses on may be perceived by some as distasteful and immoral. However, if public television is to survive and carry out its mission of enlightening as well as entertaining, it must continue to fight interference by special interests and persist in its determination to provide its viewers with honest and comprehensive examination of issues that may be controversial.

NOTES

1. Henry Morgenthau, "Dona Quixote: The Adventures of Frieda Hennock," *Television Quarterly*, Vol. 26, no. 2 (1992), 61–73.

2. The "insulating" clause is in Section [397] 398.

3. Carnegie Commission on Educational Television. *Public Broadcasting: a Program for Action: the Report and Recommendation of the Carnegie Commission on Educational Television*. New York: Harper & Row. 1967, p. 18.

4. In 1990, membership pledges fell by 11.5 percent, which netted 6.8 percent fewer dollars for public television, and it was estimated that the nationwide PBS audience had fallen about 10 percent over a five-year period.

5. In an interesting twist, the most widely watched of the basic cable channels announced that it would provide $1 million in underwriting for Charlie Rose, which is distributed on PBS. See *Quality Time: The Report of the Twentieth Century Fund Task Force on Public Television* (New York: The Twentieth Century Fund Press, 1993).

6. Federal funding now accounts for less than 17 percent of the total budget expended by the Corporation for Public Broadcasting each year.

7. Bell Atlantic, the regional Bell operating company, announced in 1995 that it may be interested in investing in the CPB.

8. Laurence Jarvik, "Getting Big Bird Off the Dole," *New York Times*, June 14, 1992, 24.

9. Mary Lu Carnevale, "Parents Say PBS Stations Exploit Barney in Fund Drives," *Wall Street Journal*, March 19, 1993, B1.

10. For the 1995 season of *Sesame Street*, CTW embarked on a new instructional pedagogy linked to the theory of "multiple intelligences," which recognizes learning other than linguistic.

11. The working title for the network is New Kids City. CTW has retained the services of the investment banking firm Allen & Co. to assist in finding investors to raise the requisite $100 million.

12. According to A. C. Nielsen, 34.3 percent of the public television audience

have four years of high school, while 24.4 percent have four or more years of college. Compared to total television households, 20.3 percent of public television households have incomes of $40,000 to $59,999, while only 18.5 percent of total television households have the same income.

13. Laurence Jarvik, "Getting Big Bird Off the Dole," *New York Times*, June 14, 1992, 24.

14. Warren Berger, "We Interrupt This Program ... Forever?" *New York Times*, January 29, 1995, sec. 2, 1.

10
Toward a Wired Nation: Cable TV

Much has been written about the abuse of television and its hypnotic effect upon viewers. Broadcast television, by its nature being directed at a mass audience, dispenses homogenized programming to its public. When cable television was first introduced, it was seen as a technology that would provide unique program services to its audience. Many hoped that cable television would create a new era in service and programming, and there is no doubt that it has brought about many changes in the entertainment marketplace: the question is whether it has lived up to its promise of providing a genuine alternative to broadcast television.

CABLE EVOLVES

In the late 1940s and early 1950s, television fever swept the nation. Television sets became a priority purchase for many households: everyone was eager to see and hear the programs that their friends and neighbors were talking about. But there were sections of the country where television signals were difficult to receive because of mountain ranges and rough terrain. People who lived in these areas were cut off from this new phenomenon of television: even if they bought television sets, reception was so poor as to be virtually useless.

Pennsylvania was one of the states where television signal distribution was difficult and television sales stagnant because of inhospitable terrain. Stagnant, that is, until a few enterprising businessmen, including several appliance dealers, in Lansford, Pennsylvania, developed a scheme to provide television service to the residents of Panther Valley. In

1950 they erected a receiving antenna in an elevated spot known as Summit Hill and ran a cable from the antenna to the community of Panther Valley. For a modest fee, and sometimes even free of charge, Panther Valley residents could enjoy their favorite television programs via cable, and appliance dealers could sell them television sets: technology and business had once again proved to be a winning partnership.

The success of the Panther Valley Community Antenna Television system created a lot of publicity for cable television. Both the *New York Times* and *Newsweek* ran stories about the unique television distribution system.[1] The individuals who first started cable television in their communities, however, could never have realized the implications their actions would come to have on the regulatory, economic, and technological aspects of modern communications in the United States.

Nevertheless, during the 1950s the growth of cable television was relatively slow and associated only with those regions that had poor broadcast television reception. At that time the broadcasting industry took little notice of cable because they were enjoying a rapid growth in television. The FCC expressed no desire to regulate cable and in a 1959 inquiry stated that it was unable to determine any impact of cable upon the television broadcasting industry.

In the 1960s, a number of competitive issues arose that did concern the broadcasting industry. Of primary concern was ownership of programming disseminated by cable companies from signals that they were picking up from broadcasting stations. During the 1960s, a number of significant court cases addressed several interrelated issues of paramount importance to both the cable television industry and the broadcasters. The debate over these issues, which is still active today, can be better understood in the context of a historical perspective.

The earliest suits that broadcasters initiated against cable named microwave carriers as the defendants. For the FCC, the relationship of microwave carriers to cable television helped to establish a regulatory stance toward the cable industry. During the late 1950s, the FCC's posture toward regulating cable television had been unclear. Cable television was transmitted by wire, not over the air. While the FCC had jurisdiction over broadcasters, cable television did not use the broadcast spectrum. Nor was cable a common carrier like the telephone or telegraph, which made oversight by the FCC problematic.

The regulatory issue became clearer, however, when microwave companies, which do utilize the broadcast spectrum, began to relay the signals of local television stations for retransmission in cable systems. Court actions questioned the right of microwave carriers to pick up broadcast signals and supply them to the cable companies who in turn distributed them to their subscribers. In a 1961 case known as *Intermountain*

Broadcasting v. Idaho Microwave, the court found in favor of the microwave company and stated that broadcasters had no authority to restrict the use of their signals after transmission. Although the case was a victory for cable television, it did not define a general policy that would address the larger issue of program ownership.

In 1963, shortly after the Intermountain case, the FCC became involved in a controversial ruling. Once again the case involved a microwave company, known as the Carter Mountain Transmission Company in Wyoming. Once again the issue in question was the distribution of broadcast signals by a microwave company to a cable facility. Carter Mountain petitioned the FCC for permission to install microwave equipment and relay the television signals of KWRB-TV, Channel 10 in Riverton, Wyoming, a local broadcast station, to three cable television systems. Initially an FCC hearing officer granted the request, but permission was revoked when the broadcast station complained. The FCC explained its reversal by citing its duty to ascertain the economic injury that may result from cable television and how this competition affects the public interest. This regulatory standard was predicated by the precedent set by *Carroll Broadcasting Co. v. FCC* in 1958. In this case the United States Court of Appeals for the District of Columbia concluded that "to license two stations where there is revenue for only one may result in no good service at all."[2]

While the cable industry was victorious in these early decisions concerning program distribution and exclusivity rights, a powerful lobbying effort by the broadcasters sought to inhibit the further growth of cable television. As a result, the FCC established a regulatory posture that was hostile toward cable television. In 1965 the FCC issued its First Report and Order that asserted the commission's jurisdiction over all cable television systems. As its rationale, the commission cited its responsibility to prevent the destruction or degradation of broadcasting from cable competition. It also adopted a number of inhibitory regulations that were designed to prevent the growth and development of cable television, especially in the major markets.

The cable television industry argued that the FCC had no jurisdiction over cable transmission, which did not use the broadcast spectrum, but the Supreme Court upheld the FCC's responsibility for regulatory oversight of cable in *U.S. v. Southwestern Cable Co.* in 1968.[3]

One of the issues that has generated great controversy between the cable and broadcasting industries has to do with the exclusivity rights of broadcast programming. Broadcasters have claimed that they have exclusive contractual rights to the programs that they broadcast by virtue of the licensing agreements with their program suppliers. In *Cable Vision v. KUTV* (1964), the broadcaster claimed that it held exclusive rights by virtue of contract to the first run of its affiliated network television programs. This case also addressed another issue: the protection of syndicated programs. The broadcaster argued that unfair competition resulted when a cable operator was allowed to import from a distant station the same program that the local broadcaster was distributing via contractual agreement over its station. Program competition due to the importation of distant signals by cable, vying with the same program distributed by local broadcasters, addresses the issue known as syndicated exclusivity. A lower court found that the existing contracts provided exclusive protection to the broadcasters. The Ninth Circuit Court of Appeals, however, reversed the lower court decision and held that broadcasters could protect their programming only if they could "demonstrate a protectable interest by virtue of the copyright laws." This case was a victory for cable television because in 1964 the only copyright legislation that existed was the Copyright Act of 1909, which made no mention of television: therefore it would be difficult for the broadcasters to claim a "protectable interest."

In 1968 the Supreme Court reversed two lower court decisions, holding that cable companies were not liable to the copyright provisions of the 1909 Copyright Act. The case, known as *Fortnightly Corp. v. United Artists Television*, involved the carriage of several motion pictures licensed for exclusive use to television stations whose signals were picked up by the Fortnightly Corporation, a microwave carrier, and distributed to a number of cable systems. Although the lower courts had decided in favor of United Artists, the Supreme Court reversed their decisions, pointing out that cable operators did not broadcast or rebroadcast television signals; they simply enhanced the capacity of viewers to receive the broadcasters' signals.

While the cable industry was victorious in the courts, they suffered in the public policy forum: the FCC continued its restrictive posture toward the industry. Soon after the Fortnightly decision, the FCC proposed rules that required full retransmission consent from all parties holding ownership in each broadcast program including networks, affiliated stations, film syndicators, and other program suppliers. In 1972 a comprehensive set of cable regulations went into effect which required cable systems to receive a certificate of compliance from the FCC. In 1988, in yet another change of policy, the FCC unanimously adopted new syndicated exclusivity rules that would protect local stations from distant signals and duplicative programming that cable systems import. These rules require cable systems to delete duplicative programming and have resulted in increased costs to cable operators. The new stipulations, which went into effect in 1989, exempt any cable operator with fewer than one thousand subscribers. The broadcasting industry lobbied for reinstatement because they felt that program exclusivity increases viewing choices, decreases program duplication, and protects their contractual programming rights to exclusive material. As part of its rationale for adopting the change, the FCC cited a radical alteration in the programming environment and the dramatically reduced costs of satellite delivery systems. As expected, there have been a number of challenges to the new syndicated exclusivity rules, whose opponents include common carriers that distribute superstation signals and other cable interests.

In 1972, the FCC initiated rules requiring cable systems with more than thirty-five hundred subscribers to originate cablecasts and create their own programming. In addition, the FCC required the enforcement of equal time rules, sponsor identification rules, and the Fairness Doctrine on cable-originated programming. The FCC rules were challenged by Midwest Video Corporation, and the case went to the Supreme Court, which once again upheld the authority of the FCC.[4] After receiving reaffirmation of its regulatory oversight of cable television, in 1972 the FCC issued the Fourth Report and Order on Cable Television Service, a comprehensive set of regulations.

In 1976, the FCC attempted to create a more comprehensive doctrine for local cablecasting by requiring cable systems with more than thirty-five hundred subscribers carrying over-the-air broadcast signals to have a twenty-channel capacity by 1986, to specify access channels for third parties, and to furnish equipment and facilities for the production and broadcast of "access" programming. Midwest Video again challenged the new rules, and in 1979 the Supreme Court upheld the company's challenge.[5]

The regulatory climate for the cable and broadcast industries was dramatically changed by the Copyright Act of 1976 and the Cable Communications Policy Act of 1984. The Copyright Act provides for a compulsory license that allows cable operators to retransmit radio and television signals as prescribed by FCC rules. The act requires that cable systems pay for distant nonnetwork television programs. Fees are computed by using a complex formula dependent upon subscriber revenues and distant signal equivalents.[6]

The Cable Communications Policy Act of 1984 created a national regulatory policy where previously none had existed. One of the most crucial areas the act addressed was the regulation of basic channel subscription rates. A basic channel service provided by the cable operator usually consists of several local broadcast stations and specialized channels like the CNN or ESPN. The basic service is distinguished from premium channels, for which the subscriber pays a separate monthly service charge. Premium channels include HBO, Showtime, and the Disney Channel, among others.

The Cable Act addressed the regulation of basic channel rates but by its definition preempted any effective regulatory oversight. It gave local governments the latitude of regulating basic rates through 1986, and thereafter the franchising authority—in most cases, the local government—could regulate basic service rates only if the cable system was without "effective competition" in the community. (Effective competition was defined as three over-the-air broadcast channels available to viewers.) Since most communities meet this standard, cable basic services rates were unregulated.

As basic service rates began to climb, the FCC in 1991 revised its definition of "effective competition." Under the new rules, "effective competition" refers to the ability to receive six over-the-air broadcast channels. With this revision, 60 percent of cable systems were now subject to basic rate regulation. The Cable Television Consumer Protection and Competititon Act of 1992 came in response to an outcry of protest from consumers annoyed at the rapid increase in basic cable subscription rates. With basic cable subscription rates having increased 50 percent, or more than three times the rate of inflation, since 1984, the act of 1992 attempted to provide consumers with some relief. The FCC's plan is to establish "reasonable" monthly fees for basic cable service provided by monopoly cable systems. Subscription rates would depend upon competitive variables including the presence of other multichannel video services (satellite, other cable companies, wireless cable, etc.) within the franchise area. Local franchising authorities will regulate rates for basic cable service using the FCC guidelines. Cable companies, if they choose, can calculate rates based upon their actual costs of providing service. If they opt for an actual cost pricing structure, the cable company must provide the FCC with detailed cost data.

The reduction rules for basic cable service rates had a negligible effect on consumers: in some cases a subscriber's monthly bill actually increased! Reed Hundt, President Clinton's appointment as chairman of the FCC, made further rate reductions a priority for his regulatory agenda. This resulted in an additional 7 percent decrease in basic subscription rates, effective May 1994. As a result of the combined decreases, the FCC found that basic cable subscription rates fell an average of 8.5 percent in twenty-five of the nation's biggest cities, with a decline of $1.50 in the average monthly cable bill.

The FCC may have been premature in creating a complex structure of regulatory rate policy that yielded so little in billing relief for the average cable television subscriber. With the entry of telephone companies into cable television programming distribution, it seems that marketplace factors and competition may be the best incentive for reducing cable rates.[7] Having this in mind, Congress passed a Telecommunications Act in 1996 that eliminated rate regulation for service beyond a basic tier by 1999.

Other regulatory issues addressed by the Cable Communications Policy Act of 1984 included approval by local governments to charge a franchise fee of up to 5 percent of a cable operator's gross revenue. The act of 1984 also dealt with channel allotments provided to communities by cable operators, allowing the establishment of public access channels for free use on a nondiscriminatory, first-come, first-served basis. Commercial access channels set aside for use by "unaffiliated programmers" were also established by the 1984 act. Other provisions in the 1984 legislation concern indecency and privacy. The government can prohibit and penalize the broadcast of obscene material over cable television: however, precedent established by the federal courts clearly suggests that only the FCC has jurisdiction in this area. In the case of public access channels, the issue of obscenity and indecency is even more difficult to enforce because of the "nondiscriminatory use" status of these channels.[8]

One of the more vexing problems affecting both local television broadcasters and cable television systems are the "must-carry" rules. These provisions require cable systems to designate channel space to over-the-air local television broadcasters. Prior to 1986 the FCC required that all cable systems carry the signals of commercial broadcast stations located within thirty-five miles of the community served by the cable operator. However, a court of appeals case vacated the must-carry rules, stating that they violated the First Amendment rights of cable operators and subscribers. The court agreed with the cable operators that the must-carry provisions compromised their editorial discretion to program the channels as they saw fit.[9]

In 1986 the FCC, supported by both the cable and broadcasting industries, announced new must-carry rules to last for a term of five years. These rules required cable systems to provide frequency space to local channels based upon designated percentages computed from the channel capacity of the system. For example, those systems with a twenty-channel capacity needed only to carry one public broadcasting station; systems with between twenty-one and twenty-seven channels had to allocate seven channels to local broadcast signals, and systems with more than twenty-seven channels were required to allocate 25 percent of their capacity to local television signals.

By designating a five-year term to these must-carry rules, the FCC hoped to provide the public with an opportunity to adjust to using an input selector device, also known as an "A/B" switch. This device allows viewers to change from cable to over-the-air broadcasting signals, giving them access to any local broadcast channels not being carried by the cable system. Such a switch, which is modestly priced, would have to be connected to an antenna, which would cost substantially more than the switch.

In 1987, a year after the FCC announced the new must-carry provisions, a U. S. Court of Appeals, in a case called *Century Communications v. FCC*, found that the new rules violated the cable operators' First Amendment rights. In addition, the court decided that the FCC failed to provide convincing evidence that it would take viewers five years to learn how to operate the "A/B" switches.

One of the more troublesome areas of the must-carry issue is the shifting of channels to different numerical assignments. There is ample evidence to suggest that lower numerical channel positions increase ratings and that cable operators reserve these spaces for services that enhance their positioning. Independent television stations suffer the most from cable channel switching and are eager to obtain relief from this problem.

The issue of must-carry and retransmission consent became a prominent component of the Cable Television Consumer Protection and Competition Act of 1992. In spite of the legislation facing a stormy approval process in Congress and a veto from President Bush, the Cable Act of 1992 passed with an overwhelming majority of both houses of Congress overriding the presidential veto.

Although the Cable Act of 1992 as a whole generated protest from the cable industry, the most controversial provisions were the retransmission consent and the must-carry rules. The legislation clearly provided a linkage between these two rules. ("Retransmission consent" is bureaucratic shorthand for permission granted to local cable operators by broadcasters to allow the cable system to retransmit the broadcast signal over their cable facilities.)

Under the "retransmission consent" and "must-carry" provisions of the Cable Act of 1992, broadcasters had the option of either demanding payment from the cable operator or forgoing the payment for a guarantee that their broadcast channel would remain on the cable system's channel inventory. If the broadcaster had filed for retransmission consent compensation and the two parties could not agree on terms, then the cable operator could summarily drop the broadcaster's channel from its programming inventory.

Some of the negative consequences of having cable operators invoke the must-carry provisions in lieu of compensation have created dissatisfaction among cable subscribers affiliated with systems that have a smaller channel capacity. For example, in Dover, New Jersey, the Sammons Communications cable system dropped its Sports Channel, which carried New York Mets' games, because it had to make room for a Christian Spanish-language station that invoked the must-carry rule. This was done even though the cable system already carried another Spanish-language channel and despite the fact that Hispanics make up less than 10 percent of the population in the community. And in Marin County, California, three broadcast stations meeting the must-carry requirement of being within a fifty-mile transmission radius of a cable system requested and qualified for must-carry status. To accommodate these stations, the Marin County cable system had to drop the arts channel, Bravo; part of the public affairs channel, C-Span; and a public station. The stations replacing these via must-carry rules include a Hispanic station, an Asian station, and a smaller public television station. (Interestingly, Asian and Hispanic ethnic groups account for only 5 percent of the population of Marin County.) However, the Cable Act of 1992 does state that public television stations cannot request compensation and must be carried by the cable operator.

The reality of must-carry and retransmission consent could have had an egregious impact upon cable subscribers. Clearly, cable subscribers did not want to lose the network-affiliated stations from their cable channel inventory. However, some network executives had indicated that they would seek payments for retransmission consent of all their owned and operated stations. This created a precedent and set the tone of negotiations for each of the network's nonowned, affiliated stations to follow.

Neither the broadcasters nor the cable operators had anything to gain by posturing for their interests. The networks could not be too cavalier about their demands because 56 percent of their prime-time viewers were in homes with cable service. On the other hand, surveys indicated that a significant number of cable subscribers would cancel their cable subscription if the service dropped CBS, NBC, or ABC.

Cable operators claimed that the issue of retransmission consent was unfair. They argued that viewers without cable don't pay for broadcast television and that cable television subscribers were thus being penalized when cable operators were required to pay for local broadcast signals. Broadcasters countered that cable systems already pay per-subscriber charges to distribute cable channels like ESPN, CNN, and TNT.

Some cable operators and broadcasters devised creative business relationships to circumvent cash compensation for retransmission consent. TCI, the nation's largest multiple-system operator (MSO), lived up to its vow of zero cash payments by negotiating noncompensatory arrangements with broadcasters. In 1992, TCI and several large group station owners became "partners" in a number of noncompensatory, retransmission-consent business arrangements. In a deal with the Fox-owned broadcast stations, TCI arranged to distribute Fox stations on its cable systems without charge in exchange for having TCI cable systems carry a new Fox cable channel (f/X) with a payment by TCI to Fox of twenty-five cents per subscriber. Shortly after the Fox arrangement was concluded, TCI announced that it had agreed to carry Times Mirror

Broadcasting Company's four television stations in return for distributing a new Times Mirror cable channel, without any per-subscriber charge paid to Times Mirror.

By enticing broadcasters with the prospects of programming a cable channel and generating additional revenue, TCI avoided having to pay directly to carry broadcast stations, and was instead able to barter with their rivals. For WPXI-TV in Pittsburgh, an NBC affiliate and a Cox Enterprises–owned station, the barter arrangement yielded minority ownership in a new news and information channel jointly owned by WPXI and TCI, with WPXI receiving a modest per-subscriber fee payment from the cable operator. Additional enticements offered by TCI and other cable operators include favorable channel placement, free cable advertising to promote new broadcast cable channels, and boosting broadcast station signals long distances, creating a larger market for the television station's audience.

Capital Cities/ABC, Inc. (now Disney/Capital Cities/ABC), owner of ABC, broke ranks with CBS and NBC by making its own nonpayment deal with the cable industry. In 1993 ABC, which owns 80 percent of ESPN, entered into an agreement with Continental Cablevision for the cable system to carry ABC's new cable network, ESPN-2 in exchange for allowing Continental to carry five ABC-owned stations and two Hearst-owned stations with payment of a fee. Instead, Continental will pay Capital Cities/ABC a monthly fee of about twelve cents a subscriber for ESPN-2.

Although the must-carry provisions have become part of the legislative landscape of cable television, the issue is far from settled. In 1994, responding to a legal challenge to the must-carry provisions, the Supreme Court in a five-to-four ruling decided that the government must present more evidence to justify the law's rationale that the retransmission requirement is necessary to preserve the economic viability of broadcast television. In so doing, the Court remanded the case to a special three-judge panel, which upheld the rule. In February 1996 the Supreme Court once again agreed to review the 1992 Cable Television Consumer Protection and Competition Act.[10]

CABLE PROGRAMMING

While regulatory and legislative issues have been important in the evolution of cable television, they are of less immediate interest to the consumer than its programming. Just as the regulatory climate for cable has changed, so has the programming environment. Cable can no longer expect to remain competitive by merely distributing programs seen on local television stations. Today, with all of the entertainment options available to consumers, cable television must offer more innovative and original programming to sustain their subscriber base.

An indication of how volatile the cable programming marketplace has become is the number of cable programming services that are waiting for channel placement on cable systems. These channels face the harsh realities of a competitive industry that makes the cost of developing and launching a new cable channel high. It is therefore not surprising that the cable system operators with the deepest pockets have diversified into the programming marketplace.

TCI provides a good example of how certain cable companies have manipulated the system to monopolize cable programming. Under the leadership of John Malone, TCI has aggressively pursued programming ventures. In 1991, responding to FCC concerns about vertical integration (ownership of both cable systems and programming companies), TCI spun off $605 million of its assets to create the Liberty Media Corporation. Liberty has partnerships in various programming services, including American Movie Classics (50 percent), Black Entertainment Television (18 percent), Courtroom Television Network (33 percent), the Family Channel (15 percent), Home Shopping Network (24 percent), QVC Home-Shopping network (22 percent) and Prime Network Sports Channel America (38 percent). Although Liberty is purported to be a separate company that also owns cable systems, John Malone and Bob Magness, founder and chairman of TCI, own 56 percent of Liberty's shareholder votes. In addition, Malone works one day a week as Liberty's chairman and has five TCI executives on its board of six directors.

As a shareholder through its subsidiary, Liberty Media, of the QVC home shopping network, TCI was a principal in the $2.2 billion acquisition of the Shopping Channel by Comcast Corporation. As a result, Liberty Media will now own up to 49 percent of QVC. In 1994, TCI purchased Tele-Cable Corporation and its universe of 740,000 subscribers. As a result, TCI's subscriber total rose to 14.7 million households, or one out of four cable homes in the country. According to FCC regulations, a cable company cannot serve more than 30 percent of homes passed by cable.

TCI has also invested in theatrical feature films. Although it once owned the United Artists movie theater chain, it sold its holdings in 1992 for $680 million. Shortly after, it invested $100 million in Carolco Pictures, earning TCI the exclusive right of distributing Carolco's films on pay-per-view cable simultaneously with their theater release.

Strategic marketing and competitive merchandising have kept TCI ahead of the programming pack. In a clever ploy, TCI peddled its low-priced Encore movie channel to subscribers using a "negative option" merchandising technique. This meant all subscribers had to pay extra for

Encore unless they explicitly notified TCI that they did not want it. After ten states sued TCI over this questionable merchandising scheme, the company eliminated its practice nationwide.

TCI has also manipulated major companies for its own gain. When NBC was contemplating an all-news cable network to rival CNN, TCI feigned an alliance with NBC. Lawrence K. Grossman, then president of NBC News, accused TCI of using the purported alliance to obtain price breaks from CNN and then abandon the broadcast network's plan. When NBC finally developed its channel, the Consumer News and Business Channel, it promised TCI that it would not be an all-news cable channel but instead would focus on business and finance.[11] By this time TCI had a substantial investment in Turner Broadcasting, owner of CNN, and had to be assured that CNBC would not compete with CNN. NBC, for its part, needed TCI's support so it could receive channel positioning and reach its 14.7 million cable subscribers, nearly 20 percent of the domestic market. As part of the deal, NBC spent $20 million for a new TCI channel called Tempo. In a 1989 Senate hearing, then Senator Al Gore called the Tempo deal a "shakedown" by TCI.

The cable television universe, of course, is larger than the United States, and TCI has also been aggressively pursuing cable programming distribution in Europe, Mexico, Latin America, and Japan. In Japan TCI purchased 18 percent of Cable Soft Network, a movie network reaching about four hundred thousand basic cable subscribers. In Great Britain, TCI is already a major cable operator with extensive cable system ownership and distribution of eight cable program services through United Artists Entertainment Programming.

Pay Television

Early experiments with over-the-air pay television faced a number of formidable obstacles: substantial financial investment, FCC ambivalence, Congressional indecision, and flagrant hostility from the motion picture industry. In addition, programming priorities at the three major television networks in the 1960s shifted to the distribution of prime-time theatrical motion picture feature films. The trend started in 1961, when NBC inaugurated *Saturday Night at the Movies*, and the other networks quickly followed suit. To this day, theatrical feature films are still an important component of the network and independent station programming mix. These factors, along with the development of pay cable television all conspired to defeat the growth of over-the-air pay, or subscription, television. In 1972 a Time Warner subsidiary, Home Box Office (HBO), made history when it transmitted the feature film *Sometimes a Great Notion* via microwave to a cable system in Wilkes-Barre, Pennsylvania. At that instant, a new entertainment service began, one that would greatly alter the shape of the entertainment marketplace. Though the first film was aired in 1972, it wasn't until three years later, when HBO became a satellite-distributed service, that it achieved a national presence.

HBO offered a simple formula to attract subscribers: a flat monthly fee no matter how many films were viewed.[12] Shortly after its satellite launch, HBO became a twenty-four-hour service, showing the same films several times a day: this allowed more flexibility for viewers. Soon HBO became a major Hollywood force, bartering for the exclusive rights to show feature films on its pay cable service.

In an effort to remain competitive, HBO also devised a number of creative business schemes. One of these, known as the "prebuy," involves HBO's investment in 25 percent of a film's production costs, with a sliding scale bonus option, which provides the studio with additional compensation from HBO if the film achieves box office success. HBO has used prebuy financing for exclusive film licensing since 1977, when it entered into such an agreement with Columbia Pictures.

At first most of Hollywood's major studios rejected the terms that HBO offered them for movie licensing. The studios, accustomed to dealing from a position of power, were not eager to have terms dictated to them by the upstart HBO. Soon, however, the all-powerful bottom line created a more hospitable reception for agreements of this kind, and since 1977 the Hollywood studios have earned hundreds of millions of dollars in pay television licensing revenues. Pay television has come to serve as a type of insurance policy for the film industry, in which eight out of ten films never recover their investment through theatrical exhibition, and six out of ten never earn a profit.

With hundreds of millions of dollars at stake, there is quite an opportunity for certain parties to become greedy. In fact, four movie studios—Columbia, MCA-Universal, Paramount, and Twentieth Century Fox—along with Getty Oil, attempted to start their own pay TV channel in 1980. Their objective was to recycle film licensing revenues back to the originating production companies without the involvement of a costly intermediary like HBO. The studios planned to distribute 150 films a year through a movie channel called Premiere, and to prohibit the licensing of their films to any other pay television service for the nine months prior to their appearance on Premiere. As expected, HBO brought suit against the venture, and the Justice Department decided to investigate on the grounds that several major film companies were conspiring to withhold their product from the marketplace. Eventually, under the pressure of a Department of Justice investigation, the film studios abandoned the $35 million venture. Two years later, Paramount and Universal did invest in a pay television service when each became shareholders in Warner-Amex

Satellite Entertainment's The Movie Channel. Ironically, Time Warner, the parent company of HBO, was named in a similar suit by Viacom, the parent company of Showtime, the second largest pay cable programming company. The $2.4 billion antitrust lawsuit charged HBO with monopolistic business practices that attempted to put Showtime out of business. After lingering for three years, and generating millions of dollars in legal fees, in 1992 Viacom settled its suit with Time Warner for $75 million. As part of the settlement, Time Warner agreed to purchase a Viacom cable system in Milwaukee for $95 million, which by industry estimates was $10 million more than its value.

Hollywood has since abandoned its antagonistic posture toward pay television, and several studios are actively aligned with HBO in production ventures. In 1985, Columbia (now Sony Pictures), CBS, and HBO formed a new film studio called Tri-Star, which produces pictures for theatrical release that are eventually licensed to HBO.

HBO has aggressively invested in, and formed partnerships with, other film studios and distribution companies. It provided a percentage of the acquisition capital to allow Orion Pictures to purchase Filmways Studios. HBO invests a certain percentage in Orion's production budget and in return receives exclusivity rights to various Orion Films.

Investment and partnerships have played a key role in HBO's efforts to secure a steady flow of exclusive films to its pay channel. To raise money for film production, HBO created Silver Screen Partners, an equity partnership among individual investors that has raised several hundred millions of dollars for production investment.

In a stunning move that occurred in 1987, HBO negotiated a five-year, $500 million deal with Paramount Pictures for exclusive licensing of eighty-five Paramount films, beginning in 1988 with the release of *Crocodile Dundee II*. Several years earlier, HBO's rival, Showtime, had engineered a similar pact with Paramount for the exclusive licensing of approximately seventy-five films through 1989. This gave HBO a lead in the exclusivity race, with two large Hollywood studios, Paramount and Warner Brothers, supplying films to its service.

Although most of HBO's investment activity has been limited to the domestic film marketplace, it has also diversified into investment abroad. In an effort to finance mini-series for domestic release and foreign theatrical exhibition, HBO aligned itself with Goldcrest, a British investment firm.

Although HBO and its parent, Time Warner Inc., are leading figures in pay cable distribution, with 20 million subscriber households and profits in excess of $200 million annually, there are a number of other regional and national companies. HBO's most prominent competitor is Showtime, founded in 1977 and owned by Viacom. In 1987 Showtime increased its subscriber base by a considerable sum after merging with Warner Amex Satellite Entertainment's The Movie Channel.

Original Programming

Although theatrical film licensing has provided cable television services with a significant portion of its programming product, the major pay and basic cable programmers have also diversified into original features and series programming. While most of the pay cable theatrical features have relatively modest budgets, some efforts have required significant financial investment and gained worldwide attention.

Typically, HBO produces about twelve original theatrical films a year, with budgets ranging from$5 to 7 million. HBO recoups the cost for films it produces by arranging coproductions, selling rights for domestic and foreign distribution and foreign theatrical distribution.

In 1993, HBO gambled on the production and distribution of *Barbarians at the Gate*, based upon the best seller by Bryan Burrough and John Helyar. This story was about the intrigue and humor behind the leveraged buyout of RJR Nabisco. Stories about corporate America are not necessarily crowd pleasers, but *Barbarians* proved to be a success for HBO; its ratings surpassed ABC, NBC, and CBS, along with the other cable networks.

The increase in original cable programming includes both the pay and basic cable marketplaces. In 1983 the basic cable expenditure on original programs, including sports, totalled $153 million; by 1995 that figure had soared to over $1 billion.

In addition to investing in miniseries and feature film products, cable programming services have also pursued the costly endeavor of series development, production, and distribution. These series range from the unsophisticated to the urbane, such as HBO's *Dream On*, which cleverly intercuts vintage Hollywood movie scenes to illustrate the inner thoughts of a frustrated male yuppie.[13]

Another comedy series that premiered on HBO in 1992 is *The Larry Sanders Show Starring Gary Shandling*. This successful series features tasteful humor and clever writing. HBO has also managed to attract top Hollywood talent to its tongue-in-cheek popular horror series *Tales from the Crypt*. It has not, however, abandoned its public service commitment and distributes a regularly scheduled documentary series, *America Undercover*, which addresses some of the more substantive issues of the day. As part of its original programming agenda, HBO has also featured concerts by some of the most accomplished artists in the world. Its August 1994 taped highlights of Barbra Streisand's successful tour was a phenomenal ratings success.

The most popular basic cable programming services are also investing heavily in original and syndicated programming. In 1995, USA Network was the highest rated, averaging a 2.2 prime time rating. USA, which is jointly owned by Time Warner, Paramount (owned by Viacom), and Matsushita (formerly MCA), features original made-for-television movies and off-network television series.14 In 1992, USA Network acquired the off-network rights to *Quantum Leap*, the successful television series produced by Universal Television, which debuted on NBC in March 1989.

Lifetime, another popular basic cable programming service that began in 1984, had an average 1995 rating and share of 1.2. The network, which is owned by Hearst/ABC Viacom, distributes a variety of programs, including paid professional medical practitioner shows, off-network series like *Moonlighting* and *Thirtysomething*, talk shows, women's shows, original television movies, and original series like *The Hidden Room*. Of all the basic cable networks, Lifetime offers one of the most eclectic programming schedules.

MTV Networks, owned by Viacom International, is most noted for its music television (MTV) and the children's Nickelodeon stations. MTV Network has been successful with its ambitious acquisition of exclusive television rights for vintage television program series, distributed on *Nick at Night*. In 1992, MTV Networks spent between $35 to 40 million for 650 hours of MTM series programming. Series acquired included *The Mary Tyler Moore Show*, *The Bob Newhart Show*, *Hill Street Blues*, and *St. Elsewhere*. The deal with MTM provides MTV Networks with an exclusive five-year term for distributing the programs. Prior to the acquisition of these television series, *Nick at Night* had been successful with rerunning episodes from the 1960s *Dick Van Dyke Show*.

Another programming benchmark for Nickelodeon was the 1992 acquisition of the animated cartoon series, *The Ren and Stimpy Show*. Viacom invested $40 million in *Ren and Stimpy*, and two other animated series: *Rugrats* and *Doug*. But it was the vile antics of Ren, the mutant Chihuahua, and Stimpy, the foul feline, that captured the love and loyalty of children, teens, college students, and adults nationwide. The networks made a mistake when they turned down John Kricfalusi's demented duo. *Ren and Stimpy's* success shows that cable television can effectively compete with the national broadcast networks in the area of program development and production.

Another bizarre cartoon pair that originated on cable, *Beavis and Butt-head*, became the highest-rated program on MTV. The brainchild of Mike Judge, the series had its premiere on MTV Network's *Liquid Television* and then became a feature on MTV.

The competition between the broadcast networks and cable television for the children's television audience has heated up since the debut of Nickelodeon in 1979. Nickelodeon, which reaches 57.4 million homes, has more children between the ages of two and eleven watching than the four major networks combined. This is significant in the competition for the children's advertising market, which averages about $500 million a year.

Nickelodeon, which has an estimated annual revenue of $245 million and profits of $95 million, was created by Warner Amex Cable for the singular purpose of providing cable operators with a free, noncommercial children's television channel. The attempt to maintain a noncommercial cable channel that was solely supported by cable operator per-subscriber fees was a noble effort but proved financially disastrous. In 1985, when Viacom acquired controlling interest in Warner Amex Cable, it repositioned Nickelodeon as an advertiser-supported channel. The revenue generated from advertising provided the network with the financial resources necessary to develop and produce original programming.

Nickelodeon's savvy, hip approach has captured the allegiance of the children's audience and has made them the largest producer of original children's television programming. In 1990 the network opened its studios in Orlando, Florida, furnishing its programming with a firm foundation of technical and creative support while incidentally providing a major tourist attraction for MCA's Universal Studio's theme park in Orlando.

The network's programming is divided into four tiers: Nick Jr. for preschoolers; Nickelodeon for older children; Nick at Night, whose spokesperson is Dick Van Dyke, featuring reruns of successful vintage television sitcoms; and Snick, a customized block of Saturday night programming.[15]

Nickelodeon has supplied a free-wheeling and creative atmosphere for its programming staff that is endorsed by its president, Geraldine Laybourne, and acted upon by an innovative writing and production team. Its programming is a diversified mix of traditional genres and brash irreverence. Indeed, it was a high-concept program, *Double Dare*, introduced in 1986, that catapulted the network into a top-rated basic cable channel and set the tone for future programming. *Double Dare* is a competitive game featuring obstacle courses loaded with hazards like mud and slime. The program became so popular that Nickelodeon created a traveling version, *Super Sloppy Double Dare*, which attracts thousands of children. Another popular program, *You Can't Do that on Television*, features comedy skits and the dreaded "green slime."

Added to Nickelodeon's programming collection are shows that are more traditional in format but still exude an element of creative license. These programs include an updated version of the 1950s science show

Mr. Wizard's World, a news series featuring Linda Ellerbee, and a preschool program, *Eureka's Castle*. The only segment of the children's programming market that Nickelodeon does not dominate is the preschool audience, which is still under the domain of PBS. In 1994 Nickelodeon announced that it would spend $30 million over the next three years to develop more preschool programming.

The network also tries to educate children about issues and events that concern them. During the 1992 presidential campaign, Nickelodeon ran a series, *Kids Pick the President*, which attempted to familiarize children with the campaign agendas of both parties. It also produced a program on AIDS, with Magic Johnson, and one on the Los Angeles riots.

While Nickelodeon tries to distance itself from its primary pay cable competitor, the Disney Channel, it nevertheless has learned a profitable lesson from Disney about the merits of licensed product merchandising. Nickelodeon has become a valuable merchandising tool, used in selling moon shoes, minitrampolines, Ren dolls, and Ren and Stimpy T-shirts. However, the network does maintain strict oversight of its product licensing and is sensitive to the whims of children.

For the most part Nickelodeon has received enthusiastic support from parents and educators. Some critics point out that even quality television is still television, by definition a passive activity, and object that it limits a child's source of information to a small number of outlets that have something to sell. But despite its critics, Nickelodeon has achieved an enormous success among American children, has displayed an ethical concern for their welfare and well-being, and has proven that television for children can be both socially responsible and fun.

Just as Nickelodeon changed the landscape of children's television, its sister network, MTV, revolutionized two industries—cable television and music recording—by creating a synergy between the two media. In 1981 Warner Amex Satellite Entertainment Corporation began distribution of MTV over cable. Bob Pittman, then a twenty-nine-year-old executive vice president of Warner Amex, helped to create a cable channel dedicated to the distribution of videos featuring popular recording artists.

The combination of television and rock music was not a new format. In 1952, Dick Clark introduced rock music to American television with *American Bandstand*, which he started on a local Philadelphia television station. In 1957, *American Bandstand* was picked up by ABC and became a nationally televised two-hour afternoon music and dance program. *American Bandstand* featured guest artists who lip-synched their song lyrics while performing to prerecorded music. This performance format later became a standard technique for music video productions.

The first music videos were seen in England and Europe, where they were shown in dance clubs and on television during the early 1970s. In

England a music-oriented television program called *Top of the Pops*, a contemporary version of American television's *Your Hit Parade*, started to accept videotaped performances of rock groups instead of live appearances. In 1975, director Bruce Gowers produced one of the first concept videos for a then unknown group called Queen, which featured their song "Bohemian Rhapsody." The response to Queen's video was overwhelming, boosting sales and providing unprecedented promotion. American record companies, eager for a vehicle to publicize their products abroad, embraced the music video concept and began to produce them for distribution in Europe. Eventually, the music videos reached American cable television. HBO used the videos as filler between movies on a segment called *Video Jukebox*. MTV elaborated on the idea and helped popularize a new art form.

Just as the music videos helped to sell records in Europe, their presence on American television rejuvenated a declining recording industry. From 1979 to 1982, the recording industry was racked by a recession that saw a precipitous decline in gross revenues and retail shipments. By 1982, record sales had hit their nadir, but they started to inch upward again as American audiences were exposed to a vast reservoir of musical styles and genres on MTV. Indeed, MTV's stature was reinforced by the cable network's ability to create a success for hitherto unknown rock groups. For example, Russell Mulcahy's stylistic video treatment of the rock group Duran Duran enabled the band to become a popular sensation in the United States; and MTV helped many other groups' and celebrity artists' fortunes to rise, among them Men at Work, Adam Ant, Stray Cats, Michael Jackson, Madonna, and Prince.

Almost from its inception, MTV has generated controversy and debate. When it first started, MTV was accused of discriminating against African-American groups and artists. At the time, the network defended its programming decisions by citing the historic segregation of black and white popular music, and pointing out that rock was more popular than contemporary rhythm and blues. The issue of racial disharmony at MTV dissipated, however, as musical styles evolved and African-American artists asserted a growing presence in the music industry. Rap music—a uniquely styled, rhythmic, urban poetry featuring African-American artists—moved from the ghetto to mainstream America and "rapper" music videos were prominently featured on MTV.

One African-American artist, Michael Jackson, along with director John Landis, created an innovative model for the design and production of future music videos: *Thriller*, a $1 million, twenty-minute music video released in 1983, featured Jackson in a ghoulish morality play, involved in a macabre dance of death with vampires, zombies, and the living undead. The video was both a commercial and an artistic success; it sold over 30 million copies, won a Grammy, and created a new artistic standard for the creation of music videos.

Although MTV does not produce the music videos it shows, it nevertheless has been criticized for promoting sexually explicit and violent videos. The portrayal of women as objects of desire and abuse on many music videos has raised the ire of feminists, who condemn the artists and the channel for perpetuating a damaging mythology of sexual stereotypes.

Two videos that exemplify the public's concern with this sexually violent genre are Michael Jackson's *Black or White* and Madonna's *Justify My Love*. *Black or White*, released in 1991, was another artistic departure for Michael Jackson. In it, Jackson explores issues of race and culture and performs startling physical transmutations, aided by the technological wizardry of "morphing."[16] At one point in the video, Jackson becomes extremely violent, battering a car with explosive outbursts. The public protested what seemed to be an endorsement of irrational violence, and Jackson, conscious of his responsibility as a role model, agreed to reedit the video and release a new version, omitting the violent segment.[17]

Madonna's *Justify My Love*, released in 1991, also created a negative sensation. A celebration of eroticism, promiscuity, and deviant sexual behavior, it featured Madonna in a number of suggestive situations involving men, women, and animals. MTV, which had established itself as the home network for Madonna videos, took the bold step of banning the video from the network. (Ironically, the video had its first national exposure on Ted Koppel's *Nightline*, giving Koppel one of his highest ratings ever.) MTV was both praised and condemned for its decision.

The issue of violence and racism in music videos was the subject of a 1986 study by Barry L. Sherman and Joseph R. Dominick. Sherman and Dominick examined 166 concept videos (those that visually portray the action of the song) and found that overall whites appeared more frequently than nonwhites, and that nonwhites were more likely to use a weapon or become victims of violence in a weapons-related incident.[18]

While music videos made MTV an international programming and distribution channel, it has also branched out into other programming genres. Video Hits One (VH1), a second MTV music video network, was introduced to showcase other musical genres, including country and western and more traditional pop music fare. And MTV has also diversified its programming schedule to include feature programs, animated series, game shows, and comedy. The network took an unusual departure from its standard programming fare when in 1992 they broadcast a documentary entitled *The Real World*. The producers of the series selected seven young strangers, four men and three women, put them together in a $30,000 renovated New York loft, and spent $1.3 million on thirteen twenty-four-minute weekly episodes, shooting fifty hours or more for each segment, and taping the participants' interactions from an integrated, confined studio loft space.[19] The producers hoped to recreate soap opera themes in a realistic living environment. Conceptually the idea was yet another attempt to capitalize on the popularity of "reality-based" television programs, and the format has spawned a number of sequels. And while continuing with new versions of *The Real World*, the same producers reconceptualized the format to produce *Road Rules* for MTV. This time the five young participants were given a luxury camper and everything else they needed to travel across the country.

Although some critics pointed out that *The Real World* "reality" was in fact artificial, it was an interesting attempt by MTV to provide its viewers with an exploration of substantive issues that would pertain to their life-styles and cultural milieu. John J. O'Connor, television critic for *The New York Times*, wrote that the show was "steadily evolving into the year's most riveting television, a compelling portrait of twentysomethings grappling with the nineties."[20]

In 1984, MTV also created a news department that in 1992 was positioned to follow the presidential campaign and election. The election year coverage, titled "Choose or Lose," featured a systematic approach to illuminating the substantive issues associated with the campaign and making them understandable to the MTV audience. The coverage included reports from the convention floors by celebrities like Ted Nugent, Dave Mustaine, and M C Lyte. Celebrities also appeared on MTV's public service announcements, urging their audience to vote. One "Rock the Vote" public service announcement featured Madonna clad only in a red bikini, black motorcycle boots, and an American flag, admonishing viewers to get out and "vote or be spanked." The band Aerosmith urged youth to vote, "even if it's for the wrong person."

One of MTV's most prominent "Choose or Lose" segments was a ninety-minute forum in which candidate Bill Clinton fielded questions from two hundred eighteen-to-twenty-four-year-olds. Cohosted by MTV's political correspondent, Tabitha Soren, and CNN's Catherine Crier, "Facing the Future with Bill Clinton" drew almost 3 million viewers during its initial and repeat broadcasts.

According to a report by the Freedom Forum Media Studies Center, "Choose or Lose" coverage was oriented more towards political education than political news. MTV spent the most time covering the abortion issue and the least time addressing environmental issues.

Although some critics objected that the type of coverage offered by MTV during the campaign trivialized the process, the network nonetheless made an effort to draw in a part of the electorate that has felt alienated by the political process. At times their approach to campaign cover-

age may have been iconoclastic and irreverent, yet it nevertheless succeeded in its goal of gaining the trust among its viewers that encouraged
them to participate in the democratic process and enabled them to make
an intelligent choice.

MTV's sense of social consciousness was not limited to election coverage. In 1995 it participated in a week-long cable campaign, "Voices
against Violence." The network's contribution was a documentary on
juvenile violence, entitled "A Generation under the Gun," featured MTV
reporter Tabitha Soren.

MTV has become a global phenomenon, reaching 180 million households in thirty-seven countries. Its distribution to Europe includes twenty-four-hour service to twelve countries. It has also expanded its reach to
other parts of the world, including Russia, Japan, and Australia.[21] An
Asian MTV service was started in 1991, while MTV Internacionál, a
Spanish-language offshoot, can be seen in five Latin American countries.
Though it began as a cable channel with a simple programming premise,
it has evolved into an international arbitrator of youth-oriented music
and style, as well as of more substantive issues.

In 1995, five leading music companies—Time Warner's Warner
Music Group, Sony, Thorn EMI PLC, Bertelsmann AG, and Polygram NV,
along with Ticketmaster Corporation—dropped plans to launch a rival
music video channel. However, in the same year TCI announced that it
was developing The Music Zone (TMZ), its own cable music network.

Themed Channels

Themed channels are another unique entertainment option offered by
cable television. With cable's ability to narrowcast, or target, a particular
audience, themed services are a natural choice, Included in the vast array
of specialized channels are those that offer comedy, legal, shopping,
financial, health, and sports programming.

Comedy Central, a joint venture between two former archrivals,
Time Warner and Viacom, offers a variety of comedy programming from
Politically Incorrect, "a *McLaughlin Report* for humorists," to *Comic Justice*,
a series featuring stand-up and sketch comedy by urban minority artists.
Comedy Central has enjoyed a moderate success with cable distribution
and subscribers.[22]

Court TV, which premiered in 1991, is dedicated to covering courtroom trials and legal issues. The channel's premiere coincided with several notable trials and hearings that provided it with substantial free publicity. Court TV covered the Clarence Thomas Senate confirmation hearings, the William Kennedy Smith rape trial, the trial of serial killer Jeffrey
Dahmer, the Rodney King beating trial, the trial of the Menendez broth-

ers who allegedly killed their parents, and of course the spectacular "Hollywood" murder trial of celebrity-athlete O. J. Simpson. All of these were high-profile events that helped to give Court TV more visibility and credibility.

In order to attract more traditional network sponsors, Court TV must increase its subscriber base, thus broadening its reach for advertisers. As of June 1993, Nielsen Media Research estimated Courtroom Television's subscriber base at 10.6 million households. Its agreement with nine of the top ten cable MSOs assures it of an increase in its subscriber base to 25 million, a threshold that should attract network advertisers. In a single year Court TV covered more than a hundred trials originating from thirty states and seventy-eight municipalities. Supplementing its live courtroom coverage, the channel is contemplating several new program formats.

Reaction to Court TV has been on the whole positive, with a few exceptions. Noted Harvard University law professor Alan Dershowitz criticized the channel, questioning "the appropriateness of having a for-profit cable channel exploiting the miseries of crime victims, criminal defendants, and other litigants in order to sell soap, dog food, and laxatives."[22] Former President Bush, commenting on the televised proceedings of the William Kennedy Smith trial, referred to the "filth and indecent material" and said that "the American people have a right to be protected against some of these excesses."[24]

The general reaction to Court TV, however, could best be summed up by Judge Mary Lupo, who presided over the William Kennedy Smith trial in the Palm Beach County Court. After the not-guilty verdict was declared, she said, "This has not been a movie made for T.V. The T.V. has come into the courthouse. The courthouse and the people associated with it have not done anything for T.V. The only difference between this case and all the other cases that we handle is that more people want to see this case."[25]

Many of the themed cable television channels have been described as niche services, fulfilling a demand to discrete target audiences. The question, of course, is how narrowly-cast a station can be and still generate a profit. Could a cable network whose subscribers average 11.6 minutes or less in viewing time, for example, be profitable?

The Weather Channel, started in 1982 by John Coleman, a former meteorologist for ABC's *Good Morning America*, fits this description and is a resounding success. The Weather Channel, which is now owned by Landmark Communications, has been consistently strong in its appeal to advertisers and subscribers. Available to 90 percent of all cable television homes, the Weather Channel has experienced regular increases in viewership, and reaches 63 percent of the country with more than 60 million subscribers. Advertisers have been receptive to the channel and to its commercial structure, which integrates commercials into twelve-minute program segments, during which time either three sixty-second or six thirty-second commercials are programmed. (No single commercial break ever lasts more than sixty seconds.) A steady increase in advertising revenues, which rose to $10.5 million in 1987 and $28.3 million in 1993, attests to the popularity of this format.

Ratings for the Weather Channel soared in December 1992, when the Northeast was plummeted with violent storms, and again during the winter of 1994, when the same region of the country was hit with a record number of snowfalls. However, it was the January 1996 blizzard that earned the Weather Channel its highest ratings, supassing even most network coverage during designated time periods on January 7.

The Weather Channel's success can be attributed to a format that provides viewers with satisfactory meteorological reporting, gives advertisers adequate exposure and sound promotional efforts, like the contest cosponsored with Columbia Pictures, timed with the release of the comedy *Groundhog Day*. Cable system operators obviously value the channel, which is included on the channel inventories of 90 percent of all cable systems.

Shopping Channels

In 1977, in Clearwater, Florida, Lowell W. Paxson, a savvy radio personality and businessman began retailing directly to radio listeners on WWQT-AM. Using radio and television to merchandise products directly to listeners and viewers was not a new phenomenon—broadcast advertising has been around for seventy-five years and has sold everything from candy to cars. However, the concept of dedicating a channel for direct merchandising to consumers was created by Paxson.

In 1982, Paxson began the Home Shopping Channel on cable television, and in 1985 he launched the Home Shopping Network (HSN), a national service distributed by satellite to broadcasters and cable systems. Although there was no prohibition against allocating cable channels dedicated exclusively to merchandising, there were regulatory constraints concerning commercial time standards that pertained to broadcasters. However, in 1984 the FCC eliminated all advertising limits on broadcasters, paving the way for networks like HSN.

By 1985 Paxson had joined with Roy Speer in building HSN into one of the most profitable broadcast/cable enterprises in the nation. When the company went public, HSN stock opened at $18 a share and ended the week with a high of $53. HSN grossed a little over $100 million in 1986, and by 1992 they were selling more than $1 billion in merchandise and shipping thousands of packages every day. Their programming is carried by about a hundred small broadcast stations and hundreds of cable systems.

With the success of HSN, it is not surprising that another shopping channel would be created to compete with it. This time, however, the primary service area would be cable television, and the principal backer would be the largest cable company in the country, TCI. The Quality, Value, Convenience Network (QVC) debuted in 1987 and was immediately picked up by a large number of cable systems around the country. TCI aggressively promoted the network and in fact was charged in Congressional testimony by HSN's CEO, Roy Speer, with systematically blocking the distribution of HSN on TCI cable systems in favor of QVC. Speer claimed that this discriminatory policy was clearly articulated for TCI cable systems serving communities in Colorado, Florida, and California. At the time TCI denied all allegations of discriminatory channel allocation.[26] Roy Speer's protests concerning TCI's business practices were muted when Liberty Media, TCI's spin-off, acquired an interest in HSN. As of 1993, Liberty Media owned 24 percent of HSN, assuming voting control of the channel, and 22 percent of QVC.

In a move that startled the industry and gave cable television's interactive media and shopping channels a new credibility, Barry Diller, former head of Fox, a man with a vast amount of leadership and programming experience in the industry, announced in December 1992 that he would purchase $25 million of QVC stock and form a voting block with the other QVC owners, Comcast Corporation and Liberty Media.[27]

The lure of selling merchandise directly to an audience of millions has also enticed traditional retailers into home shopping telemerchandising. In 1993 one of the most prominent department store retailers announced the creation of TV Macy's, a cable channel dedicated to creating the Macy's shopping experience on cable television. Partnered with Macy's are Cablevision Systems Corporation, Don Hewitt of *60 Minutes*, and Thomas F. Leahy, a former CBS executive. Hewitt and Leahy oversee the programming end, Charles Dolan's 2.1 million subscriber Cablevision Systems Corporation leads the channel affiliation effort, and Myron E. Ullman III, CEO of Macy's, provides the retail merchandising link.

Macy's, which was operating under the protection of a federal bankruptcy court when it announced its cable shopping channel, hopes that the estimated start-up cost of $50 million will generate an additional $250 million in revenue over five years. Its competitor, Saks Fifth Avenue, demonstrated the power of telemerchandising when it revealed that it had sold $570,000 of its private label "Real Clothes" on QVC in one month. Although returns on apparel can run high, the process is expedited when they can be made to a nationwide department store chain like Macy's.

The Macy's announcement was followed by other large retailers eager to cash in on the potential of home shopping profits: Catalog 1, a joint venture of Spiegel and Time Warner; and Nordstrom, which announced its version of a home shopping channel partnered with US West and J.C. Penney.

The largest obstacle facing any new cable shopping channel is competing with the formidable resources of HSN and QVC, which have a combined subscriber base of 72 million, combined sales of $2 billion, and who together control 98 percent of the home shopping television market. Recent studies have attempted to profile the home shopper and have found that she is a socially active, married, educated woman working outside the home, who shops in the stores as well. Men comprise barely 20 percent of the audience.

The dollar figures of U.S. retail merchandising are staggering—$250 billion in retail department store sales and $60 billion in catalog marketing. Enthusiastic observers predict that televised home shopping, which is presently a $2.5 billion business, may become a $30 billion business in ten years. Others are less sanguine, noting that presently only 10 percent of the television population has made a purchase via a home shopping television channel.

There are problems associated with home shopping from both the consumer's and the retailer's point of view. Consumers would like to see more major brands featured, and a substantial number feel that home shopping products are inferior in quality. They also must endure hours of viewing before the merchandise they're interested in comes up for display. (This problem will eventually be resolved by interactive television.) The retailer must deal with high return rates and credit card deadbeats.

Televised home shopping, whether on broadcast or cable television, has its share of both critics and proponents. The issue of whether such channels have any merit became a point of contention in the FCC's interpretation of the must-carry rules of the Cable Television Act of 1992. The rationale for the FCC's must-carry requirement is based upon the public interest standard that is an historical benchmark for FCC decision making. Under the act, local over-the-air broadcasters can demand channel allocation on cable systems serving their transmission area. This includes stations dedicated exclusively to home shopping programming, such as the twelve UHF stations owned by Silver King Communications.

Cable system operators are complaining that because of must-carry regulations, broadcasters requesting their signal to be carried are taxing their limited channel capacity and forcing them to drop other well-liked cable channels. Carrying yet another shopping channel, they argue, could become a burdensome requirement. They add that the public interest is not served by stations distributing programs that have as their singular purpose the merchandising, advertising, and selling of products to a large television audience.

One of those whose voice joined the protest was Representative John D. Dingell, Democrat of Michigan. In a letter to the FCC, Mr. Dingell objected to the use of the scarce radio spectrum for broadcast home shopping stations and claimed that such use "makes a mockery of the public interest responsibilities that are embodied in the Communications Act."[28]

In 1993 the FCC decided to uphold the right of over-the-air shopping stations to exercise their privilege of must-carry on local cable systems. In advocating this policy, the commission stated that the all-shopping program format attracted many viewers and was competitive with similar channels operated by cable companies. Had the FCC ruled in opposition to the shopping channels, it would have had to establish how traditional broadcast stations that stake a claim to "must carry" serve a "higher good" than the all-shopping stations. Representative Dingell condemned the decision as an abrogation of the public interest standard and an endorsement for twenty-four-hour-a-day commercialism.

Arguing the case for the public interest standard, officials at the Cable Satellite Public Affairs network (C-SPAN), protested the decision, claiming that applying the must-carry standard to home shopping stations placed C-SPAN at greater risk of being bumped from cable system channel allocation by broadcasters and shopping channels demanding "must-carry" designation.

Of course, there are those who defend the value of home shopping stations. Alan Gerson, senior vice president of HSN, supports the channel's programming as pro-social, live, interactive entertainment. The question, of course, becomes: How does one define the public interest? Which is more important—watching coverage of the Clarence Thomas Senate confirmation hearings or watching a demonstration of a motorized tie rack?

Business and Finance Channels

In the last decade, financial news has become a prominent feature in the media, with experts on both television and radio dispensing economic advice and information. The genre therefore seemed to be a natural for cable television, and in 1981 the Financial News Network (FNN), owned by UPI and International Research Network, made its debut.

FNN's programming featured timely reports about the financial markets, investments, and other money matters. The network's popularity with cable subscribers provided it with a high rate of clearance on cable systems around the country and made it an attractive takeover target. Two companies that were very interested in acquiring FNN were Dow

Jones, owner of the *Wall Street Journal*, and the Consumer News and Business Channel (CNBC), owned by NBC. The programming on FNN was a natural for Dow Jones, and the company aggressively pursued acquisition of the network.

In 1991, FNN filed for Chapter 11 bankruptcy protection, and shortly thereafter CNBC purchased FNN for $145 million in cash and $9 million in debt. A year later, CNBC shut down FNN and assimilated its programming and other assets into its own operation.

Business news can also be found on CNN. Indeed, Lou Dobbs, anchor and executive vice president of CNN, hosts two programs, *Moneyline* and *Moneyweek*, which together attract an audience of 1.2 million households.[29] In 1992 questions were expressed about Dobbs's ethical standards when it was revealed that he had accepted assignments as a paid pitchman for several Wall Street brokerage houses and for the Philadelphia Stock Exchange. Dobbs earned fees of between $5000 to $10,000 for acting as a spokesperson in videotapes for the Paine Webber Group and Shearson Lehman Brothers. These tapes were produced solely for the use of the investment companies, their clients and employees, and were not for public distribution.

While there was no evidence of impropriety, Dobbs's actions raised serious questions about the role of journalists as commercial endorsers and its effect on their professional integrity. Indeed, of all of the "beats" in journalism, financial news is one of the most likely areas for abuse. What Dobbs had chosen to do was the equivalent of an infomercial for private rather than public consumption.[30]

Black Entertainment Television

Cable television's unique capability of narrowcasting makes it especially attractive for reaching discrete audiences that have a common interest or cultural bond. Black Entertainment Television (BET), founded in 1979 by company chairman Robert Johnson, is an example of a minority-owned cable channel that has established itself as a valuable programming commodity in the competitive universe of cable television.

To help finance BET, Johnson was able to attract the support of TCI, the cable television industry's largest MSO, which still retains an 18 percent share of ownership in the network. Over the years, however, Johnson has striven to make the network financially independent and more profitable. Part of his strategy included diversifying its offerings and investment holdings. To this end, BET established two monthly magazines that have gradually grown in circulation. *Young Sisters and Brothers* (YSB), with sixty-five thousand paid subscribers, is geared toward African-American teenagers, and *Emerge,* aimed at African-American

Robert L. Johnson is the president and founder of Black Entertainment Television. Copyright and credit: Mike Carpenter. Courtesy of Black Entertainment Television.

professionals, has a circulation of about one hundred thousand.

In 1993 BET took the bold step of securing 80 percent of Action, a pay-per-view channel that reaches about 5 million homes. With its acquisition of Action, BET announced plans to begin producing movies in the $700,000 to $2 million range for the pay-per-view channel and aligned itself with Blockbuster Entertainment and Baruch Entertainment, two companies that will help finance and distribute low-cost, family-oriented movies aimed toward the African-American audience.

Eager to recapitalize the company and generate financing for expansion, Johnson went public with BET company shares, initially offered at $17 on October 30, 1991: the first day of trading closed at $23.50. Prior to the public offering, interest in the stock was enormous, with preliminary orders exceeding expectations. Eventually BET sold 4 million shares to investors who were bullish on the company's potential for growth.

The first few months of BET's life as a publicly traded company was a wild ride in valuation of the stock. Trading as low as $12 a share in March 1992, the fluctuations were attributed to disappointing earnings and an inaccurate subscriber count. Eventually, as BET grew into its new character as the first publicly traded, black-owned company on the New York Stock Exchange, its share price started to stabilize and investor confidence grew.

Under Johnson's leadership, BET has positioned itself as a competitive programming force in the cable television marketplace.[31] It has become a diversified company moving into home shopping (The BET Shop), new niche channels (BET on Jazz), and direct sales. Its subscriber base of about 30 million, with a significant potential for growth, makes BET a minority venture with a promising future.

CABLE/BROADCAST PARTNERSHIPS

Today cable television is a multibillion-dollar industry, with advertising sales in the $3 billions and sustained subscription growth. Therefore, it is not surprising that the broadcast networks have also expressed an interest in participating in the cable television industry. That interest came closer to reality in 1992, when the FCC voted to allow networks to buy cable systems. The FCC did place limitations on network ownership, based upon a percentage of the number of homes passed by cable in the cable television subscription universe.[32] The limits prescribed for cable system ownership refer to the actual possession of the hardware and distribution technology of a cable system. As of this writing, there are no regulatory limits on the number of cable programming services that a network can invest in or own. ABC is an owner of the Arts and Entertainment (A&E) Network and ESPN. CBS owned a cable system in Texas and attempted to create a cultural programming channel (CBS Cable), but after a significant investment and a great deal of promotional effort, it abandoned the attempt. In 1989, NBC, which is a 50 percent partner with Cablevision Systems Corporation, introduced CNBC and acquired its competitor, FNN, in 1991.[33]

In 1994 Fox had one of the biggest launches ever for a broadcast-sponsored basic cable network. Fox's f/X premiered in 1994 in 8 million cable homes, charging operators twenty-five cents per subscriber. The network had a $100 million programming budget for its first year and acquired thirteen hundred hours of off-network programming for f/X that consists of 70 percent reruns and infomercials. Fox used its leverage as a growing broadcasting network to persuade cable operators to pick up the channel. The deal was simple; if they carried f/X, then the cable operator could also continue to distribute the Fox broadcast affiliate in its market without paying a retransmission consent fee. Cable operators complained about Fox's heavy-handed bargaining, but the dramatic launch was evidence of how many went along with the Fox deal.

In an effort to capitalize on cable's growth and share investment burdens, several local broadcast stations have formed joint partnerships between their news organizations and those of cable TV. For example,

News 12 Long Island is a joint venture between NBC Cable and Cablevision Systems Corporation, with a reach of approximately 575,000 TV households.

Another broadcast cable alliance was formed between Turner Broadcasting's Headline News and Fox's New York City station, and a similar relationship with Fox's Chicago station WFLD-TV was also devised. Network programming partnerships have also been cautiously established between cable and broadcasting interests. ABC/Capital Cities has been the most receptive to making deals with the cable industry. In 1991 ABC broadcast six segments of an original Nickelodeon sitcom, a made-for-television Lifetime cable original movie, and a prime-time tenth-anniversary MTV special.

PAY-PER-VIEW

Although basic cable programming channels have been a growth area for the cable industry, the sale of premium or pay channels has remained relatively flat. In an effort to generate more business and capitalize on unique programming events, cable is aggressively pursuing pay-per-view (PPV) distribution. PPV allows the viewer to choose the event and pay only for those programs watched. While the attraction for PPV programming is the huge potential universe of viewers for an event, there is a downside to its strategy. Time Warner, which formed TVKO in 1990, a sports PPV network, has had modest success in scheduling PPV boxing matches.

One of TVKO's most successful events was the Holyfield-Forman fight in 1991, which earned $50 million in PPV billings from 1.45 million homes. However, in 1992, a PPV rematch between the two boxers was subscribed to by only 735,000 homes, yielding a $2.75 million loss for TVKO. Taking a lesson from its loss, TVKO restructured its financial arrangements for another 1992 bout, this one between Holyfield and Riddick Bowe. For that event, TVKO limited its involvement as a contractor, supplying production, distributing, and marketing instead of purchasing all rights, as it had done previously.[34]

One obstacle to the accessibility of PPV programming has been the cumbersome technical application necessitated by noninteractive technology, which requires either the addition of disposable traps, or addressable converter boxes and the use of the telephone to order a program. The installation of fiber optic cable systems, like the one being built by Time/Warner in Queens, New York, will create an expedient means for the marketing of PPV programming. Although fiber optic interactive technology offers great promise, lessons from the past like the failed Warner Amex interactive cable system, Qube, in Columbus, Ohio, point to the problems connected with placing too much hope on technological cures. Qube, which operated five interactive channels from 1977 to 1984, ceased operations after a $30 million loss. Warner found that after the initial novelty wore off, few subscribers used the interactive channel features.

One segment of entertainment that may offer a bonanza of PPV income is concert performance. Historically, this area of PPV has performed fairly well in the video marketplace: a 1989 Rolling Stones rock concert reached 270,000 homes at $22.50 each, in 1990 New Kids on the Block attracted 274,000 homes at $19.95 per household, a Metropolitan Opera concert generated sales to 34,000 homes at $34.95 each, and the Judds' farewell tour reached 250,000 homes and grossed in excess of $50 million.

TELEPHONE COMPANIES

While the cable companies actively pursue interactive technology to provide service for PPV television and home shopping, they do so under the specter of the telephone companies. The presence of a telephone line in almost every American home makes the local telephone company uniquely suited to providing consumers with interactive video and data services. In 1991 the FCC voted to allow telephone companies to offer video dial tone services, which could include information services and data transmission. A few weeks prior to the FCC ruling, a federal appeals court ruled that the regional Bell telephone operating companies (RBOC) could provide information services such as news, stock-market reports, and sports scores. The FCC also decided that the ban on telephone companies providing cable television programming did not apply to long-distance telephone companies like AT&T, Sprint, or MCI. The passage of the Telecommunications Act in 1996 codified the regulatory agenda for providing competition between the telephone and cable industries. It opened local phone markets to competitors like AT&T, MCI and cable companies, while the RBOCs gained access to the long-distance phone business.

The telephone companies' pursuit of cable television holdings in Great Britain became a proving ground for their entry into the U.S. cable market. Britain has encouraged competition in telecommunications by allowing the joining of cable telephone operations. Indeed, the three largest cable companies in Britain are either solely or jointly owned by American telephone companies.[35]

The American telephone companies have assumed an aggressive business posture in Britain, offering both telephone and cable service. They are operating most of the 141,000 phone lines running on cable and serve nearly three hundred thousand British telephone customers.

NYNEX has dedicated close to $3 billion for securing cable television franchises, installing fiber optic cable, and merchandising its programming services to industry and consumers.

As the regulatory environment in the United States became more receptive to telephone involvement in cable television, it is not surprising that the American telephone companies operating in Britain were the first to move into the U.S. cable marketplace. In 1993, Southwestern Bell (SBC Communications) paid $650 million for two Hauser Communications Inc. cable systems—one in Montgomery County, Maryland, and the other in Arlington, Virginia.[36]

Also in 1993 another regional Bell operating company, US West, made a bold move into the American cable market. The company invested $2.5 billion in Time Warner Entertainment, which included $1 billion to upgrade cable systems and $1.5 billion as a direct investment in Time Warner Entertainment. Like many other cable companies, Time Warner and US West are "clustering"—assembling large numbers of subscribers in the same territory—in order to achieve greater economies of scale. With that in mind, Time Warner acquired cable systems in Atlanta that are contiguous to systems owned by US West. In 1996, US West Media Group acquired Continental Cablevision for $5.3 billion in cash and stock plus assumption of $5.5 billion in debt. This acquisition gave US West access to 16.3 million households , providing it with the widest reach of any cable operator in the country. In a separate deal aimed at creating even greater clusters, Time Warner agreed to merge a third of its systems with cable companies owned by Newhouse Broadcasting.

The move by US West and Time Warner heralded a new era of cooperation and investment between two formerly antagonistic industries. Time Warner owns American Television and Communications (ATC), the country's second-largest cable system. An alliance of the two companies confirms the commitment that both telephone and cable have to upgrading and providing Americans with a modern telecommunications network.[37]

In 1993 US West announced an ambitious test of a broadband video dial tone service in Omaha, Nebraska. Eventually the test will involve sixty thousand homes and cost approximately $42.8 million. US West also expanded into the ownership of cable systems when in 1994 it spent $1.2 billion acquiring two companies that controlled 65 percent of cable television in the metropolitan Atlanta market.[38] Time Warner, its erstwhile partner and competitor, was the first cable operator in the United States to receive permission to provide telephone service when the New York State Public Service Commission approved its petition to operate a telephone service in Rochester, New York. At the same time, the commission also gave authorization for Rochester Telephone (now known as the

Frontier Corporation) to compete with Time Warner in the cable business.

The FCC gave its permission for telephone companies to provide commercial cable service when in 1994 it approved Bell Atlantic's request to provide a video dial tone service in the community of Toms River, New Jersey. However, in April 1995, Bell Atlantic reversed its position and suspended its FCC application for video dial tone services. In doing so, the company stated that it wanted to review various technological and regulatory issues. Soon after its announcement, Bell Atlantic joined with SBC Communications Inc., Bell South Corporation, and an industry trade group in filing a lawsuit challenging the FCC's authority to regulate their construction or purchasing of cable systems in their own service areas. Their rationale for the suit was based upon their right to free speech. The telephone companies want to deal directly with local governments on cable agreements, hoping to avoid FCC regulations requiring them to carry the programming of their competitors.

Even with Bell Atlantic's suspension of video dial tone applications, it remains an agressive suitor for cable television services. It is involved in a joint venture with NYNEX and Pacific Telesis Group to develop hardware and software for interactive television. Part of their interim strategy is to use wireless cable to transmit digital video signals to subscribers, eventually weaning them to wired distribution when the technology is in place. To this end, Bell Atlantic and NYNEX have invested $100 million in CAI Wireless Systems Inc. Other regional Bell operating companies have embraced the same strategy. In 1995 Pacific Telesis spent $175 million to buy Cross-Country wireless, which will allow it to offer video services to five million customers in Los Angeles and Orange Counties.

For consumers the competition between cable operators and telephone companies should mean better service and lower rates. Both the telephone and cable industries look forward to a bonanza of revenue generated from these competing services. But how do consumers view this cross-pollination of technologies? In a survey of cable subscribers, 27 percent said that they would consider going to a local telephone company for cable service, but only 8 percent responded positively to having a cable operator supply their telephone service. It appears that these technologies, which have positive name-brand recognition for their customary service, will have to win the loyalty of the consumer when branching out into new areas of service.

While the regional Bell operating companies have aggressively been pursuing their options in cable and interactive media, the allure of new technology has also attracted long distance companies. In 1993, AT&T announced that they had been involved in a secret two-year test of interactive multimedia software and hardware and a joint test of interactive television with Viacom International.[39]

REGULATORY CONCERNS

One of the unique aspects of cable television programming is its unusual freedom from censorship of language and televisual imagery. All of the films on the pay television channels are shown in their entirety, uncut and replete with nudity, gratuitous violence, simulated sex, and explicit language.[40] To many, cable television presents a new threat to public morality, with its uncensored programming and movies. A number of quasi-political and religious groups, such as Morality in Media and the Moral Majority, have mounted offensives against the sexually oriented programming available on cable. However, cable television has been judged by the federal courts to be different than broadcast television.[41]

Utah was the first state to pass legislation that attempted to define the programming limits of television. This legislation defined "unfit" programming as the displaying of "denuded" or "partially denuded" figures. In 1982, the Utah law was declared unconstitutional because it included nudity in its definition of indecency, and the Supreme Court has never ruled that the presence of nudity in programming is legally obscene.[42] Indeed, in a previous case involving a city's censorship of drive-in theaters showing movies in which female buttocks and bare breasts were visible from the street, the Supreme Court found that such a standard was defective.[43] The position of the Supreme Court was further enunciated in *Home Box Office v. Wilkinson* (1982), where the issue was presented as a matter of choice, pointing out that one does not have to purchase a television set, subscribe to cable television, or watch a television program.

The Supreme Court's position, however, has not prevented other municipalities and states from attempts at censorship. In 1990 the Montgomery County, Alabama, District Attorney's office announced indictments against Home Dish Satellite Corporation, along with GTE Corporation, the GTE Spacenet Corporation, and United States Satellite. Home Dish Satellite Corporation was distributing the X-rated American Exxxstasy Channel to thirty thousand subscribers nationwide, including twenty-two in Montgomery County, Alabama. In addition, Home Dish operated the R-rated Tuxxedo Channel, which distributed R-rated films via satellite to cable companies around the country, with thirty subscribers in Montgomery County. After the indictment was announced, the satellite carriers providing distribution service to Home Satellite denied access to their distribution facilities, effectively putting Home Satellite out of business.[44]

Another area of regulatory concern involves the question of cable franchises. In most states, municipalities can award local franchises without any oversight from state regulatory agencies. However, in some states, the Public Utilities Commission is the regulatory agency and must approve the franchise award. In other states there is an independent commission on cable television that establishes procedural guidelines that municipalities must follow. Yet the degree of autonomy that most municipalities have exercised in the franchising process led to a great deal of abuse. Since 1971, when the first cable bribery case was prosecuted, it was thought that somehow the cable franchising process could be kept from being tainted by allegations of bribery and conspiracy. Unfortunately the number of cases of municipal conspiracy and political chicanery in cable franchising awards has been too numerous, stretching from Houston to New York, where a cable television scandal sent one judge to prison.

The exclusive nature of cable television franchises is an issue that has been debated and challenged. During the peak of cable television franchising in the 1970s and early 1980s, exclusive operating franchises were routine. Most municipalities viewed the cable company as a monopoly providing the community with a noncompetitive service. However, over the last few years cable companies wishing to compete in the same geographical areas have filed suit and won.[45]

In 1986, the Supreme Court questioned the "natural monopoly" designation that most municipalities use when awarding exclusive franchises. The Court found that a Federal District judge had erred when he dismissed a legal challenge to the exclusive award of a cable television franchise in Los Angeles. The case, *Los Angeles v. Preferred Communications*, demonstrated the cable television industry's concern that various local and federal regulations violate the free speech rights of cable operators. The rationale was that cable franchise exclusivity limits freedom of speech and expression by allowing only a single monopolistic voice. In their decision the Court for the first time articulated a position that cable television activities, "plainly implicate First Amendment interests."[46] The Galloway brothers, who are the principals of Preferred Communications, had been pressing their case for six years in an effort to break the franchise monopoly held by Continental Cablevision, a Boston-based cable operator.

Although the Supreme Court did not rule on the constitutionality of the city's franchising authority, it did adopt a posture of First Amendment consideration when Associate Justice William H. Rehnquist, in writing the unanimous decision for the Court, said that "cable television partakes of some of the aspects of speech and the communication of ideas, as do the traditional enterprises of newspaper and book publishers, public speakers and pamphleteers."[47] The message the Court was sending vindicated cable operators, who have presented their position as being similar to that of newspapers, which don't have to suffer the burden of excessive regulation.

In a clear refutation of the exclusive cable franchising process, the Cable Television Act of 1992 prohibits local authorities from granting exclusive cable franchises. This could prompt "overbuilding" in a franchise area by a cable company that attempts to wire the community in competition with the established cable operator.

Even with regulatory incentives for competitive community cable service, less than 1 percent of cable communities in the United States are served by two or more providers. Frustrated by skyrocketing monthly subscription costs and poor service, some communities have attempted to start their own cable systems by passing bond issues, while others have invited cable companies in to compete with the established operator.

Challenging a larger, established cable operator can be daunting, especially when the larger operator pulls out the sales, marketing, and premium competitive bag of tricks. In Elbow Lake, Minnesota, a town of twelve hundred, the population was fed up with the expensive, shoddy cable service offered by Triax Midwest Associates, so they built their own system. The municipal system beat Triax's subscription price by $1, and quickly signed up 60 percent of households in Elbow Lake. Triax, a Denver-based MSO, countered by flying in a batallian of sales people, matching the municipality's rates, and offering subscribers an on-the-spot rebate of $100 when they signed. Elbow Lake's cable system reeled under the competition, was forced to raise rates, and now operates at a large deficit.

Of all the markets in the country, central Florida has been one of the fiercest cable competition battlegrounds. This is because Telesat, operated by the FPL Group (owner of Florida Power and Light), has attempted to compete with some of the largest cable operators in the country. In Orlando, Telesat went head to head with cable companies run by Time Warner and Cablevision Industries Corporation. The larger companies cut their rates and made subscribers who were not benefitting from the rate cut competition angry. When the Orange County Home Owners Association attempted to pass an ordinance prohibiting different prices for cable in the same market, Time Warner gave their local employees time off to attend the meeting and vote the proposed ordinance down.

Time Warner was involved in another nasty franchising battle when it used its "power of attorney" to prevent the city of Niceville, Florida, from building a $2 million cable system. After seven years, $300,000, and a victory in the Supreme Court, Niceville was finally able to start selling bonds for construction.

There have been examples, however, when cable competition works to benefit the consumer. For twenty-five years Allentown, Pennsylvania, has been served by two cable operators who have split the city in half and both run profitable companies. More recently, a municipally financed cable television system in Paragould, Arkansas, has set up a successful competition with the established operator, Cablevision Systems.

Under the 1984 Cable Act, stipulations for access to the cable system by parties other than the local government or cable operator had to be made. In most systems this is provided by public access channels that are offered on a nondiscriminatory, first-come, first-served basis. These channels were one of the benefits of the bitterly competitive municipal franchise battles of the 1960s and 1970s. Many cable companies offered to carry the public access channels along with television production facilities in order to help them win municipal franchises. As the industry matured, the channels and facilities were no longer used as a bargaining chip, and although some municipalities protested, in 1984 Congress agreed that public access should be an option rather than a requirement of municipal cable franchises.

The purpose of public access programming is to provide the community with a television forum for the discussion and exploration of local issues. In practice public access has often become synonymous with vanity programming and has generated a chaotic array of programming of dubious quality, with everything from nude talk shows to ego gratification shows. One program, *Access America*, which appeared regularly on the Comedy Central cable network, offered a compilation of segments from public access cable programming from around the country. Produced by Bo Kaprall and hosted by Fred Willard (formerly of *Fernwood Tonight*), the program traveled across the country visiting a myriad of public access sets and personalities. Programs with such diverse titles as *Doghouse, Glens Room, The Eric in His Underwear Show,* and *Beyond Vaudeville* pepper the public access landscape with outrageous humor, and tasteless—and often just plain boring—programming. *Wayne's World*, a 1992 hit movie, was a parody of cable television's public access programming.[48]

Capitalizing on the freedom of access principle and cable's nondiscriminatory allocation of channel time, a program produced by the California Chapter of the White Aryan Resistance, an arm of the Ku Klux Klan, has been making the rounds of cable access channels around the country. The program, entitled *Race and Reason*, was scheduled to be distributed on American Cablevision's Channel 20 in Kansas City, Missouri. Instead of airing the multipart series, however, the city council voted nine-to-two to eliminate the public access channel. This action prompted the local chapter of the American Civil Liberties Union (ACLU) to sue for access on behalf of the Klan, and they won. In the aftermath of the tragic 1995 bombing of a federal building in Oklahoma City, the issue of allowing unpopular, even outrageous, views to be expressed on television has become a critical concern in the public access debate.

Cable television is not just the simple installation of a wire in someone's apartment or house; but is indeed a complex technology that has brought about dramatic changes in both the communications industry and in American society. It has helped to create a new culture of programming that has redefined our political constructs and has set new standards for morality and decency.

NOTES

1. The *New York Times* article ran on December 22, 1950. The *Newsweek* piece was in the January 15, 1951 issue.

2. *Carroll Broadcasting v. FCC* (1958).

3. The case involved the importation of Los Angeles signals by Southwestern Cable into San Diego. The complainant was Midwest Television, a VHF licensee in the San Diego market. The FCC ruled that Southwestern Cable threatened instability in adjacent markets by importing near but nonlocal television stations as competitors to local broadcasters. A California Federal Court of Appeals ruled that the FCC could not restrain Southwestern Cable. The case went to the Supreme Court, which upheld the right of the FCC to regulate cable television.

4. *U.S. v. Midwest Video Corporation* (1972).

5. *FCC v. Midwest Video Corporation* (1979).

6. The Copyright Royalty Tribunal, an agency created by the Copyright Act, was empowered to adjust and distribute royalty fees to claimant copyright owners. In 1993, however, Congress passed the CRT Reform Act (PL 103-198), which abolished the five-member Copyright Royalty Tribunal, and created the Copyright Arbitration Royalty Panel (CARP), which arbitrates copyright claims on a semiannual basis. During its tenure the Copyright Royalty Tribunal distributed over $1.5 billion to various claimants.

7. Facing an explosion of complaints concerning cable rates the FCC implemented the controversial "social contract" policy. Instead of applying for a city-by-city petition for a rate increase, the FCC would engage in a single settlement per cable operator. In exchange for rate increases, cable operators agreed to upgrade systems and wire local schools. The most glaring of the FCC's largesse was the agreement to allow Time Warner to add a $1 surcharge to every monthly bill for five years to upgrade facilities. In 1996, the FCC proposed rules that would protect cable systems from rate regulation when competing against phone companies. Another FCC rule would lift rate regulations on small cable systems that serve fewer than 617,000 customers nationally. In addition, Section 301 of the Telecommunications Act of 1966 (PL104-104) will eliminate upper-tier cable-rate regulation after March 31, 1999.

8. In a case involving sexually explicit programming on a leased public access channel, Time Warner's Manhattan Cable implemented a scrambled signal policy and requested that subscribers sign a card to unscramble the explicit shows. According to the Helms amendment, cable operators can voluntarily ban sex programs on leased-access channels. Operators choosing not to ban programs

must scramble them. In July 1995 the U.S. Court of Appeals in Washington ruled that the Helms amendment did not amount to government censorship and was constitutional. The 1996 Telecommunications Act requires cable operators to scramble any program a subscriber deems unsuitable for children (section 640). In addition, it gives cable operators the right to refuse public and leased-access programs that they consider obscene or indecent (section 506). The Communications Decency Act, which makes it a felony to transmit indecent material over the Internet or on-line computer services to minors, was temporarily blocked from enforcement when a federal judge ruled that the term "indecent" was unconstitutionally vague. See "Is the Communications Decency Act Constitutinal?" *Time Digital,* April 8, 1996, TD14.

9. *Quincy Cable v. FCC,* 1985.

10. *Turner Broadcasting v. Federal Communications Commission,* Nos. 93-44 and 95-992.

11. In 1995 NBC announced that the Microsoft Corporation had purchased 50 percent of NBC's cable channel America's Talking for $100 million. The channel will be revamped as an all-news service to be jointly owned and operated by NBC and Microsoft. Rupert Murdoch in 1996 announced that Fox would start a twenty-four-hour news channel as a competitor to CNN.

12. Cable penetration in the U.S. is 63.4 percent, while pay cable is at 28.4 percent. A 1995 Roper survey found that three quarters of the public were unwilling to pay $50 a month for five hundred channels.

13. *Dream On's* last season on HBO concluded in the winter of 1996.

14. In 1996, Viacom introduced *Nick at Nite's TV Land,* a cable network dedicated to reruns of vintage television series.

15. In 1995 Seagrams acquired 80 percent of MCA from Matsushita and in 1996 the MCA Music Entertainment Group acquired 50 percent of Interscope Records Inc., the controversial company that distributes "Death Row Records," purveyor of the gangsta rap genre.

16. "Morphing," the stylistic digital video convergence of one image into another, was pioneered in films like *Terminator II.*

17. Some critics have charged Jackson with deliberately creating controversy in this way to bolster sagging sales.

18. Barry L. Sherman and Joseph R. Dominick, "Violence and Sex in Music Videos: TV and Rock 'n' Roll," *Journal of Communications,* 36, no. 1, Winter 1986, 79–93.

19. The producers referred to this arrangement as the "rock and roll Loud family," in reference to the 1973 public television documentary which followed and profiled an American family.

20. John J. O'Connor, "'The Real World,' According to MTV," *New York Times,* July 9, 1992, C15, C22.

21. In 1995 MTV went online with a weekly slate of programs available on America Online and introduced a World Wide Web site on the Internet.

22. In 1996 it was announced that *Politically Incorrect* would move to ABC's late night schedule beginning in January 1997.

23. Rich Brown, "The Trials of Court TV," *Broadcasting,* June 14, 1992, 28–30.

24. Ibid.

25. Ibid.

26. Johnnie L. Roberts, "How Giant TCI Uses Self-Dealing Hardball to Dominate Market," *Wall Street Journal*, January 27, 1992, A1, A4.

27. After two failed merger/acquisition attempts (Paramount and CBS), in 1994 Diller sold his shares in QVC. It is estimated that Diller earned $75 million on his $25 million investment in QVC during the eighteen months he was with the network. In 1995 Diller purchased control of Silver King Communications, a small group of television stations. Shortly after, Silver King gained control of Home Shopping Network when TCI agreed to exchange 80 percent of its voting stake in HSN for a share of ownership in Silver King.

28. Edmund L. Andrews, "F.C.C. Lets TV Shopping Stations Demand Access to Slots on Cable," *New York Times*, July 5, 1993, 1, 40.

29. In December 1995 CNN started a business news service, CNN Financial News (CNNfn).

30. In 1995 Sonny Bloch, a popular radio financial advisor, was indicted for allegedly defrauding his listeners of millions of dollars. CNBC's Bill Griffith raised concerns of propriety when he was paid about $10,000 as a spokesperson for a videotape called "How to Optimize Your Stock Portfolio with Options." Griffith claimed to have received permission from CNBC management. Dan Dorfman, the popular CNBC financial analyst, was fired from *Money* magazine for allegedly hindering an internal probe into insider trading. CNBC, however, stood by Dorfman and supported his denial of the allegations.

31. In January 1996 BET obtained an exclusive interview with O. J. Simpson.

32. According to FCC rules, network cable ownership cannot exceed 10 percent of the 92 million homes nationwide that are passed by cable, while local ownership was set at 50 percent of the homes that cable passes in a given market. In addition, a previous ruling prohibits a broadcaster from owning all or part of a cable system in the same community where it owns a television station. Some of these restrictions may be lifted as a result of the passage of the 1996 Telecommunications Act, which allows broadcasters to own cable systems. See Section 202, "Relaxation of One-to-a-Market," and "Cable Cross Ownership— Elimination of Restrictions."

33. In 1995 Microsoft purchased 50 percent of NBC's America's Talking cable channel for $100 million. The channel was reconfigured into an all news format as MSNBC.

34. In 1995 pay-per-view boxing accounted for 54.2 percent of all pay-per-view revenue. Boxing promoters, however, have voiced dissatisfaction with current arrangements. As a result, the 1995 Tyson-Mathis fight appeared on Fox Broadcasting, while the Oscar DeLa Hoya-Julio Cesar Chavez bout in 1996 was distributed to closed-circuit venues around the country. One of the biggest problems plaguing pay-per-view programming is theft of service. Estimates indicate that consumers stole 1.4 million pay-per-view events in 1995.

35. The companies are: NYNEX, parent of New York Telephone; US West, which has a joint 50/50 partnership with TCI; and Southwestern Bell, which operates a joint venture with Cox Cable, of which Southwestern Bell owns 75 percent. Southwestern Bell became SBC Communications and in 1996 acquired Pacific Telesis Group for $17 Billion. As a result of the merger, the new company serves 30 million residential and business telephone lines in seven states. Shortly after the Southwestern/Pacific Telesis merger, Bell Atlantic and Nynex

announced their intention to merge in a deal worth $22.1 billion. The combined company will serve 12 Eastern states from Maine to Virginia, providing local, long distance and cellular telephone service. The new company will be known as Bell Atlantic. As this book goes to press, there are three remaining independent regional Bell operating companies: Bell SouthCorp., Ameritech Corp., and U.S. West, Inc.

36. The purchase by Southwestern was within the regulatory framework since the telephone company provides service in states such as Arkansas and Texas; therefore the acquisition of the cable systems was outside their home territories.

37. US West, however, did not view the merger of Time Warner and Turner as favorable to its interests, and expressed a desire to extricate itself from the corporate relationship.

38. In 1995 US West was negotiating with Cablevision Systems Corporation, the nation's sixth-largest cable operator, for purchase of two-fifths of the company for about $600 million.

39. In 1995 AT&T announced that it would split into three companies: (1) AT&T long distance services and wireless communications; (2) a communications hardware company that would manufacture, sell, and lease telephone and network equipment, and manufacture computer chips; and (3) a computer systems company focusing on global information solutions.

40. A 1996 report compiled by the National Television Violence Study, commissioned by the National Cable Television Association, found that premium cable channels (HBO, Showtime) are the most violent, while broadcast television had the lowest violence level. In 1996, leading broadcast and cable executives met with President Clinton and endorsed a ratings system for television to be implemented in 1997.

41. In *Home Box Office v. Wilkinson* 531 F. Supp. 987 (1982), the judge noted that "there is no law that says you have to subscribe to a cable TV service any more than you have to subscribe to the *Salt Lake Tribune*."

42. *Miller v. California*, 413 U.S. 15 (1973).

43. *Erznoznik v. City of Jacksonville* (1975)

44. Various attorneys noted that this was the first time local criminal laws were deemed applicable to programs distributed nationwide by satellite.

45. *Quincy Cable v. FCC*, 768 F.2d 1434 (1985).

46. *Los Angeles v. Preferred Communications*, 476 U.S. 488 (1986).

47. Ibid.

48. In 1995 there was an attempt to amend a Senate telecommunications reform bill, with the stipulation that cable operators deny distribution of programs that contain "obscenity, indecency, or nudity" on public access or leased channels. In October 1995, Time Warner's Manhattan Cable began a policy that made available indecent leased public access programs only to customers who requested them in writing.

Bibliography

1: SYNERGY: A CONSOLIDATION OF HARDWARE AND SOFTWARE

"After the Mergers: How the Networks Fit." *New York Times*, 2 August 1995, D1.

Associated Press. "Profits Fall at Capital Cities/ABC." *New York Times*, 5 February 1991, D15.

Auletta, Ken. *Three Blind Mice: How the TV Networks Lost Their Way*. New York: Random House, 1986.

Bagdikian, Ben H. *The Media Monopoly*. 2d ed. Boston: Beacon Press, 1987.

Barnouw, Erik. *Tube of Plenty. The Evolution of American Television*. Rev. ed. New York: Oxford University Press, 1982.

Boroughs, Don. "Pressing Fast-Forward." *U.S. News and World Report*, 16 May 1994, 53.

Bruck, Connie. *Master of the Game*. New York: Penguin Books, 1995.

"Buyer-Seller Gap Spells Sluggish Station Sales." *Broadcasting*, 31 December 1990, p.35–36.

Carmody, Deirdre. "TV Guide Growth Plan: Bigger Pages." *New York Times*, 21 January 1991, D6.

Carnevale, Mary Lu. "The Word From Washington." *Wall Street Journal Reports* [television], 9 September 1994, R9.

Carnevale, Mary Lu, and Dennis Kneale. "In TV Rerun Ruling, Hollywood Interests Prove Special Indeed." *Wall Street Journal*, 10 April 1991, A1, A10.

Carter, Bill. "Big Cuts Expected for CBS." *New York Times*, 5 April 1991, D1, D7.

Carter, Bill. "CBS Employees Unsettled by Westinghouse Deal." *New York Times*, 3 August 1995, D1.

Carter, Bill. "An Old Medium Holds New Luster for Buyers." *New York Times*, 2 August 1995, A1.

Carter, Bill. "Rerun Ruling Can Only Complicate Deal-Making." *New York Times*, 10 April 1991, D6.

Carter, Bill. "Suddenly, at ABC, the Future Is Now." *New York Times*, 1 August 1995, D1.

Carter, Bill, and Richard Sandomir. "The Trophy in Eisner's Big Deal." *New York Times*, 6 August 1995, sec. 3, 1.

Cohen, Roger. "National Book Awards Predicting the Winners After the MCA Sale to 'Middle Passage' and 'House of Morgan.'" *New York Times*, 28 November 1990, C13, C18.

"Disney Facing Hurdles in Effort to Relax PTAR." *Broadcasting*, 10 December 1990, 102–103.

"Disney's Growing Empire: How the Entertainment Giants Measure Up." *Wall Street Journal*, 1 August 1995, B1.

"Disney Talks on MTM Reported." *New York Times*, 24 January 1991, D3.

Dobrzynski, Judith H., and Geraldine Fabrikant. "Tisch's Legacy: Healthy Profit, Ailing Network." *New York Times*, 2 August 1995, A1.

"Dolgen to Head Viacom Entertainment." *Broadcasting*, 21 May 1994, 6.

Fabrikant, Geraldine. "Cable Sale Called Near for Viacom." *New York Times*, 30 December 1994, D1

Fabrikant, Geraldine. "CBS Accepts Bid by Westinghouse: $5.4 Billion Deal." *New York Times*, 2 August 1995, A1.

Fabrikant, Geraldine. "Expanding in TV, Gannett Agrees to Buy Multimedia." *New York Times*, 25 July 1995, D1.

Fabrikant, Geraldine. "History Catches Up with Sony Music." *New York Times*, 18 July 1995, D1

Fabrikant, Geraldine. "Market Shrugs Off Possible Roadblock to a Viacom Cable System Sale." *New York Times*, 19 January 1995, D6

Fabrikant, Geraldine. "Media Giants Said to Be Negotiating for TV Networks." *New York Times*, 1 September 1994, 1

Fabrikant, Geraldine. "Murdoch Selling 9 U.S. Publications for $600 Million." *New York Times*, 26 April 1991, A1, D15.

Fabrikant, Geraldine. "The Record Man with Flawless Timing." *New York Times*, 9 December 1990, 4.

Fabrikant, Geraldine. "Seagrams Puts the Finishing Touches on Its $5.7 Billion Acquisition of MCA." *New York Times*, 10 April 1995, 1

Fabrikant, Geraldine. "Surprise Pact by G.E. Unit to Buy FNN." *New York Times*, 7 February 1991: D1, D19.

Fabrikant, Geraldine. "Time Warner Agrees to Acquire Cablevision." *New York Times*, 8 February 1995, D1.

Fabrikant, Geraldine. "Viacom is Winner Over QVC Fight to Get Paramount." *New York Times*, 16 February 1994, 1.

Fabrikant, Geraldine. "Walt Disney to Acquire ABC in $19 Billion Deal to Build a Giant for Entertainment." *New York Times*, 1 August 1995, 1.

Fabrikant, Geraldine, and Mark Landler. "His Place among the Moguls." *New York Times*, 19 January 1996, D1.

Fabrikant, Geraldine, and Bernard Weinraub. "Having Gotten the Part, Bronfman Plays the Mogul." *New York Times*, 4 February 1996, sec. 3, 1.

Fabrikant, Geraldine, and Bernard Weinraub. "One Deal Off. One Deal On. Well, That's Entertainment." *New York Times*, 19 June 1995, D1.

Fanning, Deirdre. "Making Japanese Bosses Stand Up and Applaud." *New York*

Times, 28 August 1987, 3, 21:1.

Feder, Barnaby J. "Murdoch's Time of Reckoning." *New York Times*, 20 December 1990, D1, D7.

"Fifth Estate Fortunes: The Top 100 Top $38 Billion." *Broadcasting*, 5 June 1989, 54–56.

Goldenson, Leonard H., and Marvin J. Wolf. *Beating the Odds: The Untold Story Behind the Rise of ABC*. New York: Charles Scribner's Sons, 1991.

Goldman, Kevin. "GE Makes a Late Bid for FNN Assets Sought in Dow Jones/Group W Offer." *Wall Street Journal*, 26 February 1991, B6:2.

Goldman, Kevin. "General Electric's NBC Unit to Acquire FNN's Media Assets for $105 Million." *Wall Street Journal*, 27 February 1991, B3.

Goldman, Kevin. "Thanks, but We'll Be Watching Reruns of 'My Favorite Martian.' " *Wall Street Journal*, 21 January 1991, B1.

Goldman, Kevin. "TV Airwaves Sizzle with 'Love' Shows." *Wall Street Journal*, 20 March 1991, B1, B3.

Jefferson, David J. and Lisa Bannon. "After Biding His Times, Michael Eisner Pounces." *Wall Street Journal*, 1 August 1995, B1.

Jensen, Elizabeth. "CBS's Tisch Is Faulted by Insiders, Affiliates for Network's Struggle." *Wall Street Journal*, 22 May 1995: p.1.

Jensen, Elizabeth. "Sharp Contrast: Why Did ABC Prosper while CBS Blinked?" *Wall Street Journal*, 2 August 1995, 1.

Jensen, Elizabeth. "Still Kicking." *Wall Street Journal Reports* [Television], 9 September 1994, R3.

Jensen, Elizabeth and John Lippman. "CBS Is Expected to Pick Lund to Succeed Stringer, Who Will Move to Bell Venture." *Wall Street Journal*, 23 February 1995, B10.

Jensen, Elizabeth and Raju Narisett. "Westinghouse Is Set to Make a Bid for CBS." *Wall Street Journal*, 18 July 1995, A3.

Johnson, Robert. "Tale of a Whale: Mysterious Gambler Wins, Loses Millions." *Wall Street Journal*, 28 June 1990, A1.

Keller, John J. and Laura Landro. "MCI Agrees to Inject as Much as $2 Billion in News Corp. in Data Highway Venture." *Wall Street Journal*, 11 May 1995, A3.

King, Thomas R. "Cable Firms Channel Efforts." *Wall Street Journal*, 9 February 1991, B6:3.

King, Thomas R. "Eisner, Katzenberg May End Feud, Saving Dream Works, Cap Cities Future." *Wall Street Journal*, 7 August 1995, B3.

King, Thomas R. and Laura Landro. "Ovitz's Surprise Move to President of Disney Transforms Hollywood." *Wall Street Journal*, 15 August 1995, A1.

Landler, Mark. "Long, Fruitful Partnership Atop Capital Cities." *New York Times*, 1 August 1995, D7.

Landler, Mark. "Two Takeovers Help Shift Focus in House Deregulation Debate." *New York Times*, 2 August 1995, D1.

Landler, Mark. "The War for Warner: You're On, Mr. Fuchs." *New York Times*, 25 June 1995, sec. 3, 1.

Landro, Laura. "Ego and Inexperience among Studio Buyers Add Up to Big Losses." *Wall Street Journal*, 10 April 1995, p.1

Landro, Laura. "Paramount Is Still Seeking a Media Firm." *Wall Street Journal*, 7 September 1990, B7.

Landro, Laura. "Paramount Taps Movie Producer for Key Role." *Wall Street Journal*, 19 March 1991, B1, B2.

Landro, Laura. "Specter of Shrinking Earnings Leaves Hollywood Home Alone with a Ghost." *Wall Street Journal*, 4 January 1991, B1, B3.

Landro, Laura. "Thrift Becomes Paramount in Hollywood as Big-Budget Films and Economy Falter." *Wall Street Journal*, 17 January 1991, B1, B6.

Landro, Laura, David P. Hamilton, and Michael Williams. "Last Action, Sony Finally Admits Billion-Dollar Mistake: Its Messed-Up Studio." *Wall Street Journal*, 18 November 1994, A1

Landro, Laura and Johnnie L. Roberts. "The Drama Ended, Two Stars Get New Script." *Wall Street Journal*, 16 February 1994, B1.

Landro, Laura, Johnnie L. Roberts, and Randall Smith. "Cable-Phone Link Is Promising Gamble, Time Warner Sees Synergy in Partnership." *Wall Street Journal*, 18 May 1993, B1, B10.

Landro, Laura, and Eben Shapiro. "Seagrams Sells Stake in Dupont so It Can Buy Control of MCA." *Wall Street Journal*, 7 April 1995, 1.

Lehner, Urban C., and Alan Murray. "Strained Alliance: 'Selling of America' to Japanese Touches Some Very Raw Nerves." *Wall Street Journal*, 19 June 1990, A1, A14.

Lev, Michael. "Sony's Columbia Unit Planning Theme Park." *New York Times*,10 January 1991, D19.

Lipman, Joanne. "Backer Loses Miller Lite to Leo Burnett." *Wall Street Journal*, 14 March 1991, B4.

Lippman, John. "What Will Jack Welch Do with NBC Now?" *Wall Street Journal*, 2 August 1995, B1.

Lohr, Steve. "A New Role for the Go-Between at Capital Cities." *New York Times*, 7 August 1995, D6.

Lowenstein, Roger. "Disney Gets Raves for Cap Cities, but Let's Talk about Mature Assets." *Wall Street Journal*, 3 August 1995, C1.

Maney, Kevin. *Megamedia Shakeout: The Inside Story of the Leaders and the Losers in the Exploding Communications Industry.* New York: John Wiley & Sons, 1995.

"Matsushita Moves on $6.1 Billion Purchase of MCA." *Broadcasting*, 31 December 1990, 36–37.

McCarthy, Michael J. "After Frantic Growth, Blockbuster Faces Host of Video-Rental Rivals." *Wall Street Journal*, 22 March 1991, A1, A5."

"Media Moguls Give the Poet Rave Reviews." *Wall Street Journal*, 1 August 1995: B1.

Metz, Robert. *CBS: Reflections in a Bloodshot Eye.* New York: Signet, New American Library, 1976.

Milbank, Dana. "Making Honda Parts, Ohio Company Finds Can Be Road to Ruin." *Wall Street Journal*, 5 October 1990, A1.

"More New Children's Players for Disney." *Broadcasting*, 7 January 1991, 45.

Narisetti, Raju. "Westinghouse Puts Curbs on CBS, Pending Purchase." *Wall Street Journal*, 7 August 1995, B5.

Norris, Floyd. "Capital Cities and CBS Have Happy Investors." *New York Times*, 2 August 1995, D1.

"Not Going to Disneyland after All." *Broadcasting*, 7 December 1990, 96.

Ono, Yumiko. "Japanese Women Are Truly Putting Aside a Tradition." *Wall Street*

Journal, 27 July 1990, A1.

Paley, William. *As It Happened: A Memoir*. Garden City, New York: Doubleday, 1979.

Pasqua, Thomas et al. *Mass Media in the Information Age*. Englewood Cliff, New Jersey: Prentice Hall, 1990.

Pember, Don R. *Mass Media Law*. Dubuque, Iowa: Brown & Benchmark, 1996.

Power, William. "Wall Street Is Back on Your TV Set, Stalking the Small Investor." *Wall Street Journal*, 28 March 1991, C1, C9.

Quinlan, Sterling. *Inside ABC American Broadcasting Company's Rise to Power*. New York: Hastings House, 1979.

Rundle, Rhonda L. "MGM, Pathe Revise and Extend Accord for Acquisition of Studio." *Wall Street Journal*, 22 June 1990, B1.

Sandomir, Richard. "Fox Outbids CBS for N.H.L. Games." *New York Times*, 10 September 1994, 31

Sanger, David E. "Tanii-san Goes Fishing in Hollywood." *New York Times*, 25 November 1990, 1, 6.

Shapiro, Eben. "Time Warner Agrees to Buy Cablevision." *Wall Street Journal*, 8 February 1995, A3.

Shapiro, Eben and Laura Landro. "Frustrated Investors Racket Up Pressure on Time Warner Chief." *Wall Street Journal*, 21 April 1995, 1.

Sharpe, Anita. "Blockbuster's Huizenga Says Outlook for Viacom Deal Remains Uncertain." *Wall Street Journal*, 25 May 1994, A8.

Sharpe, Anita. "Turner's New Leaf: Trying to Make Do." *Wall Street Journal*, 9 May 1995, B1.

Smith, Randall. "For Tisch Empire, It Looks like It's Back to the Basics." *Wall Street Journal*, 2 August 1995, C1.

Smith, Sally Bedell. *In All His Glory: The Life of William S. Paley—The Legendary Tycoon and His Brilliant Circle*. New York: Simon and Schuster, 1990.

Stanley, Robert H. *Media-Visions: The Art and Industry of Mass Communication*. New York: Praeger, 1987.

Stein, Lisa. "Cable TV Seeks to Improve Service." *TV Guide*, 3 March 1990, 53.

Sterngold, James. "Disney's Rival Studios Face Longer Competitive Odds." *New York Times*, 7 August 1995: D6.

Sterngold, James. "Hollywood 1, Japanese 0." *New York Times*, 16 April 1995: p.5

Sterngold, James. "Sony, Struggling Takes a Huge Loss on Movie Studio." *New York Times*, 18 November 1994, A1.

Stevenson, Richard W. "Taming Hollywood's Spending Monster." *New York Times*, 14 April 1991, 1, 6.

Trachtenberg, Jeffrey A. and Eben Shapiro. "Reward for the Restless: Warner Music's Top Job." *Wall Street Journal*, 4 May 1995, B1.

Turner, Richard. "Disney Retains Ex-Producers at Paramount." *Wall Street Journal*, 18 January 1991: B12.

Turner, Richard. "Disney Seeks to End Big, Big Pictures as Executive Calls for Small, Small World." *Wall Street Journal*, 30 January 1991, B1, B3.

Turner, Richard. "Disney Strategy to Increase Film Output Gets First Test in Spider Thriller-Comedy." *Wall Street Journal*, 13 January 1990, B1:3.

Turner, Richard. "Disney's Star is Foreign to U.S. Audiences." *Wall Street Journal*, 4 December 1990: B1, B3.

Turner, Richard. "Is Walt Disney Ready to Rewrite Its Own Script." *Wall Street Journal*, 26 August 1994, B1.

Turner, Richard. "Movie Studios Produce Uneven Picture with Efforts to Win More Video Buyers." *Wall Street Journal*, 6 June 1990, B1, B2.

Turner, Richard. "Muppets Seek Their Revenge against Disney." *Wall Street Journal*, 18 April 1991, B1, B6.

Turner, Richard. "Pathe Owner Parretti Finally Completes Acquisition of MGM for $1.3 Billion." *Wall Street Journal*, 2 November 1990, B1:3.

Turner, Richard. "'Pretty Woman' Lures New Video Buyers." *Wall Street Journal*, 9 January 1991, B1, B3.

Weinraub, Bernard. "Chairman of Disney Studios Resigns." *New York Times*, 15 August 1994, D1.

Weinraub, Bernard. "Clouds over Disneyland." *New York Times*, 9 April 1995: sec.3, p.1

Weinraub, Bernard. "Departure by Studio's Head Raises a Big Risk at Disney." *New York Times*, 26 August 1994, D1.

Weinraub, Bernard. "For Disney Chairman, a Deal Quenches a Personal Thirst." *New York Times*, 1 August 1995, 1.

Weinraub, Bernard. "It's a Small World, after All, Mr. Eisner." *New York Times*, 7 August 1995, D1.

"What's on the Minds of Programmers?" *Broadcasting*, 7 January 1991, 46.

"A Win for Hollywood, a Defeat for TV Competition." *Wall Street Journal*, 10 April 1991, A22.

Winans, Christopher. *The King of Cash: The Inside Story of Laurence Tisch*. New York: John Wiley & Sons, 1995.

Yoder, Stephen Kreider. "In this Bully Battle with Japan, the Cry is 'Toro, Toro, Toro,' " *Wall Street Journal* 28 September 1990, A1, A9.

Yoder, Stephen Kreider. "Japanese Players Learn Finer Points of Baseball in U.S." *Wall Street Journal*, 7 August 1990, A1.

Zier, Julie A. "CBS, Group W Form Historic Alliance." *Broadcasting & Cable*, 18 July 1994, 14.

2: STRATEGIES FOR SUCCESS: NETWORKS AND INDEPENDENT STATIONS

Gitlin, Todd. *Inside Prime Time*. New York: Pantheon Books, 1985.

Hall, Bruce Edward. "'Romper Room' Signs Off for Good." *New York Times*, 31 July 1994, sec. 2, 26.

Jensen, Elizabeth, and Mark Robichaux. "Fifth Network Sparks Interest of TV Industry." *Wall Street Journal*, 28 June 1993, B1, B6.

Sharkey, Betsy. "Anxious Parents Await the Birth of a TV Network." *New York Times*, 15 January 1995, sec. 2.

Zoglin, Richard. "Network Crazy." *Time*, 16 January 1995, 68–72.

3: THE FCC: THE AIRWAVES AND THE PUBLIC INTEREST

Andrews, Edmund L. "A Bitter Feud Fouls Lines at the F.C.C." *New York Times*, 20 November 1995, D1.

Andrews, Edmund L. "Congress Votes to Reshape Communications Industry Ending a 4-Year Struggle." *New York Times*, 2 February 1996, A1.

Andrews, Edmund L. "FCC Adopts Limits on TV Ads Aimed at Children." *New York Times*, 10 April 1991, D7.

Andrews, Edmund L. "F.C.C. Joining a Move to Curb Violence on TV." *New York Times*, 7 July 1995, 1.

Andrews, Edmund L. "Has the F.C.C. Become Obsolete?" *New York Times*, 12 June 1995, D1.

Andrews, Edmund L. "Senate Approves Far-Reaching Bill on Media Industry." *New York Times*, 16 June 1995, 1.

Andrews, Edmund L., and Geraldine Fabrikant. "The Black Entrepreneur at a Firestorm's Center." *New York Times*, 10 February 1995, D1.

Barnouw, Erik. *Tube of Plenty. The Evolution of American Television*. Rev. ed. New York: Oxford University Press, 1982.

Berniker, Mark. "FCC investigates IVDS Bidders." *Broadcasting & Cable*, 5 September 1994, 21.

Carnevale, Mary Lu. "FCC Adopts Rules on Children's TV; Critic Calls Them 'Barest Minimum,' " *Wall Street Journal*, 10 April 1991, B6.

Carnevale, Mary Lu. "FCC Panelists Near an Accord on Rerun Issue." *Wall Street Journal*, 5 April 1991, B1, B2.

Carnevale, Mary Lu. "FCC Problems in TV—Licenses Auction Grow as Interactive America Defaults." *Wall Street Journal*, 11 August 1994, A3.

Carnevale, Mary Lu. "FCC to Review Rules on Ownership of TV Stations." *Wall Street Journal*, 15 December 1994, B8.

Carter, Bill. "F.C.C. Chief Urges Repeal of Network Prime-Time Limit." *New York Times*, 17 July 1995, D8.

Cole, Barry, and Mal Oettinger. *Reluctant Regulators, The FCC and the Broadcast Audience*. Rev. ed. Reading, Massachusetts: Addison Wesley, 1978.

"Court Keeps Big Three out of Syndication until 1995." *Broadcasting & Cable*, 18 July 1994, 15.

"F.C.C. Plans to Allow TV over Phone Lines." *New York Times*, 25 October 1991, A1, D16.

"Growing Similarity between Affiliates and Indies." *Broadcasting*, 7 January 1991.

Gruley, Bryan, and Albert R. Karr. "Telecom Vote Signals Competitive Free-for-All." *Wall Street Journal*, 2 February 1996, B1.

Hickey, Neil. "Revolution in CYBERIA." *Columbia Journalism Review*, July/August 1995, 40–47.

Jensen, Elizabeth. "Violence Floods Children's TV, New Study Says." *Wall Street Journal*, 20 September 1995, B1.

Jessell, Harry A. "FCC Puts Two Stations on Indecency Notice." *Broadcasting*, 29 April 1991, 50–51.

Karr, Albert R. "FCC Clears Westinghouse Bid for CBS, Settling Dispute on Children's Programs." *Wall Street Journal*, 29 November 1995, B5.

Kolbert, Elizabeth. "TV Getting a Closer Look as a Contributor to Real Violence."

New York Times, 14 December 1994, D1.

Landler, Mark. "Disney Move Seen Clearing Regulators." *New York Times*, 1 August 1995, D5.

Landler, Mark. "House Passes Bill Curtailing Rules on Phones and TV." *New York Times*, 5 August 1995, A1.

Landler, Mark. "In TV Deregulation, Qualms about Losing Local Control." *New York Times*, 7 August 1995, A1.

McAvoy, Kim. "FCC Gets into the Children's Act." *Broadcasting & Cable*, 26 July 1993, 42–43.

McClellan, Steve. "Right-Wing Short-Wave Comes under FCC Scrutiny." *Broadcasting & Cable*, 1 May 1995, 6.

Mifflin, Laurie. "4 Networks Plan a Ratings System for Their Shows." *New York Times*, 15 February 1996, A1.

"Network Ownership: The First Seven Decades." *New York Times*, 1 August 1995, D6.

Pearl, Daniel. "FCC Investigates Special-Status Claims of Winners of Interactive-TV Licenses." *Wall Street Journal*, 31 August 1994, B2.

Pearl, Daniel. "FCC Set to Scrap Prime-Time Rule Affecting Affiliates." *Wall Street Journal*, 17 July 1995, B7.

Pearl, Daniel. "House Is Expected to Push for Radical Deregulation of Telecommunications." *Wall Street Journal*, 19 June 1995, B1.

Pearl, Daniel. "Senate Commerce Committee Considers an Auction for Digital TV Channels." *Wall Street Journal*, 31 July 1995: A2.

Pearl, Daniel. "Senate, in 81-80 Vote, Clears Overhaul of the Nation's Communications Law." *Wall Street Journal*, 16 June 1995, A3.

Pearl, Daniel. "The Shadow of Rupert Murdoch Looms Large as FCC, House Are Poised to Act on TV Matters." *Wall Street Journal*, 28 July 1995, A16.

Pearl, Daniel, and Gautam Naik. "FCC's Wireless Communication Auction Hits Snag as Federal Court Intervenes." *Wall Street Journal*, 28 July 1995, A16.

Pember, Don R. *Mass Media Law*. 6th ed. Dubuque: WCB Brown & Benchmark, 1993.

"Radio License Procedures Are Voted on at the FCC." *Wall Street Journal*, 10 April 1991, A11.

Revere, Robert Corn. "Mixed Message on the First Amendment." *Broadcasting & Cable*, 10 July 1995, 43.

Robichaux, Mark. "A Cable Empire That Was Built on a Tax Break." *Wall Street Journal*, 12 January 1995, B1.

Stanley, Robert H. *Media-Visions: The Art and Industry of Mass Communication*. New York: Praeger, 1987.

Stein, Lisa. "Networks, Studios Singing Blues over FCC Ruling." *TV Guide*, 20 April 1991, 25, 26.

Stern, Christopher. "Clinton: V-chip is not Enough." *Broadcasting & Cable*, 12 February 1996, 4.

Stern, Christopher. "Dereg Rolls in Senate: 81-18." *Broadcasting & Cable*, 19 June 1995, 6.

Stern, Christopher. "FCC Proposes 7-year TV License Terms." *Broadcasting & Cable*, 6 February 1995, 7.

Stern, Christopher. "FCC Seeks Comments on Fate of Off-Net Ban." *Broadcasting*

& Cable, 10 October 1994, 10.

Stern, Christopher. "Industry Battles Ratings, V-chip." Broadcasting & Cable, 26 June 1995, 16.

Stern, Christopher. "New Law of the Land." Broadcasting & Cable, 5 February 1996, 8.

Stern, Christopher. "Staff Shifts Help Hundt Reinvent FCC." Broadcasting & Cable, 8 August 1994, 37.

Stern, Christopher and David Tobenkin. "FCC Moves on Prime Time Access Rule." Broadcasting & Cable, 24 October 1994, 7.

Sterling, Christopher H., and John M. Kittross. Stay Tuned: A Concise History of American Broadcasting. 2d ed. Belmont, California: Wadsworth Publishing Co., 1990.

Stone, Joseph and Tim Yohn. Prime Time and Misdemeanors. New Brunswick, New Jersey: Rutgers University Press, 1992.

Tobenkin, David. "Production Big Business for Big 3." Broadcasting & Cable, 12 September 1994, 6–10.

"TV Reruns Regulations Revamped by the F.C.C." New York Times, 10 April 1991, D6.

Zoglin, Richard. "Chips Ahoy." Time, 19 February 1996, 58–61.

Zoglin, Richard. "Network Crazy." Time, 16 January 1995, 68–72.

4: A HISTORY OF PROGRAMMING: TELEVISION'S EVOLUTION

Auletta, Ken. Three Blind Mice: How the TV Networks Lost Their Way. New York: Random House, 1986.

Carter, Bill. "Cadillac-Sized Hits by the VW of Producers." New York Times, 22 January 1996, D1.

"Educating the Muses: Can Television Make the Grade?" Broadcasting & Cable, 26 July 1993, 50–54.

Fabrikant, Geraldine. "Viacom to Put Spelling Stake Up For Sale." New York Times, 11 August 1995, D1.

Felsenthal, Edward. "TV Cops May Right Wrongs, Wrong Rights." Wall Street Journal, 10 March 1993, B1 ,B8.

Goodman, Walter. "'Today' Celebrates Itself, at Night Yet." New York Times, 14 January 1992, C11, C12.

McClellan, Steve. "It's Not Just for Saturday Mornings Anymore." Broadcasting & Cable, 26 July 1993, 38.

Paley, William. As It Happened: A Memoir. Garden City, New York: Doubleday, 1979.

Sklar, Robert. Prime Time America. Life on and behind the Television Screen. New York: Oxford University Press, 1980.

Smith, Sally Bedell. In All His Glory: The Life of William S. Paley—The Legendary Tycoon and His Brilliant Circle. New York: Simon and Schuster, 1990.

Sterling, Christopher H., and John M. Kittross. Stay Tuned: A Concise History of American Broadcasting. 2d ed. Belmont, California: Wadsworth Publishing Company, 1990.

Stone, Joseph, and Tim Yohn. *Prime Time and Misdemeanors*. New Brunswick, New Jersey: Rutgers University Press, 1992.

Tartikoff, Brandon, and Charles Leerhsen. *The Last Great Ride*. New York: Turtle Bay Books, 1992.

"Television/1993." *New York Times*, 26 December 1993, 36.

Trachtenberg, Jeffrey A. "Viacom to Shed Spelling Stake to Trim Debt." *Wall Street Journal*, 11 August 1995, A3.

Zoglin, Richard. "Trekking Onward." *Time*, 28 November 1994, 72.

5: PROGRAMMING STAPLES: ENDURING GENRES

"A New Story of Sex Acts with Swaggart." *San Francisco Chronicle*, 31 January 1989, A3.

Anderson, Douglas A. *Contemporary Sports Reporting*. 2d ed. Chicago: Nelson-Hall Publishers, 1994.

Antilla, Susan. "Alarms Raised over 'Rescue 911.' " *New York Times* 1 November 1992, A4, A22:3.

Applebome, Peter. "Bakker Sentenced to 45 Years for Fraud in His T.V. Ministry." *New York Times*, 25 October 1989.

Applebome, Peter. "Blaming Others for Collapse of PTL, Bakker Completes Testimony." *New York Times*, 3 October 1989.

"At Bakker Trial, Shock Is on Wane." *New York Times*, 17 September 1989.

"At Seedy Mall, Bakkers Make Bid for Revival." *New York Times*, 10 May 1989.

"Big Names = Big Dollars." *Broadcasting & Cable*, 7 March 1994, 32.

"Bakker Aide Receives 8-Year Fraud Sentence." *New York Times*, 25 August 1989.

"Bakker and Hahn Trade Charges." *New York Times*, 28 March 1987.

"Bakker Pleads for Reduction of Prison Terms." *New York Times*, 23 August 1991.

Brown, Rich. "Cable Courts Kids." *Broadcasting & Cable*, 26 July 1993, 66–68.

Brozan, Nadine. "Chonicle." *New York Times*, 13 March 1992.

Buchert, Wendy. "Sex Scandals Hurt All Television Ministries." *USA Today*, 23 March 1989.

Carter, Bill. "CBS's 'Sports Strategy'—Everything but a Payoff." *New York Times*, 2 February 1992, 12.

Carter, Bill. "Do Double Standards Apply at Fox?" *New York Times*, 29 June 1992.

Carter, Bill. "Killing Poses Hard Questions about Talk T.V." *New York Times*, 14 March 1995, 1.

Carter, Bill. "Lessons in Broadcasting the Power of a Show for Children." *New York Times*, 19 March 1992, C20.

Castaneda, Carol J. "Swaggart: God Told Me to Keep Ministry." *USA Today*, 18 October 1991, A3.

Charren, Peggy. "Kidvid: Doing Battle with G.I. Joe." *New York Times*, 26 January 1992, 29.

Chira, Susan. "How a Friendly Ghost Became a TV Muse." *New York Times*, 11 July 1993, 26, 28.

"Church Denies Directors Mulled Reviving Channel." *Boston Globe*, 4 May 1992, 20.

Clymer, Adam. "Survey Finds Many Skeptics among Evangelists' Viewers." *New York Times*, 31 March 1987.

Coe, Steve. "More Players in Saturday Playground." *Broadcasting & Cable*, 26 July 1993, 46–48.

"The Deconstruction of Jenny and Jerry, Maury and Montel." *New York Times*, 10 December, 1995, 7.

"Donors to Bakker Got Nothing." *New York Times*, 15 November 1992.

Donovan, Sharen. "Swaggart Based Charges on Rumor." *USA Today*, 7 August 1991.

Eckholm, Eric. "From Right, a Rain of Anti-Clinton Salvos." *New York Times*, 26 June 1994, 2.

Elliott, Stuart. "Commercial Cartoon Furor Grows." *New York Times*, 5 March 1992, D1, D21.

Freeman, Mike. "Fox, Disney Power Kid's Entertainment." *Broadcasting & Cable*, 26 July 1993, 56–62.

"Falwell Hints Short PTL Term." *New York Times*, 23 March 1987.

Fineman, Howard. "God and the Grass Roots." *Newsweek*, 8 November 1993.

Franklin, James L. "Christian Science at Great Divide." *Boston Globe*, 27 December 1992, 1.

Franklin, James L. "Christian Science Was Set Aside at Monitor Radio, TV." *Boston Globe*, 26 May 1992, 1.

Franklin, James L. "Christian Scientist Local Decisions Crucial." *Boston Globe*, 28 September 1992, 13.

Franklin, James L. "Church Moves up Cable-Sale Deadline." *Boston Globe*, 6 April 1992, 1.

Franklin, James L. "Letter Chastises Church Board for Response to Critics." *Boston Globe*, 5 May 1992, 21.

Franklin, James L. "Official Says Church Spent $14M–$15M from Fund." *Boston Globe*, 13 May 1992: 1.

Friend, Tom. "Stupid Baseball Tricks." *New York Times*, sec. 6, 5 May 1996, 62–65.

Fuchsberg, Gilbert and Mark Robichaux. "IRS to Tax Sponsors' Fees to Bowl-Game Organizers." *Wall Street Journal*, 4 December 1991, B1.

"Fury: Swaggart's Lies Ruined Evangelist." *USA Today*, 13 September 1991.

Gitlin, Todd. *Inside Prime Time*. New York: Pantheon Books, 1985.

Goldman, Kevin. "Biggest Winner in NBA Finals Is NBC." *Wall Street Journal*, 8 June 1992, B1, B4.

Goldman, Kevin. "CBS Crams Olympics Coverage with Ads." *Wall Street Journal*, 13 February 1992, B3.

Goldman, Kevin. "CBS Makes Comeback with World Series." *Wall Street Journal*, 25 October 1991, B4.

Goldman, Kevin. "Humbled NBC Hopes to Avoid Sting of Seoul." *Wall Street Journal*, 20 July 1992, B1, B5.

Goldman, Kevin. "Let the Bidding Begin for the TV Rights to '96 Olympics, and Watch It Heat Up." *Wall Street Journal*, 7 August 1992, B1, B8.

Goldman, Kevin. "NBC Must Run Uphill to Win at Barcelona." *Wall Street Journal*, 27 February 1992, B5.

Goldman, Kevin. "NBC Sets Olympic Record for Ad Sales Tied to Games." *Wall Street Journal*, 28 June 1995, B1.

Goldman, Kevin, and Jacqueline Simmons. "NBC to Pay $1.27 Billion for Rights to Olympics." *Wall Street Journal*, 8 August 1995, B1.

Goodman, Walter. "Television, Meet Life. Life, Meet TV." *New York Times*, 19 June 1994, sec. 4, 1.

Goodwin, Richard N. *Remembering America: A Voice from the Sixties*. New York: Little Brown & Company, 1988.

Hagans, Gail. "Couch Parishioners Worship at the Tube." *Atlanta Journal and Atlanta Constitution*, 7 June 1992, D4.

Helyar, John. "Changing Times Fell Baseball Network." *Wall Street Journal*, 26 June 1995, B1.

Helyar, John. "A Whole New Ballgame." *Wall Street Journal Reports* [television], 9 September 1994, R9.

Horsfield, Peter G. *Religious Television, the American Experience*. New York: Longman, 1984.

Jarvis, Jeff. "The Couch Critic." *TV Guide*, 23 May 1992, 9.

Jensen, Elizabeth. "Advertisers Get More Play Time on Kids' TV." *Wall Street Journal*, 6 February 1996, B1.

Jensen, Elizabeth. "Believe It or Not, More Talk Shows are Coming." *Wall Street Journal*, 23 January 1995, B1.

Jensen, Elizabeth. "It's 8 p.m. Your Kids Are Watching Sex on TV." *Wall Street Journal*, 27 March 1995, B1.

Jensen, Elizabeth. "NBC Acquires Summer Games for $456 Million." *Wall Street Journal*, 28 July 1993, B1, B10.

Jensen, Elizabeth, and Glenn Ruffenach. "NBC High Bid for Olympics Startles Industry." *Wall Street Journal*, 29 July 1993, B1, B2.

"Jim Bakker Freed from Jail to Stay in a Halfway House." *New York Times*, 2 July 1994, 6.

"Jury Is Told That Swaggart Spread Rumors on Rival out of Jealousy." *New York Times*, 17 July 1991.

"Jury Selection Begins for Trail of a Defrocked T.V. Evangelist." *New York Times*, 9 July 1991.

King, Thomas R. "Since Shari Lewis Can't Sit Still, Kids Stand No Chance." *Wall Street Journal*, 18 December 1992, A1, A7.

King, Wayne. "Bakker, Evangelist Resigns His Ministry over Sexual Incident." *New York Times*, 21 March 1987.

King, Wayne. "Robertson Shifts Political Tack in Bid to Steer Clear of Evangelist's Battle." *New York Times*, 29 March 1987.

Kolbert, Elizabeth. "Our New Participatory Tabloid Videocracy." *New York Times*, 17 July 1994, 3.

Kolbert, Elizabeth. "We Interrupt this Program." *New York Times*, 26 June 1994, sec. 4, 18.

"Laventhol Bankruptcy Plan." *New York Times*, 25 August 1992.Lipman, Joanne. "NBC Still Has Big Chunk of Time to Unload for Summer Olympics." *Wall Street Journal*, 18 May 1992, B8.

Lippman, John, and Anita Sharpe. "Using Cox Cash, Producer Lures Stars to Studio." *New York Times*, 4 April 1995, B1.

Longman, Jere. "NBC's Triple Play Bolsters the I.O.C. and Its Chief." *New York Times*, 13 December 1995, B17.

Malone, Julia. "A Church in Strife over Secular Missteps." *Los Angeles Times*, 24 April 1992, B7.

Marcus, Frances Frank. "Swaggart Found Liable for Defaming Minister." *New York Times*, 13 September 1991.

Margolick, David. "At the Bar." *New York Times*, 15 February 1991, B6.

Maslin, Janet. "There's a Moral in TV Cartoons: Be Resourceful." *New York Times*, 4 October 1992, 2.

McClellan, Steve. "NBC Affils to Help Carry Olympic Torch." *Broadcasting & Cable*, 2 August 1993, 6,15.

McQueen, Mike. "Scandals Batter Top Evangelist." *USA Today*, 17 February 1989.

Metz, Robert. *CBS: Reflections in a Bloodshot Eye*. New York: Signet, New American Library, 1976.

Moshavi, Sharon D. "Third Quarter Baseball Sales in Slump." *Broadcasting*,17 June 1991, 44–45.

O'Connor, John J. "The Sunshine Menace of 'Wild Palms.' " *New York Times*, 16 May 1993, 34.

"New Owner Runs P.T.L. Park." *New York Times*, 14 Febrary. 1984.

Nichols, Bill. "Bakker Case Coming to Finality." *USA Today*, 28 August 1989.

"Paramount Guarantees 90 Episodes of 'Dear John.' " *Broadcasting*, 23 July 1990, 59–60.

"Pastor Tells of Guilt over Introducing Pair." *New York Times*, 29 March 1987.

Perry, James M. "Soul Mates, the Christian Coalition Crusades to Broaden Rightist Political Base." *Wall Street Journal*, 19 July 1994, A1."PTL's Creditors Set Back." *New York Times*, 24 August 1992.

Petrozzello, Donna. "Talk Show Hosts Dispute Clinton's Criticism." *Broadcasting & Cable*, 1 May 1995, 6.

Quindlen, Anna. "Talking About The Media Circus." *New York Times*, 26 June 1994, 26.

Ramirez, Anthony. "Company's News; from Evangelical TV Roots to a Stock Offering's Riches." *New York Times*, 18 April 1992.

Reinhold, Robert. "Evangelist Divided over Theology." *New York Times*, 28 March 1987.

Riddle, Lyn. "Focus; South Carolina Settling Catawba Claim." *New York Times*, 15 November 1992.

"Rider Says Swaggart Hired Her for Sex." *Washington Post*, 12 October 1991.

"Roberts Begins Fast for Funds." *New York Times*, 23 March 1987.

"Roberts Seeks More Pledges." *New York Times*, 31 March 1987.

Robichaux, Mark. "Giving College Degrees for Watching TV." *Wall Street Journal*, 1 June 1992, B1, B6.

Robichaux, Mark. "NBC Faces Loss from Olympics Pay-TV Plan." *Wall Street Journal*, 15 June 1992, B1, B2.

Robichaux, Mark. "Religious Cable Networks Fight Sin—And One Another." *Wall Street Journal*, 12 September 1995, B1.

Robichaux, Mark, and Elizabeth Jensen. "Fox Gets Rights to Tyson Match for $10 Million." *Wall Street Journal*, 15 September 1995, B1.

Rohter, Larry. "Are Women Directors an Endangered Species?" *New York Times*, 17 March 1991, 13, 20, 21.

Ruffenach, Glenn. "Let the Talks Begin: TV Networks Vow to Exercise Restraint on Olympic Fees." *Wall Street Journal*, 21 July 1993, B1, B8.

Sandomir, Richard. "For $1.27 Billion, NBC Accomplishes an Olympic Sweep." *New York Times*, 8 August 1995, A1.

Sandomir, Richard. "The Man Carrying the Ball for Murdoch." *New York Times*, 4 September 1994, sec. 3, 1.

Sandomir, Richard. "NBC Wins TV Rights to 1996 Atlanta Games." *New York Times*, 28 July 1993, B7, B11.

Sandomir, Richard. "Super Bowl, Super Rout, Super Ratings." *New York Times*, 3 February 1993, B7, B11.

"Sex, Demons and T.V. Ratings Fight Enliven Continuing Battle of Two Evangelists." *New York Times*, 21 July 1991.

Sibley, Celia. "Snellville Pastor's TV Ministry Starts Tonight." *Atlanta Constitution*, 8 December 1992, 1.

Smothers, Randal. "Bakkers Are Back in New TV Show." *New York Times*, 3 January 1989.

"Start of Deliberation in Evangelist's Lawsuits." *New York Times*, 11 September 1991.

Steinfels, Peter. "Beliefs." *New York Times*, 26 September 1992.

"Swaggart Plans to Step Down." *New York Times*, 15 October 1991.

Sharkey, Betsy. "Anxious Parents Await the Birth of a TV Network." *New York Times*, 15 January 1995, 1.

"The Baseball Network Flies Out." *Broadcasting & Cable*, 26 June 1995, 7.

Tobenkin, David. "Robertson Close to Deal on Vietnam Cable." *Broadcasting & Cable*, 30 May 1994, 32.

Toner, Robin. "Bakker's Troubles Test Faith at Religious Resort." *New York Times*, 29 March 1987.

Toner, Robin. "Preachers' Battle Transfixing the South." *New York Times*, 26 March 1987.

Tinker, Grant. *Tinker In Television From General Sarnoff to General Electric*. New York: Simon & Schuster, 1994.

Turner, Richard. "On Its Own." *Wall Street Journal Reports* [Television], 9 September 1994, R6.

"TV's Preachers: Generals in Evangelical War." *New York Times*, 26 March 1987.

6: MERCHANTS OF NEWS

"ABC, Roseanne Barr Sign Pact for Series, TV Movie." *Wall Street Journal*, 2 November 1990.

"ABC Sued over Cigarette Report." *Broadcasting & Cable*, 28 March 1994, 13.

"All Ears, Disney's Deal for ABC Makes Show Business a Whole New World." *Wall Street Journal*, 1 August 1995, A1.

Anderson, Douglas A. *Contemporary Sports Reporting*, 2d edition. Chicago: Nelson-Hall Publishers, 1994.

Arnett, Peter. *Live from the Battlefield*. New York: Simon & Schuster, 1994.

Baker, Russ. "Hidden Cameras a Million-Dollar Peek." Columbia Journalism Review, March/April 1995, 15

Barrett, Paul M. "Noriega Tapes Raise Tricky Issues but Aren't Seen Threatening Trial." *Wall Street Journal*, 14 November 1990.

Benjamin, Burton. *Fair Play. CBS General Westmoreland and How a Television Documentary Went Wrong*. New York: Harper and Row, 1988.

Benjamin, Burton. "The Documentary: An Endangered Species." Gannett Center for Media Studies. Occasional Paper No. 6, October 1987.

Bernstein, Richard. "For $64,000, What Is 'Fiction?' " *New York Times*, 4 September 1994, sec. 2, 1.

"Big Names = Big Dollars." *Broadcasting & Cable*, 7 March 1994, 32.

Bliss, Edward Jr. *Now the News: The Story of Broadcast Journalism*. New York: Columbia University Press, 1991.

Brinkley, David. *A Memoir*. New York: Alfred A. Knopf Inc., 1995.

Boyer, Peter J. "Rather Walked Off Set of CBS News." *New York Times*, 13 September 1987.

Broder, David S. "Surfeit of TV News." *Washington Post*, 8 July 1985.

Burns, John F. "Days and Nights in Baghdad." *New York Times*, 11 November 1990, sec. 6, 54.

Campbell, Richard. "Don Hewitt's Durable Hour." *Columbia Journalism Review*, September/October 1993, 25.

"Caned Teen-Ager Freed Early." *New York Times*, 21 June 1994, A3.

Carter, Bill. "Morning News Programs Draw the Young and Mobile." *New York Times*, 5 April 1993, D1, D7.

Carter, Bill. "NBC Tries Again with a News-Magazine Format." *New York Times*, 31 April 1991.

Carter, Bill. "New Surge Is Building at 'CBS Evening News.' " *New York Times*, 1 June 1992, 1.

Carter, Bill. 'Nightline,' at 15, Is Now Stronger than Ever." *New York Times*, 27 March 1995, D1.

Carter, Bill. "Sawyer Makes a New Deal with ABC." *New York Times*, 17 February 1994.

Carter, Bill. "Stations Seek More Profits on News." *New York Times*, 7 January 1991, D1, D6.

Carter, Bill. 'To Shore up Ratings, '60 Minutes' Will Cover Breaking News Stories." *New York Times*, 15 February 1996, C26.

Carter, Bill. " '20/20' Gives '60 Minutes' a Run for Its Ratings." *New York Times*, 21 April 1991, 31.

Carter, Bill. "Women Anchors Are on the Rise as Evening Stars." *New York Times*, 12 September 1992.

"CBS, Tokyo Broadcasting Link Up." *Broadcasting*, 17 September 1990, 73, 74.

Cloud, Stanley, and Lynne Olson. *The Murrow Boys: Pioneers on the Front Line of Broadcast Journalism*. New York: Houghton Mifflin Co., 1996.

Coffey, Frank. "Inside '60 Minutes.' " *TV Guide*, 6 November 1993, 18–26.

Cohen, Laurie P. and Aliz M. Freedman. "American Express Sends a Statement That's Quite Wrong." *Wall Street Journal*, 24 January 1995, 1.

Dean, Morton. "TV's Duty to Cover Terror." *New York Times*, 12 July 1985.

Elliot, Stuart. "CBS News Bends a Rule and Lets a Television Anchor Continue to Make Commercials for Radio." *New York Times*, 6 April 1994, D20.

Elliot, Stuart. "Tough Sell for Late News Shows." *New York Times*, 8 April 1992.

Fanto, Clarence. "Crisis Aftermath: Sober Second Thoughts." *New York Daily News*, 2 July 1985.

"Federal Courts Chosen for Camera Experiment." *Broadcasting*, 31 December 1990, 70.

Felsenthal, Edward. "The Torturous Story behind a *Prime Time* Story." *Wall Street Journal*, 27 July 1993, 9.

Fielding, Raymond. *The American Newsreel, 1911–1967.* Norman, Oklahoma: University of Oklahoma Press, 1972.

Fielding, Raymond. *The March of Time, 1935–1951.* New York: Oxford University Press, 1978.

Fouhy, Ed. "Toward a New Agenda in TV News." *Broadcasting & Cable,* 10 January 1994, 32.

Freedman, Alix M., Elizabeth Jensen and Amy Stevens. "Tort TV, CBS Legal Guarantees to '60 Minutes' Source Muddy Tobacco Story." *Wall Street Journal*, 16 November 1995, A1.

Freeman, Mike, and Steve McClellan. "Magazines, Talk Shows among First-Run Ideas in Works by Syndicators." *Broadcasting*, 13 July 1992, 7–8.

Gerston, Jill. "Forrest Sawyer, Gathering the Spoils of War." *New York Times*, 12 November 1992, 27, 36.

Glaberson, William. "The Press: Bought and Sold and Gray All Over." *New York Times*, 30 July 1995, sec. 4, 1.

Glaberson, William. " '60 Minutes' Case Part of a Trend of Corporate Pressure, Some Analysts Say." *New York Times*, 17 November, 1995, B14.

Goldman, Kevin. "After a Rocky Year, 'Prime Time Live' Emerges Less Live." *Wall Street Journal*, 2 September 1990.

Goldman, Kevin. "NBC Lets Group Solicit Executives for Pac Funding." *Wall Street Journal*, 30 November 1990.

Goldman, Kevin. "Newcasts Cast about for New Formats." *Wall Street Journal*, 10 January 1992, B1.

Goldman, Kevin. "Sponsors Expect Spillover of Disney Image." *Wall Street Journal*, 1 August 1995, B8.

Goldman, Kevin and Patrick M. Reilly. "Untold Story: Media's Slow Grasp of Hurricane's Impact Helped Delay Response." *Wall Street Journal*, 10 January 1992, A1.

Goldman, Kevin, and Mark Robichaux. "Camcorders Spark Two Cable Ventures." *Wall Street Journal*, 30 July 1992, B1.

Goodman, Walter. "And Now, Heeeeeeeere's a Referendum." *New York Times*, 21 June 1992, 25.

Goodman, Walter. "As Documentaries Soared, Newscasters Went on Ego Trips." *New York Times*, 30 December 1990: 35, 42.

Goodman, Walter. "Beauty and the Broadcast." *New York Times*, 26 January 1992, 29.

Goodman, Walter. "How Much Should TV Tell, and When?" *New York Times*, 29 October 1990, C20.

Goodman, Walter. "How '60 Minutes' Holds Its Viewers Attention." *New York Times*, 22 September 1993, C18.

Goodman, Walter. "Life Lessons from ABC's Nicotine Expose on 'Day One.' *New York Times*, 8 May 1994, 31.

Goodman, Walter. "Tabloid Charge Rocks Network News." *New York Times*, 13 February 1994, 29.

Goodman, Walter. "Television, Meet Life. Life Meet TV." *New York Times*, 19 June 1994, sec.4, 1.

Goodman, Walter. "Videotaped Violence: Fodder for One Set of Assumptions as Well as Another." *New York Times*, 2 May 1991, 8.

Goodman, Walter. "What Parson Rather Left Out of His Sermon." *New York Times*, 17 October 1993, 33.

Goodson, Mark. "If I'd Stood Up Earlier." *New York Times Magazine*, 13 January 1991, 22, 39, 40, 43.

Gorney, Carole. "Litigation Journalism on Trial." *Media Critic*, June 1993, 48.

Green, Michelle. "Fatal Attraction." *People*, 27 March 1995, 40.

Greenhouse, Linda. "Disdaining a Sound Bite, Federal Judges Banish TV." *New York Times*, 25 September 1994, 1.

Gremillion, Jeff. "Star School, on the Fast Track to Network News." *Columbia Journalism Review*, January/February 1995, 32.

Greppi, Michele. "Siege in Waco Ends on Live TV." *New York Post*, 20 April 1993, 2.

Grossman, Lawrence K. "CBS '60 Minutes' and the Unseen Interview." *Columbia Journalism Review*, January/February 1996, 39.

Gunther, Mark. "ABC News's Fractious All-Star Team: Make Room For Barbara." *New York Times*, 13 March 1994, 34.

Gunther, Mark. *The House That Roone Built: The Inside Story of ABC News."* New York: Little Brown & Company, 1994.

Hodson, Thomas S. "The Judge: Justice in Prime Time." *Media Studies Journal*, Winter 1992, 87.

Hughes, John. "Improving TV News." *Christian Science Monitor*, 18 September 1985.

Hughes, Kathleen A. "Hollywood Rushes Iraq Angles into Plots." *Wall Street Journal*, 21 January 1991, B1, B2.

"If It Bleeds It Leads." *Broadcasting & Cable*, 27 September1993, 48.

James, Caryn. "What's a Mother to Do?" *New York Times*, 17 March 1991, 33.

Janofsky, Michael. "A Former TV Star Is Reborn as an All Too-Human Spokeswoman for a Weight Watchers' Campaign." *New York Times*, 9 March 1994, D17.

Janofsky, Michael. "Philip Morris Accuses ABC of Libel." *New York Times*, 25 March 1994, A15.

Jensen, Elizabeth. " 'Dateline NBC' May Take on '60 Minutes.' " *Wall Street Journal*, 5 January 1996, B1.

Jensen, Elizabeth, and Suein L. Hwang. "CBS Airs Some of Wigand's Interview, Accusing Tobacco Firm, Its Ex-Chief." *Wall Street Journal*, 29 January 1996, B10.

Jensen, Elizabeth and Eben Shapiro. "Philip Morris Suit against ABC News Seeks $10 Billion, Alleges Defamation." *Wall Street Journal*, 25 March 1994, B12.

Johnston, David. "Citing Taped Talks, Lawyer for Noriega Wants Case Voided." *New York Times*, 9 November 1990, A1.

Jones, Alex S. "The Anchors, Who They Are, What They Do, the Tests They Face." *New York Times*, 27 July 1986, sec. 6, 12.

"Ka-Chung! CBS News Drops to 3rd." *Broadcasting*, 26 February 1993, 34.

King, Thomas R. "Keeping Track." *Wall Street Journal Reports* [television], 9 September 1994, R11.

King, Thomas R. "Zap." *Wall Street Journal Reports* [television], 9 September 1994, R12.

Klein, Edward. "Winning Diane. How ABC's Roone Arledge Snatched Her away from CBS." *New York Times*, 13 March 1989, 39.

Kneale, Dennis. "CBS Is Seeking a Partial Refund on Baseball Pact." *Wall Street Journal*, 30 November 1990.

Kolbert, Elizabeth. "NBC Settles Truck Crash Lawsuit, Saying Test was 'Inappropriate.' " *New York Times*, 10 February 1993, A1, A16.

Kolbert, Elizabeth. "Our New Participatory Tabloid Videocracy." *New York Times*, 17 July 1994, 3.

Kolbert, Elizabeth. "We Interrupt this Program . . ." *New York Times*, 26 June 1994, sec. 4, 18.

Kolbert, Elizabeth. "When News Producers Become Part of the News, There's Bound to Be Tension at the Network," *New York Times*, 18 October 1993, D7.

Landler, Mark. "ABC News Settles Suits on Tobacco." *New York Times*, 22 August 1995, A1, D6.

Loftus, Jack. "Are TV Webs Hostage in Beirut?" *Variety*, 26 June 1985.

MacArthur, John R. *Second Front Censorship and Propaganda in the Gulf War.* Berkeley: University of California Press, 1992.

Manegold, Catherine S. "A Grim Wasteland on News at Six." *New York Times*, 14 June 1992, 41,50.

Margolick, David. "A Peek under the Tent of the West Palm Beach Media Circus." *New York Times*, 15 December 1991, 2.

Matusow, Barbara. *The Evening Stars: The Making of the Network News Anchor.* Boston: Houghton Mifflin Company, 1983.

McClellan, Steve. "ABC News Is Number One, but . . . " *Broadcasting & Cable*, 27 September 1993, 41–42.

McClellan, Steve. "'Dateline' Faces New Complaints." *Broadcasting*, 16 August 1993, 14.

McClellan, Steve. "'Dateline' Goes for Threepeat." *Broadcasting & Cable*, 1 August 1994, 10.

McClellan, Steve. "Dateline NBC Goes Twice—Weekly." *Broadcasting & Cable*, 18 April 1994, 19.

McClellan, Steve. "Magazines Prime Earners in Prime Time." *Broadcasting & Cable*, 9 May 1994, 40.

McClellan, Steve. "Programing Overhaul in Works at CNN." *Broadcasting & Cable*, 13 June 1994, 16.

McClellan, Steve. "Sawyer Stays with ABC." *Broadcasting & Cable*, 21 February 1994, 20.

McClellan, Steve. "Tabloids Pull Out the Checkbook, Proudly." *Broadcasting & Cable*, 9 May 1994, 42.

McConnell, Chris. "Ghostbusting Finds a Home on Line 19." *Broadcasting & Cable*, 4 July 1994, 37.

McKinley, James C. "CBS Is Said to Fear Unusual Legal Challenge in '60 Minutes'

Case." *New York Times*, 17 November 1995, B14.

Meisler, Andy. "New York 1 Becomes Global Role Model." *New York Times*, 19 December 1994, D10.

Mengelkoch, Louise. "When Checkbook Journalism Does God's Work." *Columbia Journalism Review*, November/December 1994, 35.

Meyer, Thomas J. "No Sound Bites Here." *New York Times Magazine*, 15 March 1992, 46, 56–58.

Mifflin, Lawrie. "Simpson Case Gives Cable an Edge on the Networks." *New York Times*, 20 February 1995, D1.

Mifflin, Lawrie. "Weighing the Future of the Network Anchor." *New York Times*, 17 December, 1995, 37.

Mirabella, Alan. "TV's Magazine Shakeout." *Columbia Journalism Review*, March/April 1995, 11.

Mydans, Seth. "Simpson Is Charged, Chased, Arrested." *New York Times*, 18 June 1994, 1.

Myerson, Allen. "The Best Little Sideshow in Texas." *New York Times*, 9 March 1994, C1.

"News '93: An Exclusive Survey of RTNDA Members." *Broadcasting & Cable*, 27 September 1993, 46–47.

O'Connor, John J. "For a Date (Wink) or a Tease (Smirk), Try Late-Night TV." *New York Times*, 30 June 1992, C11, C16.

O'Connor, John J. "The Line Between Dramas and Lies." *New York Times*, 31 December 1992, C11, C25.

O'Connor, John. "Onscreen Journalism: Show Biz or News?" *New York Times*, 14 May 1992, C17, C20.

O'Connor, John J. "A TV 'Reality' of Dramatizations and Platitudes." *New York Times*, 20 April 1992, C11.

"Pictures Sought in Hijack Probe." *The News Media & the Law*, Summer 1985.

"Press Answers Military's Criticism of Coverage." *Broadcasting*, 14 December 1992, 8.

Quindlen, Anna. "Talking about the Media Circus." *New York Times*, 26 June 1994, 26.

Quinn, Sally: *We're Going to Make You a Star.* New York: Simon & Schuster, 1975.

Rasky, Susan F. "Terror Coverage on TV is Criticized." *New York Times*, 31 July 1985.

Rathbun, Elizabeth. "KCAL Sale Could Set Record." *Broadcasting & Cable*, 22 January 1996, 3.

Rather, Dan. "Call It Courage." Speech before the Radio Television News Directors Association Annual Convention. 29 September 1993.

Rather, Dan. *The Camera Never Blinks Twice: The Further Adventures of a Television Journalist.* New York: William Morrow and Company, 1994.

"Richard Liebner Has Talent in a Big Way. "*Broadcasting & Cable*, 7 March 1994, 27–32.

Rosenthal, A. M. "The Press and Simpson." *New York Times*, 24 June 1994, A27.

Sharpe, Anita. "Borrowed Time." *Wall Street Journal Reports* [television], 9 September 1994, R12.

Sharpe, Anita. "CNN Sticks With Hard News As Ratings Fall." *Wall Street Journal*, 9 June 1994, B1.

Shepard, Alicia C. "Fighting Back." *American Journalism Review,* January/ February 1996, 35.

"Shiite Spin Control." *The New Republic,* 15 & 22 July 1985: 11–12.

Smith, Howard K. *Events Leading Up To My Death.* New York: St. Martin's Press, 1996.

Sperber, A. M. *Murrow: His Life and Times.* New York: Freundlich Books, 1986.

"Spike for Connie and Dan." *Broadcasting & Cable,* 14 June 1993, 26.

"Station Wants to Have Its News Cake and Eat It Too." *Broadcasting,* 17 September 1990, 73.

"Television/1993." *New York Times,* 26 December 1993, 36.

Trotta, Liz. *Fighting for Air: In the Trenches with Television News.* New York: Simon & Schuster, 1991.

Urquhart, John. "When TV Anchors Smile a Lot, Is It Bias or Just Good Reporting?" *Wall Street Journal,* 11 May 1994, B1.

Viles, Peter. "Disasters Sometimes Benefit Stations." *Broadcasting & Cable,* 31 January 1994, 48.

Viles, Peter. "News Execs Grumble about Tabloid TV." *Broadcasting & Cable,* 27 Sept. 1993, 42–43.

Walley, Wayne. "Prestige of CBS Takes Direct Hit from Gulf War." *Advertising Age,* 28 January 1991, 1, 43.

"Westmoreland Vs. CBS." *U.S. News & World Report,* 1 October 1984: 44-46.

Woodward, Bob. "Mike Wallace Grand Inquisitor of '60 Minutes.' " *TV Guide,* 6 November 1993, 14–17.

7: ELECTRONIC CURRENCY: THE BOTTOM LINE OF TELEVISION

Agins, Teri. "Liz's Perfume Gets Star Role in Prime Time." *Wall Street Journal,* 15 February 1996, B1.

"As Volvo Sales Slide Do Ads Share Blame?" *Wall Street Journal,* 3 December 1990.

Beatty, Sally Goll. "Networks Are Winning Some Local Ads." *Wall Street Journal,* 27 October 1995, B5.

Berger, Warren. "The Amazing Secrets of a Television Guru." *New York Times,* 10 July 1994, sec. 2, 1.

Berniker, Mark. Nielsen Plans Internet Service." *Broadcasting & Cable,* 24 July 1995, 34.

Bishop, Jerry E. "TV Advertising Aimed at Kids Is Filled with Fat." *Wall Street Journal,* 9 November 1993, B1.

Carter, Bill. "For CBS, a Coup in Ratings Race." *New York Times,* 5 February 1991, C11, C16.

Carter, Bill. "In the Super Bowl Race, the Loser May Win Big." *New York Times,* 4 February 1991, D8.

"CBS Announces Give-Back to Affiliates." *Broadcasting,* 11 February 1991, 29.

"Chiat/Day Quits CNBC." *New York Times,* 11 January 1991, D7.

D'Orta, Christopher. "Advertising Agencies Face Stricter Scrutiny for Their Ads." *Media Law Journal,* Vol. II, no. 1, Spring 1993, 10.

Elliott, Stuart. "Ads That Crawl across the Bottom of the Television Screen Are

Scoring." *New York Times*, 13 July 1994, D16.

Elliott, Stuart. "After a Mars Move, Two Saatchi Agencies Try to Wash the Chocolate off Their Faces." *New York Times*, 23 February 1995.

Elliott, Stuart. "Big Game's Messages Got Lost among the Stars." *New York Times*, 1 February 1994, D1.

Elliott, Stuart. "For More Than a Quarter of the Advertisers, It'll Be a Super Bowl I." *New York Times*, 26 January 1996, D4.

Elliott, Stuart. "Interpublic-Ammirati Deal Expected Today." *New York Times*, 18 July 1994, D1.

Elliott, Stuart. "The Long Commercial Salaom Is Over: Here Are the Medals for Free-Style Product Pitching." *New York Times*, 1 March 1994, D22.

Elliott, Stuart. "Omnicom Gobbles Up Yet Another Big Agency." *New York Times*, 11 January 1996, D1.

Elliott, Stuart. "Super Bowl Campaigns Break Long Losing Streak." *New York Times*, 31 January 1995, D1.

Elliott, Stuart. "Super Triumphs and Super Flops." *New York Times*, 30 January 1994, 5.

Elliott, Stuart. "True North Announces Acquisition as Agencies Reveal Vast Accounts." *New York Times*, 15 January 1996, D1.

Fahey, Alison and Debra Goldman. "What the Hell Happened to DDB?" *Adweek*, 3 October 1994, 26–41.

"First-Quarter Spot: Casualty of War, Recession." *Broadcasting*, 11 February 1991, 27–28.

Foltz, Kim. "After Review, Hardee's Stays with Ogilvy." *New York Times*, 5 February 1991, D20.

Foltz, Kim. "BBDO Resigns L.A. Gear, Citing Creative Differences." *New York Times*, 4 March 1991, D7.

Foltz, Kim. "Campaign for British Knights to Escalate Sneaker Wars." *New York Times*, 20 February 1991, D17.

Foltz, Kim. "Coke and Pepsi Square Off in the Super Bowl of Colas." *New York Times*, 7 January 1991, D1, D7.

Foltz, Kim. "Coke Softens Super Bowl Ads." *New York Times*, 28 January 1991.

Foltz, Kim. "The Game a Nail-Biter, the Ads, Well . . . " *New York Times*, 29 January 1991, D19.

Foltz, Kim. "Hopes Rise for Spending Rebound as End of War Is Seen." *New York Times*, 28 February 1991, D9.

Foltz, Kim. "Saatchi Expected to Offer New Plan for Shareholders." *New York Times*, 31 January 1991, D19.

"Getting the Word Out: It's Ok to Advertise in War." *Broadcasting*, 25 February 1991, 72.

"Giant Sony TV Runs Free Ads." *New York Times*, 27 February 1991, D19.

Goldman, Kevin. "Bates's Carl Spielvogel Makes on Early Exit." *Wall Street Journal*, 21 October 1994, B5.

Goldman, Kevin. "Budweiser Fires Its Ad Agency after 79 Years." *Wall Street Journal*, 15 November 1995, B1.

Goldman, Kevin. "Catch a Falling Star: Big Names Plummet from List of Top 10 Celebrity Endorsers." *Wall Street Journal*, 19 October 1994, B1.

Goldman, Kevin. "CBS-TV to Cut Affiliate Payments by 20% Next Year." *Wall*

Street Journal, 21 November 1990, B3.

Goldman, Kevin. "Charles Saatchi Backs Brother's Venture." *Wall Street Journal,* 9 February 1995, B14.

Goldman, Kevin. "Chiat/Day to Merge with Omnicom." *Wall Street Journal,* 1 February 1995, B5.

Goldman, Kevin "Chrysler Is Sponsor in Interactive Network." *Wall Street Journal,* 9 November 1993, B6.

Goldman, Kevin "Cordiant Expected to Name Select CEO." *Wall Street Journal,* 11 July 1995, B14.

Goldman, Kevin. "Dow Jones Group Appeals Ruling against FNN Bid." *Wall Street Journal,* 9 April 1991, B6.

Goldman, Kevin. "Foote, Cone & Belding Charts New Course." *Wall Street Journal,* 12 December 1994, B7.

Goldman, Kevin "Interpublic Group, Time Warner Join in Interactive-Ad Venture." *Wall Street Journal,* 28 June 1994, B10.

Goldman, Kevin. "McDonalds to Post Golden Arches along Information Super Highway." *Wall Street Journal,* 21 July 1994, B7.

Goldman, Kevin. "NBC Gets Short End of McDonald's Tie-In." *Wall Street Journal,* 12 October 1990, B1, B4.

Goldman, Kevin. "New Saatchi Agency Expected to Unveil It Formed Alliance with Unit of Publicists." *Wall Street Journal,* 3 April 1995, B12.

Goldman, Kevin. "The Nine Lead Balloon Ad Campaigns of 1994." *Wall Street Journal,* 30 December 1994, B1.

Goldman, Kevin. "One Agency Buys Its Own Line, Advertising Itself on Television." *Wall Street Journal,* 16 November 1993, B10.

Goldman, Kevin. "Stay Tuned for No Commercials Between Shows." *Wall Street Journal,* 28 July 1994, B1.

Goldman, Kevin. "With 'Jurassic Park,' NBC Sets Sights on Monster Movies." *Wall Street Journal,* 25 January 1995, B1.

Goldman, Kevin. "Women Endorsers More Credible Than Men, a Survey Suggests." *Wall Street Journal,* 12 October 1995, B1.

Goldman, Kevin, Kyle Pope, and Tara Parker Pope. "Saatchi's Implosion: Tale of Power and Ego across Two Continents." *Wall Street Journal,* 12 June 1995, A1.

Graham, Ellen. "Changing Channels." *Wall Street Journal Reports* [television], 9 September 1994, R1.

Henderson, Angelo B. "Chrysler Backs 'Hoop Dreams' to Court Blacks." *Wall Street Journal,* 15 November 1995, B1.

Horton, Cleveland. "New Nissan Ad Jabs at Acura." *Advertising Age,* 27 June 1994, 16.

"House Votes to Restrict Ads in Children's Shows." *Broadcasting,* 30 July 1990.

Jensen, Elizabeth. "CBS Pulls Plug on Nielsen in Pittsburgh." *Wall Street Journal,* 8 February 1996, B6.

Jensen, Jeff. "Big 4 Showing No Breakaway Hits for the New Season." *Advertising Age,* 20 June 1994, 54.

Jensen, Jeff. "O. J. Case Casts Pall on Endorsers." *Advertising Age,* 27 June 1994, 50.

Jensen, Jeff. "World Cup Runneth over United States." *Advertising Age,* 20 June 1994, 76.

Jessell, Harry A. "Broadcasters Demand Place on Superhighway." *Broadcasting & Cable*, 10 January 1994, 14.

Keller, John J. "They'll Spend Lots but Lots Less than They Say." *Wall Street Journal*, 18 May 1994, B1.

Keller, John J., and Leslie Cauley. "Mad Scramble." *Wall Street Journal*, 25 October 1994, 1.

King, Thomas R. "Agencies Scramble to Prove Ads Aren't Hurt by TV War Coverage." *Wall Street Journal*, 21 February 19, B7.

King, Thomas R. "Detroit Seeks Mileage from 'Green' Ads." *Wall Street Journal*, 14 January 1991, B4.

King, Thomas R. "How a Hot Ad Agency, Undone by Arrogance, Lost Its Independence." *Wall Street Journal*, 17 April 1995, 1.

King, Thomas R. "MCI Drops Wells Rich for Small Agency." *Wall Street Journal*, 23 November 1990.

King, Thomas R. "On the Whole, Philadelphia Firms Would Rather Get More Respect." *Wall Street Journal*, 21 November 1990, B3.

King, Thomas R. "Saatchi Unveils Recapitalization Plan to Escape Burden of Preferred Shares." *Wall Street Journal*, 11 January 1991, B4.

King, Thomas R. "Super Bowl's Sponsors Watch Gulf Warily." *Wall Street Journal*, 24 January 1991, B1, B4.

Kleinfield, N.R. "The Networks' New Advertising Dance." *New York Times*, 29 July 1990, Sec. 3—1, 6.

Kneale, Dennis. "Ad Agencies Get Out Their Crystal Tubes to Predict the Winners of Fall TV Season." *Wall Street Journal*, 13 June 1990, B1, B6.

Kutz, Donald. *Just Do It: The Nike Spirit in the Corporate World*. New York: Random House, 1994.

Levin, Doron. "Audi Spending Heavily to Rebuild Image." *New York Times*, 24 January 1991, D3.

Lewis, Peter H. "Report of High Internet Use Is Challenged." *New York Times*, 13 December 1995, D12.

Lewis, Peter H. "Trying to Find Gold with the Internet." *New York Times*, 3 January 1995, C15.

Lieberman, David. "The Big-Bucks Ad Battles over TV's Most Expensive Minutes." *TV Guide*, 26 January 1991, 11–12, 14.

Lipman, Joanne. "Advertisers Elbow for Time in the Spotlight." *Wall Street Journal*, 20 July 1992, B1, B5.

Lipman, Joanne. "Agencies May Pass on Super Bowl Stars." *Wall Street Journal*, 29 January 1991, B1, B3.

Lipman, Joanne. "Brand-Name Products Are Popping Up in TV Shows." *Wall Street Journal*, 19 February 1991, B1, B6.

Lipman, Joanne. "FTC Is Cracking Down on Misleading Ads." *Wall Street Journal*, 4 February 1991, B6.

Lipman, Joanne. "FTC Zaps Misleading Commercials." *Wall Street Journal*, 19 June 1990, B1, B6.

Lipman, Joanne. "Gulf Peace Unleashes Patriotic Campaigns." *Wall Street Journal*, 5 March 1991, B7.

Lipman, Joanne. " 'Infomercial' Makers Try to Clean Up Act." *Wall Street Journal*, 4 March 1991, B3.

Lipman, Joanne. "Marketers Hope Success Is in Character." *Wall Street Journal*, 5
    June 1992, B1 ,B4.
Lipman, Joanne. "MTV Style Abandoned by Many Shops." *Wall Street Journal*, 12
    February 1991, B6.
Lipman, Joanne. "New Reebok Ads Enrage Rival by Taunting Nike's Star
    Endorsers." *Wall Street Journal*, 6 February 1991, B6.
Lipman, Joanne. "Oversupply of Celebrity Hawkers Could Trip Up Sneaker
    Makers." *Wall Street Journal*, 23 May 1990, B6.
Lipman, Joanne. "Saatchi & Saatchi Discloses Plan Revising Recapitalization
    Goals." *Wall Street Journal*, 22 February 1991, B3.
Lipman, Joanne. "Volvo Chooses Messner Vetere to Handle $40 Million Account."
    Wall Street Journal, 8 February 1991.
Lipman, Joanne. "War Generating Barrage of Patriotic Ads." *Wall Street Journal*, 28
    January 1991, B4.
Lipman, Joanne, and Joann S. Lublin. "TV War News Spurs Exodus of Sponsors."
    Wall Street Journal, 18 January 1991, B1, B12.
Lublin, Joann S. "Conflict Would Bring Sober Tone to Ads." *Wall Street Journal*, 11
    January 1991, B1, B5.
Lublin, Joann S. "WPP May Sell Stake in Ogilvy, Thompson." *Wall Street Journal*,
    8 January 1991, B8.
McCarthy, Michael J. "MagiCant's: How Coca-Cola Stumbled." *Wall Street
    Journal*, 5 June 1990, B1, B4.
McCarthy, Michael J. "Pepsi and Coke Suiting Up for '91 Super Bowl Duel." *Wall
    Street Journal*, 12 December 1990.
McClellan, Steve. "Sweepstakes Not Fair to Advertisers." *Broadcasting & Cable*, 4
    July 1994, 40.
Miller, Krystal, and Jacqueline Mitchell. "Car Marketers Test Gray Area of Truth
    in Advertising." *Wall Street Journal*, 19 November 1990, B1, B6.
Mitchell, Jacqueline. "GM Buys Rights to Block Rivals in CBS Games." *Wall Street
    Journal*, 17 January 1991, B1, B4.
"NBC Slips, Season Race Tightens." *Broadcasting*, 11 February 1991, 30.
Nielsen Media Research News. "More than 23 Million Adults Watch Television in
    Out-of-Home Locations Each Week." New York, 11 July 1995.
Oglivy, David. *Ogilvy on Advertising*. New York: Crown Publishers Inc., 1983.
Ono, Yumiko. "Tokyo TV Ads Portray Japanese as the Savvy International Type."
    Wall Street Journal, 11 October 1990, B6.
Pope, Kyle. "Charles Saatchi Quits Ad Agency He Co-founded." *Wall Street
    Journal*, 17 February 1995, B4.
Prokesch, Steven. "Refinancing Is Proposed for Saatchi." *New York Times*, 11
    January 1991, D1, D5.
Prokesch, Steven. "Saatchi Reports Progress in Refinancing Bond Issue." *New York
    Times*, 8 January 1991.
Prokesch, Steven. "Saatchi Trims Debt Burden with Revised Capital Plan." *New
    York Times*, 22 February 1991, D1, D16.
"Promoter Gets Prison Term in a Franchising Scheme." *Wall Street Journal*, 19
    February 1991, B3.
"Reebok Stunt Pushes Networks to the Edge." *Wall Street Journal*, 16 March 1990,
    B1.

Rogers, Adam. "Through a Glass, Darkly." *Newsweek*, 23 January 1995, 52.

Rothenberg, Randall. "Advertising 'Bad Boys' Grow Up in a Downturn." *New York Times*, 23 January 1991, D1, D3.

Rothenberg, Randall. "A Legend Turns to Selling Social Change to Companies." *New York Times*, 14 January 1991.

Rothenberg, Randall. "For Ad Agencies, a Costly Hard Sell." *New York Times*, 4 February 1991, D1, D8.

Rothenberg, Randall. "Messages from Sponsors Become Harder to Detect." *New York Times*, 19 November 1989, E5.

Rothenberg, Randall. "Newspapers Watch What People Watch in the TV Campaign." *New York Times*, 4 November 1990.

Rothenberg, Randall. "Study Shows Power of Public-Service Ads." *New York Times*, 8 April, 1991.

Shapiro, Eben. "CBS Joins NBC in Dropping Audience-Gauging System." *New York Times*, 4 March 1991, D7.

Simpson, Harold, and John Catanese. "Trends in Television." Television Bureau of Advertising, 1995.

Solomon, Caleb. "Gasoline Ads Canceled; Lack of Truth Cited." *Wall Street Journal*, 21 July 1994, B1.

Stevenson, Richard W. "At Saatchi's Rechristening, Angry Shareholders Are Not in the Mood for Mending Fences." *New York Times*, 17 March 1995, D5.

Stevenson, Richard W. "Saatchi Faces Uncertainty with Ouster of Its Chairman." *New York Times*, 19 December 1994, D1.

"The 'Truth in Adver-Teasing' Awards (Car-Makers Division)." *TV Guide*, 5 January 1991, 6.

Ulanoff, Stanley M. *Advertising in America. An Introduction to Persuasive Communication*. New York: Hastings House, 1977.

"USA Makes It Six in Row." *Broadcasting & Cable*, 1 January 1996, 39.

"The War in Military Ads? What War?" *New York Times*, 8 March 1991, D1, D4.

Warner, Fara. "Saab Breaks Car-Marketing Rules with Arty Campaign." *Wall Street Journal*, 3 April 1995: B12.

"WPIX (TV) Signs Up Geraldo and Joan." *Broadcasting*, 11 February 1991, 30.

8: TECHNOLOGY AND CHANGE

Abrams, Robert. "The Right to Privacy versus the Growth of Computers and Cable Television." Speech before the New York Legislative Forum, 16 March, 1982.

Adamiak, Peter T., and Eliot P. Graham. "Digital Servers." *Broadcasting & Cable*, 3 April 1995, 53.

"ADTV Standards Field Narrows." *Broadcasting*, 17 September 1990, 66.

Alderman, Ellen, and Caroline Kennedy. *The Right to Privacy*. New York: Alfred A. Knopf, 1995.

Amdur, Meredith. "The Boundless Ted Turner." *Broadcasting & Cable*, 11 April 1994, 34–36.

"Ampex Proposes Evolutionary Path to All-Digital Production." *Broadcasting*, 28

Jauary 1991, 52.

Andrews, Edmund L. "Advanced T.V. Testing Set Amid Tumult on Technology." *New York Times*, 15 November 1990, D1, D7.

Andrews, Edmund L. "Airwaves Auctions Bring $833 Million for U.S. Treasury." *New York Times*, 30 July 1994, 1.

Andrews, Edmund L. "And Now for Something Substantially Different: Digital TV." *New York Times*, 12 July 1992, 22.

Andrews, Edmund L. "Cablevision's Craving for Sports." *New York Times*, 29 August 1994, D8.

Andrews, Edmund L. "A Free-for-All in Communications." *New York Times*, 4 February 1994, D1.

Andrews, Edmund L. "The HDTV Compromise Some Experts Worry that an Accord by Rivals Doesn't Pick the Best System." *New York Times*, 21 December 1990, A1, D16.

Andrews, Edmund L. "Market Test of New Video Technology." *New York Times*, 2 June 1993, D1, D5.

Andrews, Edmund L. "New Competition in the Sky and Just in Time For the War." *New York Times*, 10 February 1991.

Andrews, Edmund L. "Six Systems in Search of Approval as HDTV Moves to the Testing Lab." *New York Times*, 18 August 1991.

Andrews, Edmund L. " Success with a Satellite Leads to a Space Network." *New York Times*, 9 July 1994, 35.

Andrews, Edmund L. "Top Rivals Agree on Unified System for Advanced T.V." *New York Times*, 25 May 1993, A1, D2.

Andrews, Edmund L. "Transition to HDTV Is Outlined." *New York Times*, 10 April 1992, D1, D5.

Andrews, Edmund L. "Two Rivals Form Pool for HDTV: Would Share Rights From U.S. Patent." *New York Times*, 8 May 1992, D1, D10.

Andrews, Edmund L. " U.S. Makes Gains in Race to Develop Advanced T.V." *New York Times*, 21 December 1990, A1, D16.

Andrews, Edmund L., and Joel Brinkley. "The Fight for Digital TV's Future." *New York Times*, 22 January 1995, sec. 3, 1.

Angus, Robert. "HDTV: The Picture Clears." *Video Business*, 7 October 1988, 18–20.

"Around the World on DBS." *Broadcasting*, 30 July 1990, 42, 44.

Berniker, Mark. "Bell Atlantic Revises Video Plans: Delays Rollout until 1997." *Broadcasting & Cable*, 26 June 1995, 32.

Berniker, Mark. "Justice Clears Cable Route for Bell South." *Broadcasting & Cable*, 8 August 1994, 12.

Berniker, Mark. "Time Warner Dials Up Rochester, N.Y." *Broadcasting & Cable*, 23 May 1994, 10.

Berniker, Mark. "US West Ventures into Cable Territory." *Broadcasting & Cable*, 27 June 1994, 33.

Berniker, Mark. "Vendors Help Cable Get into Telco Business." *Broadcasting & Cable*, 15 August 1994, 22.

Berniker, Mark. "Winner Defaults on $40 million Worth of Spectrum." *Broadcasting & Cable*, 15 August 1994, 23.

Biocca, Frank. "Communication within Virtual Reality: Creating a Space for

Research." *Journal of Communications*, 42, Autumn 1992, 5–18.

Biocca, Frank. "Virtual Reality Technology: A Tutorial." *Journal of Communications*, 42 Autumn (1992), 23–66.

Biocca, Frank, and Jaron Lanier. "An Insider's View of the Future of Virtual Reality." *Journal of Communications*, 42, Autumn 1992, 150–171.

Bishop, Katherine. "Out There: San Francisco High Tech Sex." *New York Times*, 15 November 1992, 3.

Blumenthal, Karen. "Children's Tapes Help the Sales Market Grow Up." *Wall Street Journal*, 24 December 1991, B1, B4.

Brown, Rich. "Dishing Up Full-Power DBS." *Broadcasting & Cable*, 28 March 1994, 48.

Brown, Rich. "A Telemarketable Merger." *Broadcasting & Cable*, 15 August 1994, 36.

Bryant, Adam. "Playing 'Star Trek' by the Minute: Beam Me Up, I'm Out of Change." *New York Times*, 29 September 1992, 4.

Bulkeley, William. "Gender Affects How User Sees the Computer." *Wall Street Journal*, 16 March 1994, B1.

Carlton, Jim, and Thomas R. King. "Sega-MGM Pact Will Prompt Question: Which Came First, Movie or Video Game?" *Wall Street Journal*, 27 April 1994, B9.

Carnevale, Mary Lu. "FCC's Take of $617 Million for Licenses Shows Demand for New Paging Services." *Wall Street Journal*, 1 August 1994, A3.

Carnevale, Mary Lu. "HDTV Groups Announce Plans to Merge Systems Trying to Become U.S. Standard." *Wall Street Journal*, 25 May 1993, B5.

Cauley, Leslie. "Interactive Trials Are Trials Indeed—Tough to Start and Tough to Judge." *Wall Street Journal*, 18 May 1994, B1.

Charles, Eleanor. "Virtual Reality." *New York Times*, 29 November 1992, 11.

Church, George J. "Dress Rehearsal or Opening Night?" *Time*, 16 May 1994, 68–70.

Connor, Michael. "'Videographers Record Life's Milestones." *Wall Street Journal*, 30 June 1992, B1.

"Cox and Tribune Focusing on HDTV." *Broadcasting*, 29 February 1988, 64.

Cox, Meg. "Hearst Will Launch Home Net, Services in Multimedia that Are Home-Related." *Wall Street Journal*, 18 February 1994, B1.

Cripps, Dale, and Judith Sawyer. "Hi-Def in a Decade? The Tug of War over High-Definition TV Intensifies." *Video*, December 1988, 80–83, 128.

Darlin, Damon. "Copycat Crime: Video Pirates Abroad Face a Swashbuckler Worthy of Hollywood." *Wall Street Journal*, 25 January 1992, A1, A10.

Davis, Bob. "Fading Picture: High-Definition TV Once a Capital Idea, Wanes in Washington." *Wall Street Journal*, 6 June 1991, A1, A18.

"DBS: Darkhorse or Dead Horse?" *Broadcasting*, 8 April 1991, 66.

"DBS: Making Most of Midpower." *Broadcasting*, 30 June 1990, 38.

Dominick, Joseph R., Barry L. Sherman, and Gary A. Copeland. *Broadcasting, Cable and Beyond*. New York: McGraw-Hill, 1993.

Dewitt, Philip Elmer. "Take a Trip into the Future on the Electronic Superhighway." *Time*, 12 April 1993, 50–55.

Dewitt, Philip Elmer. "The Picture Suddenly Gets Clearer." *Time*, 30 March 1992, 54, 55.

Elrich, David J. "Making It Easier to Frame Lives." *New York Times*, 6 July 1995, C2.

Elrich, David J. "New Playing in New York: Small-Dish Satellite TV." *New York Times*, 6 October 1994, C2.

Elrich, David J. "VCR Programming Made Easier." *New York Times*, 13 July 1995, C2.

Engel, Joel. "Film: A Voyage in Inner Space." *New York Times*, 1 March 1992, sec. 2, 22.

Fabrikant, Geraldine. "Time Warner and Newhouse Form a Joint Cable Operation." *New York Times*, 13 September 1994, D1.

Fagan, Gregory P. "Where Is It Now? Super VHS." *Video Review*, July 1988, 32–35, 84.

Fantel, Hans. "HDTV Faces Its Future." *New York Times*, 2 February 1992.

Fantel, Hans. "HDTV, Videodisks and Sharper Images Come to the Fore." *New York Times*, 30 December 1990, 24.

Fantel, Hans. "New Standards for Television Are in the Picture for 1993." *New York Times*, 3 January 1993, 2, 12.

Fantel, Hans. "Videodisks Make a Push for a Larger Audience." *New York Times*, 9 September 1990.

Feder, Barnaby J. "Jitters in a Showplace of Gadgets." *New York Times*, 7 June 1993, D1, D3.

Feder, Barnaby J. "Last U.S. TV Maker Will Sell Control to Koreans." *New York Times*, 18 July 1995, A1.

Feder, Barnaby J. "Selling Virtual Reality in Indiana." *New York Times*, 7 August 1995, D5.

"Filling in the Gaps about Sky Cable." *Broadcasting*, 12 March 1990, 30.

Fisher, Lawrence M. "A.T.&T. and Zenith in Venture: All-Digital System for Advanced TV Will Be Built Jointly." *New York Times*, 18 December 1990, A1, D13.

Fisher, Lawrence M. "Gateway 2000 Backs Sony/Philips Disk Format." *New York Times*, 16 June 1995, D8.

Fisher, Lawrence M. "Interactive TV Alliance Is Formed." *New York Times*, 7 June 1993, D1, D7.

Flint, Joe. "New Starz! on Cable Programming Horizon." *Broadcasting & Cable*, 7 February 1994, 26.

Foisie, Geoffrey. "Let's Make a Deal: Wireless Cable Consolidates." *Broadcasting & Cable*, 28 February 1994, 36.

Foisie, Geoffrey and Rich Brown. "At the Table with TCI and Viacom." *Broadcasting & Cable*, 8 August 1994, 6.

Gilpan, Kenneth N. "ITT Focusing on Long Term." *New York Times*, 29 August 1994, D1.

Grossman, Laurie M. "For Video Sales, It's a Green Christmas." *Wall Street Journal*, 24 December 1991, B1, B4.

"The Government Can't Do Quality . . . at All." *Broadcasting & Cable*, 15 August 1994, 41.

Hagen, Charles. "Art View; Virtual Reality: Is It Art Yet?" *New York Times*, 5 July 1992, Sec. 2–1.

Hayes, Thomas C. "Doing Business Screen to Screen." *New York Times*, 21 February 1991, D1, D15.

"HDTV Tests Planning Turns to Field Tests." *Broadcasting*, 14 January 1991, 122, 123.

"Higher Power DBS: Multichannel Promise, Threat." *Broadcasting*, 30 July 1990, 36–38.

Hornaday, Ann. "Channel Executive Seeks to Build Showtime's Slate of Original Fare." *New York Times*, 29 August 1994, D6.

"How to Look at TV, and the Future." *New York Times*, 1 November 1988, A30.

Husted, Bill. "It's All in the Mind." *Atlanta Constitution*, 29 September 1992, C1.

Imse, Ann. "Hang On for the Ride of Your Life." *New York Times*, 12 December 1993: sec. 3, p. 6.

Jessell, Harry A. "BA Hopes to Launch Video Dialtone in Fall." *Broadcasting & Cable*, 10 January 1994: 66.

Jaffe, Alfred J. "Funding Problems Bedevil HDTV Development Efforts." *Television/Radio Age*, 2 May 1988, 60–62.

Jefferson, David J. "Itochu, Iwerks Are Betting Moviegoers Will Go More for Costly Cinetropolis." *Wall Street Journal*, 16 March 1993, B7.

Jessell, Harry A. "Cable Ready: The High Appeal of Interactive Services." *Broadcasting & Cable*, 23 May 1994, 75–78.

King, Thomas R. ""3DO Faces Struggle to Keep Video-Game Player Alive." *Wall Street Journal*, 19 May 1994, B4.

Knecht, Bruce G. "Is Big Brother Watching Your Dinner and Other Worries of Privacy Watchers." *Wall Street Journal*, 9 November 1995, B1.

Kolata, Gina. "MIT Deal with Japan Stirs Fear in Competition." *New York Times*, 19 December 1990, A1, D20.

Lambert, Peter. "HDTV Push Feels Like Shove to Broadcasters." *Broadcasting*, 29 June 1992, 3, 13.

Landler, Mark. "ATT&T Enters TV Business Via Satellite Broadcasting." *New York Times*, 23 January 1996, D1.

Landler, Mark. "New! Improved? TV's Bell Telephone Hour." *New York Times*, 19 March 1995, sec. 3, 1.

Landler, Mark. "Phone Companies Clear TV Hurdle." *New York Times*, 18 March, 1995, 1.

Lewis, Peter H. "He Added 'Virtual' to 'Reality.' " *New York Times*, 25 September 1994, sec. 3, 7.

Levine, Martin. "High-Def: Tomorrow's Television . . . Today?" *Video Review*, March 1988, 28– 31, 100.

Levy, Steven. "A Night at the Feelies." *New York Times*, 18 October 1992, 29.

Lohr, Steve. "The Silver Disk May Soon Eclipse the Silver Screen." *New York Times*, 1 March 1994, A1.

Lopez, Julie Amparano, and Mary Lu Carnevale. "Glassed Houses: Fiber Optics Promises a Revolution of Sorts, If the Sharks Don't Bite." *Wall Street Journal*, 10 July 1990, A1, A10.

Lublin, Joann S. "VCR Advances May Increase Zapping." *Wall Street Journal*, 4 January 1991, B1, B3.

Markoff, John. "A Battle for Influence Over Insatiable Disks." *New York Times*, 11 January 1995, D1.

Markoff, John. "Microsoft and Rogers Plan Interactive Cable Venture." *New York Times*, 25 May 1994, D1.

Markoff, John. "A Rough Start for Digital TV." *New York Times*, 21 September 1994, D1.

Markoff, John. "Secure Digital Transactions Just Got a Little Less Secure." *New York Times*, 11 December 1995, A1.

Markoff, John. "Xerox Has New Flat Screen That Could Hold a Computer." *New York Times*, 18 May 1993, D1, D7.

McAvoy, Kim. "Al Gore: Directing Traffic onto the Superhighway." *Broadcasting & Cable*, 10 January 1994, 10.

McClellan, Steve, David Tobenkin, and Mark Berniker. "Telco Convergence Goes Hollywood." *Broadcasting & Cable*, 15 August 1994, 6–8.

McComb, Gordon. "Super Pictures From Super-VHS." *Popular Science*, January 1988, 68–70, 114.

McConnell, Chris. "Analog's Not Dead Yet." *Broadcasting & Cable*, 16 May 1994, 56.

McConnell, Chris. "Big News at NAB: Tapeless Recording." *Broadcasting & Cable*, 21 March 1994, 64.

McConnell, Chris. "Broadcasters Fending Off Spectrum Grabs." *Broadcasting & Cable*, 25 July 1994, 82.

McConnell, Chris. "Cable Blasts Non-HDTV Use of Channels." *Broadcasting & Cable*, 25 April 1994, 44.

McConnell, Chris. "DIRECTV's All-Digital Domain." *Broadcasting & Cable*, 28 March 1994: 52.

McConnell, Chris. "FCC Commissioners to Get HDTV Eyeful." *Broadcasting & Cable*, 1 August 1994, 47.

McConnell, Chris. "HDTV Field Testing Set." *Broadcasting & Cable*, 24 July 1995, 68.

McConnell, Chris. "Media Pool Tests the Tapeless Waters." *Broadcasting & Cable*, 18 July 1994, 60.

McConnell, Chris. "The Risky Business of Choosing a Format." *Broadcasting & Cable*, 17 April 1995, 57.

McDonald, Daniel G., and Michael A. Shapiro. "I'm Not a Real Doctor, but I Play One in Virtual Reality: Implications of Virtual Reality for Judgments about Reality." *Journal of Communications*, 42, Autumn 1992, 94–111.

Miller, James P. "HDTV Panel Picks Zenith Signal System." *Wall Street Journal*, 17 February 1994, B6.

Miller, Michael W. "Prodigy Unit of IBM, Sears Turns to Cable." *Wall Street Journal*, 3 June 1993, B1, B5.

Monk, John M., and Wesley Regian, and Wayne L. Shebilske. "Virtual Reality: An Instructional Medium for Visual-Spatial Tasks." *Journal of Communications*, 42, Autumn 1992, 136–148.

National TeleConsultants. "Migration to Digital." *Broadcasting & Cable*, 28 February 1994, S5–S15.

Newstadt, Richard. "Privacy and the New Media." *Privacy Journal*, vol. VIII, no. 4, February 1982.

Nilan, Michael S. "Cognitive Space: Using Virtual Reality for Large Information Resource Management Problems." *Journal of Communications*, 42, Autumn 1992, 115–133.

Ono, Yumiko. "No Class." *Wall Street Journal Reports* [television], 9 September 1994, R11.

Pascal, Zachary G. "Video Game Pioneer Tries to Blend Best of Computer, TV."

Wall Street Journal, 15 January 1991.

Pasqua, Thomas, et al. *Mass Media in the Information Age*. Engelwood Cliff, New Jersey: Prentice Hall, 1990.

Pereira, Joseph. "Video Games Help Boys Get a Head Start." *Wall Street Journal*, 16 March 1994, B1.

"Plenty of Fish in Pond Time Warner Wants to Swim in." *Wall Street Journal*, 7 March 1989, B1, B6.

Pinkwas, Stan. "Bypassing Commercials with a Clever VCR." *Popular Science*, December 1995, 36.

Pollack, Andrew. "Japan May Abandon Its System for HDTV." *New York Times*, 23 February 1994, D1.

Pollack, Andrew. "Japan Relents, Will Retain Its HDTV." *New York Times*, 24 February 1994, D1.

Pollack, Andrew. "A Milestone in High-Definition TV." *New York Times*, 3 December 1991, D1, D6.

Pollack, Andrew. "Tech Notes; All Aboard for Virtuality." *New York Times*, 5 January 1992, sec. 3–9.

Pollack, Andrew. "VS Project Hobbled by Japan's Lead." *New York Times*, 18 December 1990, D1, D13.

"Prices of HDTV Sets Sink as Sharp Creates a Cheaper Version." *Wall Street Journal*, 3 February 1992.

"Public TV: From Broadcasters toward Programmers." *Broadcasting*, 14 January 1991, 109.

Ramirez, Anthony. "New Video Previewed by Makers." *New York Times*, 3 June 1993, D5.

Ravo, Nick. "House-Hunting by Interactive Computer." *New York Times*, 22 November 1992, 1.

Reilly, Patrick M. "Camcorder Makers, with Growth Easing, Try to Bring New Markets Into the Picture." *Wall Street Journal*, 26 December 1991, B1, B2.

Reilly, Patrick M. Skeptics Question Development Progress of Two New Digital-Recording Systems." *Wall Street Journal*, 8 January 1992, B1, B2.

Reilly, Patrick M. "Video Games Get Racier as Technology Enables Makers to Target Older Players." *Wall Street Journal*, 6 January 1992, B1, B8.

Rifkin, Glenn. "Business Technology; PBS Series Will Stroll into 'Virtual Reality.'" *New York Times*, 1 April 1992, D9.

Riordan, Teresa. "Bids Soar at Auction by F.C.C." *New York Times*, 27 July 1994, D1.

Robichaux, Mark. "Creating the Box: Big Dinosaurs, Guys in Garages." *Wall Street Journal*, 18 May 1994, B1.

Robichaux, Mark. "TCI and Microsoft Set Accord to Test Interactive TV Services in Cable Systems." *Wall Street Journal*, 4 March 1994, B5.

Romano, Jay. "Speed-Up of Fiber Optic Network Debated." *New York Times*, 8 December 1991, sec. 12, 1, 22.

Rose, Frederick. "Democracy Goes On-Line in California." *Wall Street Journal*, 26 October 1994, B1.

Rothstein, Edward. "Is Home Where the TV Set Is?" *New York Times*, 3 January 1991, C1, C6.

Safire, William. "On Language: Virtual Reality." *New York Times*, 13 September 1992, sec. 6, 18.

Sanger, David E. "Invented in U.S., Spurned in U.S., a Technology Flourishes in Japan." *New York Times*, 16 December 1990, 1, 38.

Sanger, David E. "VCR's That Delete Ads Stir a Fight in Japan." *New York Times*, 9 September 1990, 1, 18.

"Satellite." *Broadcasting*, 14 January 1991, 110.

"Satellites 1990: Playing for Sky-High Stakes." *Broadcasting*, 30 July 1990, 35–36.

Schwartz, Evan I. "Demanding Task: Video on Demand." *New York Times*, 23 January 1994, sec. 3, 14.

Shannon, L. R. "Peripherals; Putting Yourself in the Picture." *New York Times*, 7 July 1992, C5.

Shapiro, Eben. "Cable-Ready. Time Warner and Other Cable Companies Have Their Sights on the Local Phone Market." *Wall Street Journal*, 20 March 1995, R8.

Shapiro, Eben. "Time Warner's Orlando Test to Start-Finally." *Wall Street Journal*, 7 December 1994, B1.

"Skypix to Subsidize Sale of First Half-Million Receivers." *Broadcasting*, 7 January 1991, 106–107.

"Sony Corp. Will Cut Price of Its HDTV Sets by 70%." *Wall Street Journal*, 2 June 1992.

"Standards Groups Try to Set Info Highway Speed Limits." *Broadcasting & Cable*, 27 June 1994, 33.

Stanley, Robert H. *Media-Visions: The Art and Industry of Mass Communication*. New York: Praeger, 1987.

Stern, Christopher. "Abrupt End to the Beginning." *Broadcasting & Cable*, 28 February 1994, 6.

Stern, Christopher. "FCC Awards PCS Advantages." *Broadcasting & Cable*, 4 July 1994, 35.

Stern, Christopher. "FCC Moves to Strengthen Wireless Cable." *Broadcasting & Cable*, 13 June 1994, 11.

Stern, Christopher. "FCC Spectrum Auctions Hit Pay Dirt." *Broadcasting & Cable*, 1 August 1994, 8.

Stern, Christopher. "Spectrum for Sale." *Broadcasting & Cable*, 25 July 1994, 87.

Stern, Christopher and Kim McAvoy. "Broadcasters Claim Stake on Superhighway." *Broadcasting & Cable*, 7 February 1994, 48.

Steuer, Jonathan. "Defining Virtual Reality: Dimensions Determining Telepresence." *Journal of Communications*, 42, Autumn 1992, 73–91.

Strauss, Neil. "Pennies That Add Up to $16.98: Why CDs Cost So Much." *New York Times*, 5 July 1995, C11.

Sukow, Randy. "HDTV Allocations Plan to Give Current Stations HDTV Channel." *Broadcasting*, 20 July 1992, 9.

"S-VHS Is Here to Stay." *Video Magazine*, December 1988.

"Technology & Media." *New York Times*, 3 June, 1995, C15–19.

" 'Time to Deliver' on Promises HDTV System is Near, Says Sikes." *Broadcasting*, 8 April 1991, 64–65.

Trachtenberg, Jeffrey. "Interactive Movies: Hot Medium or Smell-O-Vision, Part Three?" *Wall Street Journal*, 16 January 1995, B1.

Trachtenberg, Jeffrey, and David P. Hamilton. "Disk Standard Will Shake up Video Market." *Wall Street Journal*, 18 September 1995, B1.

Turner, Richard. "Studios Skip Celluloid, Go to Videotape." *Wall Street Journal*, 18 February 1994, B1.

Turner, Richard. "Tape Transfer: Disney Leads Shift from Rentals to Sales in Videocassettes." *Wall Street Journal*, 24 December 1992, 1, 30.

Weber, Jonathan. "Making 'Virtual' Centers a Reality." *Los Angeles Times*, 8 December 1992, D2.

Weber, Jonathan. "Playing Around in the Future." *Los Angeles Times*, 28 February 1993, A1.

Weinraub, Bernard. "Hollywood Dreams Lure 3 Baby Bells to Ovitz." *New York Times*, 26 October 1994, D1.

West, Don. "The Fateful Battle for the Second Channel." *Broadcasting & Cable*, 10 April 1995, 22.

Westin, Alan. "Home Information Systems: The Privacy Debate." *Datamation*, July 1982.

Wielage, Marc F. "Living in a World inside Super VHS." *High Fidelity*, November 1988: 53- 55.

Wilke, John R. "Digital Equipment Says It Will Enter Market for Massively Parallel Computers." *Wall Street Journal*, 19 March 1991, B3.

Wood, Lamont. "Virtual Reality Enters Office Landscape." *Chicago Tribune*, 14 March 1993, sec. 19, 8.

"Zenith Proposes All-Digital Transmission System." *Broadcasting*, 24 December 1990, 32–33.

Ziegler, Bart. "Building the Highway: New Obstacles, New Solutions." *Wall Street Journal*, 18 May 1994, B1.

Ziegler, Bart. "Seeing Isn't Believing." *Wall Street Journal* [technology supplement], 19 June 1995, 16.

Zoglin, Richard. "Cable Gets Dished." *Time*, 31 October 1994, 44–45.

Zoglin, Richard. "When the Revolution Comes What Will Happen to . . . " *Time*, 12 April 1993, 56–58.

9: PUBLIC BROADCASTING: ITS DWINDLING ACCOUNT

Andrews, Edmund L. "Bell Atlantic's (Mild) Interest in Public Broadcasting Deal." *New York Times*, 24 January 1995, D1.

Berger, Warren. "We Interrupt this Program . . . Forever?" *New York Times*, 29 January 1995, sec. 2, 1.

Berke, Richard L. "NBC Calls Its Venture with PBS a Success." *New York Times*, 19 July 1992, 20.

Blumenthal, Ralph. "Curriculum Update for 'Sesame Street.' " *New York Times*, 19 November 1995, 37.

Brown, Rich. "P.O.V. Gets More Money, More Flak." *Broadcasting*, 18 November 1991, 26.

Carnegie Commission on Educational Television. *Public Broadcasting: A Program for Action: The Report and Recommendations of the Carnegie Commission on Educational Television*. New York: Harper & Row, 1967.

Carnevale, Mary Lu. "Parents Say PBS Stations Exploit Barney in Fund Drives."

Wall Street Journal, 19 March 1993, B1.

Carter, Bill. "For 13, Change Brings a Chill." *New York Times*, 18 October 1994, C15.

Carter, Bill. "Producer Says a Big Bird Is Hardly a Cash Cow." *New York Times*, 30 January 1995, D8.

Cauley, Leslie. "Bell Atlantic Says It Would Help Fund Public Broadcasting in Partnership Role." *Wall Street Journal*, 23 January 1995, A3.

Cichowski, John and David Blomquist. "WNET, NJN May Merge." *Bergen Record*, 12 June 1992, 1.

Croghan, Loretto. "A Children's TV Production Company Grows Up." *New York Times*, 21 August 1994, 5.

Duggan, Ervin. "Public Broadcasting Can Be Dealt with by Reforming [It], Not Killing It." *Broadcasting & Cable*, 8 June 1992, 55.

Eggerton, John. "PBS Gets Piece of 'Wishbone.' " *Broadcasting & Cable*, 20 March 1995, 26.

"Funding Scramble Is 'Nature' of Public TV." *Broadcasting & Cable*, 31 January 1994, 22.

Goodman, Walter. "Making the Case for PBS (And It's Not So Easy.)" *New York Times*, 5 December 1993, sec. 2, 1.

Goodman, Walter. "Pull the Plug on PBS?" *New York Times*, 22 March 1992, 33.

Goodman, Walter. "A Running Debate about Public TV." *New York Times*, 18 May 1992, C18.

Gray, Jerry. "Legislative Proposal for a Public TV Merger." *New York Times*, 24 July 1992, B5.

Grimes, William. "Public-TV Offshoot Finds that the Fringe Is a Risky Place to Be." *New York Times*, 28 December 1994, C11.

Hofmeister, Sallie. "A Blue Year for the Purple-and-Green Dinosaur." *New York Times*, 20 October 1994, D1.

James, Caryn. "25 Years Later, Wiseman Goes Back to School." *New York Times*, 6 July 1994, C14.

Jarvik, Laurence. "Big Bird Goes Cold Turkey: Public Broadcasting Can Flourish without Government Subsidies." *Heritage Foundation Policy Review*, Spring 1995.

Jarvik, Laurence. "Getting Big Bird Off the Dole." *New York Times*, 14 June 1992, 24.

Jensen, Elizabeth. "Barney & Friends Public TV Prepares For Image Transplant To Justify Existence." *Wall Street Journal*, 13 January 1994, 1.

Jessell, Harr and Julie Zier. "Duggan: New Kid on the Block." *Broadcasting & Cable*, 31 January 1994, 16.

Kadish, Joanne. "NJN Girding for a Battle of Survival." *New York Times*, 17 July 1994, sec. 13, 1.

"Licensing Deal Signed by PBS." *New York Times*, 28 April 1995, D4.

Lipman, Joanne. "Cookie Monster Is Caught Moonlighting." *Wall Street Journal*, 28 April 1992, B10.

McConville, Jim. "Duggan Endorses 1% Sotation for PBS." *Broadcasting & Cable*, 17 April 1995, 55.

McClellan, Steve. "Big Bird on a Wire." *Broadcasting & Cable*, 24 July 1995, 58.

McClellan, Steve. "Children's Initiative Paying Off for PBS." *Broadcasting & Cable*, 26 July 1993, 70–72.

McClellan, Steve. "Sony Gets to 'Sesame Street.' " *Broadcasting & Cable*, 1 May 1995, 38.

Mifflin, Lawrie. "USA Networks to Sponsor Charlie Rose's PBS Program." *New York Times*, 14 November 1995, C18.

Mifflin, Lawrie. "Where Public Television Means More than a Political Football." *New York Times*, 17 April 1995, C9.

Minow, Newton N., and Craig I. LaMay. "Out of the Wasteland, a Jackpot." *New York Times*, 4 December 1994, 80.

Moshavi, Sharon D. "Cable, Public TV Produce Hybrid 'Rose.' " *Broadcasting*, 16 December 1991, 40.

O'Connor, John. "For the Right, TV Is Half the Battle." *New York Times*, 14 June 1992, 1.

"Public Television Feathers Its Nest." *U.S. News & World Report*, 18 July 1994: 52.

Rathbun, Elizabeth. "The Selling of Public TV." *Broadcasting & Cable*, 13 February 1995, 43.

Rathbun, Elizabeth. "Check It Out: WNET Pursues Money-Making Ventures." *Broadcasting & Cable*, 10 April 1995: 71.

Rathbun, Elizabeth. "PBS Overhauls Itself Amid Criticism." *Broadcasting & Cable*, 6 February 1995, 16.

Rathbun, Elizabeth. "Public TV Solution Not as Simple as V's, U's." *Broadcasting & Cable*, 3 April 1995, 79.

Stern, Christopher. "FCC Lukewarm to Hundt Plan for Kids TV." *Broadcasting & Cable*, 10 April 1995: 76.

Treaster, Joseph B. "WNET Inquiry Finds No Proof Black Unit Freed 2 Nazi Camps." *New York Times*, 8 September 1993, B1.

Zier, Julie A. "Can You Say 'Merchandising?' " *Broadcasting & Cable*, 25 July 1994, 66.

10: TOWARD A WIRED NATION: CABLE TV

"America's Watching: Public Attitudes Toward Television." Roper Starch/NTVA/NAB Report, 1995, 10–11.

Amdur, Meredith. "Targeting Germany's Growing Market." *Broadcasting & Cable*, 5 July 1993, 18.

Andrews, Edmund L. "Ambition vs. Practicality in Cable-Phone Link." *New York Times*, 2 June 1993, D5.

Andrews, Edmund L. "'Baby Bell' Entering Cable TV." *New York Times*, 16 December 1992, D1, D5.

Andrews, Edmund L. "Bill Would Free Rivals in Communications." *New York Times*, 9 June 1993, D2.

Andrews, Edmund L. "Cable Pact Is Reached by States." *New York Times*, 9 June 1993, D1, D19.

Andrews, Edmund L. "Cable TV Battling Phone Companies." *New York Times*, 29 March 1992, 1, 22.

Andrews, Edmund L. "Cable TV in Phone Challenge." *New York Times*, 28 February 1991.

Andrews, Edmund L. "Cable TV Regulation Battle Heats Up before Showdown."
    New York Times, 16 September 1992, D1, D20.
Andrews, Edmund L. "Conferees Agree to Keep Limits on Cable TV Rates for 3
    Years." *New York Times*, 6 December 1995, A1.
Andrews, Edmund L. "Congress Votes to Reshape Communications Industry,
    Ending a 4–Year Struggle." *New York Times*, 2 February 1996, A1.
Andrews, Edmund L. "F.C.C. Approves New Rate Rises for Cable TV." *New York
    Times*, 11 November 1994, D1.
Andrews, Edmund L. "F.C.C. Faulted for Delaying Cost-Saving Cable TV Rules."
    New York Times, 17 June 1993, D1, D20.
Andrews, Edmund L. "F.C.C. Lets TV-Shopping Stations Demand Access to Slots
    on Cable." *New York Times*, 5 July 1993, 1, 40.
Andrews, Edmund L. "F.C.C. Plan to Set Up 2-Way T.V." *New York Times*, 11
    January 1991.
Andrews, Edmund L. "F.C.C. Postpones Deciding If Cable Systems Must Carry
    Shopping Stations." *New York Times*, 24 June 1993, D3.
Andrews, Edmund L. "F.C.C. Split May Imperil Post Waiver for Murdoch." *New
    York Times*, 25 June 1993, B1, B4.
Andrews, Edmund L. "FCC Weighs Plan to Shrink Murdoch Role." *New York
    Times*, 22 April 1995, 25.
Andrews, Edmund L. "House Approves Plan to Regulate Cable TV." *New York
    Times*, 24 July 1992, D1, D4.
Andrews, Edmund L. "Phone Companies Could Transmit TV under F.C.C. Plan."
    New York Times, 25 October 1991, A1.
Andrews, Edmund L. "Regulatory Stance Is Called Key to the New Cable Law."
    New York Times, 7 October 1992, D1, D2.
Andrews, Edmund L. "Re-regulation of Cable Is Likely to Pass House." *New York
    Times*, 13 July 1991, D21.
Andrews, Edmund L. "Senate Bill on Cable TV Is Delayed." *New York Times*, 13
    November 1991, D1, D20.
Andrews, Edmund L. "Senate Sends President a Bill to Regulate Cable TV
    Prices." *New York Times*, 23 September 1992, D1, D2.
Andrews, Edmund L. "Time Warner's Ordinary People Play Interactive TV." *New
    York Times*, 18 December 1994, 9.
Andrews, Edmund L. "Time Warner's TV Plan Is on Display in 5 Homes." *New
    York Times*, 15 December 1994, D20.
Andrews, Edmund L. "TV Venture Is Criticized for Promises to Investors." *New
    York Times*, 14 May 1992, D5.
Andrews, Edmund L. "TV with Viewer Interaction Gets Go-Ahead from F.C.C."
    New York Times, 17 January 1992, D1, D6.
Berniker, Mark. "Bell Atlantic, Nynex Purchase CAI Wireless Systems."
    Broadcasting & Cable, 3 April 1995, 40.
Berniker, Mark. "Bell Close Disney Video Services Deal." *Broadcasting & Cable*, 24
    April 1995, 33.
Berniker, Mark. "PacTel Joins Wireless Migration." *Broadcasting & Cable*, 24 April
    1995, 35.
Bird, Laura. "ABC Tries to Cash In on Night Shopping." *Wall Street Journal*, 13
    November 1992, B1, B14.

Bradsher, Keith. "Senate Heeding Consumers' Ire Votes to Limit Cable TV Rates." *New York Times*, 31 January 1992.

Brauchli, Marcus W. "A Satellite TV System Is Quickly Moving Asia into the Global Village." *Wall Street Journal*, 10 May 1993, A1, A8.

Brown, Rich. "Arum Pulls PPV Punch." *Broadcasting & Cable*, 22 January 1996, 125.

Brown, Rich. "BET Buys 80% of Action PPV." *Broadcasting & Cable*, 14 June 1993, 42, 46.

Brown, Rich. "Black Entertainment TV Opens Up Shop." *Broadcasting & Cable*, 25 July 1994, 22.

Brown, Rich. "The Boundless Ted Turner." *Broadcasting & Cable*, 11 April 1994, 30–32.

Brown, Rich. "Cable Boosts Original Programming Slate." *Broadcasting & Cable*, 25 July 1994, 60.

Brown, Rich. "Comcast Snags Maclean Hunter." *Broadcasting & Cable*, 27 June 1994, 46.

Brown, Rich. "Cox Comes Out on Top in Times Mirror Deal." *Broadcasting & Cable*, 6 June 1994, 9.

Brown, Rich. "$900M for Hallmark Cable." *Broadcasting & Cable*, 27 June 1994, 7.

Brown, Rich. "MMDS (Wireless Cable): A Capital Ideal." *Broadcasting & Cable*, 1 May 1995, 16.

Brown, Rich. "Music Companies Want Their Own MTV." *Broadcasting & Cable*, 7 February 1994, 14.

Brown, Rich. "Original Programming Comes to Life on Cable." *Broadcasting & Cable*, 4 April 1994, 24.

Brown, Rich. "'Politically Incorrect' Mainstreams on ABC." *Broadcasting & Cable*, 15 January 1996, 6.

Brown, Rich. "PPV Outlook: Partly Sunny." *Broadcasting & Cable*, 3 April 1995, 30.

Brown, Rich. "Showtime Lifting Curtain on Five Networks," *Broadcasting & Cable*, 25 April, 1994, 12.

Brown, Rich. "Snow Sets Record for Weather Channel." *Broadcasting & Cable*, 15 January 1996, 128.

Brown, Rich. "Survey Uncovers Stay-at-Home Shoppers." *Broadcasting & Cable*, 28 February 1994, 20.

Brown, Rich. "TCI Cuts Itself In on QVC." *Broadcasting & Cable*, 25 July 1994, 14.

Brown, Rich. "Time Warner Regulates Indecency in Leased Access." *Broadcasting & Cable*, 24 July 1995, 66.

Brown, Rich. "The Trials of Court TV." *Broadcasting*, 15 June 1992, 28–30.

Brown, Rich. "VH-1, Nick Go to UK." *Broadcasting & Cable*, 5 July 1993, 17.

Browning, E.S. "AT&T Breaks Up and 'Tangerines' Come in Season." *Wall Street Journal*, 21 September 1995, C10.

Bryant, Adam. "Alphabet Soup, with a Dash of Hype." *New York Times*, 18 January 1993, D1, D4.

Bulkeley, William M. "The Videophone Era May Finally Be Near Bringing Big Changes." *Wall Street Journal*, 10 March 1992, A1, A6.

"The Cable Network Programming Universe." *Broadcasting*, 7 January 1991.

"Cable Networks Post Strong 1990 Results." *Broadcasting*, 25 February 1991.

"Cable Outsider Free TV." *New York Times*, 14 September 1993, A4.

"Cable Rates Rising Faster than Perceived Value." *Broadcasting*, 14 January 1991.

"Cable Rivals Agree to Seek Standard for Interactive TV." *New York Times*, 4 June 1993: D1.

"Cable: Up Against the [Senate] Wall." *Broadcasting*, 12 March 1990.

"Capital Cities, Time Take Opposing Views on 'Retransmissions.' " *Wall Street Journal*, 3 June 1993: B6.

Carnevale, Mary Lu. "Bill to Regulate Cable-TV Rates Clears a House Panel, Setting Stage for Fight." *Wall Street Journal*, 9 April 1992, B9.

Carnevale, Mary Lu. "Cable Bill Is Cleared by Panel." *Wall Street Journal*, 8 June 1990.

Carnevale, Mary Lu. "Cable Industry Indicates It Will Accept Reregulation Bill." *Wall Street Journal*, 6 June 1990, B1.

Carnevale, Mary Lu. "Cable-TV Industry Is Counting on Bush to Deliver Veto of Rate- Regulation Bill." *Wall Street Journal*, 27 July 1992, B8.

Carnevale, Mary Lu. "FCC Cable Rules Can Be Stretched, but Not Too Far." *Wall Street Journal*, 21 November 1994, B6.

Carnevale, Mary Lu. "FCC Favors Requiring Cable Systems to Carry Home Shopping Broadcasts." *Wall Street Journal*, 22 June 1993.

Carnevale, Mary Lu. "FCC Loosens Reins on Rates for Cable TV." *Wall Street Journal*, 13 January 1995, A6.

Carnevale, Mary Lu. "FCC Promises Faster Action on Cable Rates." *Wall Street Journal*, 18 June 1993, B2.

Carnevale, Mary Lu. "FCC Proposes to Reserve Frequencies for Interactive Service on Television." *Wall Street Journal*, 11 February 1991.

Carnevale, Mary Lu. "FCC Takes Steps to Implement New Cable Law." *Wall Street Journal*, 6 November 1992, B14.

Carnevale, Mary Lu. "FCC Votes to Allow Networks to Buy Cable Systems; Limits are Established." *Wall Street Journal*, 19 June 1992, B8.

Carnevale, Mary Lu. "How Cable Bill Will Influence Rates, Service." *Wall Street Journal*, 28 September 1992, B1, B11.

Carnevale, Mary Lu. "Rollback of Cable TV Rates is Delayed Until FCC Gets Funds to Enforce Rules." *Wall Street Journal*, 14 June 1993, B8.

Carnevale, Mary Lu. "Senate Clears Bill to Restore Regulation of Cable TV Rates, Foster Competition." *Wall Street Journal*, 3 February 1992, B3.

Carnevale, Mary Lu, John J. Keller, and Mark Robichaux. "Cable-Phone Link Is Promising Gamble US West Move Puts Pressure on Its Rivals." *Wall Street Journal*, 18 May 1993, B1, B10.

Carroll, Paul B. Reilly, Patrick M. and Johnnie L. Roberts. "Age of Interactive TV May Be Nearing as IBM and Warner Talk Deal." *Wall Street Journal*, 21 May 1992, A1, A6.

Carter, Bill. "ABC Agrees to a Cable Deal, Breaking Networks' Ranks." *New York Times*, 15 June 1993, D1, D8.

Carter, Bill. "In Its Prime, Cable TV Gets Younger." *New York Times*, 13 July 1992, D8.

Carter, Bill. "Murdoch Joins a Cable–TV Rush Into the Crowded All-News Field." *New York Times*, 31 January 1996, A1.

Carter, Bill. "A New Report Becomes a Weapon in Debate on Censoring TV Violence." *New York Times*, 7 February 1996, C11.

Carter, Bill. "Ted Turner's Time of Discontent." *New York Times*, 6 June 1993.

Carter, Bill. "Two Comedy Channels Will Merge." *New York Times*, 19 December 1990.

Carter, Bill. "Victory in a Boxing Match May Go to Pay-Per-View." *New York Times*, 8 April 1991.

Carter, Bill. "Will There Be Any Space for Outer Space on Cable?" *New York Times*, 22 September 1992, D1, D6.

Cauley, Leslie. "Baby Bells Challenge FCC With Lawsuit." *Wall Street Journal*, 28 April 1995, B7.

Cauley, Leslie. "Bell Atlantic and Nynex Discuss Merger to Form Second-Biggest Phone Firm." *Wall Street Journal*, 18 December 1995, A3.

Cauley, Leslie, and Mark Robichaux. "U.S. West Media to Pay $5.3 Billion to Buy Continental Cablevision." *Wall Street Journal*, 28 February 1996, A3.

Chartrand, Subra. "Wiretap Access Bill Is Ready." *New York Times*, 9 August, 1994, D1.

Chass, Murray. "ITT-Cablevision Deal Reported to Buy Madison Square Garden." *New York Times*, 28 August 1994, 1.

Clymer, Adam. "Congress Rebuffs Bush in Override of Cable TV Veto." *New York Times*, 6 October 1992, A1, A19.

Coe, Steve. "Cable Networks: Coming Attractions." *Broadcasting*, 20 January 1992, 12.

Coe, Steve. "Murdoch Blasts Traditional News." *Broadcasting*, 29 June 1992, 17.

Coe, Steve. "Nick's Big Deal Is the Cat's Meow." *Broadcasting*, 13 July 1992, 22–24.

Cohen, Laurie P., and Amy Stevens. "Bad News: Dan Dorfman's Woes Mount as Investigators Widen Criminal Probe." *Wall Street Journal*, 16 January 1996, A1.

"Congress Enacts Cable-TV Law." *The Record*, 6 October 1992, A1, A11.

Cushman Jr., John H. "S.E.C. Accuses 4 of Fraud at Financial News Network." *New York Times*, 29 June 1993, D1, D21.

"Danforth: Timing Crucial to Cable Reregulation Bill." *Broadcasting*, 17 Sept. 1990.

Davis, Bob. "FCC May Let Networks Buy Cable Systems." *Wall Street Journal*, 13 December 1991, B1, B4.

Davis, Bob. "FCC Pushing Phone Service That Delivers Cable TV." *Wall Street Journal*, 25 October 1991, B1, B10.

Denisoff, Serge R. *Inside MTV*. New Brunswick, New Jersey: Transaction Books, 1988.

"Despite FCC Action, Hill Likely to Move on Cable." *Broadcasting*, 17 December 1990.

Deutsch, Claudia H. "Shopping Malls: Luring Crowds and Buyers with Fun and Games." *New York Times*, 27 September 1990, 13.

"Directory Assistance: The Answers to Some Questions About AT&T's Breakup Plan." *New York Times*, September 1995, D1.

"Discovery and PBS to Study Creating National Cable Channel." *Broadcasting*, 25 June 1990.

Dominick, Joseph R., Barry L. Sherman, and Gary A. Copeland. *Broadcasting, Cable and Beyond*. New York, McGraw-Hill, 1993.

"Doug Herzog, MTV: Music Television." *Broadcasting & Cable*, 7 June 1993, 64.

"Doug McCormick, Lifetime." *Broadcasting & Cable*, 7 June 1993, 64.

Elliott, Stuart. "Defying the Skeptics, the Weather Channel Finds a Silver Lining in Mother Nature's Mood Swings." *New York Times*, 9 June 1993, D17.

Elliott, Stuart. "Pay TV Is Looking to Score Knockout." *New York Times*, 12 November 1992, D1, D21.

Elliott, Stuart. "Two Advocacy Groups Set for TV Duel." *New York Times*, 25 October 1991, D16.

Emshwiller, John R. "Cable Entrepreneurs Take on Entrenched Competitors." *Wall Street Journal*, 12 July 1990.

"Extremist Groups Spread Message Via Cable Access." *Broadcasting & Cable*, 1 May 1995, 8.

Fabrikant, Geraldine. "Black Cable Channel's Wild Ride." *New York Times*, 1 June 1992, D1, D8.

Fabrikant, Geraldine. "Cable Giant to Sell Chain of Theaters." *New York Times*, 20 February 1992, D9.

Fabrikant, Geraldine. "The King of Cable Reaches for More." *New York Times*, 30 May 1993, sec. 3, 1, 6.

Fabrikant, Geraldine. "Lin's Value Is Set at $3.3 Billion." *New York Times*, 8 March 1995, D1.

Fabrikant, Geraldine. "A Media Company's Prospects Hinge on an F.C.C. Ruling." *New York Times*, 23 June 1993, D6.

Fabrikant, Geraldine. "Merger Proposed for Two Home Shopping Giants." *New York Times*, 13 July 1993, D1.

Fabrikant, Geraldine. "A Phone Company Buys Entry into Cable Television Business." *New York Times*, 10 February 1993, A1, D2.

Fabrikant, Geraldine. "Time Deal Worrying Competitors." *New York Times*, 7 March 1989, D1, D22.

Fabrikant, Geraldine. "Time Warner Chief Proves Deal Maker." *New York Times*, 18 May 1993, D1, D20.

Fabrikant, Geraldine. "Time Warner Constructing 2-Way Cable TV System." *New York Times*, 8 March 1991.

Fabrikant, Geraldine. "TV Stations Get Ready for Cable Payment Fight." *New York Times*, 18 June 1993, D15.

Fabrikant, Geraldine. "A Very Good Year for Cable: Ad Sales Jumped 18% in '91." *New York Times*, 4 March 1992.

"FCC May Allow News Corp. to Avert Cost of Meeting Rules on TV Ownership." *Wall Street Journal*, 28 April 1995, B1.

"FCC Spells Out Role of 'Good Actor.' " *Broadcasting*, 7 January 1991.

"FCC Wants to Toughen Cable Regulations." *Broadcasting*, 17 December 1990.

Feder, Barnaby. "Mostly Stunts and Games in Chicago." *New York Times*, 3 June 1993, D6.

Flint, Joe. "Delayed Start for Fox Channel." *Broadcasting & Cable*, 12 July 1993, 16, 26.

Flint, Joe. "FCC Lets TV Networks into Cable Ownership." *Broadcasting*, 22 June 1992: 4, 16.

Flint, Joe. "NBC Planning Not One, but Three New Cable TV Networks." *Broadcasting & Cable*, 12 July 1993, 16.

Flint, Joe. "Retrans Consent: Rock vs. Hard Place." *Broadcasting & Cable*, 14 June 1993, 6–7.

Flint, Joe, and Peter Lambert. "FCC Allocates Interactive Video Spectrum." *Broadcasting*, 20 January 1992, 11.

Foisie, Geoffrey. "Barry Diller: QVC's $350 Million Man." *Broadcasting*, 14 December 1992. 14.

Foisie, Geoffrey. "Two-Way TV; Wrong-Way Cash Flow." *Broadcasting*, 16 December 1991, 51.

"Fox and TCI: The Crossover to Cable." *Broadcasting*, 10 September 1990.

"Fox Does Double Duty—Buying and Selling." *Broadcasting*, 14 January 1991.

Gerard, Jeremy. "Fledgling Cable Networks Are Poised for Flight." *New York Times*, 3 June 1990.

Goldman, Kevin. "Cable Giant Seeks NBC Affiliation." *Wall Street Journal*, 20 June 1990.

Goldman, Kevin. "Cable TV Networks Strive to Stand Out from the Crowd with Original Programs." *Wall Street Journal*, 17 December 1990.

Goldman, Kevin. "FNN Cash Flow 'Insufficient' to Meet Costs." *Wall Street Journal*, 25 October 1990, B6.

Goldman, Kevin. "NBC Cable Channel to Offer Incentives to Operators to Get Them to Carry It." *Wall Street Journal*, 13 May 1990.

Goldman, Kevin. "Network Targets Drivers at Truck Stops." *Wall Street Journal*, 3 November 1992, B1, B6.

Goldman, Kevin and Mark Robichaux. "Camcorders Spark Two Cable Ventures." *Wall Street Journal*, 30 July 1992: B1.

Goldman, Kevin and Mark Robichaux. "Games on Cable Fail to Attract Late Subscribers." *Wall Street Journal*, 29 July 1992: B1, B6.

Grossman, Laurie M. "Turner Aims to Line Up Captive Audience." *Wall Street Journal*, 21 June 1992: B1, B3.

Hansell, Saul. "A Mover of Markets." *New York Times Magazine*, 9 July 1995: p.18.

Helyar, John. "Pay-Per-View Aims for Boxing Knockout." *Wall Street Journal*, 14 January 1991.

"Herb Scannell Nickelodeon/Nick at Nite." *Broadcasting & Cable*, 7 June 1993: 66.

Holusha, John. "Trying to Take the Cable Out of Cable Television." *New York Times*, 16 December 1992, D1, D5.

"How the People of Rochester Saw the Future and Yawned." *The Economist*, 25 February 1995, 63–64.

"Ivan Seidenberg: Expanding Nynex's Entertainment Horizons." *Broadcasting & Cable*, 13 February 1995, 32.

Jensen, Elizabeth. "ABC Believes It Has Made a Perfect 'Event.' " *Wall Street Journal*, 10 May 1993, B1, B6.

Jensen, Elizabeth and Daniel Pearl. "One Dogged Lawyer Shakes Murdoch Empire." *Wall Street Journal*, 6 April 1995, B1.

Jensen, Elizabeth and Mark Robichaux. "Cable-TV Systems, Broadcasters to Play High-Stakes Game That Public May Lose." *Wall Street Journal*, 15 June 1993, B1, B2.

Jensen, Elizabeth, and Mark Robichaux. "TCI Wins Agreement with 14 Stations for Cable TV Broadcasts without Fee." *Wall Street Journal*, 18 June 1993, B2.

Jessell, Harry A. "Cable Demands Change in Rate Regs." *Broadcasting & Cable*, 28 June 1993, 28.

Jessell, Harry A. "Cable Growth Inevitable, Say Turner, Others." *Broadcasting & Cable*, 14 June 1993, 22.

Jessell, Harry A. "Pepper Has Capital Idea." *Broadcasting & Cable*, 14 June 1993, 67–68.

Jessell, Harry A. "Telcos to Go for Half a Loaf on Cable Entry." *Broadcasting*, 2 December 1991, 51.

Jessell, Harry A. "Univisa Wants Back in TV Station Ownership." *Broadcasting*, 2 December 1991, 52.

"Justices Uphold a Challenge in Cable TV Franchise Suit." *New York Times*, 2 June 1986.

Keller, John J. "Divide to Conquer: Defying Merger Trend, AT&T Plans to Split into Three Companies." *Wall Street Journal*, 21 September 1995, A1.

"Key Points of Cable Bill." *Broadcasting*, 17 September 1990.

King, Thomas R. "Cable Giant, Belatedly to Blow its Horn." *Wall Street Journal*, 10 October 1990.

King, Thomas R. "Nickelodeon Fox Film Chase Family Viewers." *Wall Street Journal*, 18 May 1993, B1, B12.

Kneale, Dennis. "Cable-TV Firm Wants to Test Phone Service." *Wall Street Journal*, 11 January 1991.

Kneale, Dennis. "Time Warner Plans Cable-TV System with 150 Channels." *Wall Street Journal*, 8 March 1991.

Kneale, Dennis. "Two Comedy Channels Make Peace and Merge." *Wall Street Journal*, 19 December 1990.

Kolbert, Elizabeth. "Cable Showdown Looms over Network Payments." *New York Times*, 21 June 1992, D6.

Kolbert, Elizabeth. "In Mounting a Campaign against Violence, Is the Cable Industry Practicing What It Preaches?" *New York Times*, 13 March 1995, D6.

Landler, Mark. "As a Beat, Business Is Booming." *New York Times*, 9 July 1995, 27.

Landler, Mark. "Bell Atlantic Halts Plan for Video Services." *New York Times*, 26 April 1995, D1.

Landler, Mark. "The Big Boys Come Calling: Rochester Is Courted by AT&T and Time Warner." *New York Times*, 23 October 1995, D1.

Landler, Mark. "Cable with a Local Twist." *New York Times*, 24 July 1995, D1.

Landler, Mark. "U.S. West's Continental Ambitions." *New York Times*, 28 February 1996, D1.

Landro, Laura. "Cable-TV Venture Sets Video Service for Doctor Offices." *Wall Street Journal*, 28 February 1990.

Landro, Laura. "Despite a Robust Basic Business, Picture Is Flawed for Cable TV." *Wall Street Journal*, 21 March 1991, B1.

Landro, Laura. "Paramount in the Dark before the Don." *Wall Street Journal*, 11 December 1990, B1.

Landro, Laura. "Tele-Communications Backs Creation of a National Pay Cable TV Network." *Wall Street Journal*, 21 February 1991.

Landro, Laura. "Tele-Communications Plan to Acquire Showtime Stake Appears to Be on Hold." *Wall Street Journal*, 17 December 1990.

Landro, Laura. "Time Warner, Concerned about Move by Seagram, Is Said to Review Options." *Wall Street Journal*, 22 June 1993, A3.

Landro, Laura, and Mark Robichaux. "Time Warner, TCI Join to Set Cable Standard." *Wall Street Journal*, 4 June 1993, B1, B2.

Langberg, Mike. "And Don't Forget to Say Cheese." *The Record*, 19 January 1992, B1, B4.

"Last Rites for a Cable Bill." *Broadcasting*, 22 October 1990.

Levine, Ed. "TV Rocks with Music." *New York Times Magazine*, 8 May 1993, 42, 55–61.

Lewin, TaMarch "Hey There, Dudes, the Kids Have Grabbed a Network." *New York Times*, 21 October 1990.

Lewis, Lisa. *Gender Politics and MTV*. Philadelphia, Pennsylvania: Temple University Press, 1990.

Lewis, Peter H. "Judge Blocks Law Intended to Regulate On-Line Smut." *New York Times*, 16 February 1996, D1.

Lipman, Joanne. "Deaf Consumers Aren't Ignored Anymore." *Wall Street Journal*, 28 February 1990.

Lublin, Joann S. "Cable TV to See If Cable Radio Means Sweet Music for Revenue." *Wall Street Journal*, 6 November 1990, B10.

Markoff, John. "Cable TV Chimes In with Some High-Tech Plans." *New York Times*, 8 June 1993, D23.

Markoff, John. "High Hurdles Await Interactive TV." *New York Times*, 14 June 1993, D6.

Markoff, John. "Turner in a Four-Year Deal to Televise N.F.L. Games." *New York Times*, 23 December 1990.

Marks, Peter. "New Focus on Cable Competition." *New York Times*, 30 January 1995, B1.

McAvoy, Kim. "Commerce OK's Info Highway Bill." *Broadcasting & Cable*, 15 August 1994, 10.

McAvoy, Kim. "Deciphering the FCC's New Cable Rules." *Broadcasting & Cable*, 11 April 1994, 50.

McAvoy, Kim. "FCC Postpones Home Shopping Vote." *Broadcasting & Cable*, 28 June 1993, 27.

McAvoy, Kim. "FCC Promises Price Drop for Most Subs." *Broadcasting & Cable*, 28 February 1994, 7.

McAvoy, Kim. "FCC Would Cap MSO's at 25% of Homes." *Broadcasting & Cable*, 28 June 1993, 9.

McAvoy, Kim. "Inouye Bill Would Let Telcos into Cable." *Broadcasting & Cable*, 7 June 1993, 91.

McAvoy, Kim. "Quello Favors Small-Operator Exemption." *Broadcasting & Cable*, 14 June 1993, 67.

McAvoy, Kim. "Tug of War over Cable Rate Reductions." *Broadcasting & Cable*, 14 February 1994, 6.

McAvoy, Kim and Christopher Stern. "Freeze Extension Angers Cable Industry." *Broadcasting & Cable*, 14 February 1994, 7.

McCarthy, Michael J. "In Reversal, Turner Broadcasting Posts Net of $7.3 Million." *Wall Street Journal*, 20 February 1991.

McCarthy, Michael J., and Peter Waldman. "Derring-Do Fades at Turner's Empire." *Wall Street Journal*, 12 October 1990, B1.

McClellan, Steve. "TBS Getting Goodwill from Games." *Broadcasting & Cable*, 25

July 1994, 17.

McConnell, Chris. "Bell Atlantic Plans More Video Networks." *Broadcasting & Cable*, 23 May 1994, 10.

Meier, Barry. "Inside the Purchasing Network at Home Shopping." *New York Times*, 10 May 1993, D1, D3.

Meisler, Andy. "Ren and Stimpy's Triumphant Return." *New York Times*, 16 August 1992, 21, 24.

"Merger Brings Comic Relief to Cable." *Broadcasting*, 24 December 1990, 26.

Mifflin, Laurie. "Cable TV Continues Its Steady Drain of Network Viewers." *New York Times*, 25 October 1995, C13.

Moshavi, Sharon D. "ABC, Garden Announce PPV Plan." *Broadcasting*, 16 December 1991, 10.

New Jersey Cable Television Association. *Code of Privacy*. Newsletter, vol. VIII, no. 1, Winter 1983.

O'Connor, John J. "MTV's Low-Cost Way of Business." *New York Times*, 18 July 1995, C22.

O'Connor, John J. " 'The Real World,' According to MTV." *New York Times*, 9 July 1992, C15, C22.

Pasqua, Thomas, et al. *Mass Media in the Information Age*. Englewood, New Jersey: Prentice Hall, 1990.

Pearl, Daniel. "House GOP Stalls Rewrite of Phone Law." *Wall Street Journal*, 22 December 1995, A2.

Pearl, Daniel. "Murdoch Wins Victory on Issue of Ownership." *Wall Street Journal*, 5 May 1995, A4.

Pearl, Daniel. "Turner Broadcasting Is Developing Multimedia Products for Home." *Wall Street Journal*, 7 February 1992.

Pepper, Bob. "Video Dial Tone Advances at FCC." *Broadcasting & Cable*, 28 October 1991, 26.

Philips, Christopher Lee. "Hollywood Takes Hill Heat on Violence." *Broadcasting & Cable*, 14 June 1993, 68.

Pollack, Andrew. "Packing Cable with Programs." *New York Times*, 22 January 1992, D1, D5.

Power, William. "CNN Business Editor Did Video Work for Brokers." *Wall Street Journal*, 24 July 1992, C1, C15.

"PPV Olympics Working for Expanding Universe." *Broadcasting*, 14 January 1991.

"Question Mark Looms over Sky Cable." *Broadcasting*, 22 October 1990.

Reilly, Patrick M. "Electronics Show Plugs into Multimedia." *Wall Street Journal*, 3 June 1993, B1, B6.

Reilly, Patrick M. "Media Firms Target Captive Audiences Taking Out of Whittle's Book." *Wall Street Journal*, 28 February 1990.

Richards, Bill. "Trojan Horse?" *Wall Street Journal* [Technology Supplement], 19 June 1995, 24.

Riggs, Michael. "The Compact Disk Is Here to Stay . . . for a While." *New York Times*, 19 January 1992, B11, B25.

Roberts, Johnnie L. "Are They Jakin' the Box?" *Newsweek*, 23 January 1995, 42.

Roberts, Johnnie L. "How Giant TCI Uses Self-Dealing, Hardball to Dominate Market." *Wall Street Journal*, 27 January 1992, A1, A4.

Roberts, Johnnie L. "ITT Cablevision Win Garden Auction with $1.09 Billion Cash

Bid to Viacom." *Wall Street Journal*, 29 August, 1994, A3.

Robichaux, Mark. "At MTV, Reality Becomes a Soap Opera." *Wall Street Journal*, 18 May 1993, B1, B8.

Robichaux, Mark. "Cable Firms Say They Welcome Competition but Behave Otherwise." *Wall Street Journal*, 24 September 1992, A1, A14.

Robichaux, Mark. "Cable Show Affords Glimpse of TV's Future." *Wall Street Journal*, 7 June 1993, B1, B6.

Robichaux, Mark. "Cable TV Firms Wonder If It's Time to Get Hooked Up." *Wall Street Journal*, 3 August 1995, B4.

Robichaux, Mark. "Cable TV Firms' Higher-Priced 'Tiers' Bring Cries of Outrage from Consumers." *Wall Street Journal*, 15 January 1992, B1, B5.

Robichaux, Mark. "FCC's 'Social Contract' for Cable Companies Draws Ire." *Wall Street Journal*, 29 January 1996, B4.

Robichaux, Mark. "For Nickelodeon, Crude 'Toon is Big Hit." *Wall Street Journal*, 27 January 1992, B1, B3.

Robichaux, Mark. "Liberty Media Plans a Network to Rival ESPN." *Wall Street Journal*, 6 January 1993, B1.

Robichaux, Mark. "MTV Is Playing a New Riff: Responsibility." *Wall Street Journal*, 9 February 1993, B1, B8.

Robichaux, Mark. "Record Firms Drop Plans to Challenge MTV With Rival Music-Video Channel." *Wall Street Journal*, 7 July 1995, B8.

Robichaux, Mark. "Store Owners Seek Funding to Split It Up." *Wall Street Journal*, 30 September 1992, A3, A6.

Robichaux, Mark. "Time Warner to Put Some Cable Systems into Venture with Newhouse Operations." *Wall Street Journal*, 13 September 1994, A2.

Robichaux, Mark. " 'Triple Cast' Plan Isn't Turning Many Viewers On." *Wall Street Journal*, 20 July 1992, B1.

Robichaux, Mark. "VH-1 Hones Its Style to Match Its Targets." *Wall Street Journal*, 6 August 1992, B5.

Robichaux, Mark. "Viewers' Horror Stories Cast Cable TV as Villain." *Wall Street Journal*, 8 March 1995, B1.

Robichaux, Mark, and Jeanne Saddler. "Cable-TV Rates Could Fall 10% Due to Ruling." *Wall Street Journal*, 2 April 1993, B1, B16.

Roman, James W. *Cablemania: The Cable Television Sourcebook*. Englewood Cliffs, New Jersey: Prentice Hall, 1983.

Romano, Jay. "Speed-Up of Fiber-Optic Network Debated." *New York Times*, 8 December 1991, sec. 12, 1, 22.

Salmans, Sandra. "Cable-TV's Losses Rise; Debt Is High." *New York Times*, 13 September 1983, D5.

Sandomir, Richard. "Cablevision's Dolan One Savvy Visionary." *New York Times*, 11 October 1994, B13.

Sandomir, Richard. "Some Shaky Precedents for New York Sports Fans." *New York Times*, 28 August 1994, 35.

Sandomir, Richard. "To Catch Triplecast Reruns, Just Switch to NBC." *New York Times*, 27 July 1992, C6.

Sandomir, Richard. "Triplecast: an Olympian Blunder or Innovation." *New York Times*, 29 June 1992, C1.

"Sci-Fi Begins $2 Million Campaign." *Broadcasting*, 28 June 1993, 38.

Scully, Sean. "CBA Calls for Four-Letter Calls." *Broadcasting & Cable*, 28 June 1993, 28.

Scully, Sean. "Midterm Review Added to EEO Compliance." *Broadcasting & Cable*, 28 June 1993, 10.

Scully, Sean. "Sports Migration to Pay TV Minimal, FCC Study Says." *Broadcasting & Cable*, 28 June 1993, 9.

Sebastian, Pamela. "It Helps to be Cool and Klutzy If You Are Selling on T.V." *Wall Street Journal*, 31 December 1990.

Shapiro, Eben. "Cable-Ready." *Wall Street Journal*, 20 March 1995, R8.

Shapiro, Eben. "Viacom Agrees to Spin Off, Then Sell Its Cable Systems." *Wall Street Journal*, 26 July 1995, A3.

Shapiro, Eben and Laura Landro. "Frustrated Investors Ratchet Up Pressure on Time Warner Chief." *Wall Street Journal*, 21 April 1995, 1.

Sheridan, Patrick J. "Nader Picks Up Baton of Cable Regulation." *Broadcasting*, 29 April 1991, 50.

Sherman, Barry L., and Joseph R. Dominick, "Violence and Sex in Music Videos: TV and Rock n' Roll." *Journal of Communications*, 36, no. 1, Winter 1986, 79–93.

Sobel, Robert. "Missing Children: Networks Blame People Meter." *Television/ Radio Age*, 7 March 1988, 40–42.

Stark, John. "Combining a Nation for the Weirdest in Cable Fare." *New York Times*, 29 March 1992, 35.

Sterling, Christopher H., and John M. Kittross. *Stay Tuned: A Concise History of American Broadcasting*. 2d ed. Belmont, California: Wadsworth Publishing Co., 1990.

Stern, Christopher. "Bell Atlantic Pulls Back VDT Applications." *Broadcasting & Cable*, 1 May 1995, 34.

Stern, Christopher. "Cable Operators Can Move Ahead Despite Rate Rollback." *Broadcasting & Cable*, 28 February 1994, 32.

Stern, Christopher. "Continental Cable, FCC Make a Deal." *Broadcasting & Cable*, 10 April 1995, 16.

Stern, Christopher. "ESPN to Launch 'Hip' ESPN 2." *Broadcasting & Cable*, 14 June 1993, 46, 48.

Stern, Christopher. "FCC Releases Final Cable Survey; Confirms Cut for Most Subscribers." *Broadcasting & Cable*, 28 February 1994, 34.

Stern, Christopher. "Macy's and Cablevision Going Shopping." *Broadcasting & Cable*, 7 June 1993, 92.

Stern, Christopher. "Nudity Clause Gives Cable Operators Pause." *Broadcasting & Cable*, 17 April 1995, 55.

Stern, Christopher, and Kim McAvoy. "Cable Feels Weight of New Rules." *Broadcasting & Cable*, 4 April 1994, 8.

"Steven Hewitt Showtime." *Broadcasting & Cable*, 7 June 1993, 66.

Stevenson, Richard W. "Britain Offers Encouraging Experience." *New York Times*, 18 May 1993, D1, D20.

Strauss, Neil. "The 'M' in MTV Loses a Little of Its Standing." *New York Times*, 13 August 1995, 27.

Strom, Stephanie. "Macy to Start Cable TV Channel, Taking Stores into Living Rooms." *New York Times*, 2 June 1993, A1, D4.

Sukow, Randy. "Gore as VP: Bad News for Cable." *Broadcasting*, 13 July 1992.

"TCI and WFLD Making News in Chicago." *Broadcasting*, 17 September 1990.

"TCI Pulls NBC's String on Exclusivity." *Broadcasting*, 25 June 1990.

"TCI Wants Its . . . TMZ." *Broadcasting & Cable*, 24 July 1995, 18.

"Telecos Sue over Cable-Entry Process." *Broadcasting & Cable*, 1 May 1995, 10.

"Telecom Vote Signals Competitive Free-for-All." *Wall Street Journal*, 2 February 1996, B1.

"Time Warner, NBC and Cablevision Alliance: More There than Meets the Eye?" *Broadcasting*, 14 January 1991.

"Time Warner Raises Stake in Turner Broadcasting." *Wall Street Journal*, 21 January 1991, B4.

Tobenkin, David. "The Wireless System That Could." *Broadcasting & Cable*, 1 May 1995, 20.

Tobenkin, David. "Warner Bros. Wants to Capture Kids." *Broadcasting & Cable*, 25 July 1994, 16.

"Top 25 Groups Brace for Retrans Showdown." *Broadcasting & Cable*, 7 June 1993, 78–82.

Trachtenberg, Jeffrey A. "High-Definition TV Has Networks, Outlets Worried about Costs." *Wall Street Journal*, November 11, 1992, A1, A6.

Trachtenberg, Jeffrey, and Eben Shapiro. "Reward for the Restless: Warner Music's Top Job."*Wall Street Journal*, 4 May 1995, B1.

Turner, Richard. "Hollywood Is Seeing the Future, and It Is Interactive Show Biz." *Wall Street Journal*, 19 May 1993, A1, A8.

Turner, Richard. "Nickelodeon's Hip Fare Stretches the Bounds of TV for Youngsters." *Wall Street Journal*, 13 July 1992, A1, A5.

"Turning Cable Networks into Phone Systems." *Wall Street Journal*, 8 January 1991.

"Viacom, AT&T Plan Video Service Launch in California Region." *Wall Street Journal*, 3 June 1993, B5.

"Viacom's New Strip Will Have MTV's Beat." *Broadcasting & Cable*, 28 June 1993, 8.

Warner-Amex Cable Communications.*Code of Privacy*. 1981.

Woletz, Robert G. "A New Formula: Into the 'Bin,' Out Comes a Hit." *New York Times*, 2 August 1992, 22.

Index

About the Author

JAMES ROMAN is Associate Professor of Media Studies at Hunter College. His publications include works on the funding and culture of both cable and public television. He is the author of *Cablemania* (1983).